Family Law
in
India

Kolkata

Eastern Law House Private Ltd.
54 Ganesh Chunder Avenue
Kolkata (Calcutta) 700 013

New Delhi

Eastern Law House Private Ltd.
36 Netaji Subhash Marg, Daryaganj
New Delhi 110 002

Family Law
in
India

by

H.K. Saharay
MA (Triple), MCom, LLB, PhD (London), Barrister

Kolkata   New Delhi
EASTERN LAW HOUSE
2011

Published and processed by
EASTERN LAW HOUSE PRIVATE LTD.
54 Ganesh Chunder Avenue
Kolkata (Calcutta) 700 013
Tel: (033) 2215-1989/2301 Fax: (033) 2215-0491
Email: elh@cal.vsnl.net.in
www.easternlawhouse.com

©
H.K. SAHARAY and
EASTERN LAW HOUSE PRIVATE LTD.
2011

Whilst all reasonable care has been taken to ensure accuracy of the contents of this book, no person associated with the creation or publishing of this book shall have responsibility for any loss or damages that may be caused to any person due to errors or omissions which may have crept in inadvertently in this publication. Disputes, if any, are subject to Kolkata jurisdiction.

ISBN 978-81-7177-239-1

Printed at
Dey's Offset, Kolkata

Preface

The word "family" refers to a group of persons of common ancestry. Law governing a family is known as family law. From jurisprudential point of view a family law has different aspects. This work on Family Laws in India has dealt with all those aspects in the context of religious law and secular law keeping an eye for the benefits of law students and beginners in legal profession. The contents of the book are divided into six parts. Part 1 deals with general aspect of family law. Part 2 relates to Hindu family law; Part 3 deals with Muslim family law; Part 4 includes Christian family law; Part 5 relates to Parsi family law and Part 6 to secular law of family. Each Part is again divided into different chapters under separate topics of family law. Part 1 under the title of General has three chapters of which chapter 1 introduces meaning of family law. Chapter 2 discusses about the institution of marriage and chapter 3 deals with other personal laws. Part 2 under Hindu Family Law starts from chapter 4 and completes in chapter 17. These chapters have elaborately dealt with Hindu Law, some importance legislations on Hindu Law and marriage during British rule, Hindu Law of marriage and divorce, legislation on Hindu marriage and divorce in post-independence era, Hindu Marriage Act 1955, Hindu Marriages (Validation of Proceedings) Act 1960, Hindu Adoptions and Maintenance Act 1956, Hindu Minority and Guardianship Act 1956, joint Hindu family, joint family property & partition, gift, wills, religious and charitable endowments, Hindu Succession Act 1956. Part 3 under Muslim Family Law begins with chapter 18 and ends in chapter 28. These chapters include introduction, Muslim Personal Law (Shariat) Application Act 1937, marriage and sonship, gifts, wakf, wills, pre-emption, succession, administration & partition, inheritance, maintenance under Muslim Law, Muslim Women (Protection of Rights on Divorce) Act 1986. Part 4 under the heading Christian Family Law includes Indian Christian Marriage Act 1872 (chapter 29), Divorce Act 1869 (chapter 30), Intestate Succession to Christian under the Indian Succession Act 1925 (chapter 31),

Converts' Marriage Dissolution Act 1866 (chapter 32). Part 5 under the heading of Parsi Family Law has two chapters, namely chapter 33 on Parsi Marriage and Divorce Act 1936 and chapter 34 on Intestate Succession to Parsi under the Indian Succession Act 1925. Part 6 under the heading of Secular Law of Family includes chapter 35 to chapter 45. These chapters discuss succinctly Special Marriage Act 1954 (chapter 35), Foreign Marriage Act 1969 (chapter 36), Family Courts Act 1984 (chapter 37), Dowry Prohibition Act 1961 (chapter 38), Guardians and Wards Act 1890 (chapter 39), Religious Endowments Act 1869 (chapter 40), Indian Succession Act 1925 (chapter 41), Maintenance under Code of Criminal Procedure 1973 (chapter 42), Maintenance and Welfare of Parents and Senior Citizens Act 2007 (chapter 43), Protection of Women from Domestic Violence Act 2005 (chapter 44), and Prohibition of Child Marriage Act 2006 (chapter 45). This book is a complete code on family law in India.

All relevant case laws of the Supreme Court and different High Courts of India and also of the foreign courts have been incorporated in appropriate places. Attempts have also been made to incorporate all the up-to-date amendments into the statutes included in this book. Different problems and their solutions by way of illustrations and leading cases are given in this book to highlight the propositions of law. Elaborate indexes will enhance the utility of the book.

It is hoped that this book will be useful to all those for whom it is meant. I sincerely appreciate the co-operation and active support of the Publishers and their staff in bringing out this book.

Bar Library Club
Calcutta High Court
15th April 2011

H.K. SAHARAY

Contents

	PAGE
Preface	[5]
Table of Cases	[25]

Part 1 – General

CHAPTER

1	**Introduction**	**3**
	Family law—meaning of	3
	Family law under German Civil Code	4
	English family law	5
	Family law in USA	5
2	**Institution of Marriage**	**6**
	Introduction	6
	Definition of marriage	7
	(i) Christian law	7
	(ii) Muslim law	8
	(iii) Hindu law	8
	(iv) Roman law	12
3	**Other Personal Laws**	**14**
	Introduction	14
	Miscellaneous Personal Laws (Extension) Act 1959 (Act 48 of 1959)	14
	(A) Objects of Miscellaneous Personal Laws (Extension) Act 1959	14
	(B) Acts extended and repealed law	15
	Secular law	15

Part 2 – Hindu Family Law

4	**Hindu Law**	**19**
	Introduction	19
	Sources of Hindu law	20
	(i) The Sruti	20
	(ii) The Smritis	20

Chapter		Page
4	**Hindu Law**—*continued*	
	(*iii*) The commentaries	21
	(*iv*) Customs or usages	21
	(*v*) Judicial decision	22
	(*vi*) Legislation	22
	Judicial interpretation on sources of Hindu law	22
	Schools of Hindu law	23
	Different sub-schools	24
	(*i*) Benares School	24
	(*ii*) Mithila School	24
	(*iii*) Dravida School	24
	(*iv*) Maharashtra School	24
5	**Some Important Legislations on Hindu Law and Marriage During British Rule**	**25**
	Introduction	25
	The Hindu Widows' Remarriage Act 1856 (Act 15 of 1856)	25
	(1) Preamble	25
	(2) Custom of remarriage	26
	(3) Rights of widow on remarriage	26
	(4) Right to adoption	28
	The Anand Marriage Act 1909	28
	Section 3 of the said Act exempted certain marriages from Act	28
	The Arya Marriage Validation Act 1937	29
	The Hindu Marriage Disabilities Removal Act 1946	29
	(1) Preliminary	29
	(2) "Gotra," or pravara meaning of	29
	Caste Disabilities Removal Act 1850	30
	(1) Preamble	30
	(2) Effect of the 1850 Act	30
	The Hindu Disposition of Property Act 1916	31
	(1) Preliminary	31
	(2) Bequest to an unborn person	31
	The Hindu Inheritance (Removal of Disabilities) Act 1928	31
	(1) Preliminary	31
	(2) No retrospective effect	31
6	**Hindu Law of Marriage and Divorce**	**32**
	Ancient Hindu law of marriage	32
	Forms of marriage	32
	Persons competent to marry	32
	Ceremonies of marriage	33
	Dissolution of marriage	33
7	**Legislations on Hindu Marriage and Divorce in Post-independence Era**	**34**
	Matrimonial laws during 1947-1955	34

CONTENTS [9]

CHAPTER		PAGE
8	**The Hindu Marriage Act 1955**	**35**

Object of the Act 35
Operation of the Act 35
Necessary changes made under the Act 36
Territorial jurisdiction of the Act 36
Concept of domicile 37
Conditions of valid Hindu marriage 37
   (i) Neither party has a spouse living at the time of marriage .. 37
   (ii) Unsoundness of mind 38
   (iii) Ages of parties to marriage 38
   (iv) Prohibited degrees 38
   (v) Parties, not sapindas 38
Ceremonies of Hindu marriage 38
   (i) Customary rites and ceremonies 39
   (ii) Saptapadi 39
   (iii) Inter caste marriage 39
   (iv) Presumption of marriage 39
Restitution of conjugal rights 40
   (i) Difference between restitution of conjugal rights and judicial separation 41
   (ii) Existence of marriage 41
   (iii) Withdrawal from the society of other spouse 41
   (iv) Reasonable excuse 41
   (v) Satisfaction of court 42
   (vi) District Court 42
   (vii) Enforcement of decree for restitution 42
   (viii) Counter claim by respondent 43
Judicial separation 43
Resumption of cohabitation 43
Grounds for judicial separation under English law 44
Nullity of marriage 44
Void marriages 44
   (i) Effect of void marriage 44
   (ii) Distinction between void and voidable marriage 45
   (iii) Grounds of void marriage in England and Australia 45
Voidable marriages 46
   (i) Impotency of a party 46
   (ii) Unsoundness of mind 47
   (iii) Consent 47
   (iv) Pregnancy at the time of marriage 48
   (v) Sub-section (2) of section 12 48
Divorce 49
   (i) Adultery 49
   (ii) Cruelty 50
   (iii) Desertion 51
   (iv) Conversion to another religion 52
   (v) Unsoundness of mind 52

Chapter		Page
8	**The Hindu Marriage Act 1955**—*continued*	
	(*vi*) Leprosy	52
	(*vii*) Venereal disease	52
	(*viii*) Renunciation	53
	(*ix*) Disappearance	53
	(*x*) Non-resumption of co-habitation after the decree of judicial separation	53
	(*xi*) Refusal to comply with decree of restitution of conjugal right	53
	Alternative relief in divorce proceedings	57
	Divorce by mutual consent	57
	Restriction on presentation of petition for divorce	58
	Remarriage by divorced person	59
	Legitimacy of children of void and voidable marriages	59
	Bigamy and punishment	60
	Punishment for contravention of section 5	61
	Jurisdiction and procedure	61
	(A) Contents of petition	62
	(B) Application of Code of Civil Procedure	62
	(C) Power of transfer of petitions	63
	(D) Expeditious trial and disposal of appeal	64
	(E) Documentary evidence	64
	(F) Proceedings to be in camera	64
	Decree in proceedings	64
	Right to make counter-claim	66
	Interim maintenance	67
	Permanent maintenance	69
	Custody of children	70
	Disposal of joint property	71
	Appeals from decrees and orders	72
	Enforcement of decrees and orders	73
	Savings and repeals	74
9	**The Hindu Marriages (Validation of Proceedings) Act 1960**	**75**
	Introduction	75
	Validation of proceedings of certain courts under the Hindu Marriage Act 1955	76
10	**The Hindu Adoptions and Maintenance Act 1956**	**77**
	Introduction	77
	Applicability of the Act	78
	Requisites of valid adoption	79
	(*i*) Capacity to adopt	79
	(*ii*) Capacity of person giving in adoption	80
	(*iii*) Person to be adopted	81
	(*iv*) Other conditions for a valid adoption	81
	Effect of adoption	83

Chapter		Page
10	**The Hindu Adoptions and Maintenance Act 1956**—*continued*	
	Prohibition of certain payments	86
	Maintenance of wife	86
	Maintenance of widowed daughter-in-law	88
	Maintenance of children and aged parents	89
	Nine classes of dependants for maintenance	90
	Maintenance of dependants	91
	Quantum of maintenance	92
	Miscellaneous	93
	(a) Charge of maintenance	93
	(b) Priority of debts	94
	(c) Effect of transfer of property on right of maintenance	94
	(d) Saving of adoption	95
11	**The Hindu Minority and Guardianship Act 1956**	**96**
	Objects of the Hindu Minority and Guardianship Act 1956	96
	Principal changes introduced in the 1956 Act	96
	Applicability of Hindu Minority and Guardianship Act	97
	Natural guardian of a Hindu minor	98
	Powers of natural guardian	100
	Testamentary guardians and their powers	101
	Certain limitations relating to guardian	102
	Considerations for appointment of guardian	102
12	**Joint Hindu Family**	**104**
	Composition of joint Hindu family	104
	Presumptions	105
	Joint family property and separate property	105
	Powers of manager or father to alienate coparcenary property	106
	A leading case	108
	Facts of the case	108
	Point for decision	108
	Decision	109
	Points decided	109
	Rights of coparceners	109
	(A) Community of interest and unity of possession	109
	(B) Share of income	109
	(C) Right to partition	109
	(D) Exclusion from joint property	109
	(E) Alienation	110
	(F) Manager	110
	Management of Hindu joint family property	110
	(A) Position	110
	(B) Rights of a manager	110
	(C) Powers of a manager	110
	(D) Liability of a manager	111
	Power of manager to start new business	111
	Liability of a coparcener	111

Chapter		Page
12	**Joint Hindu Family**—*continued*	
	Remedies of a coparcener	112
	(A) Right to sue	112
	(B) Suit for injunction	112
	(C) Suit for partition	112
13	**Joint Family Property and Partition**	113
	Meanings of words "joint", "property" and "partition"	113
	(a) Joint	114
	(b) Property	114
	(c) Partition	116
	Distinction between joint property and joint family property	117
	Ancestral property—meaning and scope of	118
	Some illustrative cases	120
	(i) Property acquired by adverse possession	120
	(ii) Income derived from practice	120
	(iii) Custom and succession to ancestral property	121
	(iv) Property acquired by gift or will from paternal ancestor	121
	Joint family property and burden of proof	121
	Proof and presumption of joint family property	122
	Separate property	123
	Partition under the Mitakshara and the Dayabhaga systems	124
	Persons entitled to claim partition	125
	Effect of partition	126
	Reunion	127
	Partition by agreement	128
	Partial partition	128
	Presumptions in a partition suit	128
	Mode of effecting partition	129
	(i) Division of status	129
	(ii) Conversion to another religion	130
	(iii) Marriage under the Special Marriage Act 1954	130
	(iv) Reference to arbitration	130
	Division of property	130
	(i) Agreement	130
	(ii) Arbitration	130
	(iii) Suit	130
	Sham partition	131
	Incidents of impartible estate	131
	Impartible estate and joint family property	131
	Relinquishment of right of succession to impartible estate	132
	Alienation of impartible estate	132
	Impartible estate and self-acquired property	132
	Partition Act 1893	132
14	**Gift**	133
	Nature and limitation	133
	Formalities	133

Chapter		Page
14	**Gift**—*continued*	
	Gift to unborn person	134
	Direction to accumulate	134
	Essentials of a valid gift	134
	(*i*) Donor	134
	(*ii*) Acceptance by donee	135
	(*iii*) Subject matter	135
	Revocation of gift	135
	Registration of gift of immovable property	135
	Definition of gift under the Gift Tax Act 1958	135
	Gift of properties of bhumidar	136
15	**Wills**	**137**
	Definition and scope	137
	Power of disposition under wills	137
	Formalities	138
	Beneficiaries under a will	138
	Construction of a will	139
	Conditions and directions in a will	139
	Factors to be considered for determination of intention of a testator	140
	No terms of will to be altered by executor	140
16	**Religious and Charitable Endowments**	**141**
	Essentials of religious endowment	141
	Dedication	142
	Proof of dedication	142
	Distinction between public and private endowments	143
	Illusory endowment	144
	Tests for public temple	144
	Deity and Image	145
	Devasthan, Math, Shebait, Mohunt	145
	Powers of shebait	146
	Duties and liabilities of shebait	147
	Pujari	148
	Mathadhipati	148
	Legal status of idol and temple	148
	Ceremonies required to become "Sanyasi"	148
	Sale of one-half share in shebaiti right	149
17	**The Hindu Succession Act 1956**	**150**
	Changes made by the Act in the traditional Hindu law of succession	150
	Abrogation of Hindu law on succession	151
	Customs of tribals	152
	Sections 4(2), 14(2)—Devolution of land on widow	152
	Devolution of interest in coparcenary property	152
	General rules of succession in case of males	153
	Changes effected under section 8 of the Hindu Succession Act	154

Chapter		Page
17	**The Hindu Succession Act 1956**—*continued*	
	Succession by Hindu females	155
	Validity of section 14 of the Hindu Succession Act 1956	158
	Is section 14 prospective or retrospective?	158
	Devolution of interest in coparcenary property	159
	Position of a female inheriting a share in a dwelling house	160
	Section 23 proviso (prior to deletion w.e.f. 09.09.2005) and after—Effect	160
	Right of a child in the womb	161
	Presumption in cases of simultaneous deaths	161
	Right of pre-emption	162
	Persons disqualified to inherit	163
	Effects of disqualification and failure of any heir to succeed	163
	Section 29A	164
	Testamentory succession	164

Part 3 – Muslim Family Law

18	**Introduction**	167
	Schools of Mahomedan law	167
	A. Sunni law	167
	(*i*) The Hanafi school	167
	(*ii*) The Maliki school	167
	(*iii*) The Shafei school	167
	(*iv*) The Hanbali school	168
	Shia laws	168
	Effect of change of sect	168
	Sources of Mahomedan law	168
	(1) The Koran	168
	(2) The Hadis	168
	(3) Ijmaa	168
	(4) Kiyas	169
	(5) Custom	169
	General rules of interpretation of the Hanafi law	169
	Application of Mahomedan law	169
	Conversion to Mahomedanism and its effect on marital rights	169
	Effect of conversion to Mahomedanism on inheritance	170
	Excommunication	170
	Religious practice	170
19	**The Muslim Personal Law (Shariat) Application Act 1937**	171
	Object	171
	Title, extent and applicability	171
	Declaration in prescribed form, necessary	171
	Rule making powers of State Government	172
20	**Marriage and Sonship**	173
	Definition of marriage	173
	Essentials of a valid Muslim marriage	173

Chapter		Page
20	**Marriage and Sonship**—*continued*	
	Marriage of fosterage	174
	Celebration of marriage	174
	Capacity for Muslim marriage	174
	Kinds of marriage	174
	Marriage by recognition	175
	Presumption of lawful marriage	175
	Points of decision	176
	Decision	176
	Reasons for decision	176
	Points decided	176
	Muta marriage	177
	Plurality of marriages	177
	Second marriage by Hindu convert	177
	Dower (mahr)	177
	Dower debt	178
	Disentitlement of dower	178
	Restitution of conjugal rights	178
	Divorce	179
	Talak	179
	Ila	179
	Zihar	179
	Talak under compulsion	180
	Judicial decree	180
	Iddat	180
	Lian	181
	Effect of conversion of a Muslim wife to other faith	181
	Custody of child	181
21	**Gifts**	**182**
	Distinction between Hiba and Hiba-bil-iwej	182
	Death-bed gifts	183
	Gift of mushaa	184
	Conditions for making valid gift	185
	Revocation of gifts	185
	Hiba-ba-shart-ul-iwaz	186
	Areeat	186
22	**Wakf**	**187**
	Conditions of valid wakf	187
	Wakf, creation of	188
	Validity of wakfnama	189
	Bequest creating wakf, when invalid	189
	Powers and functions of mutawalli	189
	Alienation of wakf property	190
	Revocation of wakf	190
	Valid objects of wakf	191

Chapter		Page
22	**Wakf**—*continued*	
	Imambara	191
	Office of imam	191
	Sajjadanashin	191
	Appointment of mutawalli	192
	Position of mutawalli	192
	Graveyard	192
	Mosque of public character	193
	Mosque	193
23	**Wills**	**194**
	Conditions for a valid will	194
	Limits of bequest by a will	194
	Kinds of executors	195
	Powers of executor	195
	Revocation of bequest	195
24	**Pre-emption**	**196**
	Origin of pre-emption under Mahommedan law	196
	Definition of pre-emption and persons entitled to pre-emption	196
	Formality for pre-emption	197
	Loss of right of pre-emption	198
	Pre-emption by a shafi	198
25	**Succession, Administration and Partition**	**199**
	Administration of estate of a deceased Mahomedan	199
	Guardian for minor and his property	200
	Devolution of property on death	200
	Partition	201
26	**Inheritance**	**202**
	General rules	202
	(1) No distinction between ancestral and self acquired property	202
	(2) Doctrine of representation	202
	(3) No transfer of the right of spes successionis	202
	(4) Life estate not recognised	203
	(5) Joint family	203
	(6) Homicide	203
	Classes of heirs	203
	Sharers	203
	Examples	205
	Residuaries	206
	Examples	207
	Distant kindred	209
	Rules of preference amongst distant kindred	209
	Example of order of succession	209
	Definition	209
	Posthumous child	210
	Simultaneous death	210

Chapter		Page
27	**Maintenance under Muslim Law**...	211
28	**The Muslim Women (Protection of Rights on Divorce) Act 1986**..	213
	Objectives of the Act	213
	Applicability and definitions of some terms	213
	Return of mohr and other properties of Muslim woman on divorce	214
	Order of maintenance to divorced Muslim woman by others	214
	Option for sections 125 to 128, Cr PC	215
	Some illustrative cases	215
	Meaning of expression	216

Part 4 – Christian Family Law

29	**The Indian Christian Marriage Act 1872**................................	219
	Preliminary	219
	Persons by whom marriages may be solemnised	219
	Time and place of solemnisation of marriage	220
	(A) Time	220
	(B) Place	221
	Marriages solemnised by licensed Ministers of Religion	221
	Registration of marriages solemnised by Minister of Religion......	222
	Marriages solemnised by or in the presence of a Marriage Registrar	223
	Marriage of Indian Christians	225
	Penalties	226
	Miscellaneous	228
30	**The Divorce Act 1869**..	229
	Objects and reasons of the Act	229
	Amendments	229
	Test of Christianity	229
	Test of domicile	230
	Test of residence	230
	Jurisdiction of court	231
	Dissolution of marriage	231
	Divorce by mutual consent	232
	Power of court to dismiss petition for dissolution	233
	Power of court in dissolving marriage	233
	Nullity of marriage	234
	Judicial separation	234
	Restitution of conjugal rights	235
	Alimony	235
	Custody of children	236
	Procedure	237
	Remarriage	237

Chapter		Page
31	**The Intestate Succession to Christian under the Indian Succession Act 1925**...	238
	As to what property deceased considered to have died intestate (section 30)	238
	Devolution of property of an intestate (section 32)	238
	(A) Where intestate has left widow and lineal descendants or widow and kindred only or widow and no kindred the following rule shall apply (section 33)	239
	(B) Special provision where intestate has left widow and no lineal descendants (section 33A).............................	239
	(C) Where intestate has left no widow, and where he has left no kindred (section 34)	239
	(D) Right of widower (section 35)	239
	Distribution of intestate property where there are lineal descendants	240
	(A) Where intestate has left child or children only (section 37)	240
	(B) Where intestate has left no child, but grandchild or grandchildren (section 38)	240
	(C) Where intestate has left only great-grandchildren or remoter lineal descendants (section 39)	240
	(D) Where intestate leaves lineal descendants not all in the same degree of kindred to him, and those through whom the more remote are descended are dead (section 40)	240
	Distribution of property of intestate where there are no lineal descendants	241
	(A) When intestate's father living (section 42)	241
	(B) Where intestate's father dead, but his mother, brothers and sisters living (section 43)............................	241
	(C) Where intestate's father dead and his mother, a brother or sister and children of any deceased brother or sister, living (section 44)...	242
	(D) Where intestate's father dead and his mother and children of any deceased brother or sister living (section 45)	242
	(E) Where intestate's father dead, but his mother living and no brother, sister, nephew or niece (section 47)	242
	(F) Where intestate has left neither lineal descendant nor parents, nor brother nor sister (section 48)	242
	Children's advancements not brought into hotchpot (section 49)	243
32	**The Converts' Marriage Dissolution Act 1866**........................	244
	Preliminary	244
	Convert deserted by the spouse	244
	Jurisdiction of court	244
	Procedure	245
	Status of children...	247

Chapter		Page
32	**The Converts' Marriage Dissolution Act 1866**—*continued*	
	Alimony	247
	Reference of question of conversion to High Court	248

Part 5 – Parsi Family Law

33	**The Parsi Marriage and Divorce Act 1936**	**251**
	Object of Parsi Marriage and Divorce Act 1936	251
	Requisites of valid Parsi marriages	251
	Unlawful remarriage and punishment of bigamy	252
	Registration of marriage	252
	Penalty for breach of certain provisions of the Act	252
	Parsi Matrimonial Courts	253
	Nullity of marriage	254
	Dissolution of marriage	254
	Divorce by mutual consent	255
	Suit for judicial separation	255
	No bar to grant decrees in certain cases	255
	Suit for restitution of conjugal rights	256
	Counter-claim and documentary evidence	256
	Alimony pendente lite	256
	Permanent alimony and maintenance	256
	Disposal of joint property	257
	Liberty to parties to remarry	257
	Custody of children	257
34	**The Intestate Succession to Parsi under the Indian Succession Act 1925**	**258**
	General principles relating to intestate succession among Parsis (section 50)	258
	Division of intestate's property among widow, widower, children and parents (section 51)	258
	Division of share of predeceased child of intestate leaving lineal descendants (section 53)	259
	Division of property where, intestate leaves no lineal descendant but leaves a widow or widower or a widow or widower of any lineal descendant (section 54)	259
	Division of property where intestate leaves neither lineal descendants nor a widow or widower nor a widow or widower of any lineal descendant (section 55)	260
	Division of property where there is no relative entitled to succeed under other provisions (section 56)	260

Part 6 – Secular Law of Family

35	**The Special Marriage Act 1954**	**263**
	Objects of the Act	263
	Amendments	263

Chapter		Page
35	**The Special Marriage Act 1954**—*continued*	
	Application and commencement of the Act	263
	Conditions for solemnisation of special marriages	263
	Notice of intended marriage	264
	Marriage Officer, Marriage Notice Book and publication	264
	Objection to marriage and procedure on receipt of objection	265
	Powers of Marriage Officer in respect of inquiry	266
	Solemnisation of marriage	266
	Registration of marriages celebrated in other forms	267
	Consequences of marriage under the Act	268
	Restitution of conjugal rights	269
	Judicial separation	269
	Void marriage	270
	Voidable marriage	270
	Some illustrative cases	271
	Legitimacy of children of void and voidable marriages	271
	Divorce and alternative relief in proceedings	271
	Some illustrative cases	272
	Irretrievable breakdown of marriage	273
	Alternative relief	273
	Divorce by mutual consent	273
	Restriction for divorce during first year of marriage and remarriage	274
	Jurisdiction and procedure	274
	Some illustrative cases	275
	Proceedings to be in camera	275
	Duty of court in passing decrees	275
	Some illustrative cases	276
	Counter-claim by respondent	276
	Alimony pendente lite	276
	Permanent alimony and maintenance	277
	Custody of children	277
	Appeals from decrees and orders	278
	Enforcement of decree and order	278
	Power to transfer petition	278
	Disposal of petition and appeal	279
	Documentary evidence	279
	Penal provisions	279
36	**The Foreign Marriage Act 1969**	**280**
	Objects and reasons	280
	Preliminary	280
	Conditions for solemnisation of foreign marriage	281
	Other formalities of foreign marriage	281
	Registration of foreign marriages	282
	Matrimonial reliefs in respect of foreign marriages (section 18)	282
	Penalty	283
	Miscellaneous	283

Chapter		Page
37	**The Family Courts Act 1984**	**284**
	Aims and objects	284
	Extent and applicability of the Act	285
	Family Courts	285
	Appointment of Judges	285
	Shifting of Family Court	286
	Counsellors, officers and employees of Family Court	286
	Jurisdiction of Family Court	286
	Some illustrative cases	287
	Exclusion of jurisdiction	287
	Duty of Family Court to endeavour for settlement	288
	Procedure for Family Court	288
	Execution of decree and order	289
	No inconsistency between s. 8 and s. 18	290
	Appeal	290
	Some illustrative cases	290
38	**The Dowry Prohibition Act 1961**	**292**
	Origin and object	292
	Evil effects of dowry	292
	Applicability of the Dowry Prohibition Act 1961	293
	Definition of dowry	293
	Illustrative cases	293
	Penalty for dowry	293
	Cognizance of offence	294
	Illustrative cases	295
39	**The Guardians and Wards Act 1890**	**297**
	Introduction	297
	Right of natural guardian to custody of child	297
40	**The Religious Endowments Act 1863**	**298**
	Introduction	298
	No power to grant perpetual lease of math properties	298
	No dedication of property before gift	298
	Filling in vacancy in Committee of Wakf	299
41	**The Indian Succession Act 1925**	**300**
	Introduction	300
	General application of Part VI dealing with succession (section 58)	301
	Person capable of making Wills (section 59)	301
	Testamentary guardian (section 60)	301
	Effect of Will obtained by fraud, coercion or importunity (section 61)	302
	Revocation of Will (section 62)	302
	Execution of unprivileged Wills (section 63)	303
	Suspicious circumstances	303
	Incorporation of papers by reference (section 64)	303

Chapter		Page
41	**The Indian Succession Act 1925**—*continued*	
	Privileged Wills (section 65)	303
	Mode of making and rules for executing, privileged Wills (section 66)	304
	Gift to attesting witness (section 67)	305
	Witness not disqualified by interest or by being executor (section 68)	305
	Revocation of Will or Codicil (sections 69, 70)	305
	Revocation of privileged Will or codicil (section 72)	305
	Revival of unprivileged Will (section 73)	305
	Construction of Wills	306
	Representative title to property of testator	306
	Grant of probate and letters of administration	307
	Alteration and revocation of grants	308
	Petition for probate (section 276)	308
	Petition for letters of administration (section 278)	309
	Petition for probate or letters of administration to be signed and verified (sections 280, 281)	309
	No change in terms of Will	309
	Succession certificates	310
	Revocation of succession certificate (section 383)	311
42	**Maintenance under Code of Criminal Procedure 1973**	**312**
	Scope of section 125, Cr PC	312
	Statutory liability to maintain	312
	Interim maintenance	313
	Quantum of maintenance	313
	Cancellation or alteration of order of maintenance	313
	Limitation	314
	Forum for maintenance proceedings	314
	Recovery of maintenance	314
	Award of maintenance from date of application or order	314
43	**The Maintenance and Welfare of Parents and Senior Citizens Act 2007**	**315**
	Objects of the Maintenance and Welfare of Parents and Senior Citizens Act 2007	315
	Extent, applicability and some definitions of the Act	315
	Overriding effect of the Act	316
	Maintenance of parents and senior citizens	316
	Jurisdiction and procedure	317
	(*a*) Constitution of Maintenance Tribunal and Appellate Tribunal (sections 7, 15)	318
	(*b*) Order of maintenance (section 9)	319
	(*c*) Alteration in allowance (section 10)	319
	(*d*) Enhancement of order of maintenance (section 11)	319
	(*e*) Option regarding maintenance in certain cases (section 12)	319

CHAPTER		PAGE
43	**The Maintenance and Welfare of Parents and Senior Citizens Act 2007**—*continued*	
	(*f*) Deposit of maintenance amount (section 13)	319
	(*g*) Award of interest where any claim is allowed (section 14)	319
	(*h*) Right of legal representation (section 17)	320
	(*i*) Maintenance Officer (section 18)	320
	Appeals (section 16)	320
	Establishment of old age homes (section 19)	320
	Medical support for senior citizens (section 20)	320
	Measures for publicity, awareness, etc. for welfare of senior citizen (section 21)	321
	Authorities to be specified for implementing the provisions of the Act (section 22)	321
	Transfer of property to be void in certain circumstances (section 23)	321
	Offences and procedure for trial and Miscellaneous matters	322
	(*a*) Exposure and abandonment of senior citizen (section 24)	322
	(*b*) Cognizance of offences (section 25)	322
	(*c*) Officers to be public servant (section 26)	322
	(*d*) Protection of action taken in good faith (section 28)	322
	(*e*) Powers of Central Government (sections 30, 31)	322
	(*f*) Powers of State Governments (sections 29, 32)	322
44	**The Protection of Women from Domestic Violence Act 2005**	323
	Objects of the Protection of Women from Domestic Violence Act 2005	323
	Extent of and some definitions in the Act	324
	Domestic incident report	324
	Domestic relationship	324
	Respondent	324
	Shared household	324
	Domestic violence	325
	Powers and duties of Protection Officer	325
	Duties and powers of service provider	326
	Duties of Government (section 11)	327
	Procedure for obtaining orders of reliefs application to Magistrate (section 12)	327
	Service of notice (section 13)	327
	Counselling (section 14)	327
	Assistance of welfare expert (section 15)	327
	Proceedings to be held in camera	328
	Right to reside in a shared household (section 17)	328
	Protection orders (section 18)	328
	Residence orders (section 19)	328
	Monetary reliefs (section 20)	329
	Custody orders (section 21)	329

Chapter		Page
44	**The Protection of Women from Domestic Violence Act 2005**—*continued*	
	Compensation orders (section 22)	329
	Grant of interim and *ex parte* orders (section 23)	329
	Court to give copies of order free of cost (section 24)	329
	Duration and alteration of orders (section 25)	329
	Relief in other suits and legal proceedings (section 26)	329
	Jurisdiction (section 27)	329
	Procedure (section 28)	330
	Appeal (section 29)	330
	Miscellaneous	330
45	**The Prohibition of Child Marriage Act 2006**	**332**
	Objects and reasons of the Act	332
	Child marriages to be voidable at the option of contracting party being a child	333
	Provision for maintenance and residence to female contracting party to child marriage (section 4)	333
	Custody and maintenance of children of child marriage (section 5)	334
	Legitimacy of children born of child marriage (section 6)	334
	Power of district court to modify orders	334
	Jurisdiction	334
	Punishment for male adult marrying a child (section 9)	334
	Punishment for solemnising a child marriage (section 10)	334
	Punishment for promoting or permitting solemnisation of child marriages (section 11)	334
	Marriage of minor child to be void in certain cases (section 12)	335
	Power of court to issue injunction prohibiting child marriage (section 13)	335
	Duties of Child Marriage Prohibition Officer	336
	Power of State Government to make rules (section 19)	336
	Amendment and repeal	336
Index		337

Table of Cases

A. Hassan *v* T. Hussain AIR 1958 Pat 232 4
A. Jayachandra *v* Aneel Kaur (2005)2 SCC 22 56
A. Nair *v* C. Amma AIR 1966 SC 411 122
A.E.T. Naidu *v* Rajammal AIR 1968 Mad 201 42
Abaji *v* Mukta (1894)18 Bom 688 133
Abdul Aziz *v* Fateh Mahomed (1911)38 Cal 518 184
Abdul Kadir *v* Salima (1886)8 All 149 173
Abdul Kasem *v* Jamila Khatun Bibi AIR 1940 Cal 251 174
Abdul Latif *v* Nyaz Ahmed (1909)31 All 343 174
Abdul Rahim *v* Sk. Abdul Zabar (2009)6 SCC 160; AIR 2010 SC 211 185
Abdul Serang *v* Pulee Bibi (1902)29 Cal 738 203
Abdur Rahim *v* Padma AIR 1982 Bom 341 282
Abdus Salam *v* Abdul Aziz (1944)48 CWN 465 192
Abhay Chandra *v* Payari Mohan (1870)5 Beng LR 347 111
Abraham *v* Abraham (1863)9 MIA 195 (PC) 30, 169
Adam *v* Gopal AIR 1974 Mad 232 90
Adams *v* Palmer (1863)51 Maine 480 6
Adhunik Grah Nirman Sahakari Samiti Ltd. *v* State of Rajasthan AIR 1989 SC 867 ... 4
Adiraju *v* A.S. Murthy (1979)2 Andh LT 85 95
Aftabuddin *v* Chandan Balasint AIR 1977 Ori 69 84
Afzalunnisa Begum *v* State of AP 2009 Cr LJ 4191 (AP) 324
Ahmed G. H. Ariff *v* CWT AIR 1971 SC 1691 192
Akshay Kumar *v* Jatindranath AIR 1955 Cal 612 26
Alluri Balas *v* Alluri Varalakshmi AIR 1976 AP 365 90
Alungaparambil Abdul Khader Shud *v* State of Kerala AIR 2007 DOC 126 (Ker) .. 268
Amarendra *v* Mansing AIR 1933 PC 155 77
Amedabad St. Zavier's College *v* State of Gujarat AIR 1974 SC 1389 15
Amer Singh *v* Tej Ram AIR 1982 Punj 282 81
Amina Khatun *v* Khalilur Rahaman (1933)8 Luck 445; AIR 1933 Oudh 246 ... 21
Amirtha *v* Sornam AIR 1977 Mad 127 (FB) 101
Ammathayee *v* Kumareson AIR 1967 SC 569 133
Amrita Lal *v* Suronoomani (1898)25 Cal 662 139
Anand Ruia *v* Vidhas Ruia 2004(1) Cal HN 685 313
Anandi *v* Nirmala AIR 2000 SC 1386 90
Anant Bhikappa Patil *v* Shankar Ramchandra Patil AIR 1943 PC 196 117
Anantha *v* Nagamuthu (1882)4 Mad 200 142

Andal *v* Sivaprakasa AIR 1963 Mad 452 159
Angat Singh *v* Dhan Kaur AIR 1964 Punj 393 89
Angrez *v* Baldeo AIR 1980 Punj 171 57
Anil Kumar Jain *v* Maya Jain AIR 2010 SC 229 .... 57, 58
Anima *v* Mohan Bai AIR 1969 Cal 304 38
Animuthu *v* Gandhi Ammal AIR 1977 Mad 372 89
Aniruddha Mitra *v* Arabinda Mitra AIR 1946 Cal 396 31
Anita Karmakar *v* Birendra Chandra Karmakar AIR 1962 Cal 88 63
Anita Laxmi *v* Laxmi Narayan AIR 1992 SC 1148 69
Anjali Kapoor *v* Rajiv Baijal (2009)7 SCC 322 297
Anjula *v* Milan AIR 1981 All 178 62
Anjum Hasan Siddiqui *v* Salma AIR 1992 All 332 214
Anjuman *v* Munshi (1971)3 SCC 814 188
Anna Saheb *v* Tarabai AIR 1970 MP 36 41
Annamalal *v* Subramanian AIR 1929 PC 1 122
Ansuva *v* Rajaih AIR 1971 AP 296 70
Anusha *v* K. Shankar Raman 1998(4) Civ LJ 389 (Kant) 290
Apaji *v* Ramchandra (1812)16 Bom 29 125
Appibai *v* Khimji (1936)60 Bom 455 33
Approvier *v* Rama Subba Aiyan (1866)11 MIA 75 (PC) 116, 124, 126, 128
Are Lachiah *v* Are Raja Mallar (1964)1 Cr LJ 237 (AP) 74
Arti Singh *v* Kanwar Pal Singh AIR 1977 Del 76 68
Arumugha *v* Valliammal AIR 1969 Mad 72 83
Aruna Basu *v* Dorothea Mitra AIR 1983 SC 916 277
Arunachala Mudaliar *v* Muruganatha AIR 1953 SC 495 .... 107, 121
Aryamusht *v* Subbaraya Setty AIR 1972 SC 1279 123
Asha Bibi *v* Nabissa Sahib AIR 1957 Mad 583 4
Asha Narang *v* Dr. Ved Prakash Narang (1997)11 SCC 667 63
Asha Qureshi *v* Afaq Qureshi AIR 2002 MP 263 271
Ashna Bibi *v* Awaljadi (1917)44 Cal 698 190
Ashok Kumar *v* Shabnam AIR 1989 Del 21 52
Ashoke *v* Raymond AIR 1976 Cal 272 80
Asifa Khatoon *v* Rubina 2009(4) Cal HN 490 330
Asrabai *v* Dhondiram ILR (1977) Bom 870 39
Atmoram *v* Bajirao AIR 1935 PC 57 22
Att.-Gen. of Ceylon *v* A.R. Arunachatam Chettiar [1957] AC 540 (PC) 105
Audh Behari *v* Gajadhar AIR 1954 SC 417 196
Authikesavalu *v* Ramanuja (1909)32 Mad 512 11
Avinash Devi *v* Dr. Khazan AIR 1960 Punj 326 .... 99, 103
Ayyapan *v* Vasantha AIR 1988 Ker 314 63
Aziz Bano *v* Muhammed (1925)47 All 823 169

B. Das *v* K. Devi AIR 1980 Ori 171 49
B.D. Charles *v* Nara Benjamin AIR 1979 Raj 156 (SB) 232
Baboolal *v* Prem Lata AIR 1974 Raj 93 71
Babu Ningappa *v* Arunkumar AIR 1988 Kant 139 78
Babu Ram *v* Keshwa Chand AIR 1978 Punj 174 103
Babubhai *v* Ujamal AIR 1937 PC 446 122
Baccha Jha *v* Judmon Jha (1886)12 Cal 348 (PC) 24
Badri Prasad *v* Dy. Director of Consolidation AIR 1976 SC 1557 39

Case	Page
Bai Kevli v Dalsukhram AIR 1945 Bom 178	140
Baikuntha Nath v Sashi Bhusan AIR 1972 SC 2531	123
Bajirao R. Tambare v Tolanbai 1980 Cr LJ 478 (Bom)	37, 45
Bakshi Ram v Shila Devi AIR 1960 Punj 304	99
Bakulabai v Gangaram (1988)1 SCC 537	312
Balabux v Rukhmabai (1903)30 Cal 725	127
Balbir Singh v Swaran Kanta AIR 1981 Raj 266	67
Baldev Sahai v R.C. Bhasin AIR 1982 SC 1091	4
Baldev Singh v State of Punjab AIR 2009 SC 913	293
Baldev v Urmila AIR 1978 SC 879	48
Baliram v Radhika AIR 1980 Pat 67	87
Balkrishen Das v Ram Narain (1903)30 IA 139 (PC)	126, 128
Balkrishna R. Kadam v Sangeeta B. Kadam AIR 1997 SC 3562	72
Balusu v Balusu (1899)26 IA 113	20
Balwant Kaur v Chanan Singh AIR 2000 SC 1908	89, 139, 155
Balwant Singh v Sardarni Balwant Kaur AIR 1957 Pepsu 1	36, 74
Balwinder Kaur v Hardeep Singh AIR 1998 SC 764	73
Balwinder v Gurpal AIR 1985 Del 14	74
Bami Reddy v Gangi AIR 1925 Mad 807	24
Banabai v Wasudeo AIR 1979 Bom 181	83
Bankim Chandra v Anjali Roy AIR 1972 Pat 80	68
Bansidhar v Seema 1992 Cr LJ 1562 (All)	289
Baqar Ali v Anjuman (1902)25 All 236	168
Basudeo v Jugal Kishore 22 CWN 841 (PC)	146
Bata v Gopal (1907)5 Cal LJ 417	125
Bathula v Bathula AIR 1981 AP 74	56
Bawi v Nath AIR 1970 J&K 130	46
Bazayet Hossein v Dooli Chand (1878)5 IA 211	199
Beer Pertab v Rajendra (1867)12 MIA 37 (PC)	137
Bengal Insurance and Real Property Co. Ltd. v Velayammal AIR 1937 Mad 521	109
Bhabani Prosad v Sarat Sundari AIR 1957 Cal 527	158
Bhagat Ram v Teja Singh AIR 1999 SC 1944	160
Bhagirathibai v Kahnujirav (1908)11 Bom 285 (FB)	24
Bhagwan Dayal v Reoti Devi AIR 1962 SC 287	104
Bhagwan Koer v Bose (1904)31 Cal 11	19
Bhagwan Krishan Gupta v Prabha Gupta 2009(3) CHN 198 (SC)	306
Bhagwan v Harihar AIR 1955 NUC 3982	130
Bhagwati Prasad v Dulhin Rameswari Kaur AIR 1952 SC 72	128
Bhalu v Hemo AIR 1969 Ori 236	68
Bhaurao Shankar Lokhande v State of Maharashtra AIR 1965 SC 1564	39, 60
Bhima Bai v Gurunath Gonda AIR 1933 PC 1	24
Bhima v Dhulappa (1905)7 Bom LR 95	41
Bhogo v Bachai AIR 1972 Punj 160	94
Bhola Umar v Kansilla AIR 1937 All 230	28
Bhola Umar v Kaunsilia AIR 1932 All 617 (FB)	27
Bholanath v Santosh AIR 1975 Pat 336	162
Bhondu v Ramdayal AIR 1960 MP 51 (FB)	27
Bhuboneshwar v Special Tahasildar AIR 1980 AP 139	90
Bhugwandeen v Myna Baee (1867)11 MIA 487 (PC)	23
Bhuri v Champi AIR 1968 Raj 139	163

Bhuru Mal v Jagannath AIR 1942 PC 13 123
Bibi Saddiqa v Saiyed Mohd. Mahmood Hasan
  AIR 1978 SC 1362; (1978)3 SCC 299 .... 180, 190, 192
Bibuni v Padmanav AIR 1956 Ori 105 4
Bihar State Board v Palat Lal AIR 1972 SC 57 143
Bijoy Krishna Ghosal v Namita Ghosal AIR 1991 Cal 34 72
Bijoychand v Kalipada (1914)41 Cal 57 142
Bimal Krishna v Jnanendra AIR 1937 Cal 338 148
Binda Prasad v Mudrika Devi AIR 1968 Pat 196 93
Bipinchandra S. Bhatt v Madhuriban Bhatt AIR 1963 Guj 250 62
Bipinchandra v Prabhavati AIR 1957 SC 176 51
Bishambhar Nath Gopi Nath v Hashim Begam AIR 1949 Oudh 56 200
Bishundas v Seogeni Rao AIR 1953 SC 280 112
Bishundeo Narain v Seogeni Bai AIR 1951 SC 280 126
Bissessur Lall v Luchmessur (1879)6 IA 233 (PC) 123
Blyth v Blyth [1966]2 WLR 634 (HL) 276
Boolchand v Janokee 25 WR 386 33
Brij Raj Singh v Sewak Ram AIR 1999 SC 2203 135
Brijnarain v Mangala Prasad (1924)28 CWN 253 (PC);
  46 All 95; 41 CLJ 232; 51 IA 129 108
Brindavan v Radhamoney (1889)12 Mad 72 11
Buddha Singh v Laltu Singh AIR 1915 PC 70 24
Bulaki v Lal Dhar AIR 1998 SC 2900 136

C. Krishna Prasad v C.I.T. (1975)1 SCC 160; AIR 1975 SC 498 .... 4, 117, 118
C. Sonnaiah v Padma AIR 1983 Kant 114 43
Cally Nath v Chundar Nath (1882) Cal 378 134
Captain Ramesh Chander Kaushal v Mrs. Veena Kaushal
  AIR 1978 SC 1807; (1978)4 SCC 70 .... 312, 313
Central Bank of India v Ram Narain AIR 1955 SC 36 97
Chaira Obula v Caova Pedda AIR 1976 AP 43 86
Chakko v Daniel AIR 1953 Trav-Co. 61 220
Chaman Lal v Mohan Lal AIR 1977 Del 97 163
Chanchal Kumari v Kewal Krishan AIR 1972 Punj 474 47
Chand Dhawan v Jawaharlal Dhawan 1993 Cr LJ 2930 (SC); (1993)3 SCC 406 70
Chanda v Nandu AIR 1965 MP 268 54
Chandan Bilasini (Smt.) v Aftabuddin Khan AIR 1996 SC 591 .... 79, 82
Chander Prabha v Prem Nath Kapur AIR 1969 Del 283 99
Chandra Kishore v Nank Chand AIR 1975 Del 175 .... 89, 90
Chandra Mohini Srivastava v Avinash Prasad Srivastava
  AIR 1967 SC 581 .... 50, 59, 66, 274
Chandrabhai K. Bhoir v Krishna Arjun Bhoir AIR 2009 SC 1645;
  (2009)2 SCC 315 .... 140, 309
Chandramathi v Pazhetti Balan AIR 1982 Ker 68 50
Chellaiyan v Sathia Krishnan AIR 1982 Mad 148 91
Chigurupati Bambasiva Rao v Chigurupati Vijayalaxmi (1997)11 SCC 84 313
Chinnaperumal v M. Ammal AIR 1976 Mad 179 66
Chinnathayi v Kulaskara AIR 1952 SC 29 132
Chiranjilal Shirilal Goenka v Jasjit Singh 1993 AIR SCW 1439 307
Chiranjilal Srilal Goenka v Jasjit Singh AIR 2001 SC 266 83

Table of Cases

Chitar Mal v Panchu Lal AIR 1926 All 392 148
Chito Mahto v Lila Mahto AIR 1991 Pat 186 120
Chotalal v Manohar (1900)26 IA 199 (PC) 147, 148
Christinamary v Vijay Siddharaj AIR 1979 Mad 100 (SB) 237
Chunilal v Suraj Ram (1909)33 Bom 433 .... 11, 33
CIT v Seth Govindram AIR 1966 SC 24 110
Clarance v Raichad AIR 1964 Mys 67 (SB) 66
Collector of Madhura v Muttu Ramlinga 10 WR 21 (PC);
  (1868)12 MIA 397 (PC) 21, 22, 23
Commissioner of Income Tax v Laxminarayan (1935)59 Bom 618 104
Commissioner of Income-Tax v Pemsel [1891] AC 531 141
Commr. Hindu Religious Endowments, Madras v
  Sri Lakshmindra Thirtha Swamiar AIR 1954 SC 282 .... 114, 148
Commr. of Gift tax, Trivandrum v T.M. Louiz AIR 2000 SC 3136 136
Commr. of Gift Tax (Andhra Pradesh) v Gollapadi 1978 Tax LR 2006 86
Commr. or Income-tax, Bombay v Ratilal Natha Lal AIR 1954 SC 503 108
Controller of Estate Duty v Haji Abdul Sattar AIR 1972 SC 2229 170
Corbett v Corbett (1971) p. 83; [1970]2 All ER 33 7
Corporation of the City of Nagpur v
  Nagpur Handloom Cloth Market Co. Ltd. AIR 1963 SC 1192 4

D. Achi v R.M.Al.Ct.C. Chettiar AIR 1954 Mad 657 26
D. Udayar v Rajarani AIR 1973 Mad 369 .... 87, 90
D.S. Agalawe v P.M. Agalawe AIR 1988 SC 845 85
Daftardar v Daftardar AIR 1972 Bom 132 48
Dalchand v Kamlabai (2000)2 SCC 209 152
Damiraiji v Chandraprabha AIR 1975 SC 784 84
Daneyl Gurumurthy v Raghu Podhan AIR 1967 Ori 63 102
Danial Latifi v Union of India AIR 2001 SC 3958 211
Darbara Singh v Karimindar Singh AIR 1979 Punj 215 100
Darshan Kumari v Surinder Kumar 1995 Supp (4) SCC 137 314
Dashrath v Pamdu (1977)79 Bom LR 426 80
Dastane v Dastane AIR 1975 SC 1534 .... 50, 66
Davaraja Raja Rao v I.T. Officer AIR 1970 AP 426 22
Debi Bhaduri v Kumarjib Bhaduri (1980)1 Cal LJ 309 73
Deivanai Achi v Kasi Vishwanathan AIR 1957 Mad 766 49
Deoki Nandan v Murlidhar AIR 1957 SC 133 .... 4, 117
Devalava v Bhimaji (1895)20 Bom 208 200
Devgonda v S.R. Patil AIR 1992 Bom 189 82
Devki v Purshotam AIR 1973 Raj 2 67
Dhani Ram v Sushila Devi AIR 1977 HP 83 73
Dhaniraiji v Chandraprabha AIR 1975 SC 784 95
Dhanraj v Suraj Bai AIR 1975 SC 1103 .... 80, 81
Dhanraj v Suraj Bai AIR 1978 Raj 7 79
Dharm Das v Shama Soondari (1843)3 MIA 229 (PC) 122
Dharmodas v Nistarani (1887)4 Cal 446 135
Dhirajkunwar v Lakhansingh AIR 1957 MP 38 159
Dinaji v Daddi AIR 1990 SC 1153 86
Dinesh v Usha AIR 1979 Bom 173 69
Dipo v Wassan Singh AIR 1983 SC 846 121

Dnyaneshwar v Anant AIR 1936 Bom 290 129
Dubey (Mrs.) v (Mr.) Dubey AIR 1951 All 529 219
Dugginal Lakshmana v D. Katamma AIR 1973 AP 302 93
Dukhi v Mabdei (1978)4 All LR 555 159
Dwarakanath v Burroda (1879)4 Cal 443 142
Dwarampudi Nagaratnamba v Kumuku Rammayya AIR 1968 SC 253 107

E.M. Pallikkaramma v K.V.P. Nair AIR 2001 SC 435 309
Earnest John White v Kathleen Olive White AIR 1958 SC 441 .... 65, 233
Ebrahim Aboobaker v Tek Chand AIR 1953 SC 298 200
Ejaz Ahmad v Khatan Begam (1917)39 All 288 192
Ekradeshwari v Homeshawar AIR 1929 PC 128 93
Elizabeth Dinshaw v Arvand M. Dinshaw AIR 1987 SC 3 71
Enatullah v Kowsher Ali (1927)54 Cal 265 198
Eramma v Veerupana AIR 1966 SC 1879 159
Fanindra v Adm. Gen. of Bengal (1901)6 Cal WN 321 142
Fazlul Rabbi v State of WB AIR 1965 SC 1722 191
Franklin Fire Ins. Co. v Shadid Com. App 68 SW 2d 1030 5

G. Apparna v G. Seethamma AIR 1972 AP 62 87
G. Sekar v Geetha (2009)6 SCC 99 161
G. v G. [1871] LR 2 P&D 287 47
G.T.M. Kothurswami v S. Veeravva AIR 1959 SC 577 156
Gajadhar v Kaunisilia (1909)31 All 161 .... 26, 27
Gajapathi Radika v Sri Gajapathi (1870)13 MIA 506 11
Ganesh Dutt v Jewach (1904)31 IA 10 105
Ganesh v Rukmani AIR 1971 Ori 65 162
Ganga Devi v Krishna Prasad Sharma AIR 1967 Ori 19 63
Ganga Devi v Sita Ram 1981 UPLT (NOC) 86 143
Ganga v Jhato (1911)38 Cal 862 28
Gangabai v Bherulal AIR 1976 Raj 153 103
Gangadhar v SLD Tribunal AIR 1991 SC 1180 81
Gangi Reddi v Tammi Raddi (1927)54 IA 136 106
Gangu v Pundlik AIR 1979 Bom 264 69
Garib Das v M.A. Hamid AIR 1970 SC 1035 189
Gaudev Kaur v Sarwan Singh AIR 1959 Punj 162 41
Gaurav Nagpal v Sumedha Nagpal (2009)1 SCC 42 103
Gauri Shankar v Hemant Kumari AIR 1936 All 301 142
Gautam Kundu v State of West Bengal AIR 1993 SC 2295 50
Gautam Sen Gupta v L.O. Sen Gupta 1998(1) CWN 406 63
Ghaidan v Godin Mendoza [2004] UKHL 30 7
Ghanshyam Lal v Kanti Devi 1979 Hindu LR 603 (Del) 41
Gian Devi v Amar Nath ILR (1975)1 Del 811 87
Giani Ram v Ramji Lal AIR 1969 SC 1144 156
Gindan v Parelal AIR 1976 MP 83 51
Girdharilal v Fateh Chand AIR 1955 MB 148 130
Girjabai v Sadashiv (1913)40 IA 40 (PC) 129
Girjabai v Sadashiv AIR 1916 PC 104 129
Githa Hariharan v Reserve Bank of India AIR 1999 SC 1149 99
Gitika Bagchi v Subhabrata Bagchi AIR 1996 Cal 246 271

Table of Cases [31]

Godabai v Narayan AIR 1973 MP 4 44
Gokal Chand v Hukum Chand AIR 1921 PC 35 106
Gokalchand v Parvin AIR 1952 SC 231 21
Golak Nath v State of Punjab AIR 1967 SC 1643 115
Gopal Lal v State of Rajasthan AIR 1979 SC 718 60
Gopal Sridhar Mahadev v Shasheebhushan Sarkar AIR 1933 Cal 109 .... 147, 148
Gopala Krishnan Nair v R. Sarasamma AIR 1980 Ker 109 74
Gour Gopal Roy v Sipra Roy AIR 1978 Cal 163 37
Govindrao v Anandibai AIR 1978 Bom 433 87
Gowli Buddanna v Commr. of IT Mysore AIR 1966 SC 1523 .... 104, 105
Gridhari Lall v Bengal Government (1868)12 MIA 448 (PC) 24
Gulam Abbas v Haji Kayyum AIR 1973 SC 554 201
Gullipilli Sowria Raj v Bandaru Pavani AIR 2009 SC 1085 44
Gulwant Kaur v Mohinder Singh AIR 1987 SC 2251 88
Gulzar v Tej Kaur AIR 1961 Punj 288 92
Guramma B.C. Deshmukh v M. Chanbasappa AIR 1964 SC 510 107
Guramma v Mallappa AIR 1964 SC 5 106
Gurbachan Singh v Kichar Singh AIR 1971 Punj 240 156
Gurdip Kaur v Chamand Singh AIR 1965 Punj 238 (FB) 89
Gurdit Singh v Darshan Singh AIR 1973 Punj 262 154
Guru Datta Sharma v State of Bihar AIR 1961 SC 1684 115
Gurudev v Malkit 1980 Hind LR 331 (Punj) 57
Gurupad v Hirabai AIR 1978 SC 1239 160

Hakim Khan v Gool Khan (1882)8 Cal 826 203
Hamilton v Mac Donald CA Ariz 503 F 2d 1138 116
Hamira Bibi v Zubaida Bibi (1916)43 IA 294 .... 169, 178
Hanmanta Laxman v D. Hanmanta AIR 1977 Bom 191 59
Hanooman parsad v Mussamat Babooee (1856)6 MIA 393 146
Hanso Patak v Harmandil Patak AIR 1934 All 851 120
Harbhajan Singh v Brij Balab Kaur AIR 1964 Punj 359 47
Hari Baksh v Babulal AIR 1924 PC 126 129
Harilal Purshottam v Lilavati Gokaldas AIR 1961 Guj 202 69
Harmohan v Kamala Kumari AIR 1979 Ori 51 45
Hashmat Ali v Nasibunnissa (1924)6 Lah 47 (PC) 21
Hasima Latifi, *in re* AIR 1962 Bom 227 268
Hayat-un-Nissa v Muhammad (1890)12 All 290 168
Hazari Mall v Ambanimath (1912)17 CWN 280 121
Hazi Mahammad Nabi v Province of Bengal AIR 1942 Cal 343 117
Himansu Sekhar Rana v Tapati Rana AIR 1995 Cal 110 42
Hira v Hansji (1913)37 Bom 295; 17 IC 941 12
Hirachand Srinivas Mahagaonkar v Sunanda AIR 2001 SC 1285; (2001)4 SCC 125 .... 43, 54
Hirakali v Ram Asrey AIR 1971 All 201 .... 59, 65
Hiralal v Lilawati AIR 1961 Guj 202 35
Howard v Marshall 48 Tex 471 5
Humeeda v Budhim (1872)17 WR 525 203
Hurpurshad v Sheo Dayal (1876)3 IA 259 (PC) 21
Hyde v Hyde [1866] LR 1 P&D 130 7

Ibrahim Goolam Ariff v Saiboo (1908)35 Cal 1 184
Ibrahim Goolam Ariff v Saido (1907)34 IA 167 184
Imambandi v Haji Mutsaddi (1918)45 IA 73 176
Inder Mal v Babu Lal AIR 1977 Raj 160 90
Inderjit Kaur v Rajinder Singh ILR (1980)2 Del 910 66
Inderjit Kaur v Union of India (1991)2 Pat LJR 104 (SC) 314
Indirabai v B.P. Patel AIR 1974 AP 303 93
Indraj v Shanti AIR 1978 All 279 73
Indranarayan v Roop Narayan AIR 1971 SC 1962 .... 122, 129
Indrawal v Radhey AIR 1981 All 151 57
Indubai v Govindrao (1980)2 Mah LR 289 63
Iqbal Bano v State of U.P. (2007)6 SCC 785 216
Iqbal Singh v Adersh 1982 All LJ 640 68
Iris Paintal v Avtar Singh Paintal AIR 1988 Del 121 273
Ishwar Das v Raj Kumar AIR 1961 Punj 275 151
Ishwar Gridher Jew v Sushila Bala Dasi AIR 1954 SC 69 147
Ishwari Bhubaneshwari v Brojo Nath Dey AIR 1937 PC 185 144

Jackson v Jackson (1912)34 All 203 237
Jadu Nath v Thakore Sita Ramji AIR 1917 PC 177 143
Jagadindra Nath Roy v Hemanta Kumari Debi (1905)32 Cal 129 145
Jagadish Kumar v Sita Devi AIR 1963 Punj 114 47
Jaganath v Narayan (1910)34 Bom 553 11
Jagannath Prasad v Ranjit Singh (1895)25 Cal 354 24
Jagat Krishna v Ajit Kumar AIR 1964 Ori 75 125
Jagdish Lal v Smt. Shyama AIR 1966 All 150 .... 41, 42
Jagdish Singh v Madhuri Devi (2008)10 SCC 497 52
Jagir Kaur v Jaswant Singh AIR 1963 SC 1521 61
Jagir Singh v State of Bihar AIR 1976 SC 997; (1976)2 SCC 942 113
Jagmohan v Ranchod Das (1945) Nag 892 125
Jagmohan v Sudesh 1979 Hind LR 303 (Punj) 57
Jagraj Singh v Birpal Kaur AIR 2007 SC 2083 66
Jai Devi v Bhishan Das AIR 1981 Punj 186 70
Jai Kaur v Sher Singh AIR 1960 SC 1118 121
Jai Prakash Khadria v Shyam Sunder Agarwala AIR 2000 SC 2172 236
Jailal v Dulari 1976 All LJ 641 92
Jairam v Nath (1907)31 Bom 54 126
Jal Kaur v Pala Singh AIR 1961 Punj 391 .... 88, 89
Jalasutram v Jalasutram AIR 1959 AP 49 68
Jamarathbee v Pralhad Dattatraya Dadpe AIR 1978 Bom 229 120
Janak Dulari v Narayan Das AIR 1959 Punj 50 75
Janakiram v Nagamony (1926)49 Mad 98 .... 105, 118
Jasbir Kaur v District Judge, Dehradun AIR 1997 SC 3397 69
Jasmet Singh v Gurnam Kaur AIR 1975 Punj 225 54
Jatindra Nath v Nagendra Nath AIR 1931 PC 268 24
Jayantilal v Asha AIR 1989 Guj 152 82
Jayantilal v Mehta AIR 1968 Guj 212 161
Jayaramchandra Iyer v Thulasi Ammal AIR 1978 Mad 95 122
Jeewanti v Kishan AIR 1982 SC 3 62
Jijabai v Pathankhar AIR 1971 SC 315 99

Table of Cases

Jivben v Dahyalal AIR 1984 Guj 6 56
Joginder Pal v Indian Red Cross Society AIR 2000 SC 3279 310
Joginder Singh v Kehar Singh AIR 1965 Punj 407 (FB) 158
Joginder Singh v Pushpa AIR 1969 Punj 397 (FB) 53
Jogindra Kaur v Shivaharan AIR 1965 J&K 95 42
Jogu Bibi v Mesal Shaikh (1936)63 Cal 415 173
John Jiban Chandra v Abinash (1939)2 Cal 12 170
Johnson v State Farm Mut. Auto Ins. Co. C.A. Mo. 252 F 2d 158 5
Jorden Dienadah v Swarnjit Singh Chopra (1982)1 DMC 224 231
Jorden Diengdeh v S.S. Chopra AIR 1985 SC 935 273
Jose v Alice 1989 Cr LJ 1527 220
Jotiram v Ramkrishna (1902)27 Bom 31 135
Jowahar Lal v Shri Thakur Radha Gopalji Maharaj (1945) All 177 106
Joyce Sumathi v Robert Dickson Brodie AIR 1982 AP 389 282
Jugmohandas v Mangaldas (1886)10 Bom 508 121
Julius v Julius AIR 1932 Oudh 142 44
Jupudi Venkata Vijaya Bhaskar v Jupudi Kesava Rao AIR 1994 AP 134 86
Jupudi Venkata Vijaya Bhaskar v Jupudi Kesava Rao AIR 2003 SC 3314 86
Jyoti Malhotra v Kewal Kishore Malhotra AIR 1983 Del 14 276
Jyoti Prasad v Chameli AIR 1975 Cal 260 90
Jyotsna v Suresh John Jagtop 2000 (1) Civ LJ 471 (Bom) 234

K. Chunilal Sawar v K.N.S. Rao AIR 1946 Mad 262 35
K. Prema S. Rao v Yadla Srinivasa Rao [2002]4 LRI 918 296
K.A. Abdul Jaleel v T.A. Shahida (2003)4 SCC 166 284
K.J.P. David v Nilmoni Devi AIR 1960 Ori 164 220
K.K. Ganguly v P. Banerjee AIR 1974 SC 1932 149
K.M.S. Rudrappa v Basamma AIR 1962 Mys 207 94
K.O. Reddy v B.V. N. Reddy AIR 1984 SC 117 105
Kaibalo v Barojo (1966)32 Cut LT 148 157
Kailasanatha v Vadivanni (1935)58 Mad 488 11
Kailash v Manmohan AIR 1975 J&K 95 65
Kalgavda v Sumoppa (1909)33 Bom 669 20
Kalwa v Union of India AIR 1964 SC 880 131
Kamala Devi v Bachulal Gupta AIR 1957 SC 434 107
Kamala Prasad v Mudliar AIR 1934 Pat 398 24
Kamala v Rupchand AIR 1958 Bom 466 67
Kamalammal v Venkatalaxmi AIR 1965 SC 1349 21
Kamani Devi v Kameshwar Singh (1946)25 Pat 58 11
Kamesharamma v S. Subramanyam AIR 1959 AP 269 93
Kanailal v Puspa Ram AIR 1979 Cal 172 89
Kanak Lata v Amal Kumar AIR 1970 Cal 328 54
Kanak Vinod Mehta v Vinod Dulerai Mehta AIR 1991 Bom 337 (DB) 287
Kanwal Ram v H.P. Administration AIR 1966 SC 614 60
Kapore Chand v Kidar Nissa AIR 1953 SC 413 178
Kapur Kaur v Kishan Singh AIR 1970 Punj 270 94
Karsondas v Gangabai (1908)32 Bom 479 118
Kartar Chand v Taravati AIR 1982 Bom 15 71
Kartar Singh v Surjan Singh AIR 1974 SC 2161 82
Kartik v Manjurani AIR 1973 Cal 545 47

Karuppana v Nachanmal AIR 1974 Mad 329 92
Kashibai v Parwatibai 1995 AIR SCW 4631 80
Kashinath v Mahadeo AIR 1977 Pat 199 82
Kashinathsa v Narsingsa AIR 1961 SC 1077 130
Kastoori Devi v Chiranjit Lal AIR 1960 All 446 74
Katama Natchair v Rajah of Shivagunga (1863)9 MIA 539 109
Katamavahi v Paradeshamma (1974)2 Andh WR 359 68
Kaulesra v Jorai (1906)28 All 233 30
Kaur Singh v Jaggar Singh AIR 1961 Punj 489 23
Kaura Devi v Indra Devi AIR 1943 All 310 38
Keogh v Keogh [1962]1 WLR 191 273
Keshow Rao v Navo, 3 Bor, 198 11
Khadal Penthi v Hulash Dei AIR 1989 Ori 137 (FB) 88
Khageswar v Aduti AIR 1967 Ori 80 42
Khajooroonissa v Rowshan Jehan (1876)2 Cal 184 194
Khazan Singh v Union of India AIR 1980 Del 60 83
Khem Chand Om Prakash Sharma v State of Gujarat (2000)3 SCC 753 313
Khub Lal v Ajodhya AIR 1916 Cal 792 142
Kiron Singh v Chaman Paswan AIR 1954 SC 340 275
Kirtikumar M. Joshi v Pradip Kumar K. Joshi AIR 1992 SC 1447 71
Kishanlal v Sudershan (1978)80 Punj LR 147 88
Kishen Devi v Shee Palton (1926)48 All 126 11
Kishore Sahu v Snehapra Sahu AIR 1943 Nag 185 (SB) 42
Kishta Bai v Ratna Bai (1979)1 Andh LT 250 154
Komalam Amma v Kumara Pillai Raghavan Pillai AIR 2009 SC 236 70
Konduru Dasaratharama v Indoor Narasa AIR 1928 Mad 601 111
Koppisatti Subbharao v State of A.P. AIR 2009 SC 2684 293
Krishna Chandra Sahu v Pradipta Das AIR 1982 Ori 114 79
Krishna Singh v Mathura Ahir AIR 1980 SC 707 .... 145, 149
Krishna v Sami (1886)9 Mad 64 (FB) 24
Krishnabai v Ananda AIR 1981 Bom 240 85
Krishnachandra Sahu v Prodipta Das AIR 1982 Ori 114 84
Krishnaji v Hanmaraddi AIR 1934 Bom 385 53
Krishnaji v Pandurang (1875)12 Bom HC 65 24
Krishnamachariar v Krishnamachariar AIR 1915 Mad 815 134
Krishnamurthi v Krishnamurthi AIR 1927 PC 139 83
Krishnamurthy v Syamanthakamani ILR (1977)1 Kant 246 41
Kulbhushan v Raj Kumari AIR 1971 SC 234 93
Kuldip Kaur v Surinder Singh AIR 1989 SC 232 314
Kulitalai Bank's *case* AIR 1955 Mad 670 111
Kumara Krishna v Sarvanga AIR 1970 SC 1795 131
Kummali Abubukker v Vengatt Marakar AIR 1970 Ker 277 8
Kumutham v Kannappan AIR 1999 SC 839; (1998)5 SCC 693 314
Kunja Bihari v Purshottam (1977)2 Cut WR 863 84
Kunjumangeli v K. Namboodripad AIR 1975 Ker 112 130
Kuppan Chetiar v Mas Goundan AIR 1937 Mad 424 128
Kusa Parida v Baishnab AIR 1966 Ori 60 98

Table of Cases

Labishwar Manjhi v Pran Manjhi (2000)8 SCC 587 152
Lakshmamma v Thayamma AIR 1974 AP 255 45
Lakshmi Ammal v R. Naicker AIR 1960 Mad 6 45
Lakshmi Chand v Ishroo Devi AIR 1977 SC 1694 120
Lakshmi Dhar v Sachit Kumar Dhar 73 Cal WN 1001 (DB) 234
Lal Man v Dy. Director of Consolidation (1998)8 SCC 693 85
Lala Gokuldas v John Kantaraj AIR 1937 Mad 895 (DB) 224
Lala Khunni Lal v Kunwar Gobind (1910)38 IA 87 (PC) 30
Lalit Kishore v Meeru Sharma AIR 2010 SC 1240 287
Lalita Prasad v Brahmanand AIR 1953 All 449 142
Lalithamma v R. Kannan AIR 1966 Mys 178 61
Lallubhai v Nirmalaben AIR 1972 Guj 174 67
Lang v Lang [1954]3 All ER 571; [1955] AC 402 52
Lata Kamat v Vilas AIR 1989 SC 1477 ..... 59, 73
Lata Singh v State of U.P AIR 2006 SC 2522 39
Latchandhara v Chinnavadu AIR 1963 AP 31 116
Laxman Singh v Keshar Bai AIR 1966 MP 166 41
Laxmibai v Limbabai AIR 1983 Bom 222 60
Leela Devi v Manoharlal AIR 1959 MP 349 51
Leela Sharma v Keshav Kumar 1980 Hind LR 171 (Del) 41
Leela v Dr. Rao Anand Singh AIR 1963 Raj 178 ..... 54, 66
Leelavathy v Sunder Athmaseelam AIR 1977 Mad 409 235
Lehja Bai v Sewanti Bai (2009)6 SCC 800 155
Lila Gupta v Laxmi Narain AIR 1978 SC 1351 59
Lily Thomas v Union of India AIR 2000 SC 1650 ..... 52, 177
Lindo v Betisario [1795]1 Hag Con 216 7
Linga Reddy v Ramchandrappa AIR 1971 Mys 194 101

M v A AIR 1993 Bom 110 283
M. Ismail Faruqui v Union of India AIR 1995 SC 605 193
M. Muthiah v Controller of E.D. Madras AIR 1986 SC 1863 85
M.D. Dhanwatey v Commr. of Income-Tax, M.P. AIR 1968 SC 682 107
M.D. Krishnan v M.C. Padma AIR 1968 Mys 226 72
M.M. Bai v Ramwati AIR 1990 MP 276 60
M.M. Malhotra v Union of India AIR 2006 SC 80 45
M.P. Chandramathy Amma v K.N. Balakrishnan Nair AIR 1982 Ker 47 72
M.P. Gangadharan v State of Kerala AIR 2006 SC 2360 286
Mackenzie v Mackenzie [1895] AC 405 50
Madanavalli v Thangavelu AIR 1961 Mad 298 27
Madanvali v Balu Padmanna AIR 1960 Mys 299 22
Madhegowda v Ankegowda AIR 2002 SC 215 102
Madho Prasad v Shakuntala AIR 1972 All 118 74
Madhu Kishwar v State of Bihar AIR 1996 SC 1864 152
Madhukar v Kusum (1982)2 Bom LR 202 47
Madhusudan Das v Narayani Bai AIR 1983 SC 114 82
Madhusudan Malhotra v Kishore Chand Bhandari (1988)1 SCWR 167 293
Mahadeo v Bainabai AIR 1975 Kant 79 84
Mahadev v Lakshman (1895)19 Bom 99 125
Mahalaxmi Vahuji v Ranchhoddas AIR 1970 SC 2025 145
Mahalingam Pillai v Amsavalli (1952)2 MLJ 289 277

Mahan Singh v Sham Kaur AIR 1973 P&H 122 84
Mahapratap Rudra Das v Pravabati Das (1993)2 DMC 54 (Ori) 288
Maharaja Pratab Narain v Subaho Koer (1877)41 All 228 (PC) 138
Mahasin v Pareshnath Thakur AIR 1954 Ori 198 143
Mahboob Sahab v Syed Ismail AIR 1995 SC 1205 200
Mahendra v Sushila AIR 1965 SC 344 ..... 48, 65
Mahomed Buksh v Hoossei Bibi (1881)15 IA 81 184
Makein, re [1955]1 All ER 57 3
Makineni Venkata Sujatha v Land Reforms Tribunal AIR 2000 SC 3191 164
Mallappa v Shivappa AIR 1962 Mys 140 156
Mallesappa v Mallappa AIR 1961 SC 1268 ..... 122, 123
Maneka Gandhi v Indira Gandhi AIR 1984 Del 428 269
Mangal Singh v Smt. Rattna AIR 1976 SC 1986 157
Mangat v Bharto AIR 1927 All 523 26
Mangoo Singh v Election Tribunal AIR 1957 SC 871 113
Manigavri v Narandas (1891)15 Bom 549 135
Manik Chand v Ramchandra AIR 1981 SC 519 100
Manisha Tyagi v Deepak Kumar AIR 2010 SC 1042 50
Maqbool v Khodaija AIR 1966 SC 1194 ..... 183, 185
Maqbul v Ghafur-un-nissa (1914)36 All 333 185
Marian Eva v State AIR 1993 HP 7 264
Mariasoosai v Clara Mary AIR 1995 Mad 35 219
Mary Sheila v Vincent Thamburaj AIR 1991 Mad 180 (SB) 287
Mary Thomas v K.E. Thomas AIR 1990 Mad 100 (FB) 287
Marya Tersa Martin v E. Martin AIR 1994 Ker 264 290
Mathew Ommen v Suseela Mathew AIR 2006 SC 786 303
Matungini v Ram Rutton (1892)19 Cal 289 (FB) 27
Mausami Moitra Ganguly v Jayant Ganguli (2008)7 SCC 673 103
Maya Ram v Samam Singh AIR 1967 Punj 353 120
Mayadevi v Jagdish Prasad (2007)3 SCC 136 51
Md. Hussain Khan v Babu Kishva (1937)64 IA 250; ILR (1937) All 655 119
Medasett v Veeramani AIR 1981 AP 123 67
Meganatha v Susheela AIR 1957 Mad 423 58
Mirza Raja v Sri Pushavati AIR 1964 SC 118 132
Mitar Sen Singh v Maqbul Hasan (1930)57 IA 313; AIR 1930 PC 251 ..... 30, 170
Mohammad Yosin v Rahmat Ilahi AIR 1947 All 201 (FB) 188
Mohan Kumar Rayana v Kamal Mohan Rayana AIR 2010 SC 1659 99
Mohanlal v Mohan Bai AIR 1958 Raj 71 65
Mohanlal v Shanto Devi AIR 1964 All 21 30
Mohd Azeem v Dist. Judge (1985)2 SCC 550 4
Mohd. Ahmed Khan v Shah Bano Begum AIR 1985 SC 945 ..... 211, 213
Mohd. Amin v Vakil Ahmad AIR 1952 SC 358 176
Mohd. Ibrahim v Mehrunisa Begum AIR 2004 Kant 261 287
Mohd. Shah v Fasihuddin AIR 1956 SC 713 ..... 188, 192
Mohd. Sulaiman Sahib v Mohd. Ismail Saheb AIR 1966 SC 792 201
Mohinder Singh v Preet Kaur AIR 1981 J&K 25 41
Mohinder v Wasson AIR 1968 Punj 389 164
Mohsin Ali v State of MP AIR 1975 SC 1518 183
Moniram v Keri (1880)7 IA 115 (PC) 30
Monji Lal v Chandrabati (1911)38 IA 122 (PC) 38

Monorama v Kalicharan (1901)31 Cal 166 142
Moolla Cassim v Moolla Abdul (1905)33 Cal 173 202
Mst. Bilkis Begum v Majid Ali Gazi 2002 (2) Cal HN 151 (SC) 216
Mst. Nandi v The Crown (1920)1 Lah 440 169
Mt. Sakina Begum v Khalifa Hafiz-ud-din (1914)194 IC 77 184
Mudigowda Gowdappa v Ramchandra Revgowda
   AIR 1969 SC 1076 .... 121, 122, 129
Muhammad Ahsan v Umardraz (1906)28 All 633 190
Muhammad Khan v Husaini Begum ILR (1919)32 All 40 (PC) 8
Mukan v Ajeet Chand AIR 1958 Raj 322 69
Mukta Bai v Kamalaksha AIR 1960 Mys 182 90
Mukundji v Parsotamlalji AIR 1957 All 77 148
Mulani v Maula Baksh AIR 1924 All 307 185
Mulchand v Amrit Bai ILR (1980) MP 838 79
Muniratnam Naidu v S. Shantamma AIR 1971 Mys 25 67
Munna Lal v State of UP AIR 1991 All 189 288
Munnalal v Rajkumar AIR 1962 SC 1493 156
Munni Lal v Biswanath AIR 1968 SC 450 197
Murudanayagam v Sola Pillai AIR 1965 Mad 200 109
Murugayi v Viramkali (1877)1 Mad 226 26
Mussadi v Chando AIR 1956 HP 45 .... 26, 27
Muthayya v Kamu AIR 1981 NOC 172 59
Muthu v Chidambara (1893)3 MLJ 261 11
Muthuraj Koilpillai v Esther Victoria Kannammal AIR 1970 Mad 237 (FB) 47
Muttammal v Sri S. Devasthanam AIR 1960 SC 601 31
Muttyjan v Ahmed Ally (1882)8 Cal 370 200

N. Nirmala v Nelson Jayakumar AIR 1999 SC 3821 103
N. Ramaiah v Nagaraj S. AIR 2001 Kant 395 137
Nafar Chandra v Ratan (1910)15 CWN 66 139
Nagamma v Ningamma AIR 1999 Kant 432 70
Naganna v Lachmi Bai AIR 1963 AP 82 54
Nagar v Khase AIR 1925 All 440 26
Nagarmal v Bajranlal AIR 1950 PC 15 111
Nagayasami Naidu v Kochadai Naidu AIR 1969 Mad 329 122
Nandarani Majumdar v Indian Airlines AIR 1983 SC 1201 278
Nandarani v Indian Airlines AIR 1983 SC 1201 70
Nandini v Sanjib AIR 1988 Bom 239 72
Nanveet Lal v Gokul (1976)1 SCC 630 139
Nar Hari Shastri v Shri. Badrinath Temple Committee AIR 1951 SC 245 147
Narain v Mohan Singh AIR 1917 All 343 26
Naranbhai v Ranchod (1902)26 Bom 141 112
Narantakath v Prakkal AIR 1923 Mad 171 169
Narayana v Karthiayani AIR 1962 Ker 122 .... 197, 198
Narayanamurthy v State of Karnataka AIR 2008 SC 2377 296
Narayanaswami Iyer v Ramakrishna Iyer AIR 1965 SC 289 122
Narayandas v Jagan Nath AIR 1950 MB 85 198
Narayanswami v Padmanabham AIR 1966 Mad 394 86
Narendra Kante v Anuradha Kante (2010)2 SCC 77 130
Narendra Kumar v Suraj Mehta AIR 1982 AP 100 68

Narendrakumar v CIT (1976)4 SCC 456 110
Naresh Kumari (Smt.) v Shakshi Lal AIR 1999 SC 928 157
Nasrat v Hamidan (1882)2 All 205 168
Nathu Mishra v Mahesh Mishra AIR 1966 Pat 196 102
Nathu Ram v Gangabhai AIR 1938 PC 228 140
Nathubhai v Chhotubhai AIR 1962 Guj 68 151
Naveen Kohli v Neelu Kohli (2006)4 SCC 558; AIR 2006 SC 1675 .... 51, 56
Navin Chander Advani v Leena AIR 2005 Bom 277 275
Nawab Zain v Director of Endowments AIR 1963 SC 985 191
Newnness alias Mewajannessa v Shaikh Mohamad AIR 1996 SC 702 203
Niboyet v Niboyet (1878)4 PD 1 7
Niranjan Umeshchandra Joshi v Mrudula Jyoti Rao AIR 2007 SC 618 303
Nirmal Dass Bose v Mamta Gulati AIR 1997 All 401 270
Nirmala v Ravendra AIR 1996 MP 227 72
Nirmoo v Nikka Ram AIR 1968 Del 260 54
Nishit Kumar Biswas v Anjali Biswas AIR 1968 Cal 105 .... 48, 65
Noor Saba Khatoon v Mohd Quasin AIR 1997 SC 3280; (1997)6 SCC 233 .... 214, 313
Nrisingha Murari Chakraborty v State of West Bengal (1977)3 SCC 7 114
Nutbehari v Nonilal 41 CWN 613 (PC) 118

O'Brien v O'Brien 89 Misc 2d 433 116
Olga Thelma Gomes v Mark Gomes AIR 1959 Cal 541 (SB) 232
Om Pati v Kartar Singh AIR 1971 Punj 35 41
Om Prakash v Shakuntala 1981 Hindu LR 92 (Raj) 57
Oma (Smt.) v Smt. Reshma 1981 Rev Dec 324 (All) 37

P. Kallioni v K. Devi AIR 1989 Ker 279 60
P. v L. (1878)3 PD 73 47
P. Venkataramana v State AIR 1977 AP 43 (FB) 44
P.A. Suramma v G. Ganapatla AIR 1975 AP 193 44
Padayachi v A. Ammal AIR 1938 Rang 59 11
Padmaraja v Gyanachandappa AIR 1976 Mys 87 162
Padmja Sharma v Ratan Lal Sharma AIR 2000 SC 1398 71
Pakkiam Solomon v Chelliah Pillai AIR 1924 Mad 18 (FB) 230
Palaniammal v Muthuvenkatacharlu AIR 1925 PC 49 130
Palanivelayutham Pillai v Ramchandran (2000)6 SCC 151 .... 302, 303
Panchamuthu Nader v TPT Charities AIR 1971 Mad 253 142
Panchappa v Sangabasawa (1900)24 Bom 89 28
Paras Ram v Kamlesh AIR 1982 Punj 60 51
Parbati Devi v Purana Patra AIR 1997 SC 2331 132
Parihar v Parihar AIR 1978 Raj 140 72
Parma Nand v Nihal Chand AIR 1938 PC 195 143
Parmeshwar v Bhagawati AIR 1950 FC 142 38
Parmeshwar v Jagmohan (1976)2 Cut WR 811 84
Parul v Bangshidhar AIR 1971 Cal 270 95
Parvati Kuer v Sarangdhar Sinha AIR 1960 SC 403 123
Pasumpon Gandhi v Shirley Gandhi AIR 2003 NOC 239 (Mad) 233
Pathumma v Raman AIR 1921 Mad 224 130
Pathuri Venkateswarlu v Damacharla Chinna Raghavulu AIR 1957 AP 604 119

Table of Cases

Pawan Kumar v State of Haryana AIR 1998 SC 958 293
Payerelal v Ram Rotti 1980 Hindu LR 691 (P&H) 57
Peter Masih v Anguina Masih AIR 1992 Del 20 232
Phankari v State AIR 1965 J&K 105 39
Phundan Lal v Arya Prithi (1911)33 All 793 142
Piare Lal Adishwar Lal v Commr. of Income-tax, Delhi AIR 1960 SC 997 108
Pigg v Clarke [1876]3 Ch D 672 3
Pillalamari Vara Prasada v P. Seshalakshmi AIR 1975 AP 239 42
Pinninti v State AIR 1977 AP 43 (FB) 61
Pistonji Kekobund Bharucha v Aloo AIR 1984 Bom 75 255
Pitra Kueri v Ujagir Rai AIR 1958 All 101 21
Poniah Nadar v Essaki Devania AIR 1955 Trav Co. 180 170
Poonam Dutta v Krisanlal Dutta AIR 1989 SC 401 71
Popat v Jagu AIR 1969 Bom 140 100
Prafulla Bala Biswas v Ila Das Cal LT 1996(2) HC 315 270
Pramatha Nath v Pradyumna AIR 1925 PC 139 .... 147, 148
Pramila Bhagat v Ajit Raj Sinha AIR 1989 Pat 163 .... 273, 276
Pranab Biswas v Mriumayee Dassi AIR 1976 Cal 156 .... 49, 50
Pranab v Ratna 98 Cal WN 931 57
Pranay Majumdar v Bina Majumdar 2007(2) CHN 13 (SC) 272
Prankishen v Mothooramohum (1865)10 MIA 403 128
Prasanna v Sureshwari AIR 1969 Ori 12 69
Preeti Singh v Sandeep Singh AIR 1995 SC 1851 57
Prem Kaur v Harnam Singh AIR 1939 Lah 125 28
Prem Prakash v Sarla AIR 1989 MP 326 (SB) 235
Prem Pratap Singh v Jagat Pratap Kunwar AIR 1944 All 97 (DB) 230
Prem Singh v Dulari Rai AIR 1973 Cal 425 36
Prema Devi v Jt. Direction AIR 1970 All 238 158
Pritma Sharma v Mohinder AIR 1984 P&H 305 62
Promotho v Radhika (1875)14 Beng LR 175 144
Pryor v Pryor [1947]1 All ER 381 237
Punjab Wakf Board v Shakur Masih AIR 1997 SC 104 189
Purabi Banerjee v Basudeb Mukherjee AIR 1969 Cal 293 (DB) 264
Purmanundas v Venayak (1883)9 IA 86 (PC) 142
Purushottam v Janki (1907)29 All 354 121
Pushpa Rani v Vijay Pal Singh AIR 1994 All 216 42
Puthiyapurayil Abdul Salam v P.P. Mariyumma AIR 2007 Ker 68 288
Puttrangamma v M.S. Ranganna AIR 1968 SC 1018 .... 126, 129

Quarry Owners Association v State of Bihar AIR 2000 SC 2870;
  (2000)8 SCC 655 113

R. Lakshmi Narayan v Santhi AIR 2001 SC 2110 38
R. Seethramamma v L.A. Collector (1079)2 Andh LT 6 90
R. v Clarke [1949]1 All ER 440 55
R.B.S.S. Munnalal v S.S. Rajkumar AIR 1962 SC 1493 115
Rabindra Nath Dutta v State AIR 1969 Cal 55 39
Radhakanta Deb v Commr. Hindu Religious Endowments, Orissa
  AIR 1981 SC 798 143
Radhakrishandas v Kaluram (1963) SCR 648 107

Case	Page
Radhikabai v Sadhuram AIR 1970 MP 14	68
Raghavamma v Chenchamma AIR 1964 SC 136	128, 129
Raghavan Nair v Lakshmikutty AIR 1961 Ker 193	98
Raghavan v Nagammal AIR 1979 Mad 200	95
Raghbir Lala v Mahammad Said AIR 1943 PC 7	53
Raghubir v Moti Kumar (1912)35 All 41 (PC)	127
Raghunada v Brozo Kishor (1876)1 Mad 69	105
Raghunath v Lakshmibai AIR 1935 Bom 298	27
Raghunath v Vijaya AIR 1972 Bom 132	47
Rahasa v Gokulanada AIR 1987 SC 962	85
Rai Bishen Chand v Mt. Asmadia Koer (1884)11 IA 164 (PC)	138
Rai Shadilal v Lal Bahadur AIR 1933 PC 85; 64 MLJ 298 (PC)	118
Raj Kali v Ram Rattan AIR 1955 SC 493	148
Raj Kumari v Trilok Singh AIR 1959 All 628	67
Raja Jogendra v Nityanand (1891)18 Cal 151	125
Rajani v Prabhakar AIR 1958 Bom 264	66
Rajashri v Rajendra AIR 1997 Bom 65	57
Rajathi v C. Ganesan AIR 1999 SC 2374	87
Rajendra Kumar v Kalyan AIR 2000 SC 3335	80, 83
Rajendra v Sharda Devi AIR 1993 MP 142	50
Rajesh Burman v Mitual Chatterjee (2009)1 SCC 398	277
Rajesh Shukla v Smt. Meena R. Shukla AIR 2006 NOC 268 (All)	290
Rajeshwari v Balchand Jain AIR 2001 MP 179	122
Rajindar Kappor v Manmohan Singh AIR 1972 Punj 142	47
Rajmohan v Gour Mohan 8 MIA 91	118
Raju v Ammani (1906)29 Mad 358	24
Rajula Bai v Suka AIR 1972 MP 57	37, 54
Ram Awadh v Krishna Nand Lal AIR 1981 All 432	39
Ram Das v Gandiabai AIR 1997 SC 1563	79, 82
Ram Kali v Sohanlal AIR 1972 Punj 419	157
Ram Kumari, in the matter of (1891)18 Cal 264	169
Ram Kunwar v Ochha Dhanpal AIR 1951 Madh Bh 96	27
Ram Laull v Mussammat AIR 1928 Oudh 338	26
Ram Narain Pathak v Urmila Devi AIR 1980 All 344	67, 73
Ram Narain v Naraini Devi 1980 All LJ 842	91
Ram Pergash v Dashan Bibi AIR 1924 Pat 420	130
Ram Saran v Domini AIR 1961 SC 1747	197
Ramalakshmi v Sivanatha (1872)14 MIA 570	124
Ramalinga v Narayana (1922)49 IA 168	128
Ramamoorthy v Sitharamamma AIR 1961 AP 131 (FB)	92
Raman Nader v Rasalamma AIR 1970 SC 1759	138
Ramanathan Chettiar v Narayana Chettiar AIR 1955 Mad 629	111
Rambir Das v Kalyan Das 1997(2) Scale 499	301
Ramchandra Anand Suryavanshi v Kalindi Ramchandra Suryavanshi AIR 1991 Bom 315	272
Ramchandra v Snehalate AIR 1977 Ori 96	87
Ramchandra v Vinayak AIR 1914 PC 1	20, 24
Ramesh Chandra Kaushal v Veena Kaushal AIR 1975 SC 1807; 1979 Cr LJ 3	68
Ramesh Nivrutti Bhagat v Dr. Surendra Manohar Parekhe AIR 2001 Bom 461	307
Ramish Francis Toppo v Violet Francis Toppo AIR 1989 Cal 128	232

Table of Cases

Ramkatori v Prakashwati ILR (1968)1 All 697 156
Ramlakshmi v Sewanantha (1890)14 MSA 570 (PC) 23
Rammi v Dy. Director 1981 All WC 204 84
Ramoki v Kameswari AIR 1975 AP 3 51
Ranchhoddas v Mahalaxmi (1952)54 Bom LR 982 143
Rangamma v Venkatarajuly AIR 1966 Mad 428 93
Ranganadha v Bhagirathi (1906)29 Mad 412 135
Rangaswami v Aravindammal AIR 1957 Mad 243 ..... 46, 62
Ranjit Kumar Bhattacharyya v Sabita Bhattacharya AIR 1996 Cal 301 228
Ranjit v Nilambar AIR 1978 Ori 48 85
Ranu Vij v Surinder Kumar AIR 1986 Del 33 62
Rao Balwant Singh v Rani Kishori (1898)25 IA 54 20
Rathnathanni v Somasundara (1921)41 MLJ 76 11
Ratnaprabhabai v Sheshrao AIR 1972 Bom 182 42
Ravanna v Suseelamma AIR 1967 Mys 165 ..... 46, 55
Ravishanker v Sharda AIR 1978 MP 44 57
Reema Aggarwal v Anupam (2004)3 SCC 199 39
Reverend Gabriel v Valliammai (1919)10 MLW 491; (1920) MWN 158 11
Rewun Persad v Radha Beeby (1846)4 MIA 137 128
Rita Roy v Satischandra AIR 1982 Cal 138 52
Robasa Khanum v Khodadad Bomanji AIR 1947 Bom 272 170
Roopa v Ladu AIR 1953 Ajmer 45 26
Roopa v Ladu AIR 1951 Ajmer 45 26
Rukmen Kanta v Faquir Chand AIR 1960 Punj 493 42
Ruli Ram v Amar Singh AIR 1994 HP 102 119
Rup Rani v Basudeo Raut AIR 1962 Pat 436 28
Russell v Russell [1895] p. 315 232

S. (Infants), re [1967]1 WLR 396 236
S. Jayakumari v S. Krishnan Nair AIR 1995 Ker 139 42
S.R. Batra v Taruna Batra AIR 2007 SC 1118 325
S.S. Baburao v B.D. Mandilik AIR 1963 MP 10 42
S.T.O. v N.K. Sarada Thampatty 1991 Supp (2) SCC 737; AIR 1991 SC 2035 116
S.v S. [1962]1 All ER 33 47
Sabir Husain v Farzanel Khan AIR 1938 PC 80 178
Sachindra Paul v Kalpana Paul 93 CWN 404 283
Sadiq Ali Khan v Jai Kishori AIR 1929 PC 152 174
Sahabjit v Indrajit (1905)27 All 203 21
Sahi Ullah v Ghulam Jabbar (1955) Lah 57 183
Sahu Ram v Bhup Singh LR 44 IA 127 109
Saira Banu v AM Abdul Gafoor AIR 1987 SC 1103 312
Sakhi Mandalani v State of Bihar (1999)5 SCC 705 295
Sakri v Chhanwarlal AIR 1975 Raj 134 66
Saligram v Raghubar dyal (1887)15 Cal 244 198
Salim Ullah v Fakir Ullah AIR 1948 All 142 4
Samar Ghosh v Jaya Ghosh (2007)4 SCC 511 ..... 51, 56
Samuasari v Anachiammal (1925)49 MLJ 554 11
Sandhya v Gopinath 86 Cal WN 665; AIR 1983 Cal 161 67
Sanjay Mishra v Eveline (1987)1 DMC 318 (MP) 267
Sankara v Anita AIR 1977 Cal 289 28

Sankaralingam v Subbon ILR 17 Mad 479 33
Santala Bewa v Badaswari Dasi AIR 1924 Cal 98 26
Santha v Cheru Kutty AIR 1972 Ker 71 101
Santhammal v Thangaraj AIR 1975 Kant 23 (SB) 236
Santi Deb Berma v Kanchan Prava Devi AIR 1991 SC 816 .... 39, 60
Santosh v Om Prakash AIR 1977 All 97 61
Sapsford v Sapsford [1954]2 All ER 373 50
Sarab Sukh v Ram Prasad (1924)46 All 130 142
Sarabai v Rabiabai (1905)30 Bom 537 179
Saraju Bala v Jyotirmoyee AIR 1931 PC 179 140
Sarangadeva v Ramaswami AIR 1966 SC 1603 298
Sardar Syedna v State of Bombay AIR 1962 SC 853 170
Sarla Mudgal v Union of India AIR 1995 SC 1531 52
Saroj Kumar Sen v Dr. Kalyan Kanta Ray AIR 1980 Cal 374 49
Sasanka Sekhar Maity v Union of India AIR 1981 SC 522 4
Satbir Singh v State of Haryana AIR 2005 SC 3546 296
Satvir Singh v State of Punjab AIR 2001 SC 2828 293
Satya Sunder Das v V. Registrar, Hindu Marriage, Orissa AIR 1963 Ori 139 62
Satya v Teja AIR 1975 SC 105 .... 37, 230
Satyanarayanamurthi v Jaggamma AIR 1962 AP 439 93
Satyendra Nath v Fulsom Bibi 36 CWN 483 182
Savitri Devi v Jiwan Chaudhury AIR 1960 Pat 548 129
Savitri Pandey v Prem Chandra Pandey AIR 2002 SC 591 52
Savitri Smt. v Govind Singh Rawat (1985)4 SCC 337 313
Sawan Ram v Kalawanti AIR 1967 SC 1761 .... 78, 82
Secy., T.N. Wakf Board v Syed Fatima Nachi AIR 1996 SC 2423 215
Seema Shrinidhi v Praveen Kumar Tiwari AIR 1999 SC 1560 63
Seshammal v State of T.N. (1972)2 SCC 11 145
Shabana Bano v Imran Khan AIR 2010 SC 305 291
Shahzad Kunwar v Ram Karan AIR 1965 SC 254 299
Shail Kumari Devi v Krishan Bhagwan Pathak AIR 2008 SC 3006 314
Shakuntala v Om Prakash AIR 1991 SC 1104 63
Sham Kaur v Hari Singh AIR 1973 P&H 71 120
Shamim Ara v State of U.P. (2002)7 SCC 518 216
Shamser Singh v Dy. Custodian General AIR 1973 J&K 89 (FB) 85
Shamsher v Rajinder AIR 1973 SC 2457 190
Shankarappa v Basamma AIR 1964 Mys 247 37
Shantabai v Ramchandra (1959)61 Bom LR 627 23
Shantaram v Hirabai AIR 1962 Bom 27 69
Shanti Devi v Ramesh Chandra AIR 1969 Pat 27 66
Sharda v Dharampal AIR 2003 SC 3450 50
Shashi Shah v Kiran Kumar Shah 1999(2) Civ LJ 65 (All) 289
Sheikh Mohd. Rafi v Khalilul Rahman AIR 1972 SC 2162 .... 197, 198
Sheo Pershard v Leela Singh (1874)12 Beng LR 188 112
Sherly Thomas v Johny AIR 2002 Ker 280 232
Shib Narain Mookerjee v Bhutnath (1918)45 Cal 475 21
Shilpa v Madhukar JT 2000(10) SC 282 314
Shivaguru v Saroja AIR 1960 Mad 216 48
Shivamurthi v Vijay Singh AIR 1972 Bom 152 101

Table of Cases

Shivnarayan Laxminarayan Joshi *v* State of Maharashtra
(1980)2 SCC 465; AIR 1980 SC 439; 1980 Cr LJ 388 115
Shoarat Singh *v* Jafri Bibi (1915)17 Bom LR 13 177
Sikhdeo *v* Mritinjoy (1939)43 Cal WN 395 23
Sirajmohmed Khan *v* Hafizunnisa Yasinkhan AIR 1981 SC 1972 269
Sitabai *v* Ramchandra AIR 1970 SC 343 105
Sivaganna *v* Udayar AIR 1961 Mad 356 107
Sivanagalingam Pillai *v* Ambalavana Pillai (1938) MWN 161 12
Skinner *v* Orde (1871)14 MIA 309 170
Sneh Prabha *v* Ravinder Kumar AIR 1995 SC 2170 90
Snighda *v* Akhil Chandra AIR 1992 Gau 95 57
Sobha Dei *v* Bhima AIR 1975 Ori 180 51
Solema *v* Hafez (1927)54 Cal 687 203
Soloman *v* Josephine AIR 1959 Mad 151 (FB) 47
Sonawanti *v* State of Punjab AIR 1963 SC 151 267
Soorjeemoney Dossee *v* Denobundo (1857)6 MIA 523 (PC) 110
Sossannamma *v* V. Abraham AIR 1957 Trav Co 277 50
Sourindra Mohan Singh *v* Hariprasad AIR 1925 PC 280 24
Sree Iswar Gopal Jieu Thakur *v* Pratapmal Bagaria AIR 1951 SC 214 147
Sri Iswar Jew *v* Sushilabala Dasi AIR 1954 SC 69 142
Sri Narayan Bal *v* Sridhar Sutar AIR 1996 SC 2371 101
State of Andhra Pradesh *v* Raj Gopal Asawa AIR 2004 SC 1933 294
State of Bihar *v* Charusila Dasi AIR 1959 SC 1002 144
State of Bombay *v* F.N. Balasara AIR 1951 SC 318 115
State of Bombay *v* Narayandas AIR 1958 Bom 68 (FB) 97
State of Haryana *v* Santra AIR 2000 SC 1888; 2000 AIR SCW 1491 .... 292, 312
State of Karnataka *v* M.V. Manjunathegowda AIR 2003 SC 809 295
State of U.P. *v* Rukmini Raman AIR 1971 SC 1687 131
State of UP *v* Sayed Abdul Jalil AIR 1972 SC 1290 .... 183, 186
State of West Bengal *v* Ashutosh Lahiri AIR 1995 SC 464 170
Subarn *v* A.M. Abdul Gafoor AIR 1987 SC 1103 212
Subash Kumar *v* Principal Officer, Mercantile Marine Dept., Madras
AIR 1991 SC 1632; (1991)2 SCC 449 113
Subash Misir *v* Thagair Misir AIR 1967 All 148 83
Subbarama *v* Saraswathi AIR 1967 Mad 85 49
Subhasini *v* Umakanth AIR 1981 Kant 115 71
Subramanyam *v* Saraswati AIR 1964 Mys 38 69
Sudarsana Maistri *v* Narasimtiulu (1902) ILR 25 Mad 149 104
Sudarsana *v* Narasimhulu (1902)25 Mad 149 .... 118, 125
Sudeep Chaudhary *v* Radha Chaudhary AIR 1999 SC 536; 1999 Cr LJ 466 313
Sudershan *v* Deepak AIR 1981 Punj 305 71
Sugra Bibi *v* Hazi Kummu AIR 1969 SC 884 190
Sukhmoy Chander Dass *v* Monohuri Dasi (1885)12 IA 103 (PC) 134
Sulochana *v* Ram Kumar AIR 1981 All 78 .... 51, 62
Sultan Begum *v* Ara Begum (1933)57 Cal LJ 459 182
Suman Bhasin *v* Neeraj Bhasin AIR 2010 SC 1777 99
Sumatiben *v* Jaswant AIR 1960 Bom 323 74
Sumedha Nagpal *v* State of Delhi (2000)9 SCC 745 99
Sumitra Devi *v* Bhikan Choudhary AIR 1985 SC 765; (1985)1 SCC 637 .... 71, 312

Sumsuddin *v* Abdul Hussein (1906)31 Bom 165 202
Sunanda *v* Venkata Subbarao AIR 1957 AP 424 59
Sunil K. Mirchandani *v* Reena S. Mirchandani AIR 2000 Bom 66 271
Suraj *v* Attar AIR 1922 Pat 378 .... 26, 27
Surajmal *v* Rukminibai AIR 2000 MP 48 67
Surendra Bhatia *v* Smt. Punam Bhatia AIR 2001 Raj 338 306
Surendra Nath *v* Pushpa (1978)2 Cal LJ 602 69
Surinder Kaur *v* Madan Gopal Singh AIR 1980 P&H 334 72
Surjit Kaur *v* Garja Singh AIR 1994 SC 135 60
Surjit Kaur *v* Tarsem Singh AIR 1978 Raj 209 66
Surjit Kaur *v* Tirath Singh AIR 1978 Punj 112 68
Surjit Kumar *v* Raj Kumari AIR 1967 Punj 172 47
Sushil Chandra *v* Bhoop Kunwar AIR 1977 All 441 85
Sushila M. Nanavati *v* Mahindra M. Nanavati AIR 1960 Bom 117 48
Sushila Nath *v* Judge Family Court AIR 1998 Ori 61 287
Swami Motor Transports (P) Ltd *v* Sankaraswamigal Mutt AIR 1963 SC 864 115
Swarajya Lakshmi *v* G.G. Padma Rao AIR 1974 SC 165 .... 9, 52
Swayamprabha *v* Chandrasekhar AIR 1982 Kant 285 50
Syed Mohd. Salie *v* Mohd. Hanifa AIR 1976 SC 1569 .... 191, 193
Syed Shah Ghulam Ghouse *v* Syed Shah Ahmed Mohiuddin
 AIR 1971 SC 2184 201

T. Srinivasan *v* T. Varalakshmi (1998)3 SCC 112 54
T.J. Poonen *v* Rathi Varghese AIR 1967 Ker 1 (FB) 230
T.M. Narayanan *v* Nishad 1990 (Supp) SCC 163(1) 313
Tagore *v* Tagore (1872)9 Beng LR 377 (PC) 135, 138
Talarierappa *v* Murthyalappa AIR 1972 Mys 31 102
Tara Chand *v* Ram Avtar AIR 1975 Punj 20 83
Tara Chand *v* Reebs Ram (1868)3 Mad HC 50 121
Tarabai *v* Balegonda AIR 1981 Bom 18 83
Tarachand *v* Narain Devi AIR 1976 Punj 300 65
Tarini Gupta *v* Gouri Gupta AIR 1968 Cal 567 87
Tarini *v* Basudeo AIR 1981 Pat 331 102
Tarlochan *v* Mohinder AIR 1963 Punj 249 68
Tehmi *v* Dinyar AIR 1976 Bom 246 257
Tej Kour *v* Hakim Singh AIR 1965 J&K 111 53
Teja Singh *v* Sarjit Kaur AIR 1962 Punj 195 42
Tejinder Kaur *v* Gurmit Singh AIR 1988 SC 839 .... 59, 73
Thakur Deyhee *v* Rai Baluk (1866)11 MIA 139 (PC) 24
Than Singh *v* Barelal AIR 1974 MP 24 100
Themmanani *v* Ammannamma (1971)1 Andh LT 233 88
Thimmakku *v* Bandhu AIR 1977 Kant 115 74
Thimmappa *v* Thimmappa AIR 1972 Mys 234 49
Thirty Hoshie Dolikuka *v* Hoshiam Shavaksha Dolikuka AIR 1982 SC 1276 257
Thoombath Haris *v* Khadeeja Sherbin AIR 2010 NOC 230 (Ker) 216
Triloke Nath *v* Principal Medical College ILR (1973) HP 1999 85
Tulsa *v* Panna Lal AIR 1963 MP 5 42

Table of Cases [45]

Udainath Misra v Chhaya Misrani AIR 1963 Ori 27 .... 36, 74
Umashankar Prasad Singh v Radha Devi AIR 1967 Pat 220 61
Umbargar v State Farm Mut Automobile Ins. Co. 254 NW 87; 218 Iowa 203 5
Upendra Kumar v Harpriya Kumar ILR (1978)2 Del 97 63
Upendra v Chintamoni AIR 1960 Cal 22 151
UPSC Wakf Board v Mohd. Alim AIR 1971 SC 1396 299
Usha v Palisetty AIR 2002 SC 400 63

V.N. Swaminathan v Angayar Kanni Ammal AIR 1964 Mad 11 98
V.T.S. Chandrasekhar v Kulandaivalu AIR 1963 SC 185 77
Vaishali v Union of India (1978)80 Bom LR 182 37
Valia v Pathakkalan AIR 1964 SC 275 183
Vankata Subbarayudu Chetty v Tanguturu Venkatiah Shastree
   AIR 1968 AP 107 39
Vanniakone v Vannichi (1928)51 Mad 1 (FB) 21
Vanugopala Ravi v Union of India AIR 1969 SC 1094 104
Vasant v Daltu AIR 1987 SC 398 85
Vasudeo v Narayan (1883)7 Bom 131 135
Vasudevan v R. Viswalakshmi AIR 1959 Ker 403 99
Vedachela v Subramania AIR 1922 PC 33 24
Veena Kapoor v Varinder Kumar AIR 1982 SC 792 71
Veena Rani v Ramesh Kumar AIR 1995 P&H 213 73
Veerarghavan v Parvarthy AIR 1974 Ker 43 65
Velamuri Venkata Sivaprasad (dead) by L.Rs. v Kothuri Venkataeswarlu
   AIR 2000 SC 434 157
Vellinayagi v T. Subramanium AIR 1969 Mad 749 48
Venkanna v Laxmi AIR 1951 Bom 57 22
Venkata Subbamma v Ramayya (1932)59 IA 112 199
Venkata v Partha Sarathy (1913)41 IA 51 140
Venkatachalapati v Subbarajadu (1890)13 Mad 298 30
Venkayamma v Veerayya AIR 1957 AP 280 158
Vervaeke v Smith (1981) Fam 77 6
Vidya Varuthi Thirtha Swamigal v Balusamy Iyer AIR 1922 PC 123 187
Vidyaben v Jagdish AIR 1974 Guj 23 159
Vidyadhar Rao v Lalita Devamma AIR 1974 AP 38 93
Vidyapurna v Vidyanidhi (1904)27 Mad 435 145
Vidyavaruti's case 48 IA 302 146
Vijaya College Trust v Kusnta Co-op. Areeanut Sales Society Ltd.
   AIR 1995 Kant 35 119
Vijayabai v State of Maharashtra 1995 Supp (2) SCC 734 295
Vijaylakshmamma v B.T. Shankar (2001)4 SCC 558 80
Vijiangam v Lakshmanam [1871]8 BHCO CJ 244 11
Vikas v State of Rajasthan AIR 2002 SC 2830 292
Vikram Vir Vohra v Shalini Bhalla AIR 2010 SC 1675 70
Vimalben Ajitbhai Patel v Vatslaben Ashokbhai Patel AIR 2008 SC 2675 88
Vinay Kumar v Purnima Devi AIR 1973 Raj 32 68

Vineet Narain *v* Union of India (1998)1 SCC 226 56
Vinod Chandra *v* Aruna AIR 1977 Del 24 66
Vinod Goyal *v* Sarita Goyal AIR 2006 Uttaranchal 37 290
Vinod *v* Mangala 1981 Bom Cr 962 69
Vira Reddi *v* Kistamma AIR 1969 Mad 235 65
Virabhatrappa *v* Irabayawwa (1969)2 Mys LJ 105 164
Vishnu Dutt Sharma *v* Manju Sharma (2009)6 SCC 379 56
Vithu *v* Govinda (1898)22 Bom 321 (FB) 26
Vitta Tayaramma *v* Chatakondu Sivayya AIR 1919 Mad 854 (FB) 27

Wahidunnissa *v* Shubrattun (1870)6 Beng LR 54 200
Waman *v* Krishnaji (1889)14 Bom 240 24
Wati Mohammed *v* Rahmat Bee AIR 1999 SC 1136 188
Wright *v* Wright AIR 1931 Cal 313 (SB) 230

Yamanaji H. Jadhav *v* Nirmala AIR 2002 SC 971 58
Yamunabai *v* Anantrao AIR 1988 SC 644 .... 60, 312
Yogeshwar Prasad *v* Jyoti Rani AIR 1981 Del 99 67

Z.B. Bukhari *v* B.R. Mehta AIR 1975 SC 1788; (1976)2 SCC 17 15
Zubeda Begum *v* Syed Shah Khursheed Ahmad Hashmi (1997)9 SCC 324 189

PART 1

General

CHAPTER
1
Introduction

Family law—meaning of

The term "Family Law" denotes the law that governs family. The word "Family" is a generic term which varies from country to country and from statute to statute. In a broad sense a family means the whole household including servants and possibly lodgers. In another sense, it means everyone who descends from a common stock, that is to say common blood relations, and includes, the husbands and wives of such persons and their children.[1] Where children are included within the meaning of family, they are meant to be legitimate children unless the context indicates contrary intention.[2] "Family" is defined in the Employees' State Insurance Act 1948[3] which means all or any of the following relatives of an insured person, namely, (i) spouse, (ii) a minor legitimate or adopted child dependent on the insured person, (iii) a child who is wholly dependent on the earnings of the insured person and who is (a) receiving education till he or she attains the age of twenty-one years, (b) an unmarried daughter, (iv) a child who is infirm by reason of any physical or mental abnormality or injury and is wholly dependent on the earnings of the insured person, so long as infirmity continues; (v) dependent parents. The word "Family" as used in s. 4 of the Partition Act 1893 must be construed in a wide sense and ought not to be restricted to persons tracing their descent from a common ancestor. This section does not suggest that the term "Family"

---

1 See *Pigg* v *Clarke* [1876]3 Ch D 672.
2 Re, *Makein* [1955]1 All ER 57.
3 Section 2(11), see also the definition of "Family" in s. 2(*ee*) of the Plantations Labour Act 1951; s. 2(*h*) of the Payment of Gratuity Act 1972.

is intended to be used in a very narrow and restricted sense.[4] Technically the word "Family" may mean the collective body of persons who live in one house and under one head of manager and includes within its fold a household consisting of parents, children and servants, lodgers or boarders, as the case may be.

Under the Mussalman Wakf Validating Act 1913, the word "Family" is intended to be used in a broad and popular sense. Popularly, the term indicates persons descended from one common progenitor and having a common lineage. It will take both agnates and cognates and relations by blood or marriage.[5] The word "Family" in popular sense includes children.[6] It always signifies a group. Plurality of persons is an essential attribute of a family. A single person, male or female, does not constitute a family. He or she would remain, what is inherent in the very nature of things, an individual, a lonely wayfarer till per chance he or she finds a mate. A family consisting of a single individual is a contradiction in terms.[7] In ultimate analysis, the concept of a family is based on marriage. In other words, marriage was rooted in the family.[8] Marriage between a man and a woman who may be strangers to each other creates a status by virtue of which law confers on them rights and obligations jointly and individually. In this context family law is concerned with the formation, dissolution and children born out of the marriage and also sometimes outside the marriage; adoption and maintenance of dependents and custody and guardianship of children, succession to property etc.

Family law under German Civil Code

A part of the German Civil Code deals with family law which contains a section relating to marriage and its effects, another section relating to parental authority and the other on guardianship.[9]

---

4   *A. Hassan* v *T. Hussain* AIR 1958 Pat 232 relying on *Salim Ullah* v *Fakir Ullah* AIR 1948 All 142; *Bibuni* v *Padmanav* AIR 1956 Ori 105.
5   *Asha Bibi* v *Nabissa Sahib* AIR 1957 Mad 583.
6   *Deoki Nandan* v *Murlidhar* AIR 1957 SC 133.
7   *C. Krishna Prasad* v *C.I.T.* (1975)1 SCC 160; AIR 1975 SC 498, see meaning of "Family" in the context of different Acts to *Adhunik Grah Nirman Sahakari Samiti Ltd.* v *State of Rajasthan* AIR 1989 SC 867; *Corporation of the City of Nagpur* v *Nagpur Handloom Cloth Market Co. Ltd.* AIR 1963 SC 1192; *Baldev Sahai* v *R.C. Bhasin* AIR 1982 SC 1091; *Mohd Azeem* v *Dist. Judge* (1985)2 SCC 550; *Sasanka Sekhar Maity* v *Union of India* AIR 1981 SC 522.
8   See E. Westermarch: *The History of Human Marriage* (1921).
9   The German Civil Code as amended on 1st January, 1975.

English family law

English family law concentrates on the creation and termination of marriage and the legal rights and duties arising out of it.[10]

Family law in USA

In the USA the definition of the term "Family" as a collection or the collective body, of persons living in one house, or under one head or manager has been criticised in judicial decisions.[11] In any case the term cannot be limited and strait-jacketed as always to mean, regardless of facts and circumstances, a collective body of persons who live in one house under one common head or manager.[12] To constitute family the following elements must be present: (1) a social status, (2) there must be a head who has a right, at least in a limited way to direct and control those gathered into the household, (3) this head must be obliged either legally or morally to support the other members, and (4) there must be a corresponding state of at least partial dependence of the other members for this support.[13] Thus, the family law in the USA shall be concerned with all these connected topics.

---

10 S.M. Cretney: *Principles of Family Law*, 4th Ed., p. 4.
11 See *Umbargar v State Farm Mut Automobile Ins. Co.* 254 NW 87, 89; 218 Iowa 203; *Howard v Marshall* 48 Tex 471, 479; *Franklin Fire Ins. Co. v Shadid* Com. App 68 SW 2d 1030, 1032.
12 *Johnson v State Farm Mut. Auto Ins. Co.* C.A. Mo. 252 F 2d 158, 161.
13 35 CJS, p. 939.

CHAPTER
2
Institution of Marriage

Introduction

The institution of marriage is as ancient as the inception of the society. The strong moral conviction of men in a civilised society and the firm belief of necessity for the preservation and well-being of the race have led most of the people to think that marriage is a natural relation, and must have existed from the infancy of mankind.[1]

Sir John Lubbock[2] says: "The lowest races have no institution of marriage; true love is almost unknown among them; and marriage in its lowest phases, is by no means a matter of affection and companionship." In primitive society there existed "communal marriage" where all men and women in a small community were regarded as equally married to one another. The term "communal marriage" is described as "promiscuous intercourse".[3] The institution of marriage was first based on practice, then on custom and ultimately it was recognised by law. Marriage is a condition of exclusiveness by each other which confers legal status of husband and wife. But now the concept of marriage is evolving away from status to contract.[4]

---

1 Sir Gooroodass Banerjee: *The Hindu Law of Marriage and Stridhana*, 5th Ed., p. 22.
2 *Origin of Civilisation*, 3rd Ed., p. 67.
3 Sir Gooroodass Banerjee, (supra), 24.
4 *Vervaeke v Smith (Messina and Attorney-General Intervenning)* (1981) Fam 77, 111; see also Weitzman: *The Marriage Contract* (1981).
   In *Adams v Palmer* (1863)51 Maine 480, 483 Appleton, CJ., said: "When the contracting parties have entered into a contract as into a new relation, the rights, duties and obligations of which rest, not upon their agreement, but upon the general law of the State, statutory or common, which defines and prescribes those rights, duties and obligations."

Definition of marriage

(i) *Christian law*. The classical definition of Christian marriage is to be found in the words of Lord Stowell in *Lindo* v *Betisario*.[5] "It is held that by some persons that marriage is a contract merely civil, by others that it is a sacred, religious and spiritual contract and only so to be considered. "I conceive that neither of these opinions is perfectly accurate. According to juster notions of the nature of the marriage contract, it is not merely either civil or religious contract. It is a contract according to the law of nature, antecedent to civil institutions, which may take place to all intents and purposes wherever two persons of different sexes engage, by mutual contracts, to live together." The legal concept of marriage is that it is the fulfilment of a contract satisfied by the solemnisation of the marriage. But marriage creates by law a relation between the parties and what is called a status of each.[6] In *Hyde* v *Hyde*[7] marriage has been defined as a voluntary union for life of one man and one woman to the exclusion of all others. The relation between the parties and the status of each of them with regard to the community which are constituted upon marriage are not imposed or defined by contract or agreement but by law.[8] Thus, marriage requires the participation of two persons, one a man and the other a woman. If two persons of the same sex continue to go through the formalities of a ceremony of marriage, the ceremony is not a marriage ceremony and the parties are not entitled to a declaratory relief, but the court in such circumstances, must grant a nullity decree.[9] This view is incorporated in the Matrimonial Causes Act 1973[10] which provides that a marriage celebrated after 31st July 1971, is void if the parties to the marriage are not respectively male and female. In *Ghaidan* v *Godin Mendoza*,[11] the House of Lords confirming the decision of the Court of Appeal held that the words "wife or husband" include a homosexual partner for the purpose of succession to a statutory tenancy. The basis of this decision is the provision of s. 3(1) of the Human Rights Act 1998 which provides the guideline for the court to interpret legislation to commensurate with the object of the European Human Rights and Fundamental Freedoms 1950.

---

5 [1795]1 Hag Con 216, 230.
6 *Niboyet* v *Niboyet* (1878)4 PD 1, 11.
7 [1866] LR 1 P&D 130, 133 per Lord Penzance.
8 Halsbury's *Laws of England*, 4th Ed., vol. 22, para 905.
9 *Corbett* v *Corbett* (*otherwise Ashley*) (1971) p. 83; [1970]2 All ER 33.
10 Section 11(c).
11 [2004] UKHL 30.

According to English law there are, four ways of celebrating marriages.[12] These are—

(1) Civil marriage; (2) Marriage according to non-Anglican religious ceremony; (3) Marriage according to the rites of the Church of England; and (4) Quaker and Jewish marriage. In civil marriages, the parties state in the notice that they intend to be married. The ceremony takes place in the office, with open doors, in the presence of the Superintendent Registrar and a Registrar. About half of the marriages in England and Wales are celebrated in this form. Marriage according to non-Anglican ceremony may be held at the places of worships. Non-conformist chapels and Roman Catholic churches are used for weddings in respect of such marriages. The Marriage Act 1949 has provided for marriages according to the rites of the Church of England. Quaker and Jewish marriages were exempted from the provisions of the Lord Hardwicke's Act, but now it is necessary for such a marriage to comply with one of the forms of civil preliminaries.

(ii) *Muslim law*. A Muslim marriage is known as *nikah* which is not a sacrament but a civil contract made with the object of procreation and legalisation of children. Consent of both the parties to the contract is necessary. In the Shafei sect the Wali conveys the consent of the wife to the Kazi.[13] The essential elements of a Muslim marriage are: (1) capacity of parties to marry, (2) offer and acceptance, (3) lawful object and (4) consideration. In *Muhammad Khan* v *Husaini Begum*[14] the Judicial Committee of the Privy Council said that in India and many communities circumstanced as the Mohammedans among whom marriages are contracted for minors by parents and guardians. If the common law doctrine were applied to such agreements, it would occasion injustice. Thus, strict rule is not applied.

(iii) *Hindu law*. Sir T. Strange[15] has said: "By no people is greater importance attached to marriage than by the Hindus". According to Hindu law marriage is regarded as one of the ten *sanskars* or sacraments.[16] It is a settled doctrine of Hindu law that one must have a son to save him from a place of torment called *put*.[17] Marriage is thus a primary means to

---

12 See *Stephen M. Cretney*, 4th Ed., pp. 28-29.
13 *Kummali Abubukker* v *Vengatt Marakar* AIR 1970 Ker 277.
14 ILR (1919)32 All 40 (PC).
15 *Elements of Hindu Law*, vol. 1, p. 35.
16 Colebrooke's Digest, B.K.V. 134, Note.
17 Manu, IX, 138.

achieve that end. It was regarded as a religious necessity. In *Swarajya Lakshmi v G.G. Padma Rao*[18] the Supreme Court has held that marriage according to Hindu law is a sacrament and a holy union for the performance of religious duties. As soon as a marriage is completed, the relation of the husband and the wife is to be considered from the point of view of the welfare of the husband and wife and also of the children, if any, of the marriage. According to Hindu law a marriage is determined by the number of parties to the relation. Amongst the Naiys of Malabar a marriage was a union between a certain number of males and a certain number of females.[19] There was a marriage between one woman and several men, related or unrelated. This type of marriage was prevalent in Tibet and Ceylon. The marriage between one man and several women was common amongst the Hindus and Mohomedans. The marriage between one man and one woman is introduced in the Hindu Marriage Act 1955. Maine[20] says, "Monogamy was rule and the approved rule, though polygamy existed to some extent. There is no real evidence of the existence of polyandry and matriarchate in Vedic times." According to Dr. Keith,[1] polyandry was not shown by a single passage to have existed amongst the Vedic Aryans. Inter-caste marriage between persons of different *vanas* or castes was not uncommon in ancient Hindu society. But from the beginning inter-caste marriages in order of castes (anuloma) were more frequent than those in the reverse order (pratiloma) till by the time of Dharmasutras and the Code of Manu, pratitoma marriage was forbidden. Finally, inter-caste marriage between *Dijas* and *Sudras* was totally forbidden by Manu and Yajnavalkya.[2] There was a universal prevalance of marriage by capture. It existed among the Jews, the Spartans and the Romans. In ancient time a marriage by capture was called the *Rakshasa* marriage which was recognised as one of the eight forms of marriage.[3] Eight forms of marriage as mentioned by different authorities on Hindu law are as follows[4]:

The gift of a daughter after decking her with costly garments and honouring her by presents of jewels, to a man learned in the Veda and of good conduct whom the father himself invites is called the Brahma rite.

---

18 AIR 1974 SC 165.
19 See Sir Gooroodass Banerjee, (supra), p. 27.
20 Mayne's Treatise on *Hindu Law and Usage*, 11th Ed., p. 101.
1 C.J.I. 1, 88, Vedic Index 1, 478-479 cited Mayne, (supra), p. 101.
2 Mayne's *Treatise on Hindu Law and Usage*, (supra), p. 103.
3 Sir Gooroodas Banerjee, (supra), p. 30.
4 Mayne's *Treatise on Hindu Law and Usage*, (supra), pp. 120-121.

The gift of a daughter to a priest who officiates at a sacrifice during the course of performance was called the Daivya rite.

When the father gives away his daughter according to the rule, after receiving from the bridegroom, for the fulfilment of the sacred law, a cow and a bull or two pairs, that was named as the Arsha rite.

The gift of a daughter by her father after he has addressed the couple with the text, "May both of you perform together your duties", and has shown honour to the bridegroom is called the Prajyapatya rite.

When the bridegroom receives a maiden, after having given as such wealth as he can afford to the Kinsmen and to the bride herself, according to his own will, that is known as Asura rite.

The voluntary union of a maiden and her lover is called the Gandharva rite.

The forcible abduction of a maiden from her home is called the Raksha rite.

When a man by stealth seduces a girl who is sleeping, intoxicated or unconscious, it is called the Paisacha rite.

Medhatithi, the commentator of Manu, says that marriage in ancient time has been classified under eight heads on the basis of different methods used for taking wives; and it does not mean that there are eight kinds of marriage."[5] The eight methods of obtaining a wife in fact resolve themselves into three forms of marriage, namely—(a) the gift of the bride, (b) the sale of the bride, and (c) the agreement between the man and the women. But in all the three forms celebration of marriage is necessary by performing rites. In the forms of marriage, such as the Brahma, the Daiva, the Prajapatya, the Arsha and the Asura, the dominion of the parents over the daughter was fully recognised and the marriage was completed by a formal transfer of the dominion over the daughter to the husband. In the Gandharva, the Rakshasa and the Paisacha forms, there was no transfer of the daughter by the parents to the husband. But in all the cases performance of marriage rites was necessary. The ancient Hindu law did not recognise rape and seduction as marriage. Abduction and rape were declared as offence by Yajnavalkya.

---

5 Medhatithi on Manu, III, 34; VIII, 366, Jha's trans, vol. II, 55-63, vol. IV, 393.

He[6] says, "He who defiles a maidan shall have his hand cut off and he shall lose his life if she be of a higher class." He who kidnapped a maiden of the same class was heavily fined, but if of superior class, was sentenced to death. Of all the forms of marriages the Brahma and the Gandharva forms of marriages were recognised as lawful for all castes. In *Brindavan* v *Radhamoney*[7] it was held that the Gandharva form of marriage coupled with performance of the prescribed ceremony or customary rites was not obsolete. The Asura form of marriage was considered by West, J. in *Vijiangam* v *Lakshmanam*.[8] He said that the very name of Asura indicated it as one derived from the aboriginal inhabitants of this country or those occupying it before the Aryan invasion and that it was the reason why it was loathed by the sages of the strict Brahmanical school. In Southern India among the Sudras the Asura form of marriage was common, if not the prevailing form.[9] In Western India although Asura marriages were forbidden, yet it had been the custom for Brahmins and others to celebrate such marriage and that no one had been expelled from the caste for such form of marriage.[10] The ceremonies for both the Asura and the Brahma forms of marriage are essential for their validity. Where money is paid to the parents of the bride as consideration for the sale of the girl, it is an Asura form of marriage. "The taint of the Asura form lies in the gratuity being paid to the giver of the bride for his benefit, not in anything paid to her; and it is the taint which determines the form."[11] Where the bridegroom or his party gives a sum of money to the father of the bride towards the expenses of the marriage, it has been held that it is equivalent to the price of the bride and that the marriage should be regarded as an Asura marriage.[12] But where the money was paid to

---

6   Yajn. II, 287, 288. "He who violates an unwilling maiden shall instantly suffer corporal punishment ... If any man, through insolence, forcibly contaminates a maiden, two of his fingers shall be instantly cut off and he shall pay a fine of six hundred panas"—Manu, VIII, 364, 367.
7   (1889)12 Mad 72; *Kishen Devi* v *Shee Palton* (1926)48 All 126, 133; see also *Gajapathi Radika* v *Sri Gajapathi* (1870)13 MIA 506. See *Padayachi* v *A. Ammal* AIR 1938 Rang 59; *Kamani Devi* v *Kameshwar Singh* (1946)25 Pat 58 (Gandharva marriage among Brahmins is valid, but its celebration is to be attended with nuptial rites and ceremonies including *homa* and *saptapadi* for its validity).
8   [1871]8 BHCO CJ 244, 254, 255.
9   *Authikesavalu* v *Ramanuja* (1909)32 Mad 512.
10 *Keshow Rao* v *Navo*, 3 Bor, 198; *Jaganath* v *Narayan* (1910)34 Bom 553; *Chunilal* v *Surajram* (1909)33 Bom 433.
11 *Chunilal* v *Suraj Ram* (1909)33 Bom 433, 442.
12 *Muthu* v *Chidambara* (1893)3 MLJ 261, *Reverend Gabriel* v *Valliammai* (1919)10 MLW 491; (1920) MWN 158; *Rathnathanni* v *Somasundara* (1921)41 MLJ 76; *Samuasari* v *Anachiammal* (1925)49 MLJ 554, *Kailasanatha* v *Vadivanni* (1935)58 Mad 488.

the parents of the bride for the purpose of paying to her third husband to procure her divorce, it was held that the marriage was not in the Asura, but in the Brahma form.[13] In many cases the marriage of a girl is delayed by her father due to shortage of fund to perform the marriage on a grander scale and he receives money from the bridegroom, or that the marriage is celebrated at the house of the bridegroom at his expenses, one cannot presume as a matter of law that there is an intention to sell the bride in consideration of money spent for expenses of the marriage. It is purely a question of fact and the interference should ordinarily be that it is not intended to be a price for the bride.[14] Under the Hindu Marriage Act 1955 a number of important changes have been brought about to codify the uniformity of marriage throughout India but preserving the prevailing customs.

(*iv*) *Roman law.* According to the Roman law, marriage was classified into *matrimonium justum* and *non-justum*. In the former case a marriage occurred when both the parties had the capacity to enter into a lawful marriage carrying along with the paternal power and other civil rights. Originally, this form of marriage was strictly confined to Roman citizens or those to whom the *jus-connubii* was conceded. The *matrimonium non-justum*, on the other hand, in which *connubium* was absent, as in the case of marriage between *Latini* or foreigners or between Romans and foreigners, though equally valid and binding marriage, did not confer the *patria notestas*, and other important civil rights.[15] Marriage was the privilege of the free alone; the union of slaves was called *contubernium*. There were three modes of contracting marriage with manus. These were called, (*a*) *confarreatio*, (*b*) *coemptio* and (*c*) *usus*.[16] *Confarreatio* was a solemn religious ceremony, before ten witnesses, in which an ox was sacrificed, and a cake of wheaten bread was divided by the priest between man and woman as an emblem of the *consortium vitae* or life in common. *Coemptio* was a kind of symbolical purchase of the wife by the husband, *per sees aes et libram*, in presence of five witnesses and the balance-holder. *Usus* was founded on prescription, by the woman cohabiting with the man as her husband for a whole year without having been absent from his house for three whole nights following each other.[17] The Roman fixed the puberty for

---

13 *Hira* v *Hansji* (1913) 37 Bom 295; 17 IC 941.
14 *Sivanagalingam Pillai* v *Ambalavana Pillai* (1938) MWN 161.
15 Lord Mackenzie: *Studies in Roman Law*, 7th Ed., pp. 94-95.
16 *Ibid*, p. 95.
17 Gai I 109-113. Becker's *Gallus*, Translated by Metcalfe, 2nd Ed., p. 158.

marriage at fourteen years of age for males and at twelve years of age for females.[18] According to Ortolan[19] marriage was not completed till the delivery of the wife to the husband which was manifested by the *deduction in domum mariti*. Parties were incapable of contracting marriage by reason of their relationship within certain degrees, either of consanguinity or affinity. But the Emperor Claudius was granted leave by the Senate to marry his niece Agrippina and that precedent was followed by some Romans. This practice was, however, suppressed by Constantine.[20] These rules as to prohibited degrees for marriage were also substantially adopted both in England and in Scotland. In the Code of Napoleon[21] the prohibited degrees were provided which are as follows:

> "In the direct line, marriage is prohibited between all ascendants and descendants, whether lawful or natural, and persons connected by affinity in the same line."

> "In the collateral line, marriage is prohibited between the brother and sister, whether lawful or natural, and persons connected by affinity in the same degree."

> "Marriage is also prohibited between uncle and niece, aunt and nephew."

---

18 UIB 11.28; Justinian Inst. 1.22 pr.
19 Institutes (9th Ed.), vol. II, p. 82.
20 Cod. Theod. 3.12.1.
21 Articles 161, 162 and 163.

CHAPTER
3
Other Personal Laws

Introduction

The word "personal" appertains to the person.[1] Personal law of a person is a law under which that person is brought up or governed either in accordance with religion or by custom. Such law governs the status of a person and applies to marriage, inheritance, guardianship, maintenance etc. A Hindu is governed by Hindu law as his or her personal law;[2] a Muslim is governed by Muslim personal law.[3] Other personal laws for the purpose of this part include Indian Christians and Parsis.[4]

Miscellaneous Personal Laws (Extension) Act 1959 (Act 48 of 1959)

(A) *Objects of Miscellaneous Personal Laws (Extension) Act 1959*. The objects of the Miscellaneous Personal Laws (Extension) Act 1959 were two-fold: (1) To extend the personal laws of certain communities to the territories comprised within the former Part B States and thereby to make the those laws generally applicable to the whole of India except the State of Jammu and Kashmir; and (2) to repeal the existing State laws which are affected consequent upon extension of personal laws as stated above.[5]

---

1. Black's *Law Dictionary*, 6th Ed., p. 1143; *Steimes' Estate*, 150 Misc. 279, 270 N.Y.S. 339.
2. See Part A dealing with Hindu Law in this work.
3. See Chapters 15, 16, 17, 18 of this work.
4. See Chapter 20 of this work.
5. See Statement of Objects and Reasons published in Gaz. of India, 31.8.1959, Pt II, s. 2, Ext, p. 918; Preamble to Act 48 of 1949.

(B) *Acts extended and repealed law.* The Acts named in Schedule I to the Act 48 or 1959 are amended in the manner specified therein with effect from 1st February 1960.[6] The following Acts, namely, (1) The Converts' Marriage Dissolution Act 1866,[7] (2) The Anand Marriage Act 1909,[8] (3) The Hindu Disposition of Property Act 1916,[9] (4) The Hindu Inheritance (Removal of Disabilities) Act 1928,[10] (5) The Hindu Gains and Learning Act 1930,[11] (6) The Muslim Personal Law (Shariat) Application Act 1937,[12] and (7) The Dissolution of Muslim Marriages Act 1939[13] have been included in Schedule I of the said Act. On and from 1st February 1960 the Acts specified in Schedule II of the Act 48 of 1959 corresponding to the Acts specified in Schedule I stand repealed in the territories to which they respectively were extended immediately before 1st February 1960.[14] There are altogether twenty local Acts specified in Schedule II of the said Act.[15]

Secular law

Secularism means a system of utilitarian ethics seeking to maximise human happiness or welfare quite independent of any religion or occult.[16] Secular law refers to a body of code which is not anti-God. It treats alike the devout, the agnostic and the atheist. It ensures that no one will be discriminated against on the ground of religion.[17] The secular laws are applicable to all irrespective of their personal law. Some of the statutes dealing with secular law are (1) The Special Marriage Act 1954, (2) The Foreign Marriage Act 1969, (3) The Family Courts Act 1984, (4) The Dowry Prohibition Act 1961, (5) The Guardian and Wards Act 1890, (6) The Indian Succession Act 1925, (7) The Protection of Women from Domestic Violence Act 2005, (8) The Maintenance and Welfare of Parents and Senior Citizens Act 2007 and (9) The Prohibition of Child Marriage Act 2006.

---

6   Act 48 of 1959, s. 3 read with Schedule I thereto.
7   Act 21 of 1866.
8   Act 17 of 1909.
9   Act 15 of 1916.
10 Act 12 of 1928.
11 Act 30 of 1930.
12 Act 26 of 1937.
13 Act 8 of 1939.
14 Act 48 of 1959, s. 4 read with Schedule II thereto.
15 See Schedule II of Act 48 of 1959.
16 *Z.B. Bukhari* v *B.R. Mehta* AIR 1975 SC 1788.
17 See *Amedabad St. Zavier's College* v *State of Gujarat* AIR 1974 SC 1389 (on secularism).

PART 2

Hindu Family Law

CHAPTER
4

Hindu Law

Introduction

Hindu law means a body of rules or commands which govern the conduct of a Hindu in relation to both Civil and Criminal matters. A person is a Hindu who is born of Hindu parents or is brought up according to the tenets of a Hindu religion in any of its forms and developments. In *Bhagwan Koer* v *Bose*[1] it has been said: "The Hindu religion is marvelously catholic and elastic. Its theology is marked by eclecticism and tolerance and almost unlimited freedom of private worship. Its social code is much more stringent, but amongst its different castes and sections it exhibits wide diversity of practice." Law as understood by a Hindu in ancient time is a branch of Dharma. The definition of Dharma is: "What is followed by those learned in the Vedas and what is approved by the conscience of the virtuous who are exempt from hatred and inordinate affection."[2] According to one view, Hindu law was the legislation by sages of semi divine authority or by ancient legislative bodies. According to the other view, the Smriti law did not wholly represent the set of rules which were administered in Hindustan.[3] A Hindu regards his laws as commands, not of any political sovereign, but of the Supreme Ruler of the Universe.[4] Even a political sovereign is also imperatively enjoined to obey such commands of the Supreme Ruler of the Universe.[5] "As obedience to the law implied only obedience to the divine will, it never wounded the

---

1 (1904)31 Cal 11, 15.
2 Manusmriti II, 1.
3 Mayne's *Treatise on Hindu Law and Usage*, 11th Ed., p. 1.
4 See Manu, 1, 58.
5 See Manu, VIII, 8.

pride of the most absolute despot; and the thought never entered the mind of a Hindu King that he could, if he chose, alter or abrogate any of the existing laws."[6] In short, it can be said that Hindu law contains its own principles of exposition.[7] In other words, Hindu law is an admixture of morality, religion and law.[8] The civil part of Hindu law deals mainly with the topics like marriage, adoption, minority and guardianship, succession, gifts, wills, partition etc.

Sources of Hindu law

According to Mayne[9] the sources of Hindu law are (*i*) the Smritis or the Dharmasastras, (*ii*) the commentaries and the Digests, and (*iii*) custom. Manu[10] and Yajnavalkye[11] have classified the sources of Hindu law into (*i*) the Sruti or the Veda, (*ii*) the Smriti or the Codes of law, and (*iii*) the approved usages. Sir Gooroodas Banerjee[12] has said that a practical division of the sources of Hindu law would be that into three classes, such as (*i*) the original authorities consisting of the texts and commentaries, (*ii*) Custom and (*iii*) Judicial decisions. In modern times, the sources of Hindu law can be divided into six classes: (*i*) the Srutis, (*ii*) the Smritis, (*iii*) the Commentaries or the Digests, (*iv*) Customs or Usages approved by law, (*v*) Judicial decisions and (*vi*) the Legislation.

(*i*) *The Sruti.* The Sruti is literally meant as what is heard. In theory it is said to be the primary source of Hindu law. It is believed to be the pronouncement of the divine Revelation. By the term Sruti it means four Vedas, such as the Rik, the Samman, the Yajus, and the Atharva along with their respective Brahmins.[13]

(*ii*) *The Smritis.* The word "Smritis" means what is recollected or remembered. The Smritis refer to the memory of the sages who were regarded as the repositories of the divine Revelation. They are also known as the Dharmasastra.[14]

---

6 Sir Gooroodass Banerjee, *The Hindu Law of Marriage and Stridhana*, 5th Ed., p. 3.
7 *Kalgavda* v *Sumoppa* (1909)33 Bom 669, 680; *Ramchandra* v *Vinayak* AIR 1914 PC 1.
8 *Rao Balwant Singh* v *Rani Kishori* (1898)25 IA 54; *Balusu* v *Balusu* (1899)26 IA 113.
9 Trestise on *Hindu Law and Usage*, 11th Ed., p. 19.
10 II, 12.
11 I, 7.
12 *The Hindu Law of Marriage and Stridhana*, 5th Ed., p. 8.
13 Manu II, 12; Yajn. 1, 7.
14 Visvarupa and Vijnaneswara on Yajnavalkya 1, 7 say that the Smritis and the Dharmasastras are synonymous.

(*iii*) *The commentaries.* The commentaries and the digests are of two classes, one dealing generally with the Hindu law and the other dealing on special topics. The Mitakshara is a running commentary on the Yajnavalkya Smriti written by Vijneshwara. The Dayabhaga is the digest of a number of Smritis written by Jimutavahana. Both of them dealt with the Hindu Law generally. There were other commentaries which were written by different scholars in different parts of India in different times. The Saraswati Vilas was written sometimes in 16th Century by Prataparudradeva Saraswati vilas dealing with general part of the Hindu Law for Southern India. But it was not regarded as the greater authority than the Mitakshara.[15] The Dottaka Mimamsa is a treatise on adoption which is a special topic of Hindu law. It was written by Nand Pandit. But the Commentators like Nand Pandit or Balam Bhatia do not carry much weight in the eye of law.[16]

(*iv*) *Customs or usages.* Customs are of various classes, namely (*a*) custom of castes, (*b*) custom of tribes, (*c*) local or territorial custom, (*d*) family custom.[17] The Supreme Court[18] has held that a custom would be binding if it derives its force of law from the fact that by long usage it has obtained the support of law. A custom must be ancient, certain and reasonable.[19] A custom which is immoral or opposed to public policy or opposed to any enactment of the legislature will not be recognised, nor enforced.[20] Continuity is an essential element for validity of a custom. The onus of proving the discontinuance will lie upon the person setting it up.[1] The Privy Council in *Collector of Madhura* v *Muttu Ramlinga*[2] held that under the Hindu system of law, clear proof of usage will outweigh the written text of the law. A custom is a rule which has obtained the force of law in a particular family, or in a particular district or in a particular sect, class or tribe.[3]

---

15 *Kamalammal* v *Venkatalaxmi* AIR 1965 SC 1349.
16 *Pitra Kueri* v *Ujagir Rai* AIR 1958 All 101.
17 Manu VIII, 3, 41; Yajn. II, 192.
18 *Gokalchand* v *Parvin* AIR 1952 SC 231.
19 See *Shib Narain Mookerjee* v *Bhutnath* (1918)45 Cal 475; *Hashmat Ali* v *Nasibunnissa* (1924)6 Lah 47 (PC).
20 *Vanniakone* v *Vannichi* (1928)51 Mad 1 (FB).
1 *Sahabjit* v *Indrajit* (1905)27 All 203; *Amina Khatun* v *Khalilur Rahaman* (1933)8 Luck 445; AIR 1933 Oudh 246.
2 10 WR 21 (PC); (1868)12 MIA 397 (PC).
3 *Hurpurshad* v *Sheo Dayal* (1876)3 IA 259 (PC).

(*v*) *Judicial decision.* The principles of *stare decisis* has been accepted as an important source of law even in respect of courts of co-ordinate jurisdiction.[4] It is the duty of Judge to administer Hindu law to ascertain the law as laid down by the Superior Courts of India such as the Privy Council.[5]

(*vi*) *Legislation.* It goes without saying that the most important source of law in modern time is the enactment of legislature. During the British Rule a number of Central and Provincial laws were passed on different subjects of Hindu law.[6] In the post independent India four major Acts have been passed on marriage,[7] succession,[8] minority and guardianship[9] and adoption and maintenance[10] concerning Hindus.

Judicial interpretation on sources of Hindu law

In interpreting Smritis as a source of Hindu law it has been held that it is not safe to merely take the dictionary meaning and apply it to the texts since the Smritis which were rendered thousands of years ago, deal with religions and moral laws as well.[11] In *Collector of Madura* v *Muttu Ramtinga Satthupathy*[12] it has been laid down by the Privy Council that in Hindu law "clear proof of usage will outweigh the written text of the law". In *Atmoram* v *Bajirao*[13] the Privy Council observed that the commentators, while interpreted as laid down in the Smritis introduced changes in order to bring it into harmony with usage followed by the people governed by the law and as a result the opinion of the commentators which prevailed in the provinces where their authority

---

4   *Venkanna* v *Laxmi* AIR 1951 Bom 57.
5   *Madanvali* v *Balu Padmanna* AIR 1960 Mys 299.
6   Some examples of Central Laws are the Caste Disabilities Removal Act 1850, the Hindu Widows, Re-marriage Act 1856, the Anand Marriage Act 1909, the Hindu Disposition of Property Act 1916, the Hindu Inheritance (Removal of Disabilities) Act 1928, the Hindu Gains of Learning Act 1930, the Hindu Women's Rights to Property Act 1937, the Hindu Married Women's Right to Separate Residence and Maintenance Act 1946, the Hindu Marriages Disabilities Removal Act 1946, the Hindu Marriages Validity Act 1949.

   Some examples of Provincial Laws are the Bombay Prevention of Hindu Bigamous Marriages Act 1946, the Bombay Hindu Divorce Act 1947, the Madras Nambudri Act 1933.
7   Hindu Marriage Act 1955.
8   Hindu Succession Act 1956.
9   Hindu Minority and Guardianship Act 1956.
10 Hindu Adoptions and Maintenance Act 1956.
11 *Davaraja Raja Rao* v *I.T. Officer* AIR 1970 AP 426.
12 (1868)12 MIA 397 (PC).
13 AIR 1935 PC 57.

was recognised. But in *Ramlakshmi* v *Sewanantha*[14] the Privy Council said, "Many of the precepts of Manu have undoubtedly been altered and modified by modern law and usage; but his authority may properly be referred to where it is necessary to resort to first principles in order to ascertain and develop the law." In any event the power of the court is not limited in interpreting the sources of Hindu law. It is said that Hindu law is not static nor is it inelastic that in interpreting the texts of Hindu law the Courts are powerless to mould it to meet situations not contemplated at the time when it was declared or in the light of consciousness of the society.[15]

Schools of Hindu law

As the authority of a commentator of Hindu law was received in some parts of India to be the prevailing law, and rejected in some other parts, there grew different schools, of Hindu law. There are five schools of Hindu law, namely, Benares, Mithila, Bengal, Dravida and Maharashtra Schools.[16] But broadly speaking there are two principal schools of Hindu law. These are—(1) the Mitakshara School, and (2) the Dayabhaga School. The Mitakshara School of Vijnaneshwara is said to be the earlier than the Dayabhaga School of Jimutavahana. The Mitakshara School prevails through out India[17] except where the Dayabhaga School prevails. Hindus living in the Punjab are governed by the Mitakshara School with some modifications in consistence with the prevailing customs.[18] The Mitakshara School is sub-divided into Benares School, Mithila School, Dravida and Maharashtra School. The names of these schools indicate the places or the territories where each school is prevalent. So far as the Dayabhaga School is concerned, it is prevalent in the Presidency of Bengal[19] and Assam.[20] It is because of different schools of thought or doctrine, there exist different Hindu laws. Law differs from school to school: first, from the Mitakshara to the Dayabhaga, and then within the Mitakshara School from one sub-school to another.[1]

---

14 (1890)14 MSA 570 (PC).
15 *Shantabai* v *Ramchandra* (1959)61 Bom LR 627.
16 Strange's *Hindu Law*, pp. 315-319.
17 *Collector of Madhura* v *Muttu Ramlinga* (1868)12 MIA 397 (PC).
18 *Kaur Singh* v *Jaggar Singh* AIR 1961 Punj 489.
19 *Collector of Madhura*, (supra). (In Midnapore the Dayabhaga School prevails). See *Sikhdeo* v *Mritinjoy* (1939)43 Cal WN 395.
20 *Collector of Madhura*, (supra).
1 *Bhugwandeen* v *Myna Baee* (1867)11 MIA 487 (PC).

Different sub-schools

Under this sub-heading the principal commentaries and digests of important authorities are dealt with.

(i) *Benares School.* The Principles of law laid down in the Mitakshara are supplemented in the Benares School by Viramitrodaya.[2] Viramitrodaya being later in time it supplements many gaps and omission left out in the earlier commentaries and it illustrates and elucidates with logical preciseness the meaning and scope of doubtful prescriptions.[3] The Viramitrodaya's prescription is declaratory in nature and acts as an exposition of what has been left doubtful by the Mitakshara.[4] The Viramitrodaya cannot be referred to where the Mitakshara is clear.[5]

(ii) *Mithila School.* The principal authorities in the Mithila School supplementing the Mitakshara are (a) Vivada Chintamani,[6] (b) Vivada Ratnakara,[7] and (c) Dattaka Mimamsa.[8]

(iii) *Dravida School.* The principal commentaries which have supplemented the Mitakshara are (a) Smriti Chandrika,[9] (b) Parasamadhaviya,[10] (c) Saraswati Vilas,[11] (d) Vayavaharanir-maya,[12] and (e) Dattaka Chandrika.[13]

(iv) *Maharashtra School.* The Principal authorities which have supplemented the Mitakshara in Maharashtra are (a) Vyavhara Mayukha,[14] (b) Samskara Kaustubha,[15] and (c) Dattaka Mimamsa.[16]

---

2   Ibid, *Gridhari Lall* v *Bengal Government* (1868)12 MSA 448 (PC); *Ramchandra* v *Vinayak* AIR 1914 PC 1; *Budha Singh* v *Laltu Singh* AIR 1915 PC 70; *Jatindra Nath* v *Nagendra Nath* AIR 1931 PC 268.
3   *Vedachela* v *Subramania* AIR 1922 PC 33; *Jatindra Nath* v *Nagendra Nath* AIR 1931 PC 268.
4   *Gridhari Lall* v *Bengal Government* (1868)12 MIA 448 (PC).
5   *Jagannath Prasad* v *Ranjit Singh* (1895)25 Cal 354.
6   *Thakur Deyhee* v *Rai Baluk* (1866)11 MIA 139 (PC); *Baccha Jha* v *Judmon Jha* (1886)12 Cal 348 (PC); *Sourindra Mohan Singh* v *Hariprasad* AIR 1925 PC 280.
7   *Thakur Deyhee,* (supra); *Kamala Prasad* v *Mudliar* AIR 1934 Pat 398.
8   *Collector of Madhura,* (supra).
9   Ibid; *Vedachela,* ibid; *Raju* v *Ammani* (1906)29 Mad 358.
10 *Bhugwandeen* v *Myna Baee,* (supra); *Collector of Madhura,* (supra).
11 *Vedachela,* (supra); *Bami Reddy* v *Gangi* AIR 1925 Mad 807; *Krishna* v *Sami* (1886)9 Mad 64 (FB).
12 *Buddha Singh* v *Laltu Singh* AIR 1915 PC 70.
13 *Collector of Madhura,* (supra); *Bhagwan Singh,* (supra).
14 *Krishnaji* v *Pandurang* (1875)12 Bom HC 65; *Bhima Bai* v *Gurunath Gonda* AIR 1933 PC 1.
15 *Bhagirathibai* v *Kahnujirav* (1908)11 Bom 285 (FB).
16 *Waman* v *Krishnaji* (1889)14 Bom 240.

CHAPTER
5

Some Important Legislations on Hindu Law and Marriage During British Rule

Introduction

During British Rule in India a number of statutes were passed touching the Hindu law and Marriage. Some of them are dealt with under this heading. These are (*i*) Hindu Widows' Remarriage Act 1856; (*ii*) Anand Marriage Act 1909; (*iii*) Arya Marriage Validation Act 1937; (*iv*) Hindu Marriage Disabilities Removal Act 1946; (*v*) Caste Disabilities Removal Act 1850; (*vi*) Hindu Disposition of Property Act 1916; (*vii*) Hindu Inheritance (Removal of Disabilities) Act 1928. Though after independence new Acts have been brought on the statute book repealing old laws relating thereto, yet the old statutory laws have both historical and legal importance. Thus those Acts are set out hereunder and are stated the legal principles laid therein.

The Hindu Widows' Remarriage Act 1856 (Act 15 of 1856)[1]

(1) *Preamble*. The Hindu Widows' Remarriage Act 1856 was passed to remove all legal obstacles to the marriage of Hindu widows. Prior to the commencement of the said Act it was known that, by the law as administered in the Civil Courts established in the territories in the possession and under the Government of the East India Company, Hindu widows with certain exceptions were held to be, by reason of their having been once married, incapable of contracting a second valid marriage, and the offspring of such widows by any second marriage were held to be illegitimate and incapable of inheriting property.

---

1 Repealed by the Hindu Widows' Remarriage (Repeal) Act 1983 (Act 24 of 1983).

Many Hindus believed that this imputed legal incapacity, although it was in accordance with established custom, yet it was not in accordance with a true interpretation of the precepts of their religion, and they desired that the Civil Law Administered by the Courts of Justice should not prevent those Hindus who might be so minded from adopting a different custom, in accordance with the dictates of their own conscience.

It was, therefore, considered just to relieve all such Hindus from such legal incapacity of which they complained and the removal of all obstacles to the marriage of Hindu widows would tend to the promotion of good morals and to the public welfare.

(2) *Custom of remarriage*. There is a custom of remarriage among the Jats of Ajmer. Thus if a custom exists, the rights and obligations of the parties to the remarriage will be governed by the said custom and not by the Act.[2] Religious ceremonies as required by custom are essential for validity of remarriage of a widow. The Hindu Widows' Remarriage Act 1856 has not dispensed with the customary law.[3] But in *Mussadi* v *Chando*[4] it has been held that the religious ceremonies, such as invocation before the sacred fire and *saptapadi* are not necessary for validity of remarriage of a Hindu widow. This Act does not validate remarriage of a Hindu widow if the parties to the marriage fall within the prohibited degrees of relationship.[5]

(3) *Rights of widow on remarriage*. Under section 2 of the Act a widow on remarriage would forfeit all her rights in the estate of her deceased husband. But there is a divergence of opinion on the question whether a widow who remarriage according to custom of caste would forfeit her right and interest in her former husband estate. According to the High Court of Allahabad[6] and the Chief Courts of Oudh and Ajmer[7] she does not forfeit her right and interest in her former deceased husband's estate. But according to the High Courts of Bombay,[8] Calcutta,[9] Patna[10] and Madras[11] she would forfeit her rights and interest. The Allahabad High

---

2 *Roopa* v *Ladu* AIR 1951 Ajmer 45.
3 *D. Achi* v *R.M.Al.Ct.C. Chettiar* AIR 1954 Mad 657.
4 AIR 1956 HP 45.
5 *Akshay Kumar* v *Jatindranath* AIR 1955 Cal 612.
6 *Gajadhar* v *Kaunisilia* (1909)31 All 161; *Narain* v *Mohan Singh* AIR 1917 All 343. *Mangat* v *Bharto* AIR 1927 All 523; *Nagar* v *Khase* AIR 1925 All 440.
7 *Ram Laull* v *Mussammat* AIR 1928 Oudh 338; *Roopa* v *Ladu* AIR 1953 Ajmer 45.
8 *Vithu* v *Govinda* (1898)22 Bom 321 (FB).
9 *Santala Bewa* v *Badaswari Dasi* AIR 1924 Cal 98.
10 *Suraj* v *Attar* AIR 1922 Pat 378.
11 *Murugayi* v *Viramkali* (1877)1 Mad 226.

Court in a Full Bench decision[12] held that a widow on her remarriage did not forfeit her right in her former husband's estate—unless it was established that there was custom of such forfeiture. There was also conflict of opinion on the question of right of a Hindu widow before remarriage by conversion to other religion in respect of her former husband's property. The High Courts of Calcutta,[13] Madras,[14] Patna[15] and Bombay[16] held that she had to cease her right in such circumstances. But the Allahabad High Court[17] held that she did not cease her right in such a situation. In *Vitta Tayaramma* v *Chatakondu*[18] the Full Bench of the Madras High Court held in construing s. 2 of the Hindu Widows' Remarriage Act: "The words any widow .... upon her remarriage in s. 2 are wide enough to cover the case of any widow of a Hindu remarrying whether or not the marriage would otherwise be prohibited by any custom or interpretation of Hindu law, and whether the remarriage was to a Hindu or to member of another religion." The said Act had no application to widow who could remarry even before the commencement of the Act and as such a Hindu widow on remarriage did not forfeit her rights in her former husband's estate which she either inherited or acquired.[19] The rule of forfeiture by a Hindu widow in the property of her husband on her remarriage was based on general principle of Hindu law in absence of any special custom prevailing in any community against such forfeiture. The court would give effect to such custom in spite of s. 2 of the 1856 Act.[20] A Hindu widow would forfeit her right to the estate of her deceased husband on her second marriage provided the said second marriage was valid. If the second marriage was not valid by reason of bar provided in another statute such as s. 4(1) of the Madras Act 6 of 1949, she did not forfeit her right.[21] Under s. 2 of the 1856 Act all rights and interests possessed by a Hindu widow ceased to exist on her remarriage and the material date of her deprivation was the date of her remarriage. Thus, she was not entitled to sue for partition of her deceased husband's share in the property.[1] Where a widow's life estate becomes absolute by virtue of the provision of s. 14 of

---

12 *Bhola Umar* v *Kaunsilia* AIR 1932 All 617 (FB).
13 *Matungini* v *Ram Rutton* (1892)19 Cal 289 (FB).
14 *Vitta Tayaramma* v *Chatakondu Sivayya* AIR 1919 Mad 854 (FB).
15 *Suraj* v *Attar* AIR 1922 Pat 378.
16 *Raghunath* v *Lakshmibai* AIR 1935 Bom 298.
17 *Gajadhar* v *Kaunisilia* (1909)31 All 161.
18 AIR 1919 Mad 854 (FB).
19 *Ram Kunwar* v *Ochha Dhanpal* AIR 1951 Madh Bh 96.
20 *Bhondu* v *Ramdayal* AIR 1960 MP 51 (FB).
21 *Madanavalli* v *Thangavelu* AIR 1961 Mad 298.
1   *Mussadi* v *Chando* AIR 1956 HP 45.

the Hindu Succession Act 1956, she would not forfeit her right to such property by her subsequent marriage, or unchastity. Section 2 of the 1856 Act would apply only to life estate and not to an absolute estate.[2]

(4) *Right to adoption.* A Hindu widow on her remarriage loses her right to give adoption of her son by her former husband unless he had expressly authorised her to do so.[3]

There is no provision in the 1856 Act depriving a widow of her right of guardianship in respect of her minor son on her remarriage.[4] Section 3 of the 1856 Act would not apply to a Hindu widow who remarries according to customary law and consequently she would not forfeit her right of guardianship of her minor children.[5] Section 3 of the 1856 Act provides for appointment of a guardian of the person of the minor but not of his property.[6]

The burden of proving custom approving remarriage lies on the widow remarrying.[7]

The Anand Marriage Act 1909[8]

This Act was passed to remove doubts as to the validity of the marriage ceremony common among the Sikhs called Anand.

Section 3 of the said Act exempted certain marriages from Act

The said Act shall apply to:

(a) any marriage between persons not professing the Sikh religion; or

(b) any marriage which has been judicially declared to be null and void.

Section 4 of the said Act provides that this Act shall not effect the validity of any marriage duly solemnised according to any other marriage ceremony customary among the Sikhs.

---

2 *Sankara* v *Anita* AIR 1977 Cal 289.
3 *Panchappa* v *Sangabasawa* (1900)24 Bom 89.
4 *Ganga* v *Jhato* (1911)38 Cal 862.
5 *Prem Kaur* v *Harnam Singh* AIR 1939 Lah 125.
6 *Rup Rani* v *Basudeo Raut* AIR 1962 Pat 436.
7 *Bhola Umar* v *Kansilla* AIR 1937 All 230.
8 Act 7 of 1909.

The Arya Marriage Validation Act 1937[9]

The Arya Marriage Validation Act 1937 was passed to recognise and remove doubts as to the validity of inter-marriages current among Arya Samajists.

Section 2 of the said Act provides that notwithstanding any provision of Hindu law, usage or custom to the contrary no marriage contracted whether before or after the commencement of this Act between two persons being at the time of the marriage Arya Samajists shall be invalid or shall be deemed ever to have been invalid by reason only of the fact that the parties at any time belonged to different castes or different sub-castes of Hindus or that either or both of the parties at any time before the marriage belonged to a religion other than Hinduism.

The Hindu Marriage Disabilities Removal Act 1946[10]

(1) *Preliminary*. The Hindu Marriage Disabilities Removal Act 1946 was passed to remove certain disabilities and doubts under Hindu law in respect of marriages between Hindus.

The said Act extended to the whole of British India.[11]

Section 2 of the said Act provides that notwithstanding any text, rule or interpretation of Hindu Law or any custom or usage, a marriage between Hindus, which is otherwise valid, shall not be invalid by reason only of the fact that the parties thereto:

(*a*) belong to the same *gotra* or *pravara*; or

(*b*) belong to different sub-divisions of the same caste.

(2) *"Gotra," or pravara meaning of.* "Gotra", means primitive stock. It means that a family descended from one of the several "Patriarchs" that is sages of Rishis. There are 120 '*gotras*'.[12] Two persons are said to be of the same *pravara* if they are descendants in the male line of the three paternal ancestors of the founder of a *gotra*.[13]

---

9 Act 19 of 1937. (Received the assent of the Governor General in Council on April 14, 1937).
10 Act 28 of 1946. (Received the assent of the Governor-General on November 22, 1946). This Act was repealed s. 30 of the Hindu Marriage Act 1955.
11 The expression "British India" was amended by the Adoption Order 1950 and the Adoption of Laws (No. 2) Order 1956.
12 *Mayne*, 10th Ed., p. 170.
13 G. Sarkar's *"Hindu Law"*, 7th Ed., p. 89.

Caste Disabilities Removal Act 1850[14]

(1) *Preamble.* It is enacted by s. 9, Regulation VII, 1832, of the Bengal Code that whenever in any civil suit the parties to such suit may be of different persuasions, when one part shall be of the Hindu and the other of the Mahammadan persuasion, or where one or more of the parties to the suit shall not be either of the Mahammadan or Hindu persuasions, the laws of those religious shall not be permitted to operate to deprive such party or parties of any property to which, but for the operation of such laws, they would have been entitled; and it will be beneficial to extend the principle of that enactment throughout India.

(2) *Effect of the 1850 Act.* The effect of the Act is to set aside the provisions of Hindu law which provided for forfeiture of property on renunciation of religion or exclusion from caste. In *Lala Khunni Lal* v *Kunwar Gobind*[15] it was held that a convert's son who was Hindu did not acquire any enforceable right to his father's share in the joint family property. The Act applies only to the actual person who changes the religion. When a person changes his religion and his personal law, that law will govern the rights of succession to his estate. Thus, the descendants of a Hindu convert to Muhammedanism cannot claim any right of inheritance to his Hindu collaterals nor can the Hindu collaterals inherit to the convert or his descendants.[16] Conversion of a member of a Hindu joint family creates partition under the Hindu law and therefore the right to survivorship does not survive unless the converts proves that he renounced the partition which his conversion *ipso facto* effected.[17] Loss of right by conversion does not involve loss of the right of guardianship.[18] This Act does not affect the usage of a Hindu temple or other religious institutions.[19] The Act does not apply to any disability under the Hindu law not based on exclusion from religion or caste.[20] A restitution of conjugal right cannot be refused to the husband on the ground that he is an outcaste.[1]

---

14 Act (21 of 1850) (Received the assent of the Governor-General-in-Council on April 11, 1850).
15 (1910)38 IA 87 (PC).
16 *Mitar* v *Maqbal* AIR 1930 PC 251.
17 *Abraham* v *Abraham* (1863)9 MIA 195 (PC).
18 *Kaulesra* v *Jorai* (1906)28 All 233.
19 *Venkatachalapati* v *Subbarajadu* (1890)13 Mad 298.
20 *Moniram* v *Keri* (1880)7 IA 115 (PC).
 1 *Mohanlal* v *Shanto Devi* AIR 1964 All 21.

The Hindu Disposition of Property Act 1916[2]

(1) *Preliminary*. The Hindu Disposition of Property Act 1916 was passed to remove certain existing disabilities in respect of the power of disposition of property by Hindus for the benefit of persons not in existence at the date of such disposition.

(2) *Bequest to an unborn person*. The power of a Hindu to make a bequest to an unborn person as provided in s. 2 of the 1916 Act is not subject to s. 112 of the Indian Succession Act 1925 and as such is not void by it.[3]

The Hindu Inheritance (Removal of Disabilities) Act 1928[4]

(1) *Preliminary*. The objects of this Act of 1928 were to amend the Hindu law relating to exclusion from inheritance of certain classes of heirs, and to remove certain doubts.

Section 2 of the said Act provides that notwithstanding any rule of Hindu law or custom to the contrary, no person governed by the Hindu law, other than a person who is and has been from birth a lunatic or idiot, shall be excluded from inheritance or from any right or share in joint family property by reason only of any disease, deformity, or Physical or mental defect.

(2) *No retrospective effect*. This Act came into force on 20th September 1928 and was not retrospective in operation. Thus, a person who was already excluded from inheritance was not entitled to claim the benefit of the Act.[5] A person who becomes subsequently insane is not disqualified to inherit, and he can claim such right by suit through the next friend.

---

2 Act No. 15 of 1916. (Received the assent of the Governor-General-in-Council on 28th September, 1916).
3 *Aniruddha Mitra* v *Arabinda Mitra* AIR 1946 Cal 396.
4 Act 12 of 1928 (Received the assent of the Governor-General-in-Council on 20th September, 1928).
5 *Muttammal* v *Sri S. Devasthanam* AIR 1960 SC 601.

CHAPTER
6

Hindu Law of Marriage and Divorce

Ancient Hindu law of marriage

With the beginning of the Rigvedic age marriage was a well-established institution and the Aryan ideal of marriage was very high.[1] When the idea of marriage emerged centuries ago, it was, for the Hindus, invested with a purely religious meaning.[2] The law laid down by the sages and commentators regarding ancient Hindu marriage varried widely due to varied Hindu tribes, castes, families and sects who were governed by different customs which were regarded as legal and important supplement to the Hindu law of marriage.[3]

Forms of marriage

Eight forms of marriage amongst Hindus in ancient time have been mentioned by Gautama, Manu, Yajnavalkya and Narada and Six by Apastamba and Vasistha.[4] These are called the Brahma, Daiva, Arsha, Prajapatya or Kaya, Asura, Gandharba, Rakshasa and Paisacha.[5] Out of these eight forms four were approved forms and the Brahma is the only one that now prevails.[6]

Persons competent to marry

All persons are deemed to be qualified for marriage unless it is shown that the law has disqualified any of them for that purpose.[7] Minor, idiots

---

1   Mayne's *Treatise on Hindu Law and Usage*, 11th Ed., p. 101.
2   See *History of Dharmashastras*, vol. II, pt. 1, pp. 428-429 by Dr. P.V. Kane.
3   Banerjee on *Marriage and Stridhana*, 5th Ed., p. 266.
4   Govt. IV 6-15; Manu III, 27-34; Yajn. 1, 58-61, Nar XII, 38-44.
5   Sir Gooroodass Banerjee on *Hindu Law of Marriage and Stridhana*, 5th Ed., p. 86.
6   *Ibid*, p. 94.
7   Banerjee on the *Hindu Law of Marriage and Stridhana*, 5th Ed., p. 36.

and lunatics, eunuch, deaf and dumb, impotent, person suffering from incurable disease, person whose elder brother remaining unmarried are described to be incompetent to marry.[8]

Ceremonies of marriage

The Asvalayana Grihyasutra recognises that the custom of different countries and of villages should be observed at the weddings though it gives the common form of marriage rites.[9] The marriage becomes complete and irrevocable on completion of the Saptapadi or ceremony of seven steps.[10] In some communities there is a custom after the actual marriage ceremony, a further ceremony to be observed before cohabitation and the man declines to perform the second ceremony, the girl may lawfully marry again.[11]

Dissolution of marriage

The provisions of the ancient Hindu law on the subject of dissolution of marriage are somewhat unique, because marriage is regarded as a sacrament and indissoluble union.[12] Manu says: "Neither by sale nor desertion, can a wife be released from her husband."[13] But Parasara declares: "If the husband be missing or dead, or retired from the world, or impotent, or degraded, in these five calamities a woman may take another husband".[14] The ground upon which divorce was most commonly granted is the mutual consent of the husband and the wife who are governed by their customary law.[15] Other grounds of dissolution of marriage by the husband under the ancient Hindu law have been described by Sir Banerjee in his celebrated Tagore Law Lectures for 1878 are: (*a*) desertion (tyaga), (*b*) wife related within the prohibited degrees or belonging to the same *gotra*.[16]

---

8   Banerjee on the *Hindu Law of Marriage and Stridhana*, 5th Ed., pp. 37-47; see Mayne's *Treatise on Hindu Law and Usages*, (11th Ed.), pp. 142-143.
9   Asvalayana Grihyasutra, 1, 7, 3-22 (Rigved as).
10 *Chunilal v Surajram* (1909)33 Bom 433; *Appibai v Khimji* (1936)60 Bom 455; see Manu VIII, 227.
11 *Boolchand v Janokee* 25 WR 386.
12 Banerjee on *the Hindu Law of Marriage and Stridhana*, 5th Ed., p. 207.
13 Manu IX, 46.
14 Parasara, Ch. IV, quoted in *Vidyasagara's Marriage of Hindu Widows*, p. 7.
15 See *Sankaralingam v Subbon* ILR 17 Mad 479.
16 Banerjee on *the Hindu Law of Marriage and Stridhana*, 5th Ed., pp. 211-214.

CHAPTER
7

Legislations on Hindu Marriage and Divorce in Post-independence Era

Matrimonial laws during 1947-1955

The Bombay Hindu Divorce Act 1947[1] was passed to provide for divorce and judicial separation among Hindus within the State of Bombay. The Hindu Marriages Validity Act 1949[2] was made to provide for marriages between Hindus including Sikhs and Jains even if they belonged to different religions, sects or castes and to treat them as valid marriages. The Madras Hindu (Bigamy Prevention and Divorce) Act of 1949[3] was passed to prohibit bigamous marriages among Hindus living in the province of Madras and to provide for divorce amongst them on certain grounds. Besides there were other Acts were passed relating to matrimonial matters which are—(1) the Madras Aliyasantana,[4] (2) the Saurashtra Prevention of Hindu Bigamous Marriage Act 1950,[5] (3) the Saurashtra Hindu Divorce Act 1952[6] and (4) the Madhya Pradesh Prevention of Hindu Bigamous Marriage Act 1955.[7]

1   Act 22 of 1947 as amended by Acts 26 and 31 of 1949.
2   Act 21 of 1949.
3   Act 6 of 1946.
4   Act 22 of 1949.
5   Act 5 of 1950.
6   Act 30 of 1952.
7   Act 10 of 1955.

CHAPTER
8

The Hindu Marriage Act 1955
(ACT 25 OF 1955)[1]

Object of the Act

The primary object of the Act is to amend and codify the law relating to marriage among Hindus.[2] This Act is not regarded as a work of art. It was not happily drafted and as such many of its provisions present difficulties of interpretation. At times it is difficult together what the legislature had in mind.[3]

Operation of the Act

The Act incorporates in itself both substantive and procedural law. A procedural law is generally retrospective in absence of specific provision to the contrary.[4] Except ss. 9, 10, 12, 13, 14 and 29(1) of the 1955 Act other provisions deal with substantive right. Section 9 provides that a petition for restitution of conjugal rights shall lie in a District Court and thereby affecting the jurisdiction of a Sub-ordinate Judge. Thus, it has been held

---

1 This Act has been amended by the Hindu Marriage (Amendment) Act 1956, the Amending Act 44 of 1961, the Marriage Laws (Amendment) Act 1976 and the Child Marriage Restraint (Amendment) Act 1978. The Hindu Marriage Act 1955 has repealed the Hindu Marriage Disabilities Removal Act 1946, the Hindu Marriage Validity Act 1949, the Bombay Prevention of Hindu Bigamous Marriage Act 1946, the Bombay Hindu Divorce Act 1947, the Madras (Bigamy Prevention and Divorce) Act 1949, the Saurashtra Prevention of Hindu Bigamous Marriages Act 1950, and the Saurashtra Hindu Divorce Act 1953. (Section 30).
2 See Preamble to the 1955 Act and also Statement of Objects and Reasons of the Bill No. 7 of 1952, Gazette of India, Ext. dt. 11.12.1952, Pt. II, s. 2, p. 67.
3 *Hiralal* v *Lilawati* AIR 1961 Guj 202.
4 *K. Chunilal Sawar* v *K.N.S. Rao* AIR 1946 Mad 262.

that a suit for restitution of conjugal rights pending in a Sub-ordinate Judge's Court at the time of the commencement of the 1955 Act cannot be governed by this Act and is not also liable to be transferred to the District Court.[5] The Act came into effect on 18th May 1955.

Necessary changes made under the Act

(A) A Hindu marriage solemnised between two Hindus as defined in s. 2(1) of the Act is valid. Thus, inter-caste marriage is not prohibited. Section 29(2) of the Act has given retrospective effect as to the validity of such marriage.

(B) Monogamy has been made compulsory. (Section 5(*i*)).

(C) Bigamy is punishable under the Penal Code.

(D) Conditions and requirements of a valid Hindu marriage are to be satisfied. (Sections 5, 7).

(E) Reliefs for matrimonial causes are provided. (Sections 10 to 13).

(F) Legitimacy of children under void and voidable marriages is recognised. (Section 16).

(G) Provisions for alimony *pendente lite*, (expenses) of proceedings, permanent alimony have been made. (Sections 24, 25).

(H) Wide discretionary powers have been conferred on the court to pass order relating to custody, maintenance and education of minor children of the spouses. (Section 26).

Territorial jurisdiction of the Act

The provisions of the Hindu Marriage Act 1955 are applicable to the whole of India except the State of Jammu and Kashmir.[6] The State of Jammu and Kashmir has been excluded from the operation of the Act by virtue of Art. 370(1) of the Constitution of India and the Constitution (Application to Jammu and Kashmir) Order 1954.[7] Where one of the parties to a marriage is not a citizen of India, but both the parties are Hindus, the law of domicile of the non-citizen will be applied to determine whether such marriage is prohibited by the law of the domicile of that party.[8] This Act will apply to all Hindus residing in India irrespective

---

5 *Balwant Singh* v *Sardarni Balwant Kaur* AIR 1957 Pepsu 1; *Udainath* v *Chhayya* AIR 1963 Ori 27.
6 Section 1(2) of the 1955 Act.
7 See Gazette of India, Ext. dt. May 14, 1954, Pt. II, s. 3.
8 *Prem Singh* v *Dulari Rai* AIR 1973 Cal 425.

of their domicile. But it will not apply to a marriage where one of the parties thereto is not domiciled in India.[9]

Concept of domicile

The concept of domicile is not uniform all over the world. Residence of a person sometimes fails to answer the qualitative test. The test of residence must answer a qualitative as well as a quantitative test. Two elements necessary for determination of domicile of a person are *factum* and *animus*. Both the elements must concur.[10]

Conditions of valid Hindu marriage[11]

The essential requirements or conditions have been set out in cls. (*i*) to (*v*) of s. 5 of the Act. A marriage between any two Hindus who have satisfied the five conditions laid down in s. 5 is valid. Even where a marriage between two Hindus belonging to different castes would not change the castes of the parties. Thus, where a woman marries a schedule caste husband would be treated as a schedule caste.[12]

(*i*) *Neither party has a spouse living at the time of marriage.* Where a marriage is solemnised in contravention of s. 5(*i*) of the Act is void.[13] The parties to such marriage are punishable for bigamy.[14] Where a widow remarriage a person who has a wife living at the time of such marries, the second marriage is void *ab initio* and as such no declaration to that effect is necessary.[15] Even in such void marriage the second wife is not entitled to maintenance under s. 125, Cr PC 1973.[16] In a proceeding for a nullity of marriage under s. 11 read with s. 5(*i*) of the Hindu Marriage Act, the existence of the first wife at the time of solemnisation of the second marriage need not be proved by direct evidence. This fact may be inferred from other proved facts.[17] In view of provisions of s. 5(*i*) of the 1955 Act a suit by a wife for a perpetual injunction against the husband forbidding him to marry for a second time is maintainable.[18]

---

9 *Gour Gopal Roy* v *Sipra Roy* AIR 1978 Cal 163.
10 *Satya* v *Teja* AIR 1975 SC 105.
11 See s. 5 of the 1955 Act.
12 *Vaishali* v *Union of India* (1978)80 Bom LR 182.
13 Section 11, the 1955 Act.
14 Section 17, *ibid*.
15 *Smt. Oma* v *Smt. Reshma* 1981 Rev Dec 324 (All).
16 *Bajirao* v *Tolanbai* 1980 Cr LJ 473.
17 *Rajula Bai* v *Suka* AIR 1972 MP 57.
18 *Shankarappa* v *Basamma* AIR 1964 Mys 247.

(ii) Unsoundness of mind. Unsoundness of mind as a ground for incapacity to marry depends on the degree of mental incapacity.[19] If a person understands that he was being married and that the ceremonies of the marriage were being held, he could not be said to be an insane and the marriage on that ground was not invalid.[20] Even where a person had been adjudicated as lunatic, it does not necessarily mean that he suffers from complete mental aberration. He may understand the ceremonies of marriage and may take active part in them.[21] This expression does not include mere eccentricity or every infirmity of mind. The ability to understand the nature of marital union and the probable consequences of such union are to be applied as a test for determining the validity of marriage.[1] In *R. Lakshmi Narayan* v *Santhi*[2] it has been held that where the spouses had short cohabitation of about a month, it cannot be inferred that the wife is unfit for marriage and procreation of children on account of mental disorder.

(iii) Ages of parties to marriage. Clause *(iii)* of s. 5 has been amended by the Child Marriage Restraint (Amendment) Act 1978. This Amendment has substituted the words "twenty one years" and "eighteen years" for the words "eighteen years" and "fifteen years" respectively.

(iv) Prohibited degrees. Clause *(iv)* of s. 5 forbids a marriage between two Hindu if they are within the degrees of prohibited relationship unless the custom or usage permits such marriage. Section 5*(iv)* is to be read with s. 3*(g)* of the Act. Section 3*(g)* defines persons who are said to be within the "degrees of prohibited relationship."[3]

(v) Parties, not sapindas. Clause (v) of s. 5 is to be read with s. 3*(f)* of the Act which defines the expression "sapinda relationship."[4]

Ceremonies of Hindu marriage[5]

There is a requirement for solemnisation of a Hindu marriage in accordance with the customary rites and ceremonies of a party thereto.

19　*Monji Lal* v *Chandrabati* (1911)38 IA 122 (PC).
20　*Kaura Devi* v *Indra Devi* AIR 1943 All 310.
21　*Parmeshwar* v *Bhagawati* AIR 1950 FC 142.
1　*Anima* v *Mohan Bai* AIR 1969 Cal 304.
2　AIR 2001 SC 2110.
3　See s. 3*(g)*.
4　See s. 3*(f)*.
5　See s. 7.

The marriage becomes complete after completing the seventh step if the *saptapadi* is included in such rites and ceremonies.[6]

(*i*) *Customary rites and ceremonies.* Merely going through some ceremonies, such as lying of the *Thali*, would not be enough for solemnisation, of marriage.[7] It is not left to the will of any caste or community to alter the customary rites and ceremonies as because the essence of custom lies in its definiteness and recognition by the community with certainty and without any variation.[8] It has been held in *Bhaurao Shankar Lokhande* v *State of Maharashtra*[9] that the word "solemnised" means to celebrate a marriage with proper ceremonies and due form.

(*ii*) *Saptapadi.* According to the rites for marriage performed by the Arya Samaj the invocation before the sacred fire and *saptapadi* are both essential.[10] In absence of solemnisation of marriage in accordance with the customary rites and usage dispensing with the ceremony of *saptapadi* there is no valid marriage even if the parties live together as husband and wife.[11] Where a marriage is performed according to the customary rites and ceremonies of one party which do not include *saptapadi*, the marriage is valid even though *saptapadi* is included in the rites and ceremonies of the other party.[12] When a factum of marriage is not established a strong presumption would arise if the parties have lived together for a long time as husband and wife that there was a wedlock between them. This presumption is rebuttable but a heavy burden would lie on a person who challenges the relationship of legal origin law leans towards legitimacy and against bastardy.[13]

(*iii*) *Inter caste marriage.* In *Lata Singh* v *State of U.P.*[14] it has been held that a major Hindu boy or a major Hindu girl has a right to undergo inter caste marriage according to the Hindu Marriage Act 1955.

(*iv*) *Presumption of marriage.* In *Reema Aggarwal* v *Anupam*[15] it has been held that if a man and a woman live together as husband and wife,

---

6 *Phankari* v *State* AIR 1965 J&K 105.
7 *Vankata Subbarayudu Chetty* v *Tanguturu Venkatiah Shastree* AIR 1968 AP 107.
8 *Rabindra Nath Dutta* v *State* AIR 1969 Cal 55.
9 AIR 1965 SC 1564.
10 *Ram Awadh* v *Krishna Nand Lal* AIR 1981 All 432.
11 *Santi Deb Berma* v *Kanchan Prava Devi* AIR 1991 SC 816.
12 *Asrabai* v *Dhondiram* ILR (1977) Bom 870.
13 *Badri Prasad* v *Dy. Director of Consolidation* AIR 1976 SC 1557.
14 AIR 2006 SC 2522.
15 (2004)3 SCC 199.

the presumption is that they live together in consequence of a valid marriage not in a state of concubinage until contrary is clearly proved.

(A) ENGLISH LAW AS TO CONCEPT OF MARRIAGE. The best known description of marriage as a legal concept under the English law is that it is the fulfilment of a contract satisfied by the solemnisation of marriage. But marriage creates by law a relation between the parties and that is called a status of each.[16]

(B) ENGAGEMENT TO MARRY NOT ENFORCEABLE UNDER ENGLISH LAW. Under the law of England and Wales an agreement between two persons to marry one another does not have effect as a contract and as such no legal action lies in England and Wales for breach of such an agreement.[17]

(C) REQUISITE OF A VALID MARRIAGE UNDER THE ENGLISH LAW. The requisite of a valid marriage under the English law are—(1) that each of the parties should as regards age and mental and physical capacity be capable of contracting marriage; (2) that they should not by reason of kinderd or affinity be prohibited from marrying one another; (3) that except where a second or subsequent polygamous marriage has been entered into under a law that permits polygamy, there should not be a valid subsisting marriage of either of the parties with any other person; (4) that the parties, understanding the nature of the contract, should freely consent to marry one another; and (5) that certain forms and ceremonies should be observed. Absence of one of the said requisites will turn the marriage either void or voidable.[18]

(D) REQUIREMENTS OF A VALID MARRIAGE IN AUSTRALIA. In Australia a marriage is valid on fulfilment of the following requirements: (*i*) the parties are of marriageable (age); (*ii*) the parties are a man and a woman; (*iii*) the parties are not already married to another; (*iv*) the parties do not fall in the category of prohibited relationships.[19]

Restitution of conjugal rights[20]

If either party to a marriage withdraws from the society of the other without reasonable cause, the aggrieved party has a right to file a petition claiming relief for restitution of conjugal rights. The court will grant the relief if there is no legal bar to such decree.

---

16 Halsbury's *Laws of England*, 4th Ed., vol. 22, para 905.
17 Halsbury's *Laws of England*, 4th Ed., vol. 22, para 902.
18 Halsbury's *Laws of England*, 4th Ed., vol. 32, para 907.
19 See Halsbury's *Laws of Australia*, 205, Family Law, pp. 49-60.
20 See s. 9.

(*i*) *Difference between restitution of conjugal rights and judicial separation.* Section 9 of the 1955 Act deals with restitution of conjugal rights, whereas s. 10 of the said Act deals with judicial separation. Section 9 grants the right of cohabitation to the aggrieved spouse, but s. 10 restricts such right of cohabitation. In both the cases existence of marriage tie is not affected.

(*ii*) *Existence of marriage.* In a suit for restitution of conjugal rights if the existence of marriage is disputed, it is for the petitioner to prove that there was a valid marriage.[21] When a particular relationship is proved to exist, such as marriage, its continuance is *prima facie* presumed.[22]

(*iii*) *Withdrawal from the society of other spouse.* If there is no legal ground, a petition for restitution cannot be dismissed simply on the ground that the wife does not like to live with him or that he is not her proper life companion.[1] Where on a difference between the husband and wife, the latter leaves the matrimonial home with the consent of her husband, that does not amount to withdrawal from the society of the husband.[2] On proof of the existence of marriage by the petitioner, the onus lies on the respondent to prove that there was justification for withdrawal from the society of the petitioner.[3]

(*iv*) *Reasonable excuse.* No definition or guideline has been laid down relating to the expression "reasonable excuse" as used in s. 9 of the Act. Generally, grounds stated in ss. 10, 12 or 13 are considered to be reasonable grounds. But the court may consider any other ground beyond those grounds as sufficient or reasonable excuse for the respondent to remain separate from the other spouse.[4] The respondent has reasonable excuse to withdraw from the society of the petitioner if the petitioner lives with another woman in the same house[5] or if the petitioner becomes blind after the marriage,[6] or if the petitioner is guilty of cruelty though it was not cruelty.[7] Where the wife was willing to live with her husband, but

---

21 *Laxman Singh* v *Keshar Bai* AIR 1966 MP 166.
22 *Bhima* v *Dhulappa* (1905)7 Bom LR 95.
1   *Anna Saheb* v *Tarabai* AIR 1970 MP 36.
2   *Leela Sharma* v *Keshav Kumar* 1980 Hind LR 171 (Del).
3   *Om Pati* v *Kartar Singh* AIR 1971 Punj 35.
4   See *Krishnamurthy* v *Syamanthakamani* ILR (1977)1 Kant 246; see also *Jagdish Lal* v *Smt. Shyama* AIR 1966 All 150.
5   *Ghanshyam Lal* v *Kanti Devi* 1979 Hindu LR 603 (Del).
6   *Mohinder Singh* v *Preet Kaur* AIR 1981 J&K 25.
7   *Gaudev Kaur* v *Sarwan Singh* AIR 1959 Punj 162.

the husband offered her to live with his parents who used to ill-treat her, it was held that the husband's offer was not *bona fide* and as such the husband was not entitled to relief under s. 9 of the Act.[8]

In the following instances the decree for restitution of conjugal rights was not granted: (*a*) the husband impotent or guilty of cruelty;[9] (*b*) physical violence to the wife;[10] (*c*) husband outwardly potent, but impotent to the wife;[11] (*d*) inordinate delay in making petition;[12] (*e*) mental pain caused to the wife by the husband.[13]

In the following cases decree for restitution of conjugal rights was granted: (*a*) agreement between husband and wife to live separately is no defence;[14] (*b*) desertion for breaking home;[15] (*c*) grievances for normal incidents of married life;[16] (*d*) untrue allegations by the wife;[17] (*e*) no allegation in the written statement that the husband was a drunkard and gambler.[18]

(*v*) *Satisfaction of court*. Where the court is satisfied about the *bona fide* of the petitioner's case, the court would granted relief to the petitioner even on uncorroborated testimony of the petitioner.[19] Where a spouse has already obtained a decree for restitution, subsequently, the other spouse cannot file a petition for restitution against the former.[20]

(*vi*) *District Court*. The words "District Court" appearing in s. 9 of the Act are to be read in the light of the definition given in s. 3(*b*) of the Act.[1]

(*vii*) *Enforcement of decree for restitution*. All decrees and orders made under the Hindu Marriage Act 1955 are enforceable in like manner as the decrees and orders of the court passed in the exercise of the original civil jurisdiction.[2]

---

8   *Jogindra Kaur* v *Shivaharan* AIR 1965 J&K 95.
9   *Khageswar* v *Aduti* AIR 1967 Ori 80.
10 *Tulsa* v *Panna Lal* AIR 1963 MP 5.
11 *Jagdish Lal* v *Shyama Madon* AIR 1966 All 150.
12 *Teja Singh* v *Sarjit Kaur* AIR 1962 Punj 195.
13 *S. Jayakumari* v *S. Krishnan Nair* AIR 1995 Ker 139.
14 *A.E.T. Naidu* v *Rajammal* AIR 1968 Mad 201.
15 *S.S. Baburao* v *B.D. Mandilik* AIR 1963 MP 10.
16 *Rukmen Kanta* v *Faquir Chand* AIR 1960 Punj 493.
17 *Himansu Sekhar Rana* v *Tapati Rana* AIR 1995 Cal 110.
18 *Pushpa Rani* v *Vijay Pal Singh* AIR 1994 All 216.
19 *Kishore Sahu* v *Snehapra Sahu* AIR 1943 Nag 185 (SB). See also *Ratnaprabhabai* v *Sheshrao* AIR 1972 Bom 182.
20 *Pillalamari Vara Prasada* v *P. Seshalakshmi* AIR 1975 AP 239.
1   See s. 3(*b*).
2   Section 28 of the 1955 Act, Or. 21, rr. 22, 32, 33.

The mode of execution of decree for restitution of conjugal right is laid down in Or. 21, rr. 32 and 33 of the Code of Civil Procedure.

(*viii*) *Counter claim by respondent*. In a proceeding for restitutional of conjugal rights, the respondent can make a counter-claim for any relief under the Act on the ground that the petitioner is guilty of adultery, cruelty or desertion.[3] Where a counter-claim for maintenance is pending in connection with a petition under s. 9 of the Hindu Marriage Act, the petitioner would not be entitled to withdraw the main petition till the disposal of the application for maintenance.[4]

Judicial separation[5]

The grounds for judicial separation are the same as those specified in s. 13 of the Hindu Marriage Act for divorce. The main grounds are— (*i*) adultery, (*ii*) cruelty, (*iii*) desertion, (*iv*) conversion to another religion, (*v*) unsoundness of mind, (*vi*) leprosy, (*vii*) venereal disease, (*viii*) renouncing the world; and (*ix*) not heard of for more than seven years.[6] A wife has four additional grounds for a decree of judicial separation. These are—(*a*) A co-wife living after the commencement of the 1955 Act, (*b*) husband guilty of rape, sodomy or bestiality, (*c*) decree obtained under s. 18 of the Hindu Adoptions and Maintenance Act or an order passed under s. 125, Cr PC in favour of the wife, and (*d*) marriage with a girl before attainment of fifteen years.[7]

Resumption of cohabitation

Section 10(2) of the Act confers extra-ordinary power on the court. On passing of a decree for a judicial separation, it is no longer obligatory on the parties to cohabit with each other. But if both the spouses jointly approach the court for rescission of the decree, it will be granted. Even where either of the parties made a petition for rescission of the decree and the other spouse does not oppose, the court may pass an order of rescission. In *Hirachand Srinivas Mahagaonkar* v *Sunanda*[8] it has been held by the Supreme Court that where a decree for judicial separation is passed, it is no longer obligatory for the petitioner to cohabit with the respondent, but the court may, on application by petition of either party rescind

---

3   Section 23A of the 1955 Act.
4   *C. Sonnaiah* v *Padma* AIR 1983 Kant 114.
5   See s. 10.
6   Section 13(1) of the 1955 Act. (See discussion under s. 13 of the Act).
7   Section 13(2), *ibid* (See discussion under s. 13 of the Act).
8   AIR 2001 SC 1285.

the decree if it considers it just and reasonable. But where an application under s. 10(2) is made, which is resisted by the other spouse, a heavy burden lies on the applicant to satisfy the court.[9] Under the Divorce Act, it has been held that resumption of cohabitation automatically annuls a decree for judicial separation.[10]

Grounds for judicial separation under English law

A petition for judicial separation is based on s. 17 of the Matrimonial Causes Act 1973 which enacts that a petition may be presented on the ground of any such fact which must be proved before a decree of divorce on the ground of irretrievable breakdown of marriage could be granted.

Nullity of marriage

A marriage under the Hindu Marriage Act 1955, can be nullified either for void marriage[11] or for voidable marriage.[12]

Void marriages[13]

A marriage becomes void for contravention of any of conditions set out in s. 5 of the Act. These are that (*i*) either party has a spouse living at the time of the marriage;[14] (*ii*) a party is incapable of giving valid consent;[15] (*iii*) the bridegroom has not completed the age of 21 years and the bride the age of 18 years;[16] (*iv*) the parties to the marriage fall within the degrees of prohibited relationship;[17] (*v*) the parties are sapindas of each other.[18]

In *Gullipilli Sowria Raj* v *Bandaru Pavani*[19] it has been held by the Supreme Court that a marriage between a Hindu and other professing other religion is null and void. It will be clear from the Preamble, ss. 2, 5, 7 and 12 of the Hindu Marriage Act 1955.

(*i*) *Effect of void marriage.* If a marriage is void for contravention of cl. (*iii*) of s. 5 it is void *ab initio* even in absence of any reference to that effect either in s. 11 or s. 12 of the Act.[20] A proceeding under s. 11 cannot be

---

9 *Godabai* v *Narayan* AIR 1973 MP 4.
10 *Julius* v *Julius* AIR 1932 Oudh 142.
11 Section 11 of the H.M. Act.
12 Section 12, *ibid.*
13 See s. 11.
14 Section 5(*i*), *ibid.*
15 Section 5(*ii*), *ibid.*
16 Section 5(*iii*), *ibid.*
17 Section 5(*iv*) read with s. 3(*g*), *ibid.*
18 Section 5(*v*) read with s. 3(*f*), *ibid.*
19 AIR 2009 SC 1085.
20 *P.A. Suramma* v *G. Ganapatla* AIR 1975 AP 193. But see *P. Venkataramana* v *State* AIR 1977 AP 43 (FB).

initiated by a party to the marriage and not by any third party. The remedy of an aggrieved third party would be under the ordinary law of the land by filing a regular suit.[21] It has been held that where a second marriage was held void the wife of such marriage is not entitled to claim maintenance.[22]

In *M.M. Malhotra* v *Union of India*[23] it has been held that where a marriage covered under s. 11 of the Act is void *ipso jure* it is void from the very inception. Any marriage subsequent to the void marriage would not be a case of plural marriage.

(ii) Distinction between void and voidable marriage. In case of a decree of a void marriage the status of children is not legitimate,[24] but in case of a voidable marriage until it is annulled by a decree the children begotten of such marriage are legitimate. A void marriage is void *ab initio* whereas a voidable marriage is valid till it is annulled by a competent court. A voidable marriage can be annulled only during the life-time of the parties to such marriage,[25] but a marriage can be declared void under s. 11 even after the death of the other spouse.[1]

(iii) Grounds of void marriage in England and Australia

(A) VOID MARRIAGE UNDER ENGLISH LAW. A marriage celebrated after 31st July 1971 is void on the following grounds: *(i)* the parties are within the prohibited degrees of relationship, or *(ii)* either party is under the age of sixteen, or *(iii)* the parties have intermarried in disregard of certain requirements as to formation of marriage, or *(iv)* that at the time of the marriage either party was already lawfully married, or *(v)* that the parties are not respectively male and female, or *(vi)* that in the case of a polygamous marriage entered into outside England and Wales either party was at the time of the marriage domiciled in England and Wales.

(See s. 11 of the Matrimonial Causes Act 1973 which replaced s. 1 of the Nullity of Marriage Act 1971).

(B) GROUNDS OF NULLITY OF MARRIAGE IN AUSTRALIA. In Australia a marriage celebrated under the (CTH) Marriage Act 1961 is either valid or void.

---

21 *Lakshmi Ammal* v *R. Naicker* AIR 1960 Mad 6; see also *Harmohan* v *Kamala Kumari* AIR 1979 Ori 51.
22 *Bajirao R. Tambare* v *Tolanbai* 1980 Cr LJ 478 (Bom).
23 AIR 2006 SC 80.
24 Unless saved by s. 16 of the H.M. Act.
25 Subject to s. 12(2) of the Act.
1 *Lakshmamma* v *Thayamma* AIR 1974 AP 255.

The former category of voidable marriage has been abolished. Thus, an application for a decree of nullity under the (CTH) Family Law Act 1975 is to be based on the ground that the marriage is void. The (CTH) Marriage Act 1961 provides that a marriage is void in five circumstances "and not otherwise".

These are—(i) The prior existing marriage of a spouse; (ii) prohibited relationship; (iii) Non-compliance with formalities; (iv) lack of real consent of a spouse; and (v) lack of marriageable age.[2]

Voidable marriages[3]

A marriage becomes voidable on any of the following grounds:

(i) The respondent was impotent at the time of the marriage and continued to be so until the institution of the suit.

(ii) The marriage is in contravention of the condition specified in s. 5(ii) of the Act which relates to unsoundness of mind of a party.

(iii) The consent of the petitioner or the guardian, as the case may be, was obtained by force or fraud.

(iv) The respondent was at the time of marriage pregnant by a person other than the petitioner.

(i) *Impotency of a party.* Impotency of a party can be discovered by the other spouse only at the time of sexual intercourse. Continuity of such impotency is to be established for the whole period commencing from the date of marriage till the date of initiation of the proceedings.[4] Where a wife has not reached the age of maturity at her first consummation, it is not possible for her to appreciate whether the husband was really impotent. In absence of any further opportunity to cohabit, it was not possible to hold that the husband continued to be impotent. However, the doctor, on examination, found the husband was potent. Thus, the petition was dismissed.[5] Impotency may arise from any of the following reasons:[6] (i) it may be due to some physical or organic defect; (ii) it may also occur on account of the existence of some loathsome or incurable disease like syphilis; (iii) it may also be due to invincible repugnance or hatred from sexual intercourse. Impotency need not be confined to only physical inability of one spouse to have sexual intercourse with other, but it may

---

2 Halsbury's *Laws of Australia*, 205 Family Law, pp. 97, 99.
3 See s. 12 as amended by the Marriage Laws (Amendment) Act 1976.
4 *Ravanna* v *Suseelamma* AIR 1967 Mys 165.
5 *Bawi* v *Nath* AIR 1970 J&K 130.
6 *Rangaswami* v *Aravindammal* AIR 1957 Mad 243.

cover such condition either of mind or of the body to render a normal or complete sexual intercourse impracticable.[7] It may happen that a person is capable of otherwise performing the sexual act, but he cannot do so with his own spouse.[8] It may also happen that one spouse was comparatively over-sexed and the other spouse could not keep with the pace with the other's desire that would not necessarily mean that the other spouse was impotent.[9] Potency so far as a whole is concerned means the power of erection of male organ and its full penetration. The discharge of seamen into the wife's body is not necessary for complete coitus.[10]

ENGLISH LAW ON IMPOTENCY. The true test of incapacity or impotency the practical impossibility of consummation of marriage.[11] The basis of the court's inference is not the structural defect, but the impracticability of consummation,[12] disability arising from mental or moral causes is sufficient, such as hysteria.[13]

(*ii*) *Unsoundness of mind*. If the respondent is lunatic at the time of the trial or at the time of presentation of the petition, it is not a ground for declaration of nullity.[14] Lunacy of a person must be taken in its ordinary sense. Insanity of a person may be intermittent or permanent. There is no hard and first rule to deduce a conclusion of insanity.[15]

(*iii*) *Consent*. Fraud vitiates the free consent of a party to marriage. But in a case[16] it has been held that the Indian Contract Act does not apply to a marriage as because s. 12(1)(*c*) (prior to the amendment) did not speak of any fraud in any general way. Where the wife was pregnant by other than her husband at the time of marriage a decree for divorce was granted in favour of the husband on the ground of fraud for suppressing the fact.[17] There is no obligation on a spouse to disclose his or her pre-marital affairs to the other. Silence in this regard does not amount to fraud.[18]

---

7 *Muthuraj Koilpillai* v *Esther Victoria Kannammal* AIR 1970 Mad 237 (FB).
8 *Jagadish Kumar* v *Sita Devi* AIR 1963 Punj 114.
9 *Rajindar Kappor* v *Manmohan Singh* AIR 1972 Punj 142.
10 *Chanchal Kumari* v *Kewal Krishan* AIR 1972 Punj 474.
11 *S.* v *S.* [1962]1 All ER 33.
12 *G.* v *G.* [1871] LR 2 P&D 287.
13 *P.* v *L.* (1878)3 PD 73.
14 *Soloman* v *Josephine* AIR 1959 Mad 151 (FB).
15 *Kartik* v *Manjurani* AIR 1973 Cal 545.
16 *Raghunath* v *Vijaya* AIR 1972 Bom 132. See also *Harbhajan Singh* v *Brij Balab Kaur* AIR 1964 Punj 359.
17 *Madhukar* v *Kusum* (1982)2 Bom LR 202.
18 *Surjit Kumar* v *Raj Kumari* AIR 1967 Punj 172.

(iv) Pregnancy at the time of marriage. The mere fact of pregnancy or even admission by the respondent in her pleadings that she was pregnant at the time of marriage is not sufficient to invoke on provisions of s. 12. It must be proved beyond all reasonable doubt that the respondent was pregnant by some one other than the petitioner at the time of marriage.[19]

The onus of proof in such a case lies on the husband to satisfy the court that all the conditions of this clause have been fulfilled.[20] In *Baldev* v *Urmila*[1] the testimony of a doctor who was an obstetrician was accepted to prove that the wife was pregnant by another person at the time of her marriage. What the court is to ensure is that the petitioner has proved beyond reasonable doubt that the respondent was pregnant by some other person and in such facts and circumstances the court can held that a prudent man would be satisfied of the allegation.[2] The proving of negative cohabitation by the husband would be too high in such a case. Thus the burden should be provisional and not a compelling one.[3]

(v) Sub-section (2) of section 12. Sub-section (2) of s. 12 provides for period of limitation to entertain an application under sub-sec. (1) of s. 12. The period of limitation for obtaining consent by force or fraud is one year from the date of cause of action.[4] Where the petitioner lives with the respondent with his or her full consent after the force had ceased to operate and after discovery of fraud, the petitioner will be deprived of his or her right. In case of pregnancy of a wife before marriage the period of limitation is one year from the date of marriage. But if any marital intercourse with the consent of the petitioner takes place after discovery of such fact the right to sue will be extinguished.[5] The delay in filing an application after expiry of the period of one year cannot be condoned by the court under s. 5 of the Limitation Act.[6] If the evidence shows that the husband and the wife lived together after the fraud was discovered, then whatever may be the period prescribed, the petition for annulment would not be maintainable.[7] Where a petition on ground mentioned in s. 12(1)(d) was filed out of time as prescribed by s. 12(2)(b)(ii), no recourse

---

19 *Sushila M. Nanavati* v *Mahindra M. Nanavati* AIR 1960 Bom 117.
20 *Shivaguru* v *Saroja* AIR 1960 Mad 216.
1 AIR 1978 SC 879.
2 *Mahendra* v *Sushila* AIR 1965 SC 344.
3 *Nishit Kumar Biswas* v *Anjali Biswas* AIR 1968 Cal 105.
4 Section 12(2)(a), H.M. Act.
5 Section 12(2)(b), *ibid.*
6 *Vellinayagi* v *T. Subramanium* AIR 1969 Mad 749.
7 *Daftardar* v *Daftardar* AIR 1972 Bom 132.

can be had under s. 23(1)(d) of the Act by reason of the fact that the bar of limitation is absolute.[8]

Divorce[9]

Grounds for presentation of a petition for divorce are—(i) adultery; (ii) cruelty; (iii) desertion; (iv) conversion to another religion; (v) insanity; (vi) incurable form of leprosy; (vii) venereal disease; (viii) renunciation; (ix) disappearance; (x) non-resumption of cohabitation after the decree of judicial separation; (xi) refusal to comply with a decree for restitutional of conjugal rights.[10] All these rights are available to both the husband and wife. But a wife has four more additional grounds for divorce. These are—(a) right of a co-wife after the commencement of the Act; (b) rape, sodomy or bestiality; (c) award of maintenance; (d) marriage with a girl below 15 years of age.[11]

(i) *Adultery.* Adultery is difficult to prove by direct evidence. It is, as a general rule proved by presumptive inferences based on (a) circumstantial evidence, (b) evidence as to non-access of the other spouse who has given birth to a child; (c) contracting of venereal disease; (d) evidence of visits to houses of ill-repute; (e) decrees made in previous proceedings or admission.[12] Testimony of eye-witness would normally require to be corroborated by circumstantial evidence.[13]

In the following cases, the court upheld the plea of adultery:

(a) Wife seen in the company of stronger after absenting herself from her house for some times.[14]

(b) Wife found alone with an unrelated person after midnight in her bed-room.[15]

(c) Letters of paramour indicating illicit relationship.[16]

(d) Admission of adultery by wife.[17]

(e) A solitary instance of voluntary sexual intercourse with other person is sufficient.[18]

---

8 *Pranab Biswas* v *Mriumayee Dassi* AIR 1976 Cal 156.
9 See section 13 of the H.M. Act as amended by the Amendment Act 44 of 1964 and the Marriage Laws (Amendment) Act 1976.
10 Section 13(1), (1A), *ibid*.
11 Section 13(2), *ibid*.
12 *Deivanai Achi* v *Kasi Vishwanathan* AIR 1957 Mad 766.
13 *Ibid*.
14 *Thimmappa* v *Thimmappa* AIR 1972 Mys 234.
15 *Subbarama* v *Saraswathi* AIR 1967 Mad 85.
16 *B. Das* v *K. Devi* AIR 1980 Ori 171.
17 *Saroj Kumar Sen* v *Dr. Kalyan Kanta Ray* AIR 1980 Cal 374.
18 *Rajendra* v *Sharda Devi* AIR 1993 MP 142.

In the following cases the plea of adultery was rejected by the court:

(a) Wife found going on the scooter of some other person.[19]

(b) Mere writing letters by some male relation to wife.[20]

(c) Wife becoming pregnant after husband's vasectomy operation without proving that the operation was successful.[21]

(d) Masturbation of co-respondent by wife.[22]

BLOOD TEST FOR DETERMINATION OF PATERNITY. In *Sharda* v *Dharampal*,[1] the Supreme Court has held that the proposition of law laid down in *Gautam Kundu* v *State of West Bengal*[2] is not an authority that under no circumstances can the court direct that blood tests be conducted. If the court is satisfied that there is a strong *prima facie* case or matrimonial court has power to order a *per se* to undergo medical test.

(*ii*) *Cruelty*. There may arise cases where cruelty may result from an indirect or overt act.[3] The word "cruelty" has not been defined in the Act. The court while dealing with cruelty must determine whether the respondent has treated him or her with such cruelty that it will be harmful or injurious for him or her to live with the respondent. Thus, the threat by the wife to her husband that she would put an end to her life or that she would make him lose his job or that she would set the house on fire and persistent abuses and insults hurled at the husband and his parents are all of such a grave order as to imperil the husband's sense of personal safety, mental happiness and reputation.[4] The word "cruelty" is not restricted to physical cruelty.[5] Where the conduct of the respondent is such as to cause harm or injury to the petitioner, that would also amount to injury which may be conveniently described as "mental" cruelty.[6] An allegation of a adultery against a spouse before filing of the petition may

---

19 *Swayamprabha* v *Chandrasekhar* AIR 1982 Kant 285.
20 *Chandra Mohini* v *Avinash Prasad* AIR 1967 SC 581.
21 *Chandramathi* v *Pazhetti Balan* AIR 1982 Ker 68.
22 *Sapsford* v *Sapsford* [1954]2 All ER 373.
1 AIR 2003 SC 3450.
2 AIR 1993 SC 2295.
3 *Pranab Biswas* v *Mriumayee Dassi* AIR 1976 Cal 156.
4 *Dastane* v *Dastane* AIR 1975 SC 1534. See *Manisha Tyagi* v *Deepak Kumar* AIR 2010 SC 1042 (Physical violence need not be established. Continued ill-treatment, cessation of marital intercourse, indifference of one spouse to the other may lead to inference of cruelty).
5 *Sossannamma* v *V. Abraham* AIR 1957 Trav Co 277.
6 See *Mackenzie* v *Mackenzie* [1895] AC 405.

amount to cruelty, but an allegation in the defence statement in the same proceedings may not amount to cruelty.[7] Mere writing several letters to wife by husband doubting the paternity of her child would not amount to cruelty.[8] Mere drinking habit,[9] mere allegation of impotency against wife[10] and non-payment of interim maintenance[11] are not cruelties.

In *Naveen Kohli* v *Neelu Kohli*[12] the Supreme Court has held that cruelty is a course or conduct of one which adversely affects the other. The cruelty may be mental or physical, intentional or unintentional. The cruelty alleged largely depends upon the type of life the parties are accustomed to or their economic and social conditions and their culture and human values to which they attach importance. In *Samar Ghosh* v *Jaya Ghosh*[13] it has been held that wife's refusal to cohabit with husband and refusal of intercourse and unilateral decision not to have any children amount to mental cruelty. In *Mayadevi* v *Jagdish Prasad*[14] the Supreme Court has highlighted the instances of mental and physical cruelty to which the husband was subjected.

(iii) Desertion. No attempt was previously made to define desertion.[15] But the Explanation added to sub-sec. (1) of s. 13 by the Marriage Laws (Amendment) Act 1976 has defined the expression "desertion" as withdrawal by a party to the marriage without reasonable cause and without consent or against the wish of such party. This expression includes also wilful neglect of the petitioner by the other party to the marriage. A desertion commences when there is a *de facto* separation without *animus* to return. It is only when both the *de facto* separation and *animus deserendi* coincide in point of time, the desertion commences.[16] In deciding the question of desertion, the court should look at the conduct of both the parties.[17] Where one spouse expels the other spouse from the matrimonial home or by his or her words or conduct makes it impossible for the other to live with him or her, as a result the other leaves, it is the former who is in desertion and not the latter, although it is the latter who actually

---

7 *Sulochana* v *Ram Kumar* AIR 1981 All 78.
8 *Paras Ram* v *Kamlesh* AIR 1982 Punj 60.
9 *Sobha Dei* v *Bhima* AIR 1975 Ori 180.
10 *Ramoki* v *Kameswari* AIR 1975 AP 3.
11 *Gindan* v *Parelal* AIR 1976 MP 83.
12 AIR 2006 SC 1675.
13 (2007)4 SCC 511.
14 (2007)3 SCC 136.
15 *Bipinchandra* v *Prabhavati* AIR 1957 SC 176.
16 Ibid.
17 *Leela Devi* v *Manoharlal* AIR 1959 MP 349.

leaves the house or terminates cohabitation.[18] This type of desertion is known as constructive desertion. In *Savitri Pandey* v *Prem Chandra Pandey*[19] it has been held that desertion under s. 13(1)(*ib*) of the 1955 Act means the intentional permanent for saking and abandonment of one's spouse by the other without that other's consent and without reasonable cause. In *Jagdish Singh* v *Madhuri Devi*[20] the Supreme Court supported the evidence considered by the Family Court why the case of the husband was believed that there was desertion on the part of the wife and that her conduct and behaviour toward the husband, his family members and daughter was cruel.

(*iv*) *Conversion to another religion*. Conversion to another religion from Hinduism as a result of which a spouse has ceased to be a Hindu is a ground for divorce.[21] The word "Hindu" is defined in the Hindu Marriage Act 1955.[22] Thus, a spouse married under the provisions of the Act may present a petition for dissolution of the marriage if the other spouse ceases to be a Hindu as defined in s. 2 of the Act by reason of his or her conversion to other religion. In *Lily Thomas* v *Union of India*[23] it has been held by the Supreme Court that conversion to other religion does not automatically bring about dissolution of marriage.

(*v*) *Unsoundness of mind*. To attract the provisions of s. 13(1)(*iii*) of the Act it must be proved that the respondent is of unsound mind or intermittently suffering from schizophrenia or mental disorder. At the same time that disease must be of such a kind and of such an extent that the petitioner cannot reasonably be expected to live with him or her. Thus only one element of that sub-section is not sufficient to obtain a decree for divorce.[24]

(*vi*) *Leprosy*. Any kind of leprosy, even if incurable, cannot be pleaded as a ground for divorce. It must be virulent, that is malignant or venomous. If it is of mild type and is capable of being arrested by treatment, though not completely curable, is not a ground for divorce.[25]

(*vii*) *Venereal disease*. Venereal disease has been made a ground for divorce provided it is in a communicable form.[26]

---

18 *Lang* v *Lang* [1954]3 All ER 571; [1955] AC 402. See *Ashok Kumar* v *Shabnam* AIR 1989 Del 21.
19 AIR 2002 SC 591.
20 (2008)10 SCC 497.
21 Section 13(1)(*ii*), H.M. Act 1955.
22 Section 2(1) and (3), *ibid*.
23 AIR 2000 SC 1650. See also *Sarla Mudgal* v *Union of India* AIR 1995 SC 1531.
24 *Rita Roy* v *Satischandra* AIR 1982 Cal 138.
25 *Swarajya Lakshmi* v *Dr. G.G. Padma Rao* AIR 1974 SC 165.
26 Section 13(1)(*v*), H.M. Act.

(*viii*) *Renunciation.* A spouse who has renounced the world by entering any religious order can be divorced on presentation of a petition by the other spouse.[1] This clause is based on the principle that a person who renounces and embraces a religious order must be treated as civilly dead. Renunciation amounting to civil death must be complete and final withdrawal from wordly affairs.[2] The mere holding of certain religious opinion by a man does not amount to civil death.[3]

(*ix*) *Disappearance.* Either the husband or the wife may present a petition for divorce where the respondent has not been heard of as being alive for a period of seven years or more by persons who would naturally have heard of it, had the respondent been alive.[4] This is based on the rule of evidence as to presumptive of life and death and also as to the burden of proof.[5]

(*x*) *Non-resumption of co-habitation after the decree of judicial separation.* Either party to marriage may make a petition for divorce for non-resumption of co-habitation for a period of one year or more after the passing of a decree for judicial separation against that party.[6] Where the wife had obtained a decree for judicial separation and had shown no intention to resume co-habitation for a period of two years following the decree, the fact that the husband was anxious to resume co-habitation with the wife but was prevented from doing so by his incarceration in jail would be of no consequence. Thus, the wife would be entitled to a decree for divorce.[7]

(*xi*) *Refusal to comply with decree of restitution of conjugal right.* Where there is a failure to comply with a decree for restitution of conjugal rights for a period of one year or more after the passing of such a decree, either party to the marriage may present a petition, for divorce.[8] A consent decree for restitution of conjugal rights was not complied with by a party against whom such decree was passed. Thus, the other party is entitled to a decree for divorce under this clause.[9] But where after obtaining the decree for restitution of conjugal rights, the husband makes no attempt to

---

1 Section (1) (*vi*), *ibid.*
2 *Krishnaji* v *Hanmaraddi* AIR 1934 Bom 385.
3 *Raghbir Lala* v *Mahammad Said* AIR 1943 PC 7.
4 Section 13(1)(*vii*), H.M. Act.
5 Sections 107 and 108 of Evidence Act 1872.
6 Section 13(1A)(*i*) read with s. 10 of the H.M. Act for judicial separation.
7 *Tej Kour* v *Hakim Singh* AIR 1965 J&K 111.
8 Section 13(1A)(*ii*), H.M. Act.
9 *Joginder Singh* v *Pushpa* AIR 1969 Punj 397 (FB).

call back the wife or remains silent, the husband is entitled to a decree for divorce.[10] Where the decree for conjugal rights has been complied with for a month only and the wife had to leave the matrimonial home on the ground of cruelty, the husband is not entitled to a decree for divorce under this clause.[11]

In *T. Srinivasan* v *T. Varalakshmi*[12] it has been held that where the husband after obtaining the decree for restitution of conjugal rights prevented the wife from performing her conjugal duties by driving her away from the house, he is not entitled to any relief under s. 13(1A) of the Act as because his act constituted misconduct under s. 23(1)(*a*) of the Act. In *Hirachand Srinivas Manganskar* v *Sunanda*[13] it has been held that the purpose of sub-sec. (1A) of s. 13 of the Hindu Marriage Act 1955 is to expand the right to apply for divorce and not to make the grant of divorce mandatory. Under this sub-section the petitioner does not have any vested right to the relief of divorce.

(*a*) ADDITIONAL GROUNDS FOR DIVORCE BY WIFE ONLY. A wife may present a petition for divorce where the husband had more than one wife before the commencement of the Hindu Marriage Act and the other wife is alive at the time of presentation of the petition.[14] This provision allows any of the wives of the respondent to present petition for divorce.[15] Where the first wife presents a petition under this sub-section for divorce, she is entitled to the decree even if he has already obtained a decree for divorce from the second wife subsequent to the filing of the petition by the first wife. The material date is the date of the presentation of the petition and not the date of passing of the decree.[16] Second marriage after the commencement of the Act is void and it is no marriage at all.[17] A compromise between the husband and the first wife made before the commencement of this Act, that she would live with her father would not take away her right under s. 13(2)(*i*) of the Act and such compromise cannot operate as an estoppel.[18] The fact that the first wife is alive at the time of the second marriage can be inferred from proved facts.[19]

10 *Kanak Lata* v *Amal Kumar* AIR 1970 Cal 328.
11 *Jasmet Singh* v *Gurnam Kaur* AIR 1975 Punj 225.
12 (1998)3 SCC 112.
13 (2001)4 SCC 125.
14 Section 13(2)(*i*), H.M. Act.
15 *Leela* v *Dr. Rao Anand Singh* AIR 1963 Raj 178.
16 *Naganna* v *Lachmi Bai* AIR 1963 AP 82.
17 *Chanda* v *Nandu* AIR 1965 MP 268.
18 *Nirmoo* v *Nikka Ram* AIR 1968 Del 260.
19 *Rajula Bai* v *Suka Dukali* AIR 1972 MP 57.

(b) RAPE, SODOMY AND BESTIALITY. Where the husband is guilty of rape, sodomy or bestiality, the wife has a right to present a petition for divorce.[20] Any attempt to commit such an offence before the solemnisation of the marriage is not covered by this provision of the Act.[21]

(I) RAPE. A man is said to commit 'rape' when except in certain cases he has sexual intercourse with a woman under any of the following situations: *(a)* against her will; *(b)* without her consent; *(c)* with her consent but it was obtained by putting her or any person in whom she is interested in fear of death or of hurt; *(d)* with her consent where the man knew that he was not her husband; *(e)* with or without her consent where she was under sixteen years of age.[1] A sexual intercourse by a man with his own wife, the wife not being fifteen years of age, is not rape. But where a wife obtains a decree of judicial separation or an order for separate maintenance, her consent to marital intercourse is thereby revived and as such any act of sexual intercourse thereafter by the husband with the wife by force amounts to rape.[2]

(II) SODOMY. It generally means unnatural sexual offence against man, woman or animal. A person who voluntarily has carnal intercourse against the order of nature with any man, woman or animal is punishable.[3]

(III) BESTIALITY. It ordinarily means an act relating to a beast. Dictionary meaning of the word is a sexual relation between a human being and lower animal.[4]

(c) AWARD OF MAINTENANCE. Where in a suit under s. 18 of the Hindu Adoptions and Maintenance Act 1956 or in a proceeding under s. 125 of the Code of Criminal Procedure, a decree or an order passed against the husband awarding maintenance to the wife and since then the parties have not cohabited for a period of one year or more, the wife is entitled to present a petition for divorce.[5]

(d) MARRIAGE WITH A GIRL BELOW FIFTEEN YEARS OF AGE. Where a marriage is solemnised with a girl before she attained the age of fifteen years and she has repudiated the marriage after attaining that age but before attaining the age of eighteen years, the wife will have the right to present a petition

---

20 Section 13(2)(*ii*), H.M. Act.
21 *Revanna* v *Suseelamma* AIR 1967 Mys 165.
 1 Section 375 of the Indian Penal Code.
 2 *R.* v *Clarke* [1949]1 All ER 440.
 3 Section 377 of the Indian Penal Code.
 4 See Webster's *Seventh New Collegiate Dictionary.*
 5 Section 13(2)(*iii*), H.M. Act.

for divorce.[6] A petition under the provision of this section may be filed after repudiation and also on completion of the age of 18 years.[7]

(e) GRANT OF DIVORCE ON IRRETRIEVABLE BREAKDOWN OF MARRIAGE. In *Vishnu Dutt Sharma* v *Manju Sharma*[8] a Bench of two judges of the Supreme Court has held that if divorce is granted on the ground of irretrievable breakdown of the marriage by the Supreme Court, that would amount to adding a clause to s. 13 of the Hindu Marriage Act to the effect that irretrievable breakdown of the marriage is also a ground for divorce. Thus, this can be done only by the legislature and not by a court. It is for Parliament to enact or amend the law and not for the court.

In this regard earlier decisions of the Supreme Court are quite contrary to proposition of law laid down in *Vishnu Dutt Sharma's* case. In *Naveen Kohli* v *Neelu Kohli*[9] a three-Judge Bench of the Supreme Court has held that if it is found that the breakdown is irreparable, then divorce should not be withheld. Two other three-Judge Benches in *A. Jayachandra* v *Aneel Kaur*[10] and in *Samar Ghosh* v *Jaya Ghosh*[11] granted divorce on the ground of irretrievable breakdown of marriage. In *Vineet Narain* v *Union of India*[12] the Supreme Court has held that the Supreme Court has ample power under Art. 32 read with Art. 142 of the Constitution to make orders which will have the effect of law by virtue of Art. 141 of the Constitution.

(A) *GROUND OF DIVORCE IN ENGLAND.* The sole ground on which a petition for divorce may be presented to the court by either party to a marriage is that the marriage has broken down irretrievably.[13]

(B) *GROUND OF DIVORCE IN AUSTRALIA.* Under the (CTH) Family Law Act 1975, an application for dissolution of marriage is made on the sole ground that the marriage has broken down irretrievably. In such proceedings the ground will be held to be established if the court is satisfied that the parties have separated and thereafter have lived separately and apart for a continuous period of not less than twelve months immediately, preceding the date of the filing of the application.[14]

---

6 Section 13(2)(*iv*), *ibid*.
7 *Bathula* v *Bathula* AIR 1981 AP 74. See also *Jivben* v *Dahyalal* AIR 1984 Guj 6.
8 (2009)6 SCC 379.
9 (2006)4 SCC 558.
10 (2005)2 SCC 22.
11 (2007)4 SCC 511.
12 (1998)1 SCC 226.
13 Matrimonial Causes Act 1973, s. 1(1) replacing Divorce Reform Act 1969, s. 1.
14 Halsbury's *Laws of Australia* 205, Family Law, pp. 84-85.

Alternative relief in divorce proceedings[15]

Where a petition for dissolution of marriage is presented, except in so far as the petition founded on grounds as set out in cl. (*ii*) relating to conversion to another religion; cl. (*vi*) relating to renounciation; and cl. (*vii*) relating to disappearance for more than seven years in sub-sec. (1) of s. 13, the court may pass instead a decree for judicial separation.[15] This power has been exercised by the court in the undernoted cases.[16]

Divorce by mutual consent[17]

A petition for dissolution of marriage may be presented to the District Court on the ground—(*i*) that they have been living separately for a period of one year or more; (*ii*) that they have not been able to live together; and (*iii*) that they have mutually agreed that their marriage be dissolved.[18] On presentation of the petition, a date of hearing is to be fixed not earlier than six months and not later than eighteen months. If the petition is not withdrawn in the meantime, the court shall, on being satisfied, pass a decree for divorce.[19] The court may make necessary enquiries as it considers fit and proper. But it is not necessary for the parties to prove any of the grounds mentioned in s. 13 of the Act.[20] This power to dissolve by mutual consent of the parties may also be exercised by the appellate court provided there is no collusion or the decree will not be otherwise illegal.[21] Even where a petition for dissolution of marriage has been presented by one party, it can be converted into a fresh petition for divorce by mutual consent.[22] It is the duty of the court to satisfy whether the mandatory provisions under s. 23(1)(*bb*) of the Act have been complied with and there was no force, fraud or undue influence to obtain consent of a party.[23] In *Preeti Singh* v *Sandeep Singh*[24] the divorce was granted by mutual consent of the parties under direction of the Supreme Court. Where one spouse withdraws consent from divorce by mutual

---

15 See s. 13A, H.M. Act.
16 *Angrez* v *Baldeo* AIR 1980 Punj 171; *Payerelal* v *Ram Rotti* 1980 Hindu LR 691 (P&H); *Om Prakash* v *Shakuntala* 1981 Hindu LR 92 (Raj); *Snighda* v *Akhil Chandra* AIR 1992 Gau 95.
17 See s. 13B, H.M. Act.
18 Section 13B(1), *ibid*.
19 Section 13B(2), *ibid*.
20 *Ravishanker* v *Sharda* AIR 1978 MP 44.
21 *Indrawal* v *Radhey* AIR 1981 All 151; *Gurudev* v *Malkit* 1980 Hind LR 331 (Punj).
22 *Jagmohan* v *Sudesh* 1979 Hind LR 303 (Punj).
23 *Rajashri* v *Rajendra* AIR 1997 Bom 65; *Pranab* v *Ratna* 98 Cal WN 931.
24 AIR 1995 SC 1851. See *Anil Kumar Jain* v *Maya Jain* AIR 2010 SC 229.

consent before passing of decree, no court other than the Supreme Court can pass divorce decree.[25]

In *Yamanaji H. Jadhav* v *Nirmala*[26] it has been held by the Supreme Court that customary divorce by consent is not recognisable by court unless specifically permitted by law.

Restriction on presentation of petition for divorce

No petition for dissolution of marriage can be presented to a District Court unless at the date of the presentation of the petition one year has elapsed since the date of the marriage.[27] But the District Court may entertain a petition for divorce even before expiry of one year from the date of the marriage on the ground that the case is one (*i*) of exceptional hardship to the petitioner, or (*ii*) of exceptional depravity on the part of the respondent. But where it appears to the court at the hearing of the petition that the petitioner obtained the leave to present the petition by any misrepresentation or concealment of the nature of the case, the court may pronounce a decree subject to the condition that the decree shall come into effect after expiry of one year from the date of the marriage. Alternatively, the court may dismiss the petition without prejudice to the right of the petitioner to file a petition after expiry of the said one year upon substantially the same facts as pleaded in the petition so dismissed.[1] A petitioner was married to the respondent in the forenoon and in the afternoon she came to know that the respondent had already married another woman and had a child by her. It was held that there was sufficient ground to grant leave to the petitioner under the proviso to s. 14 of the Act.[2] The grant of leave by the court under the proviso to s. 14 of the Act is discretionary and the appellate court will not usually interfere with such discretion unless the trial court has proceeded on wrong principle of law or has failed to consider the material question of fact or has caused gross injustice to the aggrieved party.[3]

In disposing an application under s. 14 for leave the court shall take into consideration the interest of any children of the marriage and also the possibility of reconciliation between parties before the expiry of the said one year.[4]

---

25 *Anil Kumar Jain* v *Maya Jain* AIR 2010 SC 229.
26 AIR 2002 SC 971.
27 Section 14(1), H.M. Act.
1 Section 14(1) proviso, *ibid*.
2 *Meganatha* v *Susheela* AIR 1957 Mad 423.
3 *Ibid*.
4 Section 14(2), H.M. Act.

Remarriage by divorced person

After dissolution of a marriage by a decree of divorce and when there is no any other legal bar to such dissolution, it is lawful for either party to the marriage to marry again.[5] The object of this section is to give effect to the judgment as a judgment *in rem*.[6] In *Chandra Mohini* v *Avinash Prasad*[7] it has been held by the Supreme Court that where a person immediately after the decree of divorce remarries, it would not take away the right of the wife to challenge the impugned decree by appeal and as such the second marriage by that person would be illegal. Where a marriage was held in contravention of the old proviso to s. 15[8] it was not to be considered as void but voidable.[9] Where a decree is passed under s. 11 or s. 12, it is also covered by s. 15 of the Act. Thus, a second marriage contracted during the pendency of the appeal is not lawful and the husband cannot raise the plea that the appeal is infructuous.[10]

Legitimacy of children of void and voidable marriages[11]

Where a child is born of void marriage whether or not a decree of nullity is granted in respect of that marriage under this Act or whether or not the marriage is held to be void otherwise than a petition under this Act, such child is deemed to be legitimate and it will be entitled to inherit the property of its parents only.[12] Similarly, where a child is born of a voidable marriage in respect of which a decree of nullity is granted, the child shall be the legitimate child of their parents. The said child shall be entitled to inherit the property of its parents only.[13] The child of a void marriage would not be entitled to step into the shoes of its father for inheriting coparcenary property.[14] This section has no application to a marriage which is said to be not selemnised.[15] Section 16 is intended to uphold the legitimacy of paternity a child born out of void marriage, but this section

---

5 Section 15, H.M. Act.
6 *Sunanda* v *Venkata Subbarao* AIR 1957 AP 424; see *Hirakali* v *Ram Asrey* AIR 1971 All 201.
7 AIR 1967 SC 581.
8 *Omitted* by Act 68 of 1976.
9 *Lila Gupta* v *Laxmi Narain* AIR 1978 SC 1351.
10 *Lata Kamat* v *Vilas* AIR 1989 SC 1477. See also *Tejinder Kaur* v *Gurmit Singh* AIR 1988 SC 839.
11 See s. 16, H.M. Act.
12 Section 16(1), (3), H.M. Act.
13 Section 16(2), (3), *ibid*.
14 *Hanmanta Laxman* v *D. Hanmanta* AIR 1977 Bom 191.
15 *Muthayya* v *Kamu* AIR 1981 NOC 172.

has not extended similar protection to the mother of the child.[16] This section does not purport to confer legitimacy on children born of a marriage which was not valid under the law in force prior to the commencement of this Act.[17] Long cohabitation of a man with a woman raises presumption of marriage by the prevailing custom in the community. Thus, a child born of such cohabitation is entitled to the benefit under s. 16 of the Act.[18] This section has removed the disability of a child to inherit the property of its parents.[19]

Bigamy and punishment

If a marriage is solemnised after the commencement of this between two Hindus and the marriage is void on the ground that a party to such marriage has a spouse leaving the provisions of ss. 494 and 495 of the Indian Penal Code 1860 shall apply.[20] Section 494 of the Indian Penal Code prescribes punishment for a term not exceeding seven years and also with fine for marrying again during life-time of husband or wife. Section 495, IPC deals with offence for concealment of former marriage from person with whom subsequent marriage is contracted. The punishment for this offence as prescribed under this section is imprisonment for a term not exceeding ten years and also fine. In order to attract the provisions of s. 17 of the Hindu Marriage Act the second marriage is to be solemnised in accordance with proper ceremonies and form. Mere going through certain ceremonies with intention of marrying cannot be deemed to be the ceremonies prescribed by law or approved by the custom.[1] Section 495, IPC and s. 17, H.M. Act are to be read together to appreciate the purports of these sections. Merely because the second marriage is void under s. 17 of the H.M. Act, it cannot be said that s. 494, IPC is not attracted.[2] When there is no plea that the marriage was solemnised in accordance with customary rites and usage, there cannot be any inference as to the performance of essential ceremonies for a valid marriage even if both the parties are living together as husband and wife.[3]

---

16 *Yamunabai* v *Anantrao* AIR 1988 SC 644.
17 *P. Kallioni* v *K. Devi* AIR 1989 Ker 279.
18 *M.M. Bai* v *Ramwati* AIR 1990 MP 276.
19 *Laxmibai* v *Limbabai* AIR 1983 Bom 222.
20 Section 17, H.M. Act.
1 *Bhaurao* v *State of Maharashtra* AIR 1965 SC 1564; *Kanwal Ram* v *H.P. Administration* AIR 1966 SC 614.
2 *Gopal Lal* v *State of Rajasthan* AIR 1979 SC 718.
3 *Santi Deb Berma* v *Kanchan Prava Devi* AIR 1991 SC 816; *Surjit Kaur* v *Garja Singh* AIR 1994 SC 135.

Punishment for contravention of section 5

If a marriage is solemnised in contravention of cl. (*iii*) of s. 5 which forbids marriage below the prescribed age of twenty-one for the bridegroom and of eighteen years for the bride, every person is punishable with simple imprisonment for not more than fifteen days or with fine for a sum not exceeding one thousand rupees or with both.[4] Similarly, if a marriage is solemnised in contravention of condition specified in cl. (*iv*) or cl. (*v*) of s. 5, every person who procures a marriage of himself or herself shall be punished with imprisonment for a period not exceeding one month or with fine which may extend to one thousand rupees or with both.[5] Where a marriage is solemnised in contravention of provision of s. 5(*iii*) of the Act, there are two civil consequences, namely, the party procuring the marriage is punishable under s. 18(*a*) of the Act and the aggrieved party can also obtain a decree for divorce under s. 13(2)(*iv*) of the Act.[6] Besides, if the wife is below 18 years of age and has also repudiated the marriage can file a complaint under s. 496 of the Indian Penal Code.

Jurisdiction and procedure

A petition under this Act shall be presented to the District Court within whose local limits of ordinary original civil jurisdiction any of the following facts may relate: (*a*) the marriage was solemnised; (*b*) the respondent at the time of the presentation of the petition resides; (*c*) the parties to the marriage last resided together; (*d*) in case the wife is the petitioner, where she is residing on the date of presentation of the petition; (*e*) the petitioner is residing at the time of the presentation of the petition and the respondent is residing outside the territories of India or has not been heard of seven years or more.[7] A petition filed in a matrimonial suit under this Act is a plaint.[8] A person resides in a place which he or she has chosen as his or her permanent or temporary abode. Whether a person has chosen a particular place as his or her abode depends on facts of each case.[9] Visits by husband or wife to the other cannot be termed as casual or flying but

---

4 Section 18(*a*), H.M. Act. See also, ss. 9, 10 and 11 of the Prohibition of Child Marriage Act 2006.
5 Section 18(*b*), *ibid*.
6 *Pinninti* v *State* AIR 1977 AP 43 (FB).
7 Section 19, H.M. Act. This section is substituted by the Marriage Laws (Amendment) Act 1976.
8 *Umashankar Prasad Singh* v *Radha Devi* AIR 1967 Pat 220.
9 *Lalithamma* v *R. Kannan* AIR 1966 Mys 178; *Santosh* v *Om Prakash* AIR 1977 All 97; *Jagir Kaur* v *Jaswant Singh* AIR 1963 SC 1521.

these will come within the meaning of the word 'resides' or 'resided'.[10] The enjoyment of marital relations is not relevant in such cases.[11] The word "resides" does not connote the place of origin. It is a flexible one and has many shades of meaning and it takes its colour and content from the context in which it appears and cannot be read in isolation.[12]

(A) *Contents of petition.* Every petition presented under this Act shall contain the facts for the reliefs claimed and except a petition under s. 11 of the Act shall also state that there is no collusion between the parties.[13] Every such petition shall be verified in the manner required by law for verification of a plaint and at the hearing statements contained in the petition may be referred to as evidence.[14] Where an original petition for divorce did not contain the ground of cruelty but it was subsequently included in reply to the written statement of the wife, it was held that no relief on the ground of cruelty could be granted.[15] The provisions of this section would apply to a petition filed in a District Court and not to an application made for registration of marriage required under Rules framed under this Act.[16] In an *ex parte* matter the court cannot pass a decree only on affidavit of the petitioner, but must examine the petitioner himself.[17] There is a conflict of decisions as to whether a party suffering from physical or mental disability would have to undergo medical examination. The High Court of Madras has held that the Courts have discretion in ordering a physical examination of the respondent suffering from any such disability or disease subject to protection from violence due to natural delicacy and sensibility.[18] On the other hand, the High Court of Gujarat has held that in absence of specific provision in any Act the court has no jurisdiction to order compulsory medical examination as because this would interfere with the personal liberty of a citizen.[19]

(B) *Application of Code of Civil Procedure.* All proceedings under the Act shall be governed, as far as possible, by the Code of Civil Procedure 1908 subject to the specific provisions contained in this Act and rules framed

---

10 *Pritma Sharma* v *Mohinder* AIR 1984 P&H 305.
11 *Ranu Vij* v *Surinder Kumar* AIR 1986 Del 33.
12 *Jeewanti* v *Kishan* AIR 1982 SC 3.
13 Section 20(1), H.M. Act.
14 Section 20(2), *ibid*.
15 *Sulochana* v *Ram Kumar* AIR 1981 All 78.
16 *Satya Sunder Das* v *V. Registrar, Hindu Marriage, Orissa* AIR 1963 Ori 139.
17 *Anjula* v *Milan* AIR 1981 All 178.
18 *Rangaswami* v *Aravindammal* AIR 1957 Mad 243.
19 *Bipinchandra S. Bhatt* v *Madhuriban Bhatt* AIR 1963 Guj 250.

by the High Court.[20] In absence of specific provisions in the Code of Civil Procedure the court has inherent power. In exercise of this power the court may stay further proceedings under the Act if an order of interim maintenance under s. 24 of the Act is not complied by a party against whom such order is passed.[1] Under Or. 11 read with s. 141, CPC the court may pass an order for interrogations in connection with application for interim maintenance under s. 24 of the H.M. Act.[2] An *ex parte* decree of divorce can be set aside by the court in exercise of power under s. 151, CPC.[3] In case of conflict between the provisions of s. 20 of the Code of Civil Procedure and those of s. 19 of the H.M. Act, the former cannot be invoked.[4] In accordance with r. 11 of the Hindu Marriage (Kerala) Rules 1963 the adulterer is a necessary co-respondent to a petition for divorce. Non-compliance with such mandatory provision renders a petition not maintainable.[5] In *Asha Narang* v *Dr. Ved Prakash Narang*[6] an application under Or. 41, r. 27, CPC was filed for the first time in second appeal, it was held by the Supreme Court that Or. 41, r. 27 was not attracted in that case. In service of summons in a matrimonial suit Or. 5, r. 19A, CPC is applicable.[7]

(C) *Power of transfer of petitions.* The District Court and the competent court under the Code of Civil Procedure has power to transfer certain cases arising out of matrimonial causes under the H.M. Act by the same parties to the suits to one District Court for joint hearing of their cases.[8] In an application for transfer of a matrimonial case from the court of District Judge, Bokaro, to the court of District Judge at Delhi, the Supreme Court gave liberty to parties to file petition for divorce by mutual consent before the transferee court at Delhi.[9] In *Usha* v *Palisetty*[10] it has been held that under Art. 139A of the Constitution of India the Supreme Court has power to transfer a matrimonial case to a court having no jurisdiction under the Hindu Marriage Act.

---

20 Section 21, H.M. Act.
1 *Anita Karmakar* v *Birendra Chandra Karmakar* AIR 1962 Cal 88.
2 *Ganga Devi* v *Krishna Prasad Sharma* AIR 1967 Ori 19.
3 *Indubai* v *Govindrao* (1980)2 Mah LR 289.
4 *Upendra Kumar* v *Harpriya Kumar* ILR (1978)2 Del 97.
5 *Ayyapan* v *Vasantha* AIR 1988 Ker 314.
6 (1997)11 SCC 667.
7 *Gautam Sen Gupta* v *L.O. Sen Gupta* 1998(1) CWN 406.
8 Section 21A, H.M. Act as inserted by the Marriage Laws (Amendment) Act 1976.
9 *Seema Shrinidhi* v *Praveen Kumar Tiwari* AIR 1999 SC 1560. See also *Shakuntala* v *Om Prakash* AIR 1991 SC 1104 (a case under s. 22, CPC).
10 AIR 2002 SC 400.

(D) *Expeditious trial and disposal of appeal.* The trial of a petition under this Act shall be completed within six months from the date of service of notice of the petition on the respondent.[11] Every appeal under this Act shall be heard as expeditiously as possible and endeavour shall be made to conclude the hearing of such appeal within three months from the date of service of notice of appeal on the respondent.[12]

(E) *Documentary evidence.* Notwithstanding any provision in any other Act no document shall be inadmissible in any proceeding at the trial of a petition under this Act on the ground that it is not duly stamped or registered.[13] These provisions supersede s. 35 of the Indian Stamp Act 1899[14] and s. 49(c) of the Registration Act 1908.[15]

(F) *Proceedings to be in camera.* Every proceeding under this Act shall be conducted *in camera* and no such matter shall be printed or published except a judgment of the High Court or of the Supreme Court.[16] If any person prints or publishes any matter in contravention of provisions contained in sub-sec. (1) of s. 22, he shall be punishable with fine for a sum not exceeding one thousand rupees.[17]

Decree in proceedings[18]

Section 23 deals with proceedings like restitution of conjugal rights (s. 9), judicial separation (s. 10) void marriage (s. 11), voidable marriage (s. 12), divorce (s. 13), and divorce by mutual consent (s. 13B). Clauses (*a*), (*c*), (*d*) and (*e*) of sub-sec. (1) of s. 23 set out the circumstances which must be considered by the court in the proceedings under ss. 9, 10, 11, 12 and 13 of the Act. Clause (*b*) of sub-sec. (1) forbids the petitioner not to be accessory in any manner, nor has the petitioner connived or condoned the acts of respondent the ground specified in cl. (*i*) of sub-sec. (1) of s. 13. Clause (*bb*) of sub-sec. (1) deals specifically with the divorce by mutual consent. Sub-section (2) of s. 23 has no application to any proceeding relating to reliefs sought on any ground specified in cl. (*ii*), cl. (*iii*), cl. (*iv*), cl. (*v*), cl. (*vi*) or cl. (*vii*) of sub-sec. (1) of s. 13. This sub-sec. (2) has also

---

11 Section 21B(2), H.M. Act. This section is inserted by the Marriage Laws (Amendment) Act 1976.
12 Section 21B(3), *ibid.*
13 Section 21C, *ibid.*
14 Act 2 of 1899.
15 Act 16 of 1908.
16 Section 22(1) H.M. Act. This section is substituted by the Marriage Laws (Amendment) Act 1976.
17 Section 22(2), *ibid.*
18 See section 23, H.M. Act.

no application to the proceedings for nullity of marriage. Sub-section (3) confers power on the court to bring about reconciliation between parties through a third party. Sub-section (4) gives right to a party in divorce proceedings a copy of decree of divorce free of cost from the court. Section 23 does not grant any discretion to the court on the grant of a decree for judicial separation or divorce. The court must be satisfied that a ground specified in s. 13 exists and the conditions enumerated in s. 23 and also satisfied. Thereafter the court can grant a decree for judicial separation or divorce.[19] It is obligatory on the court to consider all aspects mentioned in s. 23 of the Act even if parties give their consent.[20] Satisfaction of the court under s. 23 is to be based on materials on record and not on a mere probabilities and circumstances.[21] The word "satisfied" means satisfaction by proof beyond reasonable doubt, the standard of proof drawn from criminal law is not a proper analogy.[1] In a proceeding under this Act the court can arrive at the satisfaction contemplated by s. 23 of the Act on the basis of legal evidence in accordance with the provisions of the Indian Evidence Act which would include admissions of the parties alone unless the court is of the view that they were collusive or contradicted by facts.[2] It is the duty of the court to pass a decree only if it is satisfied that the case of the petitioner has been proved.[3] Even where the petitioner has proved all the allegations against the respondent, the court is entitled to refuse the relief asked for, if the court is satisfied that the petitioner is himself or herself responsible for the situation.[4] The burden of proving that the petitioner had not taken any advantage of his or her own wrong lies on the party who seeks the relief for divorce.[5] The word "wrong" used in s. 23(1)(*a*) of the Act means an act causing some injury to the other side.[6] The word "condonation" implicitly means that the act condoned was temporarily suspended. If a husband knowing the adultery of his wife with another person cohabits with her, it implies that he has condoned the act of his wife's adultery. Mere delay in filing the petition

---

19 *Veerarghavan* v *Parvarthy* AIR 1974 Ker 43.
20 *Hirakali* v *Ram Asrey Awasthi* AIR 1971 All 201.
21 *Nishit Kumar* v *Anjali Biswas* AIR 1968 Cal 105.
1 *Vira Reddi* v *Kistamma* AIR 1969 Mad 235.
2 *Mahendra* v *Sushila* AIR 1965 SC 364.
3 *Earnist John White* v *Kathileen* AIR 1958 SC 441.
4 *Tarachand* v *Narain Devi* AIR 1976 Punj 300.
5 *Kailash* v *Manmohan* AIR 1975 J&K 95.
6 *Mohanlal* v *Mohan Bai* AIR 1958 Raj 71.

is not condonation.[7] Normal sexual intercourse is evidence of both forgiveness and reconciliation. It may be rebutted by evidence sufficient to negative the intent to forgive.[8] Connivance can be inferred only when the circumstances are such that a reasonable man could have foreseen that a marital offence was probable on the wife being left alone in the company of another young person.[9] So far as delay is concerned, it depends upon facts and circumstances of each case. There is no absolute rule that there had been unreasonable delay.[10] Ten years' delay was held to be fatal.[11] But in another case, 13 years' delay was held to be not fatal.[12] The court should not pass a decree on a compromise, because compromise leads to suspect collusion.[13] The court should "in the first instance" make an attempt to bring about reconciliation between the parties. The words "in the first instance" denote that the court must make an endeavour before granting relief, and the court means the trial court.[14] In *Jagraj Singh* v *Birpal Kaur*[15] it has been held by the Supreme Court that appearance of parties in matrimonial dispute can be ensured by issuance of non-bailable warrant. The view that the court has no power to issue non-bailable warrant and should the matter *ex parte* would defeat the provisions under s. 23 of the Act providing for reconciliation of matrimonial disputes. Under sub-sec. (4) of s. 23 it is the duty of a party to apply for a copy of decree. If no application is made, the period of limitation will not be saved.[16]

Right to make counter-claim

In any proceeding for divorce, or judicial separation or restitution of conjugal rights, the respondent, in addition to opposing the relief on ground of petitioner's adultery, cruelty or desertion, may make a counter-claim for any relief under this Act on that ground. If the court is satisfied as to the ground agitated by the respondent in his or her defence, the court may grant him or her any relief to which he or she is entitled under

---

7   *Rajani* v *Prabhakar* AIR 1958 Bom 264. See *Chandra Mohini* v *Avinash Prasad* AIR 1967 SC 581.
8   *Dastane* v *Dastane* AIR 1975 SC 1534.
9   *Clarance* v *Raichad* AIR 1964 Mys 67 (SB).
10 *Vinod Chandra* v *Aruna* AIR 1977 Del 24; *Chinnaperumal* v *M. Ammal* AIR 1976 Mad 179.
11 *Shanti Devi* v *Ramesh Chandra* AIR 1969 Pat 27.
12 *Leela* v *Rao Anand Singh* AIR 1963 Raj 178.
13 *Inderjit Kaur* v *Rajinder Singh* ILR (1980)2 Del 910.
14 *Sakri* v *Chhanwarlal* AIR 1975 Raj 134.
15 AIR 2007 SC 2083.
16 *Surjit Kaur* v *Tarsem Singh* AIR 1978 Raj 209.

this Act as if he or she had presented a petition seeking such relief on that ground.[17] A counter-claim cannot be allowed at the appellate stage.[18] The option of making counter-claim is not barred even if it is not made initially. The party may take any ground mentioned in the section as a defence in the main petition.[19] In a divorce petition by husband for divorce, prayer for permanent alimony made by wife in her written statement was granted without any separate application having been made by the wife following the broader view indicated in s. 23A of the Act.[20]

Interim maintenance

In any proceeding under this Act either party to such proceeding may make an application for maintenance *pendente lite* and expenses of proceeding provided the petitioner has no independent income sufficient for his or her support and the necessary expenses of the proceedings. The court, on being satisfied, may pass an order directing the respondent to pay to the petitioner the expenses of the proceedings and monthly maintenance during the proceeding a sum as having regard to the petitioner's own income and the income of the respondent.[21] The expression "petitioner" and "respondent" used in s. 24 of the Act refer to petitioner and respondent in the application under this section and not in the original petition.[1] Proceedings under this section would include any appeal.[2] Though there is no specific provision to vary an order passed under this Act, the court in exercise of inherent power may vary an order of maintenance provided there is a change in the circumstances justifying the same.[3] Once an order passed under this section, subsequent dismissal of the original petition would not discharge the liability already incurred.[4] In deciding question of interim maintenance the conduct of the spouse is not material as because s. 24 is not controlled by s. 23 or any other provision of the Act.[5] An application under s. 24 may be disposed of by way of a summary proceeding, the court may decide the issue on the

---

17 Section 23A, H.M. Act as inserted by the Marriage Laws (Amendment) Act 1976 (s. 17).
18 *Sandhya* v *Gopinath* 86 Cal WN 665; AIR 1983 Cal 161.
19 *Medasett* v *Veeramani* AIR 1981 AP 123.
20 *Surajmal* v *Rukminibai* AIR 2000 MP 48.
21 Section 24, H.M. Act.
1 *Kamala* v *Rupchand* AIR 1958 Bom 466; *Raj Kumari* v *Trilok Singh* AIR 1959 All 628.
2 *Ram Narain Pathak* v *Urmila Devi* AIR 1980 All 344.
3 *Devki* v *Purshotam* AIR 1973 Raj 2.
4 *Muniratnam Naidu* v *S. Shantamma* AIR 1971 Mys 25.
5 *Lallubhai* v *Nirmalaben* AIR 1972 Guj 174; *Yogeshwar Prasad* v *Jyoti Rani* AIR 1981 Del 99. But see also, *Balbir Singh* v *Swaran Kanta* AIR 1981 Raj 266.

basis of affidavits of the parties concerned.[6] By the amending Act 49 of 2001 it is now provided that an application for interim maintenance shall, as far as possible to be disposed of within sixty days from the date of service of notice on the opposite party. Generally, the quantum of maintenance is fixed on the basis of an estimate of the average monthly income of the respondent after allowing certain uncertainties and to divide it by the total number of dependents including the wife and then to grant her a share.[7] There are two views with regard to grant of interim maintenance under s. 24 to children. One view is that the court has no power to grant interim maintenance under s. 24 to the children excepting the wife.[8] The other view is that the court has power to grant interim maintenance not only to the wife but also to the children under s. 26 though there is no specific prayer.[9] A mere pre-existing order under s. 125, Cr PC would not oust the jurisdiction of the civil court under this section.[10] The fact that the wife is maintained or supported by her father or brother cannot be taken into consideration for determination of her alimony nor was the fact that she was well-educated and capable of earning. Sufficient independent income of the petitioner is not equivalent to saying she had potential earning capacity.[11] An order on a petition under this section shall be made at the first instance of the proceedings.[12] The grant of interim alimony cannot be postponed till the passing of the final order on the ground that marriage itself is in dispute.[13] In *Ramesh Chandra Kaushal* v *Veena Kaushal*[14] the Supreme Court has held that remedies under s. 24 of the H.M. Act and under s. 125, Cr PC are quite independent and the decision under the former section is not final. There are conflicting views on fixation of quantum of maintenance under this section. One view is that in absence of special circumstances interim maintenance should be paid at the rate of one-fifth of the net income of

---

6   *Vinay Kumar* v *Purnima Devi* AIR 1973 Raj 32; see also *Bhalu* v *Hemo* AIR 1969 Ori 236.
7   *Radhikabai* v *Sadhuram* AIR 1970 MP 14.
8   *Bankim Chandra* v *Anjali Roy* AIR 1972 Pat 80.
9   *Katamavahi* v *Paradeshamma* (1974)2 Andh WR 359; *Narendra Kumar* v *Suraj Mehta* AIR 1982 AP 100. But see also *Iqbal Singh* v *Adersh* 1982 All LJ 640.
10 *Surjit Kaur* v *Tirath Singh* AIR 1978 Punj 112.
11 *Radhikabai* v *Sadhuram* AIR 1970 MP 14.
12 See *Jalasutram* v *Jalasutram* AIR 1959 AP 49; *Tarlochan* v *Mohinder* AIR 1963 Punj 249.
13 *Arti Singh* v *Kanwar Pal Singh* AIR 1977 Del 76.
14 AIR 1975 SC 1807; 1979 Cr LJ 3.

the respondent.[15] But this view has been dissented from some other High Courts.[16] While ordering the expenses for proceedings the court should take into consideration the income of the respondent against whom such order is passed.[17] In *Anita Laxmi* v *Laxmi Narayan*[18] it has been held by the Supreme Court where the wife could not attend proceedings due to grant of meagre amount of expenses and an *ex parte* decree was passed, it was liable to be set aside. Where husband conceals his true income, an adverse inference may be drawn against him.[19]

Permanent maintenance

A court exercising jurisdiction under this Act may pass an order for permanent alimony and maintenance.[20] Where a party to a matrimonial proceeding makes an application for permanent alimony and maintenance, the court shall pass an order thereon either at the time of passing of the decree or at any time subsequent thereto. By such order the respondent is directed to pay to the applicant for her or his maintenance such sum or such monthly or periodical sum for a term not exceeding the life of the applicant having regard to the respondent's own income and other property, if any, the income and other property of the applicant, the conduct of the parties and other circumstances of the case and such payment may be secured, if necessary, by a charge on the immovable property.[1] A divorced wife can apply for maintenance under this section.[2] The existence of a decree is a condition precedent for invoking the jurisdiction of the court under s. 25 of the Act. Thus, where the husband withdrawn a petition under s. 10 of the Act, an application under s. 25(1) is not maintainable.[3] The expression "at any time of passing any decree or at any time subsequent thereto" appearing in s. 25(1) means at any time of passing any decree covered by the Act and not at the time of dismissing the petition for a relief provided under this Act or any time subsequent thereto.[4] A court can pass an order of maintenance by consent

---

15 *Mukan* v *Ajeet Chand* AIR 1958 Raj 322; *Prasanna* v *Sureshwari* AIR 1969 Ori 12; *Surendra Nath* v *Pushpa* (1978)2 Cal LJ 602.
16 See *Subramanyam* v *Saraswati* AIR 1964 Mys 38; *Dinesh* v *Usha* AIR 1979 Bom 173.
17 *Gangu* v *Pundlik* AIR 1979 Bom 264.
18 AIR 1992 SC 1148.
19 *Jasbir Kaur* v *District Judge, Dehradun* AIR 1997 SC 3397.
20 See section 25, H.M. Act.
1 Section 25(1), *ibid*.
2 *Vinod* v *Mangala* 1981 Bom Cr 962.
3 *Shantaram* v *Hirabai* AIR 1962 Bom 27.
4 *Harilal Purshottam* v *Lilavati Gokaldas* AIR 1961 Guj 202.

of parties in which case no formal application is necessary.[5] Either party to the proceedings under s. 25 may make an application to the court subsequent to the passing of the order for variation, modification or rescission of the order.[6] The order of permanent maintenance at the instance of party against whom it is passed may be rescind by the court on any of the following grounds: (*i*) that the party in whose favour the order was passed has remarried; or (*ii*) that the party being the wife has not remained chaste; or (*iii*) that the party being husband has had sexual intercourse with any woman outside wedlock.[7] Where a party after obtaining a decree of maintenance resumes cohabitation with other party, the decree would be nullified.[8] In *Chand Dhawan* v *Jawaharlal Dhawan*[9] the Supreme Court has held that while the court passing the decree affecting the marital status has power to grant permanent alimony under s. 25 of the Act which may be altered or modified in future by the court as the situation may warrant. A suit for declaration of a decree for permanent alimony in favour of a divorced wife for charge on the estate of the deceased husband can be converted into an execution application by way of a measure of *ex debito justitiae*.[10] A decree of permanent maintenance is not extinguished on the death of the husband. The decree is executable against the estate of the husband in the hands of the heirs and there is no personal liability.[11]

In *Komalam Amma* v *Kumara Pillai Raghavan Pillai*[12] the Supreme Court has held that maintenance necessarily must encompass a provision for residence. An estranged wife cannot be denied right of residence in matrimonial home. Provision for residence may be made either by giving a lump sum in money or property in lieu thereof.

Custody of children[13]

In any proceeding under this Act the court may pass interim order as to the custody, maintenance and education of minor children keeping in view their wishes. The court may also from time to time revoke, suspend or vary any such order.[14] The court has discretion to grant maintenance

---

5   *Jai Devi* v *Bhishan Das* AIR 1981 Punj 186.
6   Section 25(2), H.M. Act.
7   Section 25(3), *ibid*.
8   *Ansuva* v *Rajaih* AIR 1971 AP 296.
9   1993 Cr LJ 2930 (SC); (1993)3 SCC 406.
10 *Nandarani* v *Indian Airlines* AIR 1983 SC 1201.
11 *Nagamma* v *Ningamma* AIR 1999 Kant 432.
12 AIR 2009 SC 236.
13 See section 26, H.M. Act.
14 See *Vikram Vir Vohra* v *Shalini Bhalla* AIR 2010 SC 1675 (Orders as to custody and visitation rights are interlocutory orders and can be moulded and changed as per needs of child).

pendente lite to children where wife is not entitled to maintenance under s. 24 of the Act.[15] Under this section maintenance can be granted only to minor children and not to adults.[16] In *Sumitra Devi* v *Bhikan Choudhary*[17] it has been held by the Supreme Court that an illegitimate minor child is entitled to maintenance under s. 125, Cr PC. In *Poonam Dutta* v *Krisanlal Dutta*[18] the Supreme Court while dealing with custody of a child has considered the paramount interest of the child and directed the parties not to do anything which would adversely affect the interest of the child and also its physical and mental condition. In *Veena Kapoor* v *Varinder Kumar*[19] the Supreme Court has held that it is the well settled principle that in matters concerning custody of minor children the paramount consideration is the welfare of minor and not a legal right of a party to custody. Where the father was facing charge for death caused to the mother of minor children under s. 498A, IPC, the Supreme Court declined to give custody of the minor children to their father though he had preferential right. The custody of the children was given to the maternal uncle of the children with certain directions.[20] In allowing a writ of *habeas corpus* against the father who abducted the child to India from the custody of its mother in USA the Supreme Court has held that whenever a question arises before a court regarding the custody of a minor child, the matter is to be decided not on consideration of the legal rights of the parties, but on the paramount consideration of the welfare of the minor.[21]

In *Padmja Sharma* v *Ratan Lal Sharma*[22] it was held by the Supreme Court that where both the parents of the child were employed, they would have to pay the maintenance of the child in proportion of their salaries.

Disposal of joint property

In a proceeding under this Act the court may make such provisions in the decree with respect to any property presented, at or about the time of marriage, which belong jointly to both the husband and wife.[23] The

---

15 *Baboolal* v *Prem Lata* AIR 1974 Raj 93; *Subhasini* v *Umakanth* AIR 1981 Kant 115; *Sudershan* v *Deepak* AIR 1981 Punj 305.
16 *Kartar Chand* v *Taravati* AIR 1982 Bom 15.
17 AIR 1985 SC 765.
18 AIR 1989 SC 401.
19 AIR 1982 SC 792.
20 *Kirtikumar M. Joshi* v *Pradip Kumar K. Joshi* AIR 1992 SC 1447.
21 *Elizabeth Dinshaw* v *Arvand M. Dinshaw* AIR 1987 SC 3.
22 AIR 2000 SC 1398.
23 Section 27, H.M. Act.

matrimonial court has no jurisdiction to make an order in respect of property presented subsequent to the marriage.[1] The word "belong" appearing in this section does not reflect the title to the property in legal sense of ownership, but denotes connection with property having his or her possession.[2] A married woman is an absolute owner of her *stridhan*, and if *stridhan* is placed in the custody of her husband or in-laws, they would be deemed to be trustees and are bound to return them as and when demanded by the married woman.[3] The scope of s. 27 is that property which the spouses had received individually or collectively as presents on or about the time of the marriage for their joint use in day-to-day life.[4] In *Balkrishna R. Kadam* v *Sangeeta B. Kadam*[5] the Supreme Court has laid down the proposition of law underlying s. 27 of the Act. It is not the property which is given to the wife at the time of marriage only but includes the property given to the parties before or after the marriage as well provided such property relates to the marriage. The expression "at or about the time of marriage" is to be construed to include such property which is given at the time of marriage and also the property given before or after the marriage to the parties to become their "joint property". The court can pass an order under s. 27 of the Act at a post-decreetal stage.[6]

Appeals from decrees and orders[7]

All decrees made by the court in any proceeding under this Act is appealable except the decree as to costs. Every such appeal shall lie to the court to which appeal will ordinarily lie from the decision of the trial court.[8] The Appeal Court has power to take into consideration the events which have happened after the passing of the decree.[9] A decision given under ss. 9 to 13 of the Act is a decree and is as such appealable and court-fees are to be paid accordingly.[10] Orders made by the court in any proceeding under this Act under s. 25 or s. 26 except the order of costs are appealable provided they are not interim orders. Such appeals will lie to

---

1 *M.D. Krishnan* v *M.C. Padma* AIR 1968 Mys 226.
2 *Surinder Kaur* v *Madan Gopal Singh* AIR 1980 P&H 334.
3 *Nirmala* v *Ravendra* AIR 1996 MP 227.
4 *Nandini* v *Sanjib* AIR 1988 Bom 239.
5 AIR 1997 SC 3562.
6 *Bijoy Krishna Ghosal* v *Namita Ghosal* AIR 1991 Cal 34.
7 See section 28, H.M. Act.
8 Section 28(1) and (3), *ibid*.
9 *Parihar* v *Parihar* AIR 1978 Raj 140.
10 *M.P. Chandramathy Amma* v *K.N. Balakrishnan Nair* AIR 1982 Ker 47.

the court to which appeals will ordinarily lie against the decisions of the trial court.[11] An appeal would not lie against an order under this section even if the application was made prior to the amendment of s. 28.[12] No appeal lies against an order of stay.[13] There is absolute prohibition on the right of appeal against the costs only.[14] Every appeal under this Act is to be preferred within a period of ninety days from the date of the decree or order.[15] The period of limitation prescribed under sub-sec. (4) of s. 28 is applicable in respect of first appeal and not in respect of second appeal for which the period of limitation is 90 days.[16] Delay in filing an appeal may be condoned under s. 29 of the Limitation Act 1963.[17] In *Balwinder Kaur v Hardeep Singh*[18] the wife alleged that fraud was committed in getting the petition filed through her and she never wanted divorce and the circumstances showed that what she said was *prima facie* probable. In the facts and circumstances of the case the High Court was not justified in rejecting the appeal. Where the trial court passed the decree for dissolution of the wife against which the wife preferred an appeal during which the husband married for second time, it was held that such marriage would not render the appeal infructures.[19] In *Tejinder Kaur v Gurmit Singh*[20] it has been held by the Supreme Court that it is incumbent on the successful husband to ascertain whether an appeal is pending in the High Court or the time for filing special leave petition to the Supreme Court has expired before he remarried after dissolution of marriage.

Enforcement of decrees and orders

All decrees and orders made by the court in a proceeding under this Act are enforceable as if these are decrees and orders made by the court in exercise of its original civil jurisdiction.[1] Sections 36 to 74 and Or. 21 of the Code of Civil Procedure deal with the procedures of execution of decree and order of a civil court. 'Court' in this section will mean "district court" which has only jurisdiction to deal with petition under this Act.[2]

---

11 Section 28(2)(3), H.M. Act.
12 *Ram Narain Pathak v Urmila Devi* AIR 1980 All 344.
13 *Dhani Ram v Sushila Devi* AIR 1977 HP 83.
14 Section 28(3), H.M. Act.
15 Section 28(4), *ibid*.
16 *Indraj v Shanti* AIR 1978 All 279.
17 *Debi Bhaduri v Kumarjib Bhaduri* (1980)1 Cal LJ 309.
18 AIR 1998 SC 764.
19 *Veena Rani v Ramesh Kumar* AIR 1995 P&H 213 relying on *Lata Kamat v Vilas* AIR 1989 SC 1477.
20 AIR 1988 SC 839.
1   Section 28A, H.M. Act.
2   Section 19, *ibid*.

Savings and repeals

A marriage solemnised between Hindus before the commencement of the Hindu Marriage Act is otherwise valid and shall not be declared invalid by reason of the fact that the parties thereto belonged to the same *gotra* or *pravara* or belonged to different religions, castes or sub-division of the same caste.[3] Any principle or custom of Hindu law under which intercaste marriage was considered invalid is now nullified and as such, such marriage is valid under s. 29(1) of the Act with retrospective effect.[4] Any right recognised by custom or conferred by any special enactment to obtain the dissolution of a Hindu marriage, whether solemnised before or after the commencement of the Act has not been taken away or affected under this Act.[5] The right to claim dissolution of Hindu marriage in accordance with the custom and recognised by the custom would continue to be recognised as dissolved marriage.[6] In the Barai Chaurasiya Community a marriage may be dissolved by mutual consent of the parties.[7] But a custom in the community of Komma Reddio, for dissolution of marriage observing certain formalities has not been recognised as a valid divorce.[8] The right to dissolution of marriage under the Travancore Nair Act 1100 continues to be operative by reason of s. 29(2) of the H.M. Act.[9] There is a custom amongst the Sikh Jats of Amritsar District to dissolve marriage otherwise than under the provisions of the Hindu Marriage Act.[10] Any proceeding pending under any law in force for the time being touching any matrimonial causes has not been affected and such proceeding may be continued and determined as if this Act had not been passed.[11] The proceedings pending on the date of commencement of the H.M. Act are not affected by this Act and they would continue to be considered and determined according to the law to which they relate.[12] Any marriage solemnised between two Hindus under the Special Marriage Act 1954, is affected by the provisions of this Act.[13]

---

3 Section 29(1), *ibid*.
4 *Kastoori Devi* v *Chiranjit Lal* AIR 1960 All 446.
5 Section 29(2), H.M. Act.
6 *Are Lachiah* v *Are Raja Mallar* (1964)1 Cr LJ 237 (AP).
7 *Madho Prasad* v *Shakuntala* AIR 1972 All 118.
8 *Thimmakku* v *Bandhu* AIR 1977 Kant 115.
9 *Gopala Krishnan Nair* v *R. Sarasamma* AIR 1980 Ker 109.
10 *Balwinder* v *Gurpal* AIR 1985 Del 14.
11 Section 29(3), H.M. Act.
12 *Sumatiben* v *Jaswant* AIR 1960 Bom 323; *Balwant Singh* v *Sardarni Balwant Kaur* AIR 1957 Pepsu 1; *Udainath Misra* v *Chhaya Misrani* AIR 1963 Ori 27.
13 Section 29(4), H.M. Act.

CHAPTER
9

The Hindu Marriages (Validation of Proceedings) Act 1960[1]

Introduction

The Hindu Marriages (Validation of Proceedings) Act 1960 was passed with a view to validating certain proceedings under the Hindu Marriage Act 1955. Section 19 of the Hindu Marriage Act has conferred jurisdiction on the "District Court" as defined in s. 3(4) of the said Act to entertain and determine the reliefs sought under the said Act. Section 21 of the Punjab Courts Act 1918 assigns power of the District Judge on the Additional Judge who in discharge of his functions exercises the same powers as a District Judge. In a decision[2] of the Punjab High Court it was held that the court of Additional District Judge could not be regarded as a principal court of civil jurisdiction within the meaning of "District Court" as defined in the Hindu Marriage Act and that a District Judge to whom a petition under the Hindu Marriage Act was presented could not transfer it to an Additional Judge for trial. The Punjab Courts Act 1918 extends to the Union Territory of Delhi by virtue of a notification issued under the Delhi Laws Act 1912 and as a result of the said notification issued by the Delhi Administration and the State Government of the Punjab on 24th August 1959, and 26th January 1960, respectively under s. 3(*b*) of the Hindu Marriage Act 1955, the courts of Additional Judges have now jurisdiction to deal with matters arising under that Act. Legal steps were necessary to validate decrees and orders passed by

---

1 Act XIX of 1960.
2 *Janak Dulari* v *Narayan Das* AIR 1959 Punj 50.

the Additional District Judges before the issue of the above-mentioned notifications and it was also possible that the judgement of the Punjab High Court might also affect decrees and orders, if any, passed under the Hindu Marriage Act 1955. Thus the Hindu Marriages (Validation of Proceedings) Act 1960 has sought to validate all proceeding taken and decrees and orders passed by any of the courts specified in s. 2 of this Act which exercised jurisdiction under the Hindu Marriage Act 1955.[3] This Act extended to the whole of India except the State of Jammu & Kashmir.[4]

Validation of proceedings of certain courts under the Hindu Marriage Act 1955

All proceedings in which decrees and orders passed before the commencement of this Act by any of the following courts exercising jurisdiction under the Hindu Marriage Act shall be deemed to be valid in law as if such jurisdiction had been exercised by a district court: (*i*) the court of an additional judge; (*ii*) additional district judge; (*iii*) joint district judge; (*iv*) assistant district judge; (*v*) assistant judge; and (*vi*) any other court not below the rank of a court of a subordinate judge.[5]

---

3 See Statement of Objects and Reasons for the Bill, Gazette of India, 1960 Extra. Pt. II, s. 2, p. 8.
4 Section 1(2), Hindu Marriages (Validation of Proceedings Act).
5 Section 2, *ibid*.

CHAPTER
10

The Hindu Adoptions and Maintenance Act 1956[1]

Introduction

This Act has been passed to amend and codify the law relating to adoptions and maintenance amongst Hindus.[2] The old law of adoption was mainly based on religious consideration rather than secular one. The Privy Council recognised that the religious motive was the dominant object of adoption secular motive was secondary.[3] This view was also confirmed by the Supreme Court.[4] But this concept of adoption has undergone serious change under the Hindu Adoptions and Maintenance Act 1956. An adoption is to be made after the commencement of this Act in accordance with the provisions contained in Chapter 2 of the Act and any adoption made in contravention of the said provisions shall be void.[5] Besides there are also important changes with regard to (*i*) capacity to adopt;[6] (*ii*) capacity to give in adoption;[7] (*iii*) persons capable of being adopted;[8] (*iv*) conditions of adoption;[9] (*v*) effect of adoption.[10] So far as law of maintenance is

---

1 Act 78 of 1956 as amended by Act 58 of 1960 and Act 45 of 1962.
2 See Preamble to the H.A. & M. Act 1956.
3 *Amarendra* v *Mansing* AIR 1933 PC 155.
4 *V.T.S. Chandrasekhar* v *Kulandaivalu* AIR 1963 SC 185.
5 Section 5, H.A. & M. Act.
6 Sections 7, 8, *ibid*.
7 Section 9, *ibid*.
8 Section 10, *ibid*.
9 Section 11, *ibid*.
10 Section 12, *ibid*.

concerned this Act has brought changes only with regard to (*i*) maintenance of illegitimate child;[11] and (*ii*) maintenance of daughter-in-law.[12]

Applicability of the Act

This Act extends to the whole of India except the State of Jammu and Kashmir.[13] This Act applies to a Hindu as provided in s. 2(1) and (3) of the Act. It will not apply to any member of Scheduled Tribe as described in cl. (25) of Art. 366 of the Constitution of India unless the Central Government by notification directs otherwise.[14] This Act has also no application to the Renoncants of Union Territory of Pondicherry.[15] This Act supersedes the authority of any text, rule or interpretation of Hindu law or any custom or usage in force before the commencement of this Act with regard to any matter for which provision has been made.[16] Besides, any other law in force immediately before the commencement of this Act shall cease to apply to a Hindu if it is inconsistent with the provisions contained in this Act.[17] An adoption is to be regulated only by application of the provisions of Chapter 2 of the Hindu Adoptions and Maintenance Act 1956. An adoption made in contravention of the provisions of this Act shall be void.[18] An adoption which is void shall create no right in favour of the adoptee in the adoptive family, but shall save the right of succession in the family of his or her birth.[19] The expression "by or to a Hindu" appearing in s. 5(1) of the Act has been constructed by the Supreme Court in *Sawan Ram* v *Kalawanti*.[20] The Supreme Court in that case has viewed that by provision of s. 5(1) of the Act an adoption is of two kinds: one is adoption by a Hindu, and the other is an adoption to a Hindu. Where there is no partition of a Hindu joint family and a widow of a coparcener adopts a child according to the provisions of this Act, the effect of such adoption relates back to the death of the coparcener and adoptee is entitled to a share of his late adoptive father.[1]

---

11 Sections 20, 22, *ibid*.
12 Section 21, *ibid*.
13 Section 1(2), H.A. & M. Act.
14 Section 2(2), *ibid*.
15 Section 2(2A), *ibid*.
16 Section 4(*a*), *ibid*.
17 Section 4(*b*), *ibid*.
18 Section 5(1), *ibid*.
19 Section 5(2), *ibid*.
20 AIR 1967 SC 1761.
1 *Babu Ningappa* v *Arunkumar* AIR 1988 Kant 139.

Requisites of valid adoption

The requisites of a valid adoption are: (i) the person adopting has the capacity and right to take adoption; (ii) the person giving in adoption has the capacity to do so; (iii) the person adopted is capable of being taken in adoption; and (iv) the adoption is made in compliance with the other conditions as laid down in Chapter 2 of the Hindu Adoptions and Maintenance Act.[2] All these four conditions are cumulative and each of them must be complied with.[3]

In *Ram Das* v *Gandiabai*[4] it has been held by the Supreme Court that if step-father spent money on up-keep of children and on marriage, it would not mean that step-son was adopted by step-father. In *Smt. Chandan Bilasini (dead) by LRs.* v *Aftabuddin Khan*[5] it has been held that where adoption took place by ceremony of giving and taking the adoption was valid.

(i) *Capacity to adopt.* A person competent to contract has the capacity to adopt a son or a daughter. But if he has a wife living, he shall not adopt except with the consent of his wife unless she has renounced the world or she has ceased to be a Hindu or she has been declared to be of unsound mind by a competent court. If that person has more than one wife living at the time of adoption, the consent of all the wives is necessary unless any one of them is debarred by reason of the proviso stated in the section.[6] Consent of wife to an adoption by husband is a condition precedent. Subsequent consent cannot validate a void adoption. The proviso to s. 7 prescribes that the husband has no right to adopt a child without prior consent of his wife. Thus, an adoption without the consent of the wife is void.[7] Consent of wife need not be directly proved, but can be inferred from circumstances.[8] A female like a male has also capacity to take in adoption provided the following conditions are fulfilled: (a) she is of sound mind; (b) she is not minor; and (c) she is not married, or if married, her marriage has been dissolved or her husband is dead or he has renounced the world completely or ceased to be a Hindu or is declared to be of unsound mind by a competent court.[9] An unmarried woman

---

2 Section 6, H.A. & M. Act.
3 *Dhanraj* v *Suraj Bai* AIR 1978 Raj 7.
4 AIR 1997 SC 1563.
5 AIR 1996 SC 591.
6 Section 7, H.A. & M. Act.
7 *Krishna Chandra Sahu* v *Pradipta Das* AIR 1982 Ori 114.
8 *Mulchand* v *Amrit Bai* ILR (1980) MP 838.
9 Section 8, H.A. & M. Act.

under the provisions of this section can adopt a child even if she has an illegitimate child in existence. Under the old Hindu law she had no capacity to take in adoption.[10] A married woman whose husband is not disqualified as laid down in cl. (c) of s. 8 cannot take in adoption even if her husband consents thereto.[11]

In *Vijaylakshmamma* v *B.T. Shankar*[12] it has been held that after death of a Hindu male having more than one wife, a widow need not obtain permission from co-widow or junior widow in order to carry out an effective adoption for herself and to the deceased husband. Interest of junior or co-widow is protected by proviso (c) to s. 12 of the Act.

In *Kashibai* v *Parwatibai*[13] the Supreme Court has held that where one of two wives of a person taking a child in adoption not only declined to participate in adoption proceedings but also declined to give consent for said adoption, the adoption is hit by s. 7 of the Act and hence is not valid.

In *Rajendra Kumar* v *Kalyan (dead) by LRs.*[14] it has been held that where adoption of a child was taken by a widow to her husband, the Shastric law would apply, since, the Act is silent on this point. Thus, in absence of husband's authority to widow to adopt a child, adoption is invalid.

(ii) *Capacity of person giving in adoption.* No person other than (a) father, or (b) mother, or (c) guardian of a child has capacity to give the child in adoption.[15] Where the father is alive, he is alone competent to give in adoption. But if the mother of the child is alive, the father shall not exercise this right without her consent unless the mother has completely renounced the world or has ceased to be a Hindu or is declared to be of unsound mind by a competent court.[16] Both the "father" and the "mother" would not include "adoptive father" and the "adoptive mother".[17] The mother has also right to give a child in adoption if the father is dead, or has completely renounced the world, or has ceased to be a Hindu, or is declared to be of unsound mind by a competent court.[18] The word "mother" used in this section does not include "step-mother".[19] Where

---

10 *Ashoke* v *Raymond* AIR 1976 Cal 272.
11 *Dashrath* v *Pamdu* (1977)79 Bom LR 426.
12 (2001)4 SCC 558.
13 1995 AIR SCW 4631.
14 AIR 2000 SC 3335.
15 Section 9(1), H.A. & M. Act.
16 Section 9(2), *ibid*, as amended by Act 45 of 1962.
17 Explanation (i) to s. 9, *ibid*.
18 Section 9(3), *ibid*.
19 *Dhanraj* v *Suraj Bai* AIR 1975 SC 1103.

both the father and the mother are dead or have completely renounced the world or have abandoned the child or have been declared to be of unsound mind by a competent court or the parentage of the child is not known, the guardian of the child may give the child in adoption with previous permission of the court to any person including the guardian himself.[20] Before granting any permission to a guardian, the court shall be satisfied that the adoption is for the welfare of the child having regard to the age, and if possible, wishes of the child and in such adoption no payment or reward in consideration has been made or agreed upon except such as the court may direct.[21] The expression "guardian" used in this section would mean (*a*) a person having care of the person of a child or both of his person and property, (*b*) a guardian appointed by the will of the child's father or mother, (*c*) a guardian appointed by a court.[22] The word "court" as used in this section would mean the City Civil Court or a District Court within whose jurisdiction the child to be adopted resides.[23]

(*iii*) *Person to be adopted.* A person cannot be taken in adoption unless the following conditions are fulfilled: (*a*) he or she is a Hindu; (*b*) he or she has not been adopted; (*c*) he or she is not married in absence of any custom contrary thereto; (*d*) he or she has not completed the age of fifteen years in absence of any custom contrary thereto.[24] Among the Jats of Haryana there is an existing custom to adopt a married person and also a person above the age of 15 years. Since such custom is judicially recognised, it need not be proved.[25] Even if there is a custom under which a major can be given in adoption, still it is necessary that he must be given in adoption by his parents or guardian and he cannot of his own go in for adoption although he is an orphan.[1]

(*iv*) *Other conditions for a valid adoption.* In addition to the aforesaid requirements, there are other six conditions to be complied with for a valid adoption.[2] These are: (*a*) if the adoption is of a son, the adoptive

---

20 Section 9(4), *ibid* as amended by Act 45 of 1962.
21 Section 9(5), *ibid*.
22 Explanation to s. 9, *ibid* as amended by Act 45 of 1962.
23 Explanation (*ii*) of s. 9, *ibid*.
24 Section 10, *ibid*.
25 *Amer Singh* v *Tej Ram* AIR 1982 Punj 282. See *Gangadhar* v *SLD Tribunal* AIR 1991 SC 1180. (Once the custom permits adoption of child of any age prevailing in Bombay State and it is judicially recognised, it need not be proved in subsequent cases.)
1 *Dhanraj* v *Suraj Bai* AIR 1975 SC 1103.
2 Section 11, H.A. & M. Act.

father or mother by whom the adoption is made must not have a Hindu son, son's son or son's son's son, whether legitimate or adoptive, living at the time of adoption; (b) if the adoption is of a daughter, the adoptive father or mother by whom the adoption is made must not have a Hindu daughter or son's daughter, legitimate or illegitimate, living at the time of adoption; (c) if the adoption is by a male and the person to be adopted is a female, the adoptive father must be older than the adoptive daughter by at least twenty one years; (d) if the adoption is by a female and the person to be adopted is a male, the adoptive mother must be older than the adoptive son by at least twenty one years; (e) the same child cannot be adopted simultaneously by two or more persons; (f) the child to be adopted must be actually given and taken in adoption by the parents or guardian concerned with intent to transfer the child from the family of its birth or from a place where it is brought up to the family of its adoption. But the performance of *datta homam* shall not be essential to the validity of an adoption.

In *Sawan Ram* v *Kalawanti*[3] it has been held by the Supreme Court that an adoption by a married woman or a widow is an adoption not only to herself but also to her husband or the deceased husband, as the case may be. The Act has not provided any substitute for actual physical delivery of the child to the adoptive father or mother.[4] Where an adoption ceremony is observed and the giving and taking takes place, there cannot be any other intention rather than intention to transfer.[5] In an inter-country adoption primary consideration of a court would be the welfare of the child.[6] Motive of adoption is not relevant for considering the validity of adoption.[7] Performance of *datta homam* is necessary in some cases but not in the case of twice-born classes when adopted boy belongs to same *gotra* as the adoptive father.[8] In *Chandan* v *Aftabuddin*[9] it was held that entire evidence on record showed that adoption took place by ceremony of giving and taking. Thus, adoption was valid. In *Ram Das* v *Gandiabai*[10] it has been held by the Supreme Court that adoption was not finally established on record.

3   AIR 1967 SC 1761.
4   See *Kashinath* v *Mahadeo* AIR 1977 Pat 199.
5   *Kartar Singh* v *Surjan Singh* AIR 1974 SC 2161.
6   *Jayantilal* v *Asha* AIR 1989 Guj 152.
7   *Devgonda* v *S.R. Patil* AIR 1992 Bom 189.
8   *Madhusudan Das* v *Narayani Bai* AIR 1983 SC 114.
9   AIR 1996 SC 591.
10 AIR 1997 SC 1563.

Effect of adoption

An adopted child is deemed to be the child of its adoptive parents for all purposes from the date of adoption and ceases all ties in the family of its birth.[11] There are three limitations in this regard. These are: (*a*) the adopted child cannot marry any person whom he or she could not have done if he or she continued in the family of his or her birth; (*b*) any property which is vested in the adopted child before the adoption shall continue to belong to adoptee subject to any obligation attached thereto; (*c*) the adopted child shall not divest any person of any estate which vested in him or her before the adoption.[12] A person from Juleha caste which is a Scheduled caste adopted a child of Jat family. It was held that the adopted son was entitled to all the benefits available to that caste.[13] In *Rajendra Kumar* v *Kalyan*[14] adoption of son by a Hindu widow in 1967 after death of her husband was taken. Findings in previous suit to which widow was a party would operate as *res judicata* in a subsequent suit by her adopted son. In absence of any provision to the contrary it can be inferred from the provisions of ss. 12 and 13 of the Act that the adopted child would be the son of the widow and her deceased husband.[15] Subject to any agreement to the contrary an adoption does not deprive the adoptive father or mother of the power of transfer of his or her property *inter vivos* or by will.[16] Even in absence of s. 13 expressly protecting the right to property to the adoptive father or mother, this right would not be affected by an adoption.[17] Where an adoptee was a minor, an arrangement was made whereby the widow of the adoptive father had to enjoy his property during her life time. It was held that such arrangement was valid by custom.[18] In *Chiranjilal Srilal Goenka* v *Jasjit Singh*[19] it has been held by the Supreme Court that right of adoptive parent to dispose property by will is limited by agreement between parties in respect of adoption. Offer letter not reflecting any agreement but was a unilateral offer giving child

---

11 Section 12, H.A. & M. Act.
12 Proviso to s. 12, *ibid.*
13 *Khazan Singh* v *Union of India* AIR 1980 Del 60; *Tarabai* v *Balegonda* AIR 1981 Bom 18.
14 AIR 2000 SC 3335.
15 *Subash Misir* v *Thagair Misir* AIR 1967 All 148. But see also for contrary view, *Arumugha* v *Valliammal* AIR 1969 Mad 72.
16 Section 13, H.A. & M. Act.
17 *Tara Chand* v *Ram Avtar* AIR 1975 Punj 20; see also *Banabai* v *Wasudeo* AIR 1979 Bom 181.
18 *Krishnamurthi* v *Krishnamurthi* AIR 1927 PC 139.
19 AIR 2001 SC 266.

on adoption. Thus it does not restrain adoptive father to execute a will. A Hindu wife after adoption is deemed to be the adoptive mother.[20] Where there are more than one wife living at the time of adoption, the seniormost wife will be deemed to be the adoptive mother, and the others to be a step-mothers.[21] Similarly where a widower or a bachelor adopts a child and marries subsequently, that wife will be deemed to be step-mother.[22] Similarly where a widow or unmarried woman adopts a child and marries subsequently, her husband will be regarded as the step-father of the child.[23] An adoption which is made in accordance with the provisions of this Act cannot be cancelled either by the adoptive father or mother or the adopted child, nor can he or she return to the family of his or her birth.[24] Section 15 of the Act is prospective in its operation and applies to adoption after the commencement of the Act. An adoption which had taken place prior to the commencement of this Act which was revocable by custom can be revoked after the commencement of the Act.[1] Whenever a registered document is produced before the court showing the record that the adoption made was signed by both the giver and taker of child in adoption, the court shall presume that the adoption was made in compliance with the provisions of this Act unless and until it is disproved.[2] This presumption cannot be drawn when there are more than one document relating to adoption.[3] No presemption would arise where the deed of adoption was signed by the person taking in adoption and not by the person giving in adoption for any reason whatsoever.[4] The presumption drawn under s. 16 is rebuttable presumption.[5] Where there was no ceremony for giving and taking of the child in adoption the presumption under this section would stand rebutted.[6] No presumption can be drawn where the guardian of an orphan child signed the document of adoption without obtaining prior permission of the court as required under s. 9 of the Act.[7] Section 16 lays down a rule of evidence and there

---

20 Section 14(1), H.A. & M. Act.
21 Section 14(2), *ibid.*
22 Section 14(3), *ibid.*
23 Section 14(4), *ibid.*
24 Section 15, *ibid.*
1   *Damiraiji* v *Chandraprabha* AIR 1975 SC 784.
2   Section 16, H.A. & M. Act.
3   *Aftabuddin* v *Chandan Balasint* AIR 1977 Ori 69.
4   *Rammi* v *Dy. Director* 1981 All WC 204; *Mahadeo* v *Bainabai* AIR 1975 Kant 79; *Krishnachandra Sahu* v *Prodipta Das* AIR 1982 Ori 114.
5   *Mahan Singh* v *Sham Kaur* AIR 1973 P&H 122.
6   *Kunja Bihari* v *Purshottam* (1977)2 Cut WR 863.
7   *Parmeshwar* v *Jagmohan* (1976)2 Cut WR 811.

is no necessity of a registered deed to prove adoption.[8] The presumption cannot arise in relation to adoption taking place prior to the commencement of this Act.[9] The onus of invalidity of a document lies on the person challenging it.[10] Where factum of adoption was not proved either by registered document, or examination of the priest present at the ceremony or evidence of change of name or evidence of any neighbour showing that the child was living with adoptive mother, dismissal of a suit by trial court was proper.[11]

In *Lal Man* v *Dy. Director of Consolidation*[12] it has been held that where the High Court was satisfied on the basis of evidence that in fact there was no valid adoption, the Supreme declines to interfere with such findings of the High Court.

In *M. Muthiah* v *Controller of E.D. Madras*,[13] it has been held that where according to custom prevailing among Nattukottai of Tamil Nadu an adopted son does not lose interest in joint family property of his natural birth and agreement to that effect being produced, the adopted son was entitled to share in such property. In *D.S. Agalawe* v *P.M. Agalawe*,[14] a joint family consisted of two brothers one of whom died and consequently the property passed into the hands of a sole surviving coparcener. The widow of the deceased brother adopted a child after coming into force this Act. Adopted son and widow, it has been held by the Supreme Court, are entitled to file a suit for partition against the surviving brother, as proviso to s. 12 is not a bar. No question of divesting the sole coparcener of his estate is involved. By virtue of proviso (c) to this section upon adoption of a child by a brother's widow, shares of other members of joint family get decreased. They are not divested of any estate vested in them. The said proviso does not preclude adopted child from claiming his share. To interpret the said proviso to include cases of devolution by survivorship on death of member of joint family, would be to deny and practical effect to adoption made by widow of such member.[15]

---

8   *Triloke Nath* v *Principal Medical College* ILR (1973) HP 1999.
9   *Ranjit* v *Nilambar* AIR 1978 Ori 48; *Shamser Singh* v *Dy. Custodian General* AIR 1973 J&K 89 (FB).
10 *Sushil Chandra* v *Bhoop Kunwar* AIR 1977 All 441; *Krishnabai* v *Ananda* AIR 1981 Bom 240.
11 *Rahasa* v *Gokulanada* AIR 1987 SC 962.
12 (1998)8 SCC 693.
13 AIR 1986 SC 1863.
14 AIR 1988 SC 845.
15 *Vasant* v *Daltu* AIR 1987 SC 398.

A sole surviving coparcener is entitled to dispose of coparcenary property as if it was his separate property. But if he takes in adoption, he ceases to be sole surviving coparcener and is not entitled to deal with joint family property as his separate property.[16] In *Dinaji* v *Daddi*,[17] it has been held that adopted son is entitled to his rights only after the death of adoptive mother. She may, however, relinquish her property in favour of her adopted son by an agreement.

Prohibition of certain payments

No person shall receive or agree to receive any payment or other consideration for the adoption of any person. Similarly, no person shall make or give or agree to make or give any person any payment or reward, the receipt of which is prohibited.[18] If any person contravenes such prohibition, he shall be punishable with imprisonment for a term not exceeding six months or with fine or with both.[19] But no prosecution for such offence can be initiated without prior sanction of the State Government or an Officer authorised by the State Government in this behalf.[20] This section upholds the principle of public policy to the effect that there may not be any trafficking in children.[21]

In *Jupudi Venkata Vijaya Bhaskar* v *Jupudi Kesava Rao*[1] an ante-adoption agreement was entered into between plaintiff-adopted son and adoptive parents that he will not set up any claim with regard to certain properties of adoptive father. Such ante-adoption agreement is valid. It does not amount to reward in consideration of adoption. It is also not hit by s. 17 of the Act.

Maintenance of wife

A Hindu wife is entitled to maintenance from her husband during her life time.[2] This provision applies to a woman who is legally married and not to a woman whose marriage is void.[3] There are conflicting views of

---

16 *Jupudi Venkata Vijaya Bhaskar* v *Jupudi Kesava Rao* AIR 1994 AP 134.
17 AIR 1990 SC 1153.
18 Section 17(1), H.A. & M. Act.
19 Section 17(2), *ibid*.
20 Section 17(3), *ibid*.
21 *Commr. of Gift Tax (Andhra Pradesh)* v *Gollapadi* 1978 Tax LR 2006.
1 AIR 2003 SC 3314.
2 Section 18(1), H.A. & M. Act.
3 *Narayanswami* v *Padmanabham* AIR 1966 Mad 394. But see also *Chaira Obula* v *Caova Pedda* AIR 1976 AP 43 (second wife whose marriage in void is also entitled to maintenance).

different High Courts as to whether interim maintenance can be granted to wife under s. 18 of the Act. The High Courts of Calcutta,[4] Orissa,[5] Andhra Pradesh[6] have held that a court has no power to grant interim maintenance under s. 18 of the Act. On the other hand, the High Courts of Madras,[7] Patna[8] and Delhi[9] have held that the court has power to grant interim maintenance. It is to be noted that under s. 18(1) a Hindu wife is entitled to maintenance *proprio vigore*, that is without filing any petition for divorce, judicial separation or restitution of conjugal rights, whereas s. 25 of the Hindu Marriage Act does not confer such right on a wife.[10] In *Rajathi* v *C. Ganesan*[11] it has been held that under s. 18 of the Hindu Adoptions and Maintenance Act 1956 a Hindu wife whether married before or after the commencement of this Act, shall be entitled to be maintained by her husband during her life-time even while considering the petition under s. 125, Cr PC.

A Hindu wife without forfeiting her right of maintenance is also entitled to live separately from her husband on any of the following grounds:[12]

(a) if the husband is guilty of desertion, that is to say, of abandoning her without reasonable cause and without her consent or against her wish or of wilfully neglecting her;

(b) if the husband has treated her with such cruelty as to cause reasonable apprehension in her mind that it will be harmful or injurious to live with him;

(c) if the husband has been suffering from a virulent form of leprosy;

(d) if the husband has any other wife living;

(e) if the husband keeps a concubine in the same house in which the wife is living or he habitually resides with a concubine elsewhere;

(f) if the husband has ceased to be a Hindu by conversion to another religion;

(g) if there is any other cause justifying her living separately.

---

4 *Tarini Gupta* v *Gouri Gupta* AIR 1968 Cal 567.
5 *Ramchandra* v *Snehalate* AIR 1977 Ori 96.
6 *G. Apparna* v *G. Seethamma* AIR 1972 AP 62.
7 *D. Udayar* v *Rajarani Ammal* AIR 1973 Mad 369.
8 *Baliram* v *Radhika* AIR 1980 Pat 67.
9 *Gian Devi* v *Amar Nath* ILR (1975)1 Del 811.
10 *Govindrao* v *Anandibai* AIR 1978 Bom 433.
11 AIR 1999 SC 2374.
12 Section 18(2), H.A. & M. Act.

But the wife shall forfeit her right of separate residence and maintenance by her husband if (*i*) she is unchaste, or (*ii*) ceases to be a Hindu by conversion to another religion.[13]

In *Vimalben Ajitbhai Patel* v *Vatslaben Ashokbhai Patel*,[14] it has been held by the Supreme Court that ss. 18 and 19 of the Hindu Adoptions and Maintenance Act 1956 prescribe the statutory liabilities in regard to maintenance of wife by her husband and only on his death upon the father-in-law. Mother-in-law, thus, cannot be fastened with any legal liability to maintain her daughter-in-law from her own property or otherwise.

Like the Hindu Marriage Act, the Hindu Adoptions and Maintenance Act has not provided any special form for enforcement of the right of maintenance. Thus, the remedy would be by way of a suit under the Code of Civil Procedure.[15] Right of Hindu wife for maintenance can be enforced by a civil suit under s. 9 of CPC but not under this Act. In the absence of express provisions in any law or under CPC for grant of interim maintenance, it can be granted under s. 151, CPC. Denial of matrimonial relationship is no ground to refuse interim maintenance.[16] Land obtained by a Hindu widow in lieu of maintenance becomes her absolute property under s. 14(1) and (2) of the Hindu Succession Act.[17]

Maintenance of widowed daughter-in-law

A Hindu widowed daughter-in-law is entitled to maintenance by her father-in-law provided and to the extent that she is unable to maintain herself (*i*) out of her own earnings or other property, or (*ii*) where she has no property of her own, is unable to obtain maintenance (*a*) from the estate of her husband or her father or mother, or (*b*) from her son or daughter, if any, or his or her estate.[18] Widowed daughter-in-law is a dependent[19] and is entitled to maintenance under certain circumstances.[20] The expression "maintenance" includes provision for food, clothing, residence, education, medical attendance and treatment.[1] Where the

---

13 Section 18(3), *ibid*.
14 AIR 2008 SC 2675.
15 See *Kishanlal* v *Sudershan* (1978)80 Punj LR 147; *Themmanani* v *Ammannamma* (1971)1 Andh LT 233.
16 *Khadal Penthi* v *Hulash Dei* AIR 1989 Ori 137 (FB).
17 *Gulwant Kaur* v *Mohinder Singh* AIR 1987 SC 2251.
18 Section 19(1), H.A. & M. Act.
19 Section 21(*vii*), *ibid*.
20 *Jal Kaur* v *Pala Singh* AIR 1961 Punj 391.
1 Section 3(*b*)(*i*), H.A. & M. Act.

father-in-law has no means to maintain his widowed daughter-in-law from any coparcenary property in his possession out of which the daughter-in-law has not obtained any share, this obligation of the father-in-law cannot be enforced. Besides, such obligation shall cease on the re-marriage of the daughter-in-law.[2] The father-in-law's liability to maintain his daughter-in-law confines to income of coparcenary property received and owned by him.[3] The expression "coparcenary property" appearing in s. 19(2) does not mean coparcenary property as understood in the Mitakshara Law, but it would mean any ancestral property as the expression understood in the Punjab customary law.[4] The Calcutta High Court[5] has held that sub-sec. (2) of s. 19 has no application to the parties belonging to the Dayabhaga School of law. But s. 19(1) applies to parties belonging to both the Dayabhaga and the Mitakshara Schools of law. The quantum of liability of the father-in-law depends on his means to earn from any coparcenary property in his possession under the proviso to the section.[6] But the obligation to maintain the daughter-in-law comes to an end on her remarriage.[7]

In *Balwant Kaur* v *Chanan Singh*[8] it has been held that in view of the provisions of s. 19 of the Hindu Adoptions and Maintenance Act 1956 read with s. 14 of the Hindu Succession Act 1956 the destitute widowed daughter has pre-existing right of maintenance in her favour *qua* the estate of the testator and it is this right which though circumscribed as life interest in the Will.

Maintenance of children and aged parents

A Hindu is under obligation during his or her life-time to maintain his or her legitimate or illegitimate children and his or her aged or infirm parents.[9] This obligation of a Hindu is personal and irrespective of the father or mother holding any property.[10] Maintenance in the case of an unmarried daughter includes the reasonable expenses of and incidental

---

2 Section 19(2), *ibid*.
3 *Jal Kaur* v *Pala Singh* AIR 1961 Punj 391.
4 *Angat Singh* v *Dhan Kaur* AIR 1964 Punj 393; *Gurdip Kaur* v *Chamand Singh* AIR 1965 Punj 238 (FB).
5 *Kanailal* v *Puspa Ram* AIR 1979 Cal 172.
6 *Animuthu* v *Gandhi Ammal* AIR 1977 Mad 372.
7 *Animuthu* v *Gandhi Ammal* AIR 1977 Mad 372.
8 AIR 2000 SC 1908.
9 Section 20(1), H.A. & M. Act.
10 *Chandra Kishore* v *Nank Chand* AIR 1975 Del 175.

to her marriage.[11] Maintenance and marriage expenses for the daughter are the legal obligation of the father and as such any property given to her at the time of marriage cannot be termed as a gift.[12] An illegitimate daughter who could not claim maintenance before the commencement of the Act can now claim maintenance under this Act but not for a period prior to the Act.[13] A legitimate or illegitimate child may claim maintenance from his or her father or mother as long as the child remains minor.[14] The obligation to maintain a person's aged or infirm parents or a daughter who is unmarried extends in so far as any of them is unable to maintain himself or herself out of his or her own earnings or other property.[15] The word "Parent" includes a childless step-mother.[16] The right of an infirm mother to be maintained by sons does not entitle her to live in the house of her sons' families.[17]

Though there is no express provision to grant interim maintenance by court, yet it appears to be implied.[18] If the person obliged to maintain has property, the court has power to create charge on the said property.[19] An obligation to maintain an unmarried daughter includes an obligation to provide for expenses of her marriage, irrespective of any property.[20]

Nine classes of dependants for maintenance

There are nine classes of "dependants" for the purposes of Chapter 3 of the Act which deals with maintenance. They are as follows:

(*i*) his or her father;

(*ii*) his or her mother;

(*iii*) his widow so long as she does not remarry;

---

11 Section 3(*b*)(*ii*), H.A. & M. Act.
12 *R. Seethramamma* v *L.A. Collector* (1079)2 Andh LT 6; see also *Bhuboneshwar* v *Special Tahasildar* AIR 1980 AP 139.
13 *Mukta Bai* v *Kamalaksha* AIR 1960 Mys 182.
14 Section 20(2), H.A. & M. Act; see *Adam* v *Gopal* AIR 1974 Mad 232.
15 Section 20(3), H.A. & M. Act.
16 Explanation to s. 20, *ibid*.
17 *Anandi* v *Nirmala* AIR 2000 SC 1386.
18 See *Jyoti Prasad* v *Chameli* AIR 1975 Cal 260; *Chandra Kishore* v *Nanak Chand* AIR 1975 Del 175; *D. Udayar* v *Rajarani* AIR 1973 Mad 369; *Inder Mal* v *Babu Lal* AIR 1977 Raj 160.
19 *Alluri Balas* v *Alluri Varalakshmi* AIR 1976 AP 365.
20 *Chandra Kishore* v *Nanak Chand* AIR 1975 Del 175. See *Sneh Prabha* v *Ravinder Kumar* AIR 1995 SC 2170 (daughters are entitled to more financial assistance at the time of their marriage).

(iv) his or her son, son of his predeceased son, grand son of predeceased son of his predeceased son, so long as he is minor provided none is able to obtain maintenance from the estate of his father or mother's estate in case of a grand son and from the estate of his father or mother or father's father or father's mother in case of a great grand-son;

(v) his or her unmarried daughter or the unmarried daughter of his predeceased son or the unmarried daughter of a predeceased son of his predeceased son, as long as she remains unmarried: provided that she is unable to obtain maintenance in the case of a grand-daughter from her father's or mother's estate and in the case of a great grand-daughter from the estate of her father or mother or father's father or father's mother;

(vi) his widowed daughter provided she is unable to obtain maintenance—(a) from the estate of her husband; or (b) from her son or daughter, if any, or his or her estate; or (c) from her father-in-law or his father or the estate of either of them;

(vii) any widow of his son or of a son of his predeceased son, as long as she does not remarry, provided that she is unable to obtain maintenance from her husband's estate, or from her son or daughter, if any, or his or her estate, in the case of a grand-son's widow, also from her father-in-law's estate;

(viii) his or her minor illegitimate son, as long as he is minor;

(ix) his or her illegitimate daughter, as long as who remains unmarried.[1]

Maintenance of dependants

The heirs of a deceased Hindu are bound to maintain the dependants of the deceased out of the estate inherited by them from the deceased.[2] The word "estate" is to be construed as interest which anyone has in lands or in any other subject of the property, whether such property is heritable under general law or any special or local law.[3] A brother is not bound to maintain his sister if he has not inherited any property from his father. If a brother incurs expenses for marriage of his sister that does not mean that other brothers are required to contribute to such expenses.[4] Where a

---

1 Section 21, H.A. & M. Act.
2 Section 22(1), *ibid.*
3 *Ram Narain* v *Naraini Devi* 1980 All LJ 842.
4 *Chellaiyan* v *Sathia Krishnan* AIR 1982 Mad 148.

dependant has not obtained, by testamentary or intestate succession, any share in the estate of a Hindu, dying after the Act, the dependant shall be entitled to maintenance from those who take the estate.[5] Where a Hindu after bequeathing all his estate to his son died intestate, the son is bound to maintain the widow as a dependant.[6] A daughter who got a share in the estate of her father who died intestate was not entitled to claim any additional provision for her marriage expenses from the coparceners.[7] The liability of a person who takes the estate shall be in proportion to the value of the share or part of the estate taken by him or her.[8] But no person shall be liable to contribute to the maintenance of others if he or she, himself or herself, is dependant though he or she has obtained a share or part of the value of the deceased.[9] The combined effect of ss. 21 and 22 of the Act is that only the dependants mentioned in s. 21 dying after the commencement of the Act and who have not obtained any share in the estate of such person have a right of maintenance.[10]

Quantum of maintenance

The award of maintenance is the discretion of court which the court determines with reference to special consideration in some cases and to general consideration in other cases.[11] In determining the quantum of maintenance, specially for wife, children or aged or infirm parents the court shall consider (*a*) the position and status of parties; (*b*) the reasonable wants of the claimant; (*c*) if the claimant is living separately, whether there is any justification in doing so; (*d*) the value of the claimant's property and any income derived therefrom or from the claimant's own earnings, or from any other source; (*e*) the number of persons entitled to maintenance under this Act.[12] Generally in determining the amount of maintenance in other cases the court shall consider the following; (*a*) the net value of the estate of the deceased after providing for the payment of his debts; (*b*) the provision, if any, made under a will of the deceased in respect of the dependants; (*c*) the degree of relationship between the two; (*d*) the reasonable wants of the dependant; (*e*) the past relation between the dependant and the deceased; (*f*) the value of the property of the dependant

---

5 Section 22(2), H.A. & M. Act.
6 *Gulzar* v *Tej Kaur* AIR 1961 Punj 288.
7 *Karuppana* v *Nachanmal* AIR 1974 Mad 329. See also *Jailal* v *Dulari* 1976 All LJ 641.
8 Section 22(3), H.A. & M. Act.
9 Section 22(4), *ibid.*
10 *Ramamoorthy* v *Sitharamamma* AIR 1961 AP 131 (FB).
11 Section 23(1), H.A. & M. Act.
12 Section 23(2), *ibid.*

and any income derived therefrom; or from his or her earnings, or from any other source; (g) the number of dependants entitled to maintenance under this Act.[13] Determination of maintenance is not a matter of mathematical certainty, but it is fixed judiciously by the court after taking all the factors into account.[14] The quantum of maintenance depends upon gathering together of all the facts of the situation, the amount of free estate, the past life of the married parties, and the families, a survey of the conditions and necessities and rights of the members on a reasonable view of change or circumstances possibly required in the future, regard being had to the scale and mode of living and to the age-habits, wants and class of life of the parties. Section 23(2) has not departed from these principles as enunciated in *Ekradeshwari* v *Homeshawar*[15] except to a limited extent envisaged in sub-cls. (d) and (e) of sub-sec. (2) of s. 23.[16] If the claimant has separate property, it will not disqualify her to claim maintenance, but this factor will be taken into account while determining the amount of maintenance.[17] Section 23 is not retrospective and as such no claim arising prior to the Act can be considered for determining maintenance.[18] The claimant to maintenance must be a Hindu.[19] The amount of maintenance fixed by a decree of court or by agreement made either before or after this Act may be altered subsequently if there is a material change in the circumstances justifying such alteration.[20] Where a decree for maintenance does not contain any provision for making an application by either party for increase or reduction, the party desiring to have the quantum of maintenance varied must file a suit and not an application.[1] Abnormal rise in cost of living would be a ground for increasing maintenance.[2]

Miscellaneous

(a) *Charge of maintenance.* A dependant's claim for maintenance shall not be a charge on the estate of the deceased or any portion thereof, unless

---

13 Section 23(3), *ibid*.
14 *Satyanarayanamurthi* v *Jaggamma* AIR 1962 AP 439.
15 AIR 1929 PC 128.
16 *Kulbhushan* v *Raj Kumari* AIR 1971 SC 234.
17 *Dugginal Lakshmana* v *D. Katamma* AIR 1973 AP 302.
18 *Vidyadhar Rao* v *Lalita Devamma* AIR 1974 AP 38.
19 Section 24, H.A. & M. Act.
20 Section 25, *ibid*. See also *Kamesharamma* v *S. Subramanyam* AIR 1959 AP 269.
 1 *Binda Prasad* v *Mudrika Devi* AIR 1968 Pat 196; see also *Rangamma* v *Venkatarajuly* AIR 1966 Mad 428.
 2 *Indirabai* v *B.P. Patel* AIR 1974 AP 303.

one has been created (*i*) by the will of the deceased; (*ii*) by the decree of court; (*iii*) by agreement between the dependant and the owner of the estate or portion, or (*iv*) otherwise.[3] In a suit by wife for maintenance, the wife was entitled to claim a charge under s. 39 of the Transfer of Property Act and this right was not taken away by s. 27 of the Hindu Adoptions and Maintenance Act.[4] Section 27 of the said Act empowers the court to create a charge for maintenance on the property, but the court cannot grant possession of any property in lieu of maintenance.[5]

(*b*) *Priority of debts*. Subject to the provisions of charge as contained in s. 27 of the Act debts of every description contracted or payable by the deceased shall have priority over the claims of the dependants for maintenance under this Act.[6]

(*c*) *Effect of transfer of property on right of maintenance*. Where a dependant has a right to receive maintenance out of an estate and such estate or any part thereof is transferred, the right to receive maintenance may be enforced against the transferee provided the transferee has notice of such right of maintenance out of the concerned estate or if the transfer is gratuitous, but not against the transferee who has received the property for consideration and without notice of the right of maintenance.[7] The provisions of s. 28 of the Hindu Adoptions and Maintenance Act are similar to those in s. 39 of the Transfer of Property Act 1882.[8] If the transferee has notice of claim of maintenance and he gets the property, the claim can be enforced against the estate even if the transfer is for valuable consideration, or where the transfer is gratuitous, the claim for maintenance can be enforced against the estate though the transferee has no notice of such claim.[9] A wife, not being dependant, cannot enforce her right of maintenance by way of charge on her husband's property under

---

3 Section 27, H.A. & M. Act.
4 *K.M.S. Rudrappa* v *Basamma* AIR 1962 Mys 207.
5 *Bhogo* v *Bachai* AIR 1972 Punj 160.
6 Section 26, H.A. & M. Act.
7 Section 28, *ibid*.
8 Section 39 of the Transfer of Property Act reads as follows:
"Where a third person has a right to receive maintenance, or a provision for advancement or marriage, from the profits of immovable property, and such property is transferred the right may be enforced against the transferee, if he has notice thereof or if the transfer is gratuitous; but not against a transferee for consideration and without notice of the right, nor against such property in his hands."
9 *Kapur Kaur* v *Kishan Singh* AIR 1970 Punj 270.

this section, but she is entitled to claim a charge under s. 39 of the Transfer of Property Act.[10] Section 28 of the Act has no application to a transfer made by the father-in-law of his separate property either gratuitously or otherwise even if he is under legal obligation to maintain his widowed daughter-in-law.[11] This section applies to transfer *inter vivos* and not to a bequest or legacy.[12]

(*d*) *Saving of adoption*. The provision of this Act shall not affect any adoption made before the commencement of this Act and the validity and effect of such adoption shall be determined as if this Act had not been passed.[13] This section saves only the validity and affect of adoption made prior to the Act, and not the revocability or illegality of adoption.[14]

---

10 *Raghavan* v *Nagammal* AIR 1979 Mad 200.
11 *Parul* v *Bangshidhar* AIR 1971 Cal 270.
12 *Adiraju* v *A.S. Murthy* (1979)2 Andh LT 85.
13 Section 30, H.A. & M. Act.
14 See *Dhaniraiji* v *Chandraprabha* AIR 1975 SC 784.

CHAPTER
11

The Hindu Minority and Guardianship Act 1956[1]

Objects of the Hindu Minority and Guardianship Act 1956

This Act was passed to amend and codify certain parts of law relating to minority and guardianship among Hindus.[2] Prior to this Act the law relating to minority and guardianship to govern a Hindu is to be found in the old Hindu law and the Guardians and Wards Act 1890[3] and the Indian Majority Act 1875.[4] Apart from the provisions of the 1956 Act, any other residuary matters for which specific provisions are to be found in the earlier two Act may be referred to.

Principal changes introduced in the 1956 Act

Unlike the old law the Hindu Minority and Guardianship Act does not recognise any other person as natural guardian of a minor as provided in s. 6 of the Act. Under the old law the father was not only the natural guardian of his children, but also preferred to the their mother in respect of their custody. Under the 1956 Act the mother will have ordinarily the right of custody of her child who has not completed the age of five years.[5] Unlike the old law the Act does not recognise a person who has ceased to be a Hindu or who has finally and completely renounced the world as a natural guardian of a minor child.[6] The Act restricts the power of a

---

1 Act 32 of 1956.
2 See Preamble to H.M. & G. Act.
3 Act 8 of 1890.
4 Act 9 of 1875.
5 Section 6(*a*), H.M. & G. Act.
6 Section 6, Proviso, *ibid*.

natural guardian to alienate the property of a minor even for legal necessity without prior permission of the court.[7] Under the 1956 Act a widow is entitled to appoint a testamentary guardian of her children[8] which she could not do under the old Act. Under old Hindu law, a minor could be the natural guardian of his minor wife or child, but under the 1956 Act, a minor is incompetent to act as the natural guardian or a guardian of the property of any minor.[9] Under the old law a *de facto* guardian had power to alienate the property of a minor for legal necessity, but a *de facto* guardian under the 1956 Act is not entitled to dispose of or deal with the property of a Hindu minor.[10]

Applicability of Hindu Minority and Guardianship Act

This Act applies to the whole of India except the State of Jammu and Kashmir. This Act also applies to all Hindus who are domiciled in a territory to which this Act extends, but they are living outside for the time-being.[11] There must exist two elements to determine domicile of a person: first the residence of a person of a particular kind, and secondly, the intention of a particular kind. In other words, there must be present both the *factum* and the *animus*.[12] The territories of the State of Jammu and Kashmir are excluded from the purview of this Act by virtue of Art. 370 of the Constitution of India and the Constitution (Application to Jammu and Kashmir) Order 1954. The provisions of this Act shall apply in addition to and not, except as expressly provided in this Act in derogation of the Guardians and Wards Act 1890.[13] Thus, this Act in effect supplement the Guardians and Wards Act 1890. This Act applies (*a*) to any person who is a Hindu by religion; (*b*) to any person who is a Buddhist, Jaina or Sikh by religion; and (*c*) to any other person domiciled in the territories to which this Act extends, but who is not a Muslim, Christian, Parsi or Jew by religion.[14] The following persons are Hindus by religion: (*i*) Any child, legitimate or illegitimate, both of whose parents are Hindus; (*ii*) Any child, legitimate or illegitimate, one of whose parents is a Hindu and who is brought up as a member of the tribe, community,

---

7 Section 8, *ibid*.
8 Section 9(3), *ibid*.
9 Section 10, *ibid*.
10 Section 11, *ibid*.
11 Section 1(2), *ibid*.
12 See *Central Bank of India* v *Ram Narain* AIR 1955 SC 36; *State of Bombay* v *Narayandas* AIR 1958 Bom 68 (FB).
13 Section 2, H.M. & G. Act.
14 Section 3(1), *ibid*.

group or family to which such parent belongs; and (*iii*) any person who is a convert or reconvert to the Hindu.[15] The expression "Hindu" used in this Act shall be construed as if included a person who though not a Hindu by religion, is nevertheless a person to whom this Act applies by virtue of the provisions contained in s. 3.[16] This Act shall not apply to (1) the members of any Scheduled Tribes within the meaning of cl. (25) of Art. 366 of the Constitution of India unless the Central Government, by notification in the Official Gazette directs otherwise.[17] (2) the Renoncants of the Union Territory of Pondicherry.[18] This Act overrides any text, rule or law that was in force immediately before the commencement of this Act which is inconsistent with any of provisions contained in this Act.[19] There is no inconsistency between the provisions of ss. 7 and 17 of the Guardians and Wards Act 1890 and s. 13 of the Hindu Minority and Guardianship Act 1956, but in case of any conflict between the provisions of the former Act and those of 1956 Act the latter would prevail over the former.[20] Section 6(*a*) of the H.M. & G. Act was held to override s. 15 of the Madras Marumakkattayam Act 1952.[1] There is apparent conflict between the Indian Majority Act and the Hindu Minority and Guardianship Act with regard to attainment of majority. The latter Act has fixed the age of majority at 18 years, but the former Act extended the period of majority beyond 18 years when a court appoints a guardian for a minor. It was held that there was no conflict between the provisions of the said two Acts and by virtue of s. 2 of the H.M. & G. Act, the said two Acts are to be read together and construed that they are complementary to each other. Thus, for the purpose of appointment of a guardian one is required to look to the Guardians and Wards Act read with the Indian Majority Act.[2]

Natural guardian of a Hindu minor[3]

A natural guardian means a guardian mentioned in s. 6 of the H.M. & G. Act. Section 6 lays down the question of natural guardian may arise in three types of cases. In case of a boy or an unmarried girl the natural guardian is the father and after him is the mother provided the custody

---

15 Section 3(1) Explanation, H.M. & G. Act.
16 Section 3(3), *ibid*.
17 Section 3(2), *ibid*.
18 Section 3(2A), *ibid* as inserted by the Pondicherry (Extension of Laws) Act 1968.
19 Section 5, H.M. & G. Act.
20 *Kusa Parida* v *Baishnab* AIR 1966 Ori 60.
1 *Raghavan Nair* v *Lakshmikutty* AIR 1961 Ker 193.
2 See *V.N. Swaminathan* v *Angayar Kanni Ammal* AIR 1964 Mad 11.
3 Section 6, H.M. & G. Act.

of a minor upto the age of five years shall ordinarily be with the mother.[4] In case of illegitimate boy or an illegitimate unmarried girl, the natural guardian is the mother and after her the father.[5] In case of a married girl, the natural guardian is the husband.[6] The natural guardian of a Hindu minor has control in respect of minor's person as well as minor's property, but such property shall not include minor's undivided interest in joint family property. A person is not entitled to act as a natural guardian of a Hindu minor under the following circumstances:[7] (*a*) he has ceased to be a Hindu; or (*b*) he has completely and finally renounced the world by becoming a hermit (*vanaprastha*) or an ascetic (*yati* or *sanyasi*). It is noteworthy that the expressions "father" and "mother" used hereinabove would not include a step-father and a step-mother.[7] In the absence of the father, the mother even if she has subsequently remarried, becomes the natural guardian of her child and while appointing a legal guardian of her child she should be given preference over other relatives if she is otherwise fit.[8] Even where the father is alive, but does not take any interest in the minor and is as good as non-existent, the mother would be the natural guardian of minor.[9] Mother is entitled to the custody of a child where it is less than five years of age.[10] Where the mother had left the child of 2½ years with its father for about 10 months without caring its welfare, it was held that the father was entitled to retain the custody of the child.[11] The natural guardianship of adopted son who is minor passes, on adoption, to the adoptive father and after him to the adoptive mother.[12] In *Sumedha Nagpal* v *State of Delhi*,[13] the question relating to custody of minor child cannot be decided merely upon the rights of parties under the law, *viz.*, right of mother under s. 6(*a*) proviso of this Act. Welfare of the child is the primary consideration.

In *Githa Hariharan* v *Reserve Bank of India*[14] it has been held that if the father is unable to take care of the minor because of his physical and/or

---

4   Section 6(*a*), *ibid*.
5   Section 6(*b*), *ibid*.
6   Section 6(*c*), *ibid*.
7   Section 6, Explanation, *ibid*.
8   *Bakshi Ram* v *Shila Devi* AIR 1960 Punj 304.
9   *Jijabai* v *Pathankhar* AIR 1971 SC 315.
10 *Chander Prabha* v *Prem Nath Kapur* AIR 1969 Del 283. See also, *Avinash* v *Dr. K. Singh* AIR 1960 Punj 326.
11 *Vasudevan* v *R. Viswalakshmi* AIR 1959 Ker 403.
12 Section, 7, H.M. & G. Act.
13 (2000)9 SCC 745. See *Mohan Kumar Rayana* v *Kamal Mohan Rayana* AIR 2010 SC 1659; *Suman Bhasin* v *Neeraj Bhasin* AIR 2010 SC 1777.
14 AIR 1999 SC 1149.

mental incapacity, the mother can act as natural guardian of the minor and all her actions would be valid during the life time of the father who would be deemed to be "absent" for the purposes of s. 6(*a*) of the Hindu Minority and Guardianship Act 1956 and s. 19(*b*) of the Guardians and Wards Act 1890.

Powers of natural guardian[15]

The natural guardian of a minor has power to do all acts which are necessary or reasonable and proper (*i*) for the benefit of the minor, or (*ii*) for the realisation, protection or benefit of the minor's estate. The natural guardian cannot, however, bind the minor by a personal covenant.[16] Though personal contract is not binding on the minor, yet the minor on attaining majority can enforce such contract if it is advantageous to him, and the other party to the contract would be bound by it.[17] Similarly, the other party can also enforce a contract entered into by a natural guardian of a minor if the contract is for the benefit of the minor.[18] The natural guardian cannot, without the previous permission of the court, (*a*) mortgage or charge or transfer by way of sale, gift or exchange any immovable property of the minor, or (*b*) lease any property for a term exceeding five years or for a term extending more than one year beyond the date on which the minor will attain majority.[19] Thus, a natural guardian enters into an agreement to sell minor's property and gives possession of the property to the purchaser, the doctrine of part performance will not apply, as because the agreement will not be enforceable against the minor.[20] Sub-section (2) of s. 8 of the Act refers only to alienation of immovable property of a minor by a natural guardian, but where the natural guardian purchases minor's property for himself for the benefit of the minor, it does not require the permission of the court.[1] The expression "any person claiming under him" in sub-sec. (3) of s. 8 of the Act would include a transferee from the minor after attaining majority. Thus, where the father of a minor daughter sold her property as the natural guardian, and on attaining majority she sold the same property to another person, such transferee was held to be competent to file a suit

---

15 Section 8, *ibid*.
16 Section 8(1), *ibid*.
17 *Popat* v *Jagu* AIR 1969 Bom 140.
18 *Manik Chand* v *Ramchandra* AIR 1981 SC 519.
19 Section 8(2), H.M. & G. Act.
20 *Darbara Singh* v *Karimindar Singh* AIR 1979 Punj 215.
1 *Than Singh* v *Barelal* AIR 1974 MP 24.

to set aside the sale by the father during minority of his daughter.[2] Where an agreement to purchase immovable property is entered into by the natural guardian on behalf the minor, no permission of the court would be required.[3] A transfer of property by the natural guardian of a minor without permission of the court can be avoided by the minor by his conduct without going to the court for setting aside the sale.[4] Permission for alienation of minor's property from the court can be sought only by the natural guardian, and not by the intending purchaser.[5] The procedure for permission of the court in respect of alienation of minor's property by the natural guardian is laid down in sub-sec. (5) of s. 8 of the Act. The word "court" appearing in s. 8 of the Act means (*i*) the City Civil Court, or (*ii*) A district court, or (*iii*) A court empowered under s. 4A of the Guardians and Wards Act 1890 within whose jurisdiction the immovable property of a minor situates.[6]

In *Sri Narayan Bal* v *Sridhar Sutar*,[7] it has been held that s. 8 in view of express terms of ss. 6 and 12 of the Act would not be applicable where a joint Hindu family property is sold/disposed of by the Karta involving an undivided interest of the minor in the said joint Hindu family property.

Testamentary guardians and their powers[8]

A testamentary guardian is a guardian appointed by the will of minor's father or mother.[9] A Hindu father entitled to act as the natural guardian of his minor child may appoint a guardian by will in respect of minor's person or property or both. No testamentary guardian can be appointed in respect of undivided interest in joint family property.[10] The testamentary appointment of guardian made by the father will not have any effect if the father predeceases the mother, but such appointment will revive if the mother dies without appointing any person by will as guardian.[11] A Hindu widow entitled to act as the natural guardian of her minor legitimate child may by will appoint a guardian in respect of minor's person or property or both except the undivided interest of the minor in

---

2 *Amirtha* v *Sornam* AIR 1977 Mad 127 (FB).
3 *Linga Reddy* v *Ramchandrappa* AIR 1971 Mys 194.
4 *Santha* v *Cheru Kutty* AIR 1972 Ker 71.
5 *Shivamurthi* v *Vijay Singh* AIR 1972 Bom 152.
6 Sub-section (6) of s. 8, H.M. & G. Act.
7 AIR 1996 SC 2371.
8 Section 9, H.M. & G. Act, 1956.
9 See s. 4(*b*)(*ii*), H.M. & G. Act.
10 Section 9(1) read with s. 12, *ibid*.
11 Section 9(2), H.M. & G. Act.

joint family property.[12] A Hindu mother as the natural guardian of her illegitimate child may appoint a testamentary guardian in respect of such minor's person or property or both.[13] A testamentary guardian will have right to act as the minor's guardian only after the death of testator and to exercise all the rights of a natural guardian.[14] The right of the testamentary guardian in respect of minor girl shall cease to have effect on her marriage.[15]

Certain limitations relating to guardian

A minor cannot act as guardian of the property of any minor.[16] A *de facto* guardian of a minor has no right to dispose of or deal with the property of a Hindu minor.[17] The sale of minor's property by *de facto* guardian is void.[18] A sale of property of a minor by a *de facto* guardian cannot be validated by the minor on attaining the majority.[19] Section 11 would not apply to a sale by the manager of joint Hindu family property including minor's interest therein, provided the sale is for legal necessity.[20] Another limitation has been imposed on the power of a guardian. Where a minor has an undivided interest in a joint family property and the property is under the management of an adult member of the family, no guardian shall be appointed for the minor in respect of such undivided interest. This limitation does not, however, affect the jurisdiction of the High Court to appoint a guardian in respect of such interest.[1]

In *Madhegowda* v *Ankegowda*,[2] it has been held that sale of minor's property by sisters acting as *de facto* guardian is in contravention of s. 11 of the Act and therefore is *per se* invalid.

Considerations for appointment of guardian

In appointment or declaration of any person as a guardian of a Hindu minor by a court, the paramount consideration is the welfare of the

---

12 Section 9(3) read with s. 12, H.M. & G. Act.
13 Section 9(4), H.M. & G. Act.
14 Section 9(5), *ibid*.
15 Section 9(6), *ibid*.
16 Section 10, *ibid*.
17 See section 11, *ibid*.
18 *Daneyl Gurumurthy* v *Raghu Podhan* AIR 1967 Ori 63.
19 *Talarierappa* v *Murthyalappa* AIR 1972 Mys 31.
20 *Nathu Mishra* v *Mahesh Mishra* AIR 1966 Pat 196; *Tarini* v *Basudeo* AIR 1981 Pat 331.
1   Section 12, H.M. & G. Act 1956.
2   AIR 2002 SC 215.

minor.[3] No person shall be entitled to be a guardian under any law in force regarding marriage among Hindus, if the court is of opinion that his or her guardianship is not for the welfare of the minor.[4]

In *N. Nirmala* v *Nelson Jayakumar*,[5] it has been held that custody of minor child can be granted to the father, but the mother is to be given the visiting right as well as the right to keep the child in her custody during school vacation. In *Mausami Moitra Ganguly* v *Jayant Ganguli*,[6] the Supreme Court has held that better financial resources, love for child or statutory presumptions are no doubt relevant considerations, but welfare of the minor child is the paramount consideration. Similarly, in *Gaurav Nagpal* v *Sumedha Nagpal*,[7] the Supreme Court has held that the principles regarding custody of a minor child are well-settled. The paramount consideration of the court in determining the question as to who should be given custody of a minor child is the "welfare of the child" and not rights of parents under a statute for the time being in force or what parties say.

---

[3] Section 13(1), *ibid*, see also *Avinash Devi* v *Dr. Khazan* AIR 1960 Punj 326; *Gangabai* v *Bherulal* AIR 1976 Raj 153; *Babu Ram* v *Keshwa Chand* AIR 1978 Punj 174.
[4] Section 13(2), H.M. & G. Act 1956.
[5] AIR 1999 SC 3821.
[6] (2008)7 SCC 673.
[7] (2009)1 SCC 42.

CHAPTER
12

Joint Hindu Family

Composition of joint Hindu family

A joint Hindu family consists of all male members who have lineally descended from a common ancestor and includes their wives and unmarried daughters.[1] A daughter after marriage ceases to be a member of a Hindu joint family. After marriage she becomes a member of her husband's joint family.

The tie of joint Hindu family is *sapindaship*. The members of the joint family are united by birth, marriage and adoption. The undivided Hindu family under the Mitakshara law is based on community of interest and unity of possession among persons descended from a common ancestor in the male line.[2] Where the *sapinda* relationship exists, there is no limit to the number of persons in joint Hindu family. Both male and female may be the members of a joint Hindu family.[3] A joint Hindu family may consist of a male and a female member. Property of a joint Hindu family does not lose its identity even if the family is represented by a single coparcener.[4] A Hindu joint family is not a legal or juristic entity with separate existence without its members. It is purely a creature of law and cannot be created by act of parties, because the basic principle of joint family is the tie of *sapindaship* arising by birth, marriage or adoption.[5] The joint status of a Hindu family continues unless it is determined by act of members or by operation of law.

1 *Commissioner of Income Tax* v *Laxminarayan* (1935)59 Bom 618.
2 *Vanugopala Ravi* v *Union of India* AIR 1969 SC 1094.
3 *Sudarsana Maistri* v *Narasimtiulu* (1902) ILR 25 Mad 149.
4 *Gowli Buddanna* v *Commr. of IT Mysore* AIR 1966 SC 1523.
5 *Bhagwan Dayal* v *Reoti Devi* AIR 1962 SC 287.

Presumptions

There may be presumption that there is a Hindu joint family, but there can be no presumption that the joint family possesses joint family property.[6] The possession of joint estate is not an essential requisite to constitute a joint family. A family may be joint without having property of its own.[7] The normal condition of a joint Hindu family is that it has joint estate and is joint in food and worship.[8] A Hindu family ceases to be joint when the members of the family have their separation with regard to estate. Severance in food and worship of the members of a Hindu family does not operate as separation of a joint Hindu family.[9] The following are examples of Hindu joint family:

(a) A, a male Hindu, B, wife of A, and C, unmarried daughter of A.[10]

(b) A, a male Hindu, and B, widow of deceased brother of A.[11]

A family does not cease to be joint merely on temporary reduction of coparcenary to a single individual.[12]

Joint family property and separate property

The term "joint family property" is also described technically in the Mitakshara law as "coparcenary property". Separate property includes self-acquired property.

Joint family property may be classified according to the source from which it comes into (i) ancestral property, and (ii) separate property of coparceners thrown into common coparcenary stock. Where property jointly acquired by the members of a joint family with the aid of ancestral property it is joint family property. But if members of a joint family acquire property jointly without the aid of ancestral property, it may or may not be joint family property. It depends on the facts and circumstances of the case.

There are three main sources of joint family property, namely (1) ancestral property, (2) acquisition of property with the aid of joint family property by members of the joint family, and (3) abandonment of

---

6 *K.O. Reddy* v *B.V. N. Reddy* AIR 1984 SC 117.
7 *Janakiram* v *Nagamony* (1926)49 Mad 98.
8 *Raghunada* v *Brozo Kishor* (1876)1 Mad 69.
9 *Ganesh Dutt* v *Jewach* (1904)31 IA 10.
10 *Gowli Buddanna* v *CIT, Mysore* AIR 1966 SC 1523.
11 *Sitabai* v *Ramchandra* AIR 1970 SC 343.
12 *Att.-Gen. of Ceylon* v *A.R. Arunachatam Chettiar* [1957] AC 540 (PC).

separate claim over any property by a member of a joint family. The incidents of a joint family property are the following:

(a) It devolves by survivorship and not by succession.

(b) It is the property in which the male issue of the coparceners acquires an interest by birth.

(c) Every coparcener has a joint interest and joint possession.

The incidents of separate or self-acquired property are as follows: (a) Such property belongs exclusively to a member of a joint family. (b) No other member of the coparcenary acquires any interest in it by birth. (c) The owner of such property has right to sell, bequeath or dispose it in any manner he likes. (d) Such property is not liable to partition. (e) It devolves by succession, and not by survivorship.

Separate property may be acquired in the following ways: (1) Property inherited from a person other than his father, grandfather or great grand father. (2) Small gift made through affection by a father out of ancestral movable property. (3) Government grant. (4) Property lost to the family but recovered by a member without the assistance of joint family. (5) Income of separate property. (6) Share on partition. (7) Property held by sole surviving coparcener. (8) Separate earnings. (9) Gains of learning. Prior to the Hindu Gains of Learning Act 1930 property acquired as gains of science or learning with the aid and assistance of joint family property by a member of the family was the joint family property.[13] But the provisions of the Hindu Gains of Learning Act 1930 have overruled that rule.

Powers of manager or father to alienate coparcenary property

A manager or the father can alienate property by way of a gift within reasonable limit for pious purposes. This must be by an act *inter vivos* and not by way of testament.[14] It was held in *Jowahar Lal* v *Shri Thakur Radha Gopalji Maharaj*,[15] that even a fraction of a coparcenary property cannot be alienated by a will for a charitable purpose by member of a joint Hindu family. But now s. 30 of the Hindu Succession Act 1956 confers power on a Hindu to dispose of any property by will which he is capable of disposing. On examining the whole question the Supreme Court held in *Guramma* v *Mallappa*,[16] that a father is capable of making a gift of

---

13 *Gokal Chand* v *Hukum Chand* AIR 1921 PC 35.
14 *Gangi Reddi* v *Tammi Raddi* (1927)54 IA 136.
15 (1945) All 177.
16 AIR 1964 SC 5.

immovable property to a daughter within a reasonable limit. In *Kamala Devi* v *Bachulal Gupta*,[17] the Supreme Court considered the meaning of the expression "pious purposes". It is the imperative religious duty and moral obligation of the father to give a girl in marriage to suitable husband and direct spiritual benefit is conferred upon the father by such a marriage. The Madras High Court in *Sivaganna* v *Udayar*,[18] held that a father has no power to make a gift of ancestral immovable property to wife.

Illustrations

(a) The father in a joint family of a Mitakshara school can sell his self-acquired immovable property to a stranger without the concurrance of his sons. He can also make a gift of his self-acquired property to one of his sons to the detriment of another and can further make even an unequal distribution amongst his heirs.[19]

(b) A manager of a Hindu undivided family entered into a transaction and a junior member of the said family who was a major or believed to be major joined him. It was held that the transaction was deemed to be on behalf of the family and was binding on it. Even where such a transaction was entered into solely by a manager, it would be binding on the family. The position would not change if the junior members were minor.[20]

(c) A *Karta* of a joint Hindu family transferred certain coparcenary properties by way of gift to his concubine in recognition of her past services. It was held that the gift was invalid.[1]

(d) There were certain antecedent debts incurred by the grand-father and the father of the minor sons and to satisfy the said debts, joint family properties were alienated. It was held that the transaction was valid including the right, title and interest of the minors.[2]

(e) There were certain alienations of joint family property by the father when one of the sons was in the womb. It was held that alienations were voidable at the instance of that son in the womb born subsequently.[3]

(f) M was one of the partners in a partnership firm representing the Hindu undivided family consisting of himself and his two minor sons. M was paid remuneration for rendering services to the firm. Was the remuneration paid by the firm to M his individual income or income of the undivided Hindu family? It was held that the remuneration paid to M was the income of the Hindu undivided family.[4]

---

17 AIR 1957 SC 434.
18 AIR 1961 Mad 356.
19 *Arunachala Mudaliar* v *Muruganatha* AIR 1953 SC 495.
20 *Radhakrishandas* v *Kaluram* (1963) SCR 648.
 1 *Dwarampudi Nagaratnamba* v *Kumuku Rammayya* AIR 1968 SC 253.
 2 *Mehar Chand* v *Kushi Ram* CA No. 250 of 1954 decided by the Supreme Court on April 25, 1958.
 3 *Guramma B.C. Deshmukh* v *M. Chanbasappa* AIR 1964 SC 510.
 4 *M.D. Dhanwatey* v *Commr. of Income-Tax, M.P.* AIR 1968 SC 682.

(g) A Hindu undivided family consisted of S and T. S was appointed the Treasurer of a Bank. As the Treasurer S had to furnish security to the Bank of certain properties of the Hindu undivided family. Was the salary of S assessable as profits and gains of the Hindu undivided family or as salary under the Income-Tax Act? It was held that it was assessable as salary.[5]

(h) A Hindu undivided family consisted of A, his son B, his wife C, his son's wife D and his unmarried daughter E. A and B executed a trust deed in respect of certain properties belonging to the joint family. The effect of the said trust deed was that the income of the property was to be enjoyed by A during his life time and after his death the said income was to be enjoyed by B alone with a right of residence provided in favour of C. After B's death the income of the said trust property was to be enjoyed by D and the natural born sons in existence at the time of the death of the survivor of A and B. There was an express power of revocation of the trust deed reserved to the said A by a clause therein. A died without revoking the trust deed and B enjoyed the income of the trust property. Is the income of the trust property assessable as income of the joint family? It was held that the income of the trust property could not be included in the income of the assessee undivided family.[6]

A leading case

Brijnarain v *Mangala Prasad* (1924)28 CWN 253 (PC); 46 All 95; 41 CLJ 232; 51 IA 129.

Facts of the case

Sitaram had two minor sons. He was a member of a Hindu joint family governed by the law of the Mitakshara school. He mortgaged the joint ancestral properties in 1905 and 1907. It was known for which purpose the loan was raised by Sitaram. Again in 1908, he executed another mortgage for the purpose of paying off the earlier mortgages. A decree was passed on this mortgage in 1912. The minor sons filed a suit against the mortgagees and their father Sitaram for a declaration that the mortgage as well as the decree were void as they were against them. The trial court decided that as the sons were not properly represented in the suit, they were not bound by the decree. This decision was affirmed by the High Court at Allahabad. The mortgagees preferred an appeal to the Privy Council.

Point for decision

Was a mortgage of joint ancestral property executed by the father to pay off his two earlier mortgages on the same property binding on his minor sons?

---

5 *Piare Lal Adishwar Lal* v *Commr. of Income-tax, Delhi* AIR 1960 SC 997.
6 *Commr. or Income-tax, Bombay* v *Ratilal Natha Lal* AIR 1954 SC 503.

Decision

As the previous mortgages were not executed for immoral object of the father, the mortgages constitute good antecedent debts as to make the subsequent mortgage binding on the sons.

Points decided

(1) A mortgage executed by the father of a joint family estate not for immoral purpose is a good antecedent debt. The subsequent mortgage by the father to liquidate the earlier mortgage is, therefore, binding on the son.

(2) In *Sahu Ram* v *Bhup Singh*,[7] the observation that the debt must be antecedent in fact as well as in time, is a good law but others are not.

Rights of coparceners

The rights of coparceners in the property of joint Hindu family are as follows:

(A) *Community of interest and unity of possession.* The Privy Council in *Katama Natchair* v *Rajah of Shivagunga* (1863)9 MIA 539 observed "there is community of interest and unity of possession between all the members of the family."

(B) *Share of income.* A member of a Mitakshara joint family is not definite about his share in the joint family till partition. Thus, no definite share of income can be claimed by a coparcenary. But a coparcener in a Dayabhaga joint family is definite about his share and as such is entitled to a definite share of income. The manager of a joint Hindu family may allot to individual member a portion of family property to enable him to maintain himself out of the income of that property. Any saving made by an individual member of that income is the separate property of that member.[8]

(C) *Right to partition.* Every adult coparcener is entitled to enforce partition of joint family property.

(D) *Exclusion from joint property.* Clear evidence would be necessary to exclude a coparcener from enjoyment of joint family property. Onus is on the party claiming exclusion from joint property to the knowledge of the coparcener concerned.[9]

---

7 LR 44 IA 127.
8 *Bengal Insurance and Real Property Co. Ltd.* v *Velayammal* AIR 1937 Mad 521.
9 *Murudanayagam* v *Sola Pillai* AIR 1965 Mad 200.

(E) *Alienation*. A coparcener has no right to alienate his coparcenary interest by gift. But in the Dayabhaga law a male coparcener has right to dispose of his share by will or by way of gift.[10]

(F) *Manager*. A manager of a joint Hindu family has certain special power of disposition over the coparcenary property.

Management of Hindu joint family property

Management of Hindu joint family property vests in an elderly coparcener who is call *karta* or manager of the joint Hindu family. There cannot be two *kartas* in the same family. A widow cannot be a *karta* of a joint Hindu family.[11] A junior member of a joint Hindu family can act as *karta* with the consent of all other members.[12]

(A) *Position*. The manager of Hindu joint family is neither an agent nor a trustee of the other coparceners in the family. He has no longer proprietary interest or rights in the joint family property. He represents the interest of the joint family and its property as a whole. He is the guardian of the interest of the minor coparcenary members in respect of joint family property. He cannot receive remuneration as a *karta* of the family. The position of the manager is to be determined with reference to judicial decisions.

(B) *Rights of a manager*. The manager of Hindu joint family has the following rights: (*a*) He has a right of possession of the joint family property. (*b*) He can manage the joint property and its affairs in the greatest interest of the coparceners. (*c*) He represents the family as a whole in any transaction with outsiders. (*d*) He is entitled to equal contribution from all other coparceners for any money spent for the cause or benefit of the joint family.

(C) *Powers of a manager*. The manager has implied power to do all things necessary for the benefit of the members and also of the estate of the Hindu family. The manager has power (*i*) to contract debts for the benefit of the family as a whole, (*ii*) to give valid discharge for debts due to the joint family, (*iii*) to acknowledge debt on behalf of the joint family, (*iv*) to refer disputes involving joint family property to arbitration; (*v*) to enter into *bona fide* compromise with a third party, (*vi*) to prosecute and defend

---

10 *Soorjeemoney Dossee* v *Denobundo* (1857)6 MIA 523 (PC).
11 *CIT* v *Seth Govindram* AIR 1966 SC 24.
12 *Narendrakumar* v *CIT* (1976)4 SCC 456.

suits or other proceedings, and (*vii*) to dispose of the joint family property for the benefit or legal necessity of the family.

The Manager has no power (*i*) to revive a debt barred by limitation,[13] (*ii*) to relinquish a debt due to joint family,[14] or (*iii*) to start new business.

(D) *Liability of a manager*. The manager is liable to the members of a joint Hindu family: (*i*) for misapplication of the family property and fund,[15] (*ii*) for accounts on partition.[16]

Power of manager to start new business

The *karta* or manager of joint Hindu family cannot start a new business so as to bind the other members of the family. If a manager starts a new business with the consent of the adult members of the family, only they are personally and jointly liable with manager for the liability of the new business. The minor coparceners are not liable at all and their interests in the joint family property are unaffected.

There is one exception to this principle which is laid down in *Kulitalai Bank's* case.[17] In that case the Madras High Court has held that the manager of a trading family or one whose *Kulachara* (hereditary vocation) is trade is not personally liable for starting a new business. He can bind all the members of the joint Hindu family by his act. Any limitation on the power of a trading family will amount to curtailment of the spirit of commercial adventure.

The manager of a joint Hindu family is personally liable if he enters into partnership with a stranger. He can bind only those coparceners who will consent to such undertaking.

Liability of a coparcener

A coparcener is liable for the debts of the joint family only to the extent of his undivided interest in the coparcenary property. The separate or self acquired property of a coparcener is not liable for the debt of the joint family unless the coparcener has rendered himself personally liable for such debt.

---

13 *Nagarmal* v *Bajranlal* AIR 1950 PC 15.
14 *Konduru Dasaratharama* v *Indoor Narasa* AIR 1928 Mad 601.
15 *Abhay Chandra* v *Payari Mohan* (1870)5 Beng LR 347.
16 *Ramanathan, Chettiar* v *Narayana Chettiar* AIR 1955 Mad 629.
17 AIR 1955 Mad 670.

Remedies of a coparcener

Where a coparcener is excluded from joint possession or enjoyment of joint family property, he has the following remedies:

(A) *Right to sue*. An aggrieved coparcener may sue to enforce his right to joint possession and enjoyment of joint family property.[18] He is not bound to file a suit for partition. He files the suit for declaration of title.

(B) *Suit for injunction*. A coparcener may sue to restrain by injunction other coparceners or members from altering the condition of the joint family property or from committing any unauthorised act, such as waste.[19]

(C) *Suit for partition*. A coparcener may also sue for partition of the joint family property. A minor coparcener has also right to claim partition and the court may refuse or grant it at its discretion.[20] A coparcener may maintain a suit for partition even if he is not in actual possession of any property.

---

18 *Naranbhai* v *Ranchod* (1902)26 Bom 141.
19 *Sheo Pershard* v *Leela Singh* (1874)12 Beng LR 188.
20 *Bishundas* v *Seogeni Rao* AIR 1953 SC 280.

CHAPTER
13

Joint Family Property and Partition

Meanings of words "joint", "property" and "partition"

Real meaning of a word is determined with reference to the colour, shade and the other words accompanying it. Every word of a language is impregnated with and is flexible to connote different meanings, when used in different context. That is why it is said words are not static but dynamic. The court must adopt the dynamic meaning of a word if it aims at upholding a provision of a statute. In the *Quarry Owners Association* v *State of Bihar*[1] it has been held by the Supreme Court that dynamic meaning of a work often saves many statutes from being declared as void. It dissolves the onslaught of any rigid and literal interpretation of a statute. It gives full thrust and satisfaction to achieve the objectivity which the legislature intended. In *Subash Kumar* v *Principal Officer, Mercantile Marine Dept., Madras*[2] it has been held by the Supreme Court that the meanings of words are to be understood according to their subject matter. The general rule of construction of words is not only to look at the words but to look at the context, the collocation and the object of such words relating to such matter and interpret the meaning according to what would appear to be the meaning intended to be conveyed by the use of the words under the circumstances.[3] In *Mangoo Singh* v *Election Tribunal*[4] Justice S.K. Das speaking for the court of three Judges Bench has observed: "We have been referred to several meanings of the word 'demand' in standard English dictionaries and Law Lexicons. When the context makes the

---

1 AIR 2000 SC 2870; (2000)8 SCC 655.
2 AIR 1991 SC 1632; (1991)2 SCC 449.
3 *Jagir Singh* v *State of Bihar* AIR 1976 SC 997; (1976)2 SCC 942.
4 AIR 1957 SC 871 (para 9).

meaning of a word quite clear, it becomes unnecessary to search for and select a particular meaning out of the diverse meanings a word is capable of, according to lexicographers." Thus, while dealing with the meanings of the words like "joint", "property" and "partition" it is necessary to bear in mind the aforesaid principles laid down by the Supreme Court of India.

(a) *Joint.* Black's *Law Dictionary*[5] defines the word "joint". It means "united"; combined; undivided; done by or against two or more unitedly; shared by or between two or more; coupled together in interest or liability." This term is used to express common property interest enjoyed or a common liability incurred by two or more persons. Thus, it is one in which obligators being two or more in number bind themselves jointly but not severally, and which must, therefore be prosecuted in a joint action against them all, distinguished from "joint and several" obligation. Wharton's *Law Lexicon*[6] gives meaning of the word "joint" as "combined; shared amongst many; in the same possession." Thus, the word "joint" is to be understood as a common to two or more. Rights and obligations in respect of any subject-matter may be ascribed to two or more jointly and not severally.

(b) *Property.* Property means a tangible thing capable of ownership. The word "property" has been defined in the Century Dictionary which is an encyclopaedic lexicon of the English language, as follows: "The right to the use or enjoyment or the beneficial right of disposal of anything that can be the subject of ownership, estate; especially ownership of tangible things ....; anything that may be exclusively passed and enjoyed ....; possessions."[7] The word "property" was used in Art. 19(1)(f) (since deleted and now in Art. 300A of the Constitution) of the Constitution of India. The Supreme Court has dealt with the meaning of this word in different cases. In *Commr. Hindu Religious Endowments, Madras* v *Sri Lakshmindra Thirtha Swamiar*[8] the Supreme Court has held that the word "property" should be given a liberal and wide connotation and should be extended to those well recognised types of interest which have the insignia or characteristics of proprietary right. The ingredients of both office and property, of duties and personal interest, are blended together in the rights of a Mahant and the Mahant has the right to enjoy the property or beneficial interest so long as he is entitled to hold his office. The phraseology used in Art. 19(1)(f) (prior to amendment) of the Constitution

---

5   6th Ed., p. 837.
6   14th Ed., (First Indian Reprint 1993), p. 540.
7   See *Nrisingha Murari Chakraborty* v *State of West Bengal* (1977)3 SCC 7, 9.
8   AIR 1954 SC 282.

is wide and *prima facie* it takes in its sweep both abstract and concrete rights of property.[9] Property includes both movable and immovable property.[10] Property has been defined in the context of Art. 31 of the Constitution as a legal concept and it is the sum of a bundle of rights and in the case of tangible property it would include the right of possession, the right to enjoy, the right to destroy, the right to retain, the right to alienate and so on.[11] HIDAYATULLAH, J., in his concurring judgment with the majority view in *Golak Nath* v *State of Punjab*[12] has quoted from Noyes[13] regarding the definition of property which reads as follows: "Property is any protected right or bundle of rights (interest or thing) with direct or indirect regard to any external object (*i.e.*, other than the person himself) which is material or *quasi* material (*i.e.*, a protected process) and which the then and there organisation of society permits to be either private or public, which is connoted by the legal concepts of occupying, possessing or using". Section 14(1) of the Hindu Succession Act 1956 in dealing with the absolute interest of a Hindu female has used the word "property" in Explanation thereto. In *R.B.S.S. Munnalal* v *S.S. Rajkumar*[14] the Supreme Court has held that the expression "property" in that context shall be given the widest connotation. The expression includes property acquired by a Hindu female by inheritance or devise or at a partition, or in lieu of maintenance or arrears of maintenance or by gift from any person before or after the marriage, or by her own skill or exertion, or by purchase or by prescription or in any other manner whatsoever. According to s. 409 of the Indian Penal Code 1860 property includes chose-in-action.[15] From jurisprudential point of view all property can be broadly divided into corporeal and incorporeal.[16] Corporeal property is the right of ownership in material things; incorporeal property is any other proprietary right *in rem*. Incorporeal property is itself of two kinds, namely (1) *jura in re aliena* or encumbrances, whether over material or immaterial things, for example, leases, mortgages and servitudes; and (2) *jura in propria* over immaterial things, for example patents, copyrights and trade marks which are also known as intellectual property.

---

9 *Swami Motor Transports (P) Ltd* v *Sankaraswamigal Mutt* AIR 1963 SC 864.
10 *State of Bombay* v *F.N. Balasara* AIR 1951 SC 318.
11 *Guru Datta Sharma* v *State of Bihar* AIR 1961 SC 1684.
12 AIR 1967 SC 1643 (at p. 1709).
13 The Institution of Property (1936), p. 436.
14 AIR 1962 SC 1493.
15 *Shivnarayan Laxminarayan Joshi* v *State of Maharashtra* (1980) 2 SCC 465; AIR 1980 SC 439; 1980 Cr LJ 388.
16 Salmond on *Jurisprudence*, 12th Ed., p. 413.

(c) *Partition.* Generally speaking, the word "partition" means severance of jointness. In technical sense of American law partition means any division of real or personal property between co-owners, resulting in individual ownership of interests of each. Division between several persons of property which belongs to them as co-owners, it may be compulsory (judicial) or voluntary.[17] Partition severs unity of possession.[18] Under the English law partition actions are now obsolete.[19] Today a legal estate is not capable of subsisting or of being created in an undivided share in land.[20] Previously, with a view to the more convenient and perfect partition or allotment of the premises, equity frequently decreed a pecuniary compensation to one of the parties for 'owelty', *i.e.*, equality of partition so as to prevent any injustice or unavoidable inequality. Under the Hindu law partition means the division of title and division of property; a physical division of the family property, may be brought about either by a suit for partition or in pursuance of an agreement between the members dividing the property. The division of right likewise may be a matter of agreement between the parties. The members of an undivided family may agree among themselves with regard to any particular property that they shall enjoy the same thereafter in certain defined shares. The disruption of joint status may also be brought about by a definite and unambiguous indication by one member of intention to separate himself and to enjoy the share in severally.[1] The Supreme Court in *S.T.O.* v *N.K. Sarada Thampatty*[2] has ascribed a different meaning to the word "partition" while dealing with s. 171 of the Income Tax Act 1961 and the Explanation added thereto. This definition is different from the general principles of Hindu law. It contains a deeming provision under which partition of the property of HUF is accepted only if there has been actual physical division of the property. In the absence of any such proof, the HUF shall be deemed to continue for the purpose of assessment of tax. Any agreement between the members of the joint family effecting partition or a decree of the court for partition cannot terminate the status of HUF unless it is shown that the joint family property was physically divided in accordance with the agreement or decree of the court.

---

17 *O'Brien* v *O'Brien* 89 Misc 2d 433.
18 *Hamilton* v *Mac Donald* CA Ariz 503 F 2d 1138.
19 Halsbury's *Laws of England*, 4th Ed., vol. 16, para 1263.
20 Law of Property Act 1925, s. 1(6).
 1 *Latchandhara* v *Chinnavadu* AIR 1963 AP 31 relying on *Appovier* v *Rama Subba Aiyan* 11 Moo Ind App 75.
 2 1991 Supp (2) SCC 737; AIR 1991 SC 2035.

Distinction between joint property and joint family property

Joint property is one in which two or more persons have joint right title and interest in a particular property, for example, property of a partnership firm or a club or association is a joint property of partners, or members who compose the firm, club or association. They may not be related to each other by blood through any parental lineage. But in case of joint family property, the property belongs to a family consisting of parents and children related to each other by blood or affinity or who can claim as descendants of a common ancestor. The word "family" in its popular sense means children and when the settlor recites that he has no children, that is an indication that the dedication is not for the benefit of the family but for the public.[3] But in *Anant Bhikappa Patil* v *Shankar Ramchandra Patil*[4] it was held by the Judicial Committee that the power of a Hindu widow to adopt did not come to an end on the death of the sole surviving coparcener. The Judicial Committee further held that on the death of a sole surviving coparcener a Hindu joint family cannot be finally brought to an end while it is possible in nature or law to add a male member to it. The family cannot be at an end while there is still a potential mother if that mother in the way of law brings in a new male member. If a son is adopted, he becomes a preferential heir in the family. This proposition of law relating to joint Hindu family as laid down by the Judicial Committee of the Privy Council was not approved by the Supreme Court in *C. Krishna Prasad* v *CIT*.[5] In that case it has been held by the Supreme Court that family connotes a group of people related by blood or marriage. According to Shorter Oxford English Dictionary the word "Family" means the group consisting of parents and their children whether living together or not. In wider sense, those who are nearly connected by blood or affinity, a person's children regarded collectively those descended or claiming descent from a common ancestor; a house, kindred, lineage; a race; a people or group of peoples. According to Aristotle (Politics 1), it is the characteristic of a man that he alone has any sense of good and evil or just and unjust and the association of living beings who have the sense make a family and a State. It would follow from the above that the word "family" always signifies a group. Plurality or persons is an essential attribute of a family. A single person, male or female does not constitute a family. He or she would remain what is inherent in the very nature of

---

3 *Deoki Nandan* v *Murlidhar* AIR 1957 SC 133 following *Hazi Mahammad Nabi* v *Province of Bengal* AIR 1942 Cal 343.
4 AIR 1943 PC 196.
5 AIR 1975 SC 498.

things, an individual, a lonely wayfarer till perchance he or she finds a mate.[6] In the context of above discussion joint property herein denotes joint family property and not in the ordinary sense of joint property. Thus, all ancestral properties are joint properties[7] and not *vice versa*. Because if a member of joint family by dint of his own labour and skill without any aid or assistance of joint fund acquires any property and keeps it apart from joint family property, it shall be treated his personal or individual property. Similarly a gift to a member of Hindu joint-family from a relation is not ancestral property.[8]

There is no presumption that a family being joint possesses joint property.[9] Possession of property is not under the Mitakshara law a necessity for the constitution of joint family though where persons live together joint in food and worship, it is difficult to conceive of their possessing no property whatsoever, such as ordinary house-hold articles which they enjoy in common. Hindu law does not require that properties of a joint family should be immovable properties or that they should be of appreciable value.[10] The primary basis for joint property under the Hindu law is that the property in question is ancestral property.

Ancestral property—meaning and scope of

A joint family and its coparcenary with all its incidents are purely a creature of Hindu law and cannot be created by act of parties as the fundamental principle of the joint family is the tie of *sapindaship* arising by birth, marriage or adoption.[11] The coparcenary property is also known as ancestral property. The term in its technical sense, is applied to property which descends upon one person in such a manner that his male issues acquire certain rights in the property as against him.[12] If a father under the Mitakshara law attempted to dispose of property, the question arises whether it was ancestral property. The answer to that question is that property is ancestral property in the hands of the father if it has been inherited by him as unobstructed property; but if it has been inherited by the father as obstructed property, it is not ancestral property. Mayne[12] has given reasons for this distinction between unobstructed property and

---

6 *C. Krishna Prasad* v *CIT* AIR 1975 SC 498, para 6 at pp. 499-500.
7 *Rajmohan* v *Gour Mohan* 8 M.I.A. 91.
8 *Nutbehari* v *Nonilal* 41 CWN 613 (PC).
9 *Rai Shadilal* v *Lal Bahadur* AIR 1933 PC 85; 64 MLJ 298 (PC).
10 *Janakiram* v *Nagamony* (1926)49 Mad 98.
11 Mayne's *Treatise on Hindu Law and Usage*, 11th Ed., p. 338; *Sudarsana* v *Narasimhulu* (1902)25 Mad 149; *Karsondas* v *Gangabai* (1908)32 Bom 479.
12 Mayne's *Treatise on Hindu Law and Usage*, 11th Ed., pp. 339-340.

obstructed inheritance relating to ancestral property.[13] In the former case the father had an effective vested interest in the property before the inheritance fell in, and therefore his own issue acquired by birth a similar interest in that property. Thus, when the property actually devolved upon him, he took it subject to the interest they had already acquired. But in the latter case, the father had no such interest in property before the descent took place, therefore when that event occurred, he received the property free of all claims upon it by his issue, and *a fortiori*, by any other person. Hence all property which a man inherits from a direct male ancestor, not exceeding three degrees higher than himself, is ancestral property, and is atonce held by himself in coparcenary with his own male issue. But where the father has inherited from a collateral relation, as for instance from a brother, nephew, cousin or uncle, it is not ancestral property in his hands in relation to male issue. Consequently, his male issues have no equal rights as coparceners. They cannot restrain him in dealing with if, nor can they compel him to give them a share of it. On the same principle, property which a man inherits from his mother or maternal grandfather or maternal uncle or other collateral relation in the maternal line is not ancestral property. It has been held by the Privy Council[14] that the term "ancestral property" must be confined to property descending to the father from his male ancestor in the male line and that it is only in that property that the son acquires by birth an interest jointly with and equal to that of his father. The property inherited from females cannot be ancestral property.

An important question though incidently arose in *Vijaya College Trust v Kusnta Co-op. Areeanut Sales Society Ltd.*[15] for determination what is ancestral property. It has been held in that case that property inherited by a male Hindu from his father, father's father or father's father's father is ancestral property. The property inherited from females cannot be ancestral.

It is now well settled legal proposition of law that the share allotted to a coparcener on partition of ancestral property retains the character of ancestral property in the hands of male hair only. This question has been dealt with in *Ruli Ram v Amar Singh*[16] having regard to the present position of law under the Hindu Succession Act 1956.

---

13 Mayne's *Treatise on Hindu Law and Usage*, 11th Ed., pp. 339-340.
14 *Md. Hussain Khan v Babu Kishva* (1937)64 IA 250; ILR (1937) All 655, followed in *Pathuri Venkateswarlu v Damacharla Chinna Raghavulu* AIR 1957 AP 604.
15 AIR 1995 Kant 35.
16 AIR 1994 HP 102.

Under the Punjab custom the expression "ancestral property" has a special connotation.[17] When a property is alleged to be ancestral, it is not sufficient to prove that the last male holder had inherited it from the grandfather, and as such it was his ancestral property. It has also to be established further that it had devolved from a common ancestor of the parties. In other words, the party asserting it to be ancestral must show—

(*a*) that it was owned by the common ancestor; and

(*b*) that it had descended to the party or parties concerned by inheritance and in no other manner.

Both these elements are positive and if either of them is missing the property cannot be said to be ancestral. Both of them must be cogently established and the law does not accept mere conjectures, surmises or assumptions as a substitute for the proof. The best way of doing it is by adducing direct proof. In most cases such direct proof may be forthcoming from the revenue records. However sometimes property may be traced to a common ancestor in a heavy antiquity and for doing so, evidence of authentic revenue record may either be scarce or non-existent. When the land in lieu of which proprietary rights therein is in dispute and it was ancestral *qua* his son, the land in dispute is to be regarded as ancestral *qua* the son.[18] Under the Hindu law there is presumption of jointness, but in absence of any document of settlement, the court has no other option but to draw a presumption that the properties in question were ancestral properties.[19]

Some illustrative cases

(*i*) *Property acquired by adverse possession*. A coparcener under the Hindu law acquired certain property by adverse possession in accordance with the modern laws of limitation, such property cannot be termed as "ancestral property".[20]

(*ii*) *Income derived from practice*. In *Lakshmi Chand* v *Ishroo Devi*[1] it has been held that income from practice of a hereditary profession (in the instant case hereditary priest) will not be joint family property.

---

17 *Sham Kaur* v *Hari Singh* AIR 1973 P&H 71.
18 *Maya Ram* v *Samam Singh* AIR 1967 Punj 353.
19 *Chito Mahto* v *Lila Mahto* AIR 1991 Pat 186.
20 *Jamarathbee* v *Pralhad Dattatraya Dadpe* AIR 1978 Bom 229.
 1 AIR 1977 SC 1694 approving *Hanso Patak* v *Harmandil Patak* AIR 1934 All 851.

(*iii*) *Custom and succession to ancestral property.* In *Dipo* v *Wassan Singh*[2] it has been held by the Supreme Court that property inherited from paternal ancestors is ancestral property as regards the male issue of the propositus, but it is his absolute property and not ancestral property as regards other relations.

In *Jai Kaur* v *Sher Singh*[3] the question of succession to ancestral property under custom arose. The Supreme Court decided that according to the custom of Hindu Grewal Jats of Ludhiana district in the Punjab, collaterals have no preferential right over daughter.

(*iv*) *Property acquired by gift or will from paternal ancestor.* The general rule is that property acquired by gift or will from any person is not ancestral property as held in *Arunachala* v *Murugantha*,[4] but previously there were different judicial opinions of the High Courts in India. According to the High Court of Calcutta it is ancestral.[5] According to the Madras High Court it is ancestral unless the donor or testator clearly indicates that it should be separate.[6] According to the Allahabad High Court it is separate unless there is a clear intention that it would be treated as ancestral.[7] According to the Bombay High Court it is separate unless the intention of the donor or testator was that it would be treated as ancestral.[8]

Joint family property and burden of proof

There is no presumption of joint property. There must be unequivocal and definite intention of severance of joint status. The burden of proof in respect of particular property whether it is joint proper or separate property has been discussed at length along with other points in *Mudigowda* v *Ramchandra*[9] in which principles of law on different aspects of joint family have been laid down. There are as follows: (1) A definite and unambiguous indication of intention by one member and to enjoy his share in severality will amount in law to a division of status. (2) There is no presumption that a Hindu family merely because it is joint possesses any joint property. (3) If the expression of intention is a mere pretence, there is no separation of the joint family status.

---

2 AIR 1983 SC 846.
3 AIR 1960 SC 1118.
4 AIR 1953 SC 495.
5 *Hazari Mall* v *Ambanimath* (1912)17 CWN 280.
6 *Tara Chand* v *Reebs Ram* (1868)3 Mad HC 50.
7 *Purushottam* v *Janki* (1907)29 All 354.
8 *Jugmohandas* v *Mangaldas* (1886)10 Bom 508.
9 AIR 1969 SC 1076.

It is thus the settled principle of law that there is no presumption that joint family possesses joint property. Merely because a family is joint, every property purchased or held by its members is not a property of joint family. The burden of proving it to be so is on the party asserting it.[10]

Proof and presumption of joint family property

(*i*) There is no presumption that a joint family possesses joint property. It is for the person who alleges that the property is joint family property, or ancestral property to prove it.[11]

(*ii*) In the case of father and sons, the presumption that they are joint is stronger.[12]

(*iii*) There is no presumption when the property stands in the name of a female.[13]

(*iv*) Though there is no presumption that a joint family possesses joint property, yet it is well settled that once it is admitted or proved that a family is joint and possesses some joint property, the presumption of law is that all property held by or in the hands of any individual member is joint property. But if any member of joint family claims any property as his separate property, the burden rests on him to show that it is separate property.[14]

(*v*) When a manager or *karta* of joint family claims any immovable property as his separate property, the onus is on him to prove it.[15]

(*vi*) There is no presumption of joint property when any property is acquired in the name of a junior member of *tarward* under the Marumakkathayam law.[16]

(*vii*) When a joint family property is sold and a member of joint family purchases it in his own name and the source of money is not sufficiently explained, the newly acquired property would be presumed to be joint property.[17]

---

10 *Rajeshwari* v *Balchand Jain* AIR 2001 MP 179 (para 13).
11 *Annamalal* v *Subramanian* AIR 1929 PC 1; *Mudigowda* v *Ramchandra* AIR 1969 SC 1076.
12 *Indranarayan* v *Roop Narayan* AIR 1971 SC 1962.
13 *Nagayasami Naidu* v *Kochadai Naidu* AIR 1969 Mad 329.
14 *Dharm Das* v *Shama Soondari* (1843) 3 MIA 229 (PC); *Babubhai* v *Ujamal* AIR 1937 PC 446; *Narayanaswami Iyer* v *Ramakrishna Iyer* AIR 1965 SC 289.
15 *Mallesappa* v *Mallappa* AIR 1961 SC 1268.
16 *A. Nair* v *C. Amma* AIR 1966 SC 411.
17 *Jayaramchandra Iyer* v *Thulasi Ammal* AIR 1978 Mad 95.

(*viii*) There is no presumption of joint property when a member remains in possession of the entire properties of the family even after severance in status and subsequently acquires property, that cannot be regarded as joint family property.[18]

(*ix*) Mere existence of a nucleus is not enough, the presumption arises only when it is proved that nucleus is substantial for acquisition of a property.[19]

(*x*) When a manager acquires an immovable property claiming the consideration paid out of his own separate funds and not out of the joint family fund which was in his possession and charge, it is for him to prove by clear and satisfactory evidence that the purchase consideration money proceeded out of his separate fund. The onus of proof in such a case must be placed on the manager and not on his coparceners.[20]

(*xi*) When it appears that joint family had sufficient ancestral property, but at the material point of time some members of the joint family had their separate funds and properties and any of them acquires or deals in a transaction for benefit of himself, the onus is shifted on those who claim such acquisition as joint family property.[1]

(*xii*) No presumption can arise in case of trade or business on the ground that special considerations exist in relation to a trade or business.[2]

(*xiii*) There is no presumption of law that an insurance policy must be regarded as a separate property when there is no clear intention that the policy is to be treated as a separate asset, otherwise the presumption is that the income would become a joint family property.[3]

Separate property

Mayne's *Treatise on Hindu Law and Usage*[4] has laid down that there are four classes of properties which may be described as separate properties held by coparceners. These are: (1) Property which comes to a man as obstructed heritage *(sapratileandhadaya)* is his separate property. (2) Property may be self-acquired; such self-acquisition may be made by any one while even in a state of union. (3) Property which a man takes at

---

18 *Aryamusht* v *Subbaraya Setty* AIR 1972 SC 1279.
19 *Baikuntha Nath* v *Sashi Bhusan* AIR 1972 SC 2531.
20 *Mallesappa* v *Mallappa* AIR 1961 SC 1268.
1 *Bissessur Lall* v *Luchmessur* (1879)6 IA 233 (PC).
2 *Bhuru Mal* v *Jagannath* AIR 1942 PC 13.
3 *Parvati Kuer* v *Sarangdhar Sinha* AIR 1960 SC 403.
4 11th Ed., p. 351.

a partition will be his separate property as regards those from whom he has severed but will be ancestral property as regards his own male issue. (4) So too, family property vested in the last surviving male member of a coparcenary will be his separate property subject to its becoming at any moment coparcenary property when he has male issue or when an adoption is made to him or to a predeceased coparcener in the family.

Partition under the Mitakshara and the Dayabhaga systems

According to the Mitakshara law the partition means the adjustment into specified portion of diverse rights which extend to the whole estate. But according to the Dayabhaga law partition means the determination of the fractional interest of each person so that each member can deal exclusively with the identified portion. In the Mitakshara law every member has indefinite or unascertained right over the whole estate. Partition ascertains the interest of every member. The movable and immovable properties are the properties which are subject to partition. There are two types of properties, namely partible and impartible. Partible properties are divisible among the members of the family on partition. But in impartible property the members have the right to enjoy property jointly or by turn. The examples of impartible properties are tanks, gardens, works of art, apparel, rare jewellary, etc.

According to the Mitakshara law the only property that can be divided on partition is coparcenary property. Separate property is not partitioned, nor is the property which by custom or otherwise descends to a particular member of the family to the exclusion of other members, such as, a major principality.[5] In the Mitakshara law partition consists in a numerical division of the property by which the proportion of every coparcener in the property is determined. On the other hand, in the Dayabhaga law partition consists in separating the shares of the coparceners, and assigning to the coparceners specific portion of the property. In both the Schools of law one thing is common so far as partition is concerned. The true test of partition in both the cases is the intention of the parties to separate. But the effect of the intention is different in the two Schools. In the Mitakshara law the intention is manifested by mere agreement between the coparceners without any actual division of the property by metes and bounds.[6] In the Dayabhaga law such an agreement is not sufficient manifestation of the intention to separate. There must be something more

---

5 *Ramalakshmi* v *Sivanatha* (1872)14 MIA 570.
6 *Appovier* v *Rama Subba Aiyan* (1886)11 MIA 75.

than such an agreement.[7] There must be separation of shares and assignment of specific portion to each coparcener.

Proviso to s. 6(1) of the Hindu Succession Act 1956 as amended by Act 39 of 2005 saves any disposition or alienation including any partition or testamentary disposition of property which had taken place before 20th December 2004.

There may be partial partition either in respect of the property or in respect of the persons between the coparceners.[8] The members of a joint Hindu family may make a division and severance of interest in respect of a part of the joint estate while retaining their status as a joint family and holding the rest as the properties of a joint and undivided family.[9] There may also be partial partition as regards the persons separating.

Persons entitled to claim partition

Every coparcener has right to claim a partition of the joint family property. In Bombay it has been held that a son is not entitled to a partition without the consent of his father if the father is joint with his own father, brothers or other coparceners. But the son can do so if the father is separate from them.[10] A minor coparcener can sue for partition unless the partition sought for is for the benefit of the minor.[11] A son in the womb of his mother is entitled to the benefit of partition if it is made when he is in the womb. If no share is reserved for him at the time of partition while he was in the womb, he is entitled to reopen the partition for allotment of his share.[12] An illegitimate son of a *sudra* does not acquire interest in his father's property by birth. He is not therefore entitled to partition against his father during his life time.[13]

A purchaser of the whole or any portion of the joint family property is entitled to partition either by a sale in execution of a decree or by a voluntary transfer.

The wife of a coparcener has no right to claim partition. But if a partition is made between her husband and sons, she is entitled to a share in partition.

---

7   *Bata* v *Gopal* (1907)5 Cal LJ 417.
8   *Sudarsanam* v *Narasimhulu* (1902)25 Mad 149.
9   *Jagmohan* v *Ranchod Das* (1945) Nag 892.
10 *Apaji* v *Ramchandra* (1812)16 Bom 29.
11 *Mahadev* v *Lakshman* (1895)19 Bom 99.
12 *Jagat Krishna* v *Ajit Kumar* AIR 1964 Ori 75.
13 *Raja Jogendra* v *Nityanand* (1891)18 Cal 151.

Illustrations

(a) A had a wife B, two sons by B, namely C and D, and another son F by a predeceased wife, E. F sued for partition. In such case, A, B, C, D and F were entitled to one-fifth share each.[14]

(b) A, B, C and D were coparceners in a joint Hindu family of whom D was minor. There was a partition among the said coparceners. D on attaining majority challenges that the division is unfair and unjust. What is the effect of such partition? Would it make any difference if in a partition suit D as a minor was properly represented and the decree was passed? It was held *Bishundeo Narain* v *Seogeni Bai*[15] that in case of mutual partition where a minor cannot consent in law, on attaining majority he can assail the partition by showing that the division was unfair and unjust and in such case, the court will set aside it. But if a decree is passed in a suit where the minor was properly represented before the court, the decree is binding him as well as other adult parties unless the minor can show that there was fraud or negligence on the part of his next friend or guardian *ad litem*.

Effect of partition

The effect of partition is to dissolve the coparcenary. Partition destroys the status of jointness as between members of coparcenary and alters the character of joint property. Separating members hold their respective shares as their separate property. Where partition of property has not been made by metes and bounds, a right to division by metes and bounds always exists.[16]

Partition of property does not affect the status of jointness of the dividing members as members of joint family if they so decide. In *Balkrishen Das* v *Ram Narain*[17] it was held that the separating members after partition might elect to have a partition of their shares by metes and bounds or continue to live together and enjoy their property in common as before. Whether they did one or the other would affect the mode of enjoyment but not the tenure of the property or their interest in it.

In *Puttrangamma* v *M.S. Ranganna*[18] the plaintiff in the original suit, Savoy Ranganna, was living with the defendants as a member of a joint Hindu family till 7th January 1951. The plaintiff was in fact the *Karta* of the joint family. The plaintiff had four daughters; two of them were widows, one was living with her husband. Two widowed daughters and another daughter were living with the joint family. The plaintiff was admitted in a nursing home on 4th January 1951 on account of his sickness. In order to protect the interest of his daughters, he issued a notice dated

---

14 *Jairam* v *Nath* (1907)31 Bom 54.
15 AIR 1951 SC 280.
16 *Approvier* v *Rama Subba Aiyan* (1866)11 MIA 75 (PC).
17 (1903)30 IA 139 (PC).
18 AIR 1968 SC 1018.

8th January 1951 to the defendants declaring his unequivocal intention to separate from them. The notice was sent by registered post, but on the request of some well-wishers who promised a family settlement, he asked the postal authority to withdraw the notice. Contrary to expectation no settlement was arrived at. So the plaintiff instituted a suit on 13th January 1951 for partition of his share of the joint family properties. The defendants contended that there was no separation of status either because of the notice of 8th January 1951 or because of institution of the suit on 13th January 1951. With regard to the notice the defendants contended that since it was withdrawn, there was no communication. With regard to the institution of the suit they contended that the plaintiff being 85 years of age did not understand the contents of the plaint or affixation of his signature or thumb impression thereon as well as on the *vakalatnama*. The trial court granted a decree for the plaintiff who was substituted by his three daughters on his death. On appeal to the Mysore High Court the decree passed by the trial court was reversed. Hence the matter came up before the Supreme Court by a certificate of fitness. The question arose whether there was a separation of status? The decision was affirmative for the reason that a member of a joint Hindu family subject to the Mitakshara law can bring about his separation in status by an unequivocal declaration of his intention to separate himself from the family, even though no actual division takes place; and the commencement of a suit for partition is sufficient to effect a severance in interest even before the decree. The points of law laid down were as follows:

(1) When once a communication of the intention to separate is made, it is not thereafter open to the coparcener to nullify its effect so as to restore the family to its original joint status.

(2) In the case of intention of separation it is immaterial whether the other coparceners give their assent to the separation or not.

(3) The question of subsequent agreement between the members to reunite in a joint Hindu family is a question of fact to be proved as such.

Reunion

A reunion in estate can be made between persons who were parties to the original partition.[19] No writing is necessary for a reunion of the separated parties. The question whether the separated coparceners are reunited is a question of fact.[20]

---

19 *Balabux* v *Rukhmabai* (1903)30 Cal 725.
20 *Raghubir* v *Moti Kumar* (1912)35 All 41 (PC).

To constitute reunion there must be an intention of the parties to reunite in estate and interest.[1]

The effect of reunion is to constitute a joint family of the separate members and to restore to them the former status of a joint Hindu family.[2]

Partition by agreement

It has been held in *Appovier* v *Rama Subba Aiyan*,[3] by the Privy Council that the true test of partition of property according to the Hindu law is the intention of the coparceners to become separate owners in defined shares of joint property. Thus, when the members of the undivided Hindu family agree among themselves to divide their property in defined shares, the character of undivided property and joint enjoyment is taken away from the subject-matter so agreed to be dealt with. If a property is genuine, it will severe the joint status even if the motive is to defeat the claims of creditors.[4]

Partial partition

A partition between the coparceners may be partial. A partial partition may be affected either in respect of the property or in respect of the persons making it.[5] Members of a joint family may make division and severance of interest in respect of part of the joint estate while retaining their status as a joint family and holding the rest of the properties as joint and undivided.[6] There may be also partial partition as regards the persons separating. This situation arises when there is no general partition amongst all the members of the family.

Presumptions in a partition suit

(1) Once a partition is proved, the presumption is that all joint property was partitioned and divided among the members.[7]

(2) Once a partial partition as to property is proved, the presumption is that all the property was partitioned.[8]

---

1 *Balkishen Das* v *Ram Narain* (1903)30 IA 139 (PC).
2 *Prankishen* v *Mothooramohum* (1865)10 MIA 403.
3 (1866)11 MIA 75.
4 *Kuppan Chetiar* v *Mas Goundan* AIR 1937 Mad 424.
5 *Rewun Persad* v *Radha Beeby* (1846)4 MIA 137.
6 *Ramalinga* v *Narayana* (1922)49 IA 168.
7 *Raghavamma* v *Chenchamma* AIR 1964 SC 136.
8 *Bhagwati Prasad* v *Dulhin Rameswari Kaur* AIR 1952 SC 72.

(3) Once a partial partition as to persons is proved, there is no presumption that the remaining members of the family are also separated or united.[9]

(4) When two or more coparceners remain separate, there is no presumption that there was a partition between each of them or their descendants.[10]

(5) The law presumes that the members of a Hindu family are joint. The presumption is stronger in the case of a father and son.[11]

Mode of effecting partition

Partition may be effected by the modes of (*i*) division of status, (*ii*) conversion to another religion, (*iii*) marriage under the Special Marriage Act 1954, and (*iv*) reference to arbitration.

(*i*) *Division of status.* A member of a joint family shall make a definite and unequivocal declaration to the effect that he wants to separate himself from other members of the family. This is his exclusive right which he can exercise at any time according to his sweetwill. The intension of such declaration must be in unambiguous term and be clearly expressed.[12] Mere separate residence does not constitute severance of joint status.[13] Consent of other members of the family for unequivocal declaration to separate oneself or actual partition of the property is not essential for division of status.[14] In *Girjabai* v *Sadashiv*,[15] the Judicial Committee of the Privy Council has held that "there is no room for doubt that 'separation' which means the severance of the status of jointness is a matter of individual volition." The intention to separate from the joint family is required to be communicated to all the other members of the family.[16] A minor may sever connection from the joint family by an unequivocal declaration through his guardian.[17]

---

9 *Raghavamma* v *Chenchamma* AIR 1964 SC 136.
10 *Hari Baksh* v *Babulal* AIR 1924 PC 126.
11 *Indranarayan* v *Roopnarayan* AIR 1971 SC 1962.
12 *Girjabai* v *Sadashiv* (1913)40 IA 40 (PC); *Mudigowda Gowdappa* v *Ramchandra Revgowda* AIR 1969 SC 1076.
13 *Savitri Devi* v *Jiwan Chaudhury* AIR 1960 Pat 548.
14 *Mudigowda* v *Ramchandra* ante.
15 AIR 1916 PC 104.
16 *Dnyaneshwar* v *Anant* AIR 1936 Bom 290.
17 *Puttorangamma* v *Ranganna* AIR 1968 SC 1018.

(ii) Conversion to another religion. Conversion of a member of a Hindu joint family to any other religion, such as Islam or Christianity operates as partition or severance of the status of jointness.[18]

(iii) Marriage under the Special Marriage Act 1954. Where a member of a Hindu joint family marriages under the Special Marriage Act 1954, he shall be deemed to effect his severance from the joint family.

Illustration

A had two sons B and C. C had a son D by his first wife. After the death of the first wife D married F under the Special Marriage Act. B and D were living with A till he died. After the death of A, C claimed a right of survivorship with regard to A's self-acquired property. It was held that by reason of C's marriage under the Special Marriage Act, C ceased to be a member of the joint family and as such was not entitled to any share. D was a coparcener by birth and D was entitled to half share with B in respect of self-acquired property of D's grandfather.[19]

(iv) Reference to arbitration. Reference to arbitration to determine share of property of a coparcener amounts to severance of the joint status.[20]

Division of property

Division of property of a joint family on partition may be effected *(i)* by agreement, *(ii)* by arbitration, and *(iii)* by suit.

(i) Agreement. By mutual consent of all the members of a joint family, division of property may be effected.[1] Such agreement for division of property is binding on the minor unless it can be shown that division has become unfair and prejudicial to his interest. In such case the court may decline to enforce it.[2]

(ii) Arbitration. Members of joint family may agree to appoint an arbitrator for division of joint family property. In this case also a minor member is binding by the award unless his interest is adequately protected. An unregistered award for division of property is not admissible to prove the terms of partition, but oral evidence may be produced in this respect.[3]

(iii) Suit. Property may be partitioned by institution of a suit by a member of a joint family. A decree is necessary for allotment of definite shares. A suit may also be filed on behalf of a Hindu minor for partition of joint family property.

---

18 *Ram Pergash* v *Dashan Bibi* AIR 1924 Pat 420; *Pathumma* v *Raman* AIR 1921 Mad 224.
19 *Girdharilal* v *Fateh Chand* AIR 1955 MB 148.
20 *Kashinathsa* v *Narsingsa* AIR 1961 SC 1077.
1 *Palaniammal* v *Muthuvenkatacharlu* AIR 1925 PC 49.
2 *Kunjumangeli* v *K. Namboodripad* AIR 1975 Ker 112. See also, *Narendra Kante* v *Anuradha Kante* (2010)2 SCC 77 (registration of deed of family settlement is not necessary).
3 *Bhagwan* v *Harihar* AIR 1955 NUC 3982.

Sham partition

If the circumstances disclose by evidence that there was no intention to arrive at a partition in fact, mere execution of a deed does not constitute genuine partition but a sham partition.

Illustration

The father desires to defeat his creditors and to save the property for his sons. He executes a deed of partition. The father thereafter continues the management of the property and looks after the interest of his sons in a suit prosecuted against him. It is held that the deed of partition is a nominal transaction which was never intended to be acted upon and was never given effect to.[4]

Incidents of impartible estate

The nature and incidents of impartible estate is now well settled by law. Impartibility is essentially a creature of custom. The junior members of a joint family in the case of ancient right in impartible joint family estate take no right in the property by birth and, therefore, have no right of partition having regard to the very nature of the estate. Secondly, they have no right to interdict alienations by the head of the family either for necessity or otherwise. The right of junior members of the family for maintenance is governed by customs. Thirdly, the income of the impartible estate is the individual income of the holder of the estate and is not the income of the joint family.[5]

Impartible estate and joint family property

An estate which is impartible by custom cannot be said to be separate or exclusive property of the holder of the estate. If the holder has got the estate as an ancestral estate and he has succeeded to it by primogeniture, it will be part of the joint estate of the undivided Hindu family. In case of an ordinary joint family property the members of the family can claim four rights: (1) the right of partition; (2) the right to restrain alienations by the head of the family except for necessity; (3) the right of maintenance; and (4) the right of survivorship. In case of impartible estate the first of these rights cannot exist. The second is also incompatible with the custom of impartibility. The right of maintenance and the right of survivorship still remain. It is by reference to these two rights, the impartible estate has in the eye of law to be regarded as joint family property.[6]

---

4   *Kalwa* v *Union of India* AIR 1964 SC 880.
5   *Kumara Krishna* v *Sarvanga* AIR 1970 SC 1795.
6   *State of U.P.* v *Rukmini Raman* AIR 1971 SC 1687.

Relinquishment of right of succession to impartible estate

A member of a joint family owning an impartible estate can on behalf of himself and his heirs renounce his right of succession. But any such relinquishment must operate for the benefit of all members. The surrender must be in favour of all the branches of the family or in favour of the head of the family as representing all its members.[7]

Alienation of impartible estate

A holder of an impartible estate can alienate the estate by gift *inter vivos*, or even by a will, though the family is undivided. The only limitation on this power would flow from a family custom to the contrary or from the condition of the tenure which has the same effect.[8]

Impartible estate and self-acquired property

Unless the power is excluded by custom or statute, the holder of impartible estate, by a declaration of his intention, can incorporate with the estate self-required immovable property, and thereupon the property accrues to the estate and is impressed with all its incidents including a custom of descent by primogeniture. But this theory of incorporation has no application to movable property. It cannot, however, be said that by a family custom movable property cannot be treated as impartible.[8]

Partition Act 1893

If there cannot be any amicable settlement for partition of joint property, a shareholder can take recourse to the Partition Act 1893. Under s. 2 of the said Act the court has power to order sale instead of division in partition suit. Under s. 4 of the said Act a transferee of share in dwelling house can institute a partition suit. In *Parbati Devi* v *Purana Patra*[9] the title of the appellant as co-sharer was denied by the respondents, *i.e.*, other co-shareholders. The appellant claimed purchase of share in the said property as successor-in-interest of *A* who had purchased the same in court sale. Certificate of sale was issued by the court and the entry in court's register proved the title of the said *A*. It was held that the appellant was a co-owner with the respondents and was entitled to $1/3$ share on partition of the suit property under s. 8 of the said Act any order for sale made by the court, that shall be deemed to be a decree within the meaning of s. 2 of the Code of Civil Procedure.

---

7 *Chinnathayi* v *Kulaskara* AIR 1952 SC 29.
8 *Mirza Raja* v *Sri Pushavati* AIR 1964 SC 118.
9 AIR 1997 SC 2331.

CHAPTER
14
Gift

Nature and limitation

A gift is the relinquishment of one's own right over a particular property without consideration and the creation of proprietory right of another person over the same.

Section 122 of the Transfer of Property Act 1882 defines gift as the transfer of certain existing movable or immovable property made voluntarily and without consideration, by one person, called the donor, to another, called the donee, and accepted by or on behalf of the donee.

A Hindu can dispose of his separate and self acquired property by way of gift. A coparcener under the Mitakshara law cannot dispose of his coparcenary interest by gift. But a coparcener under the Dayabhaga law can dispose of his coparcenary interest by gift.

Gifts of immovable property made by a father-in-law to a daughter-in-law are admitted in Hindu law and such gifts form part of *stridhan*. But a father-in-law cannot dispose of any ancestral property by gift to a daughter-in-law.[1]

A female can dispose of her *stridhan* by gift.

Formalities

A person competent to enter into contract can make a gift. A gift may be made orally or in writing, but acceptance of a gift is essential. A gift is not valid unless it is accompanied by delivery of the subject-matter of the gift from the donor to the donee.[2] Mere registration without delivery of

---

1   *Ammathayee* v *Kumareson* AIR 1967 SC 569.
2   *Abaji* v *Mukta* (1894)18 Bom 688.

possession is not sufficient. A gift once made is irrevocable unless it was obtained by fraud or undue influence.

Gift to unborn person

Generally, a gift to an unborn person is not valid. But that rule of the Hindu law has undergone changes under different statutes. At present the rules are as follows: (*a*) If a gift to an unborn person is preceded by a prior disposition, it shall be for the whole residue. (*b*) The gift shall not offend the rule against perpetuity. (*c*) If a gift is made to a class of persons with regard to some of which it is void, it shall not fail with regard to other persons. (*d*) Where a gift to an unborn person is void, any subsequent gift thereunder is also void.

Direction to accumulate

A direction to accumulate with gift of accumulation is recognised by Hindu law. It fails only when it offends the fundamental rule of Hindu law. The direction is required to be examined whether (*i*) the object is illegal, (*ii*) the effect of carrying out the direction is inconsistent with the Hindu law, and (*iii*) the direction is unreasonable or against the public policy. If the object of direction is to create a perpetuity, it is bad in law.[3] If the effect of a direction is to make a gift in favour of a donee in future without gift in *praesenti*, it is inconsistent with the Hindu law and as such is illegal.[4]

Essentials of a valid gift

The essentials of a valid gift are: (*i*) capacity of donor, (*ii*) acceptance by donee, and (*iii*) existence of subject matter of gift.

(*i*) *Donor*. A person of sound and disposing state of mind who has attained the age of majority may make a gift under Hindu law.[5] A person attains the age of majority when he has attained the age of eighteen years under s. 3 of the Indian Majority Act 1875. But if the property of a minor is under the superintendence of the Court of Ward, he shall be deemed to have attained his majority when he shall have completed his age of twenty-one years. Before passing of this Act of 1875 a Hindu attained the age of discretion (majority) at the age of sixteen.

---

3 *Sukhmoy Chander Dass* v *Monohuri Dasi* (1885)12 IA 103 (PC).
4 *Cally Nath* v *Chundar Nath* (1882) Cal 378.
5 *Krishnamachariar* v *Krishnamachariar* AIR 1915 Mad 815.

(*ii*) *Acceptance by donee.* A donee must be a person in existence at the material date of the gift.[6] A gift made in favour of a person not in existence at the date of the gift is void. A child in the womb at the date of the gift is a person in existence in the eye of law.[7] A gift may be made in favour of a minor, lunatic, two or more persons or a class of persons.[8] A gift to an idol is valid. A gift may be made orally or in writing, but its acceptance is essential in all cases.[9] Acceptance may be made verbally, mentally or corporeally. According to Hindu law "in order to give complete validity to a gift of land as between the donor and the donee, the donee must be put in possession."[10]

(*iii*) *Subject matter.* A Hindu may make the whole or part of his property by way of gift. But the subject matter of a gift must be in existence and under absolute control having right of disposition by the donor.

Revocation of gift

A gift once made validity is irrevocable. It is revocable only if it can be shown that the gift was obtained by fraud or undue influence.[11] In case of gift of land it may be revoked before delivery of possession.[12]

Registration of gift of immovable property

Section 123 of the Transfer of Property Act 1882 provides that for the purpose of making a gift of immovable property the transfer must be effected by a registered instrument signed by or on behalf of the donor and attested by at least two witnesses. In *Brij Raj Singh* v *Sewak Ram*[13] a question arose whether a gift deed was valid. It was held that if the deed in question is a registered deed and one of two attesting witnesses is examined to prove the deed, nothing more is required to satisfy the requirements of s. 123 of the said Act of 1882.

Definition of gift under the Gift Tax Act 1958

Section 2(*xii*) of the Gift Tax Act 1958 defines gift as the transfer of one person to another of any existing movable or immovable property made voluntarily and without consideration in money or money's worth and

---

6 *Ranganadha* v *Bhagirathi* (1906)29 Mad 412.
7 *Tagore* v *Tagore* (1872)9 Beng LR 377.
8 *Jotiram* v *Ramkrishna* (1902)27 Bom 31.
9 *Dharmodas* v *Nistarani* (1887)4 Cal 446.
10 *Vasudeo* v *Narayan* (1883)7 Bom 131.
11 *Manigavri* v *Narandas* (1891)15 Bom 549.
12 *Vasudeo* v *Narayan* (1883)7 Bom 131.
13 AIR 1999 SC 2203.

includes the transfer or conversion of any property referred to s. 4, deemed to be a gift under that section. In *Commr. of Gift tax, Trivandrum* v *T.M. Louiz*[14] it has been held that if a retiring partner receives the value of his share in partnership assets less liabilities without taking into account of goodwill of the firm, there is no element of gift of goodwill by the retiring partner to the continuing partners.

Gift of properties of bhumidar

Gift of properties of bhumidar under s. 24 of the U.P. Zamindari Abolition and Land Reforms Act 1951 requires sanction. It has been held in *Bulaki* v *Lal Dhar*[15] that the sanction of competent officer even if given on the next day of the gift would not invalidate the alienation of property by way of gift.

---

14   AIR 2000 SC 3136.
15   AIR 1998 SC 2900.

CHAPTER
15
Wills

Definition and scope

The expression "will" is defined in s. 2(h) of the Indian Succession Act 1925 as "the legal declaration of the intention of a testator with respect to his property which he desires to be carried into effect after his death." The differences between a transfer and a will are well settled. A transfer under the Transfer of Property Act 1882 is a conveyance of an existing property by one living person to another (that is transfer *inter vivos*). On the other hand, a will does not involve any transfer, nor effect any transfer *inter vivos*, but is a legal expression of the wishes and intention of a person in regard to his properties which he desires to be carried into effect after his death. A will regulates succession and provides for succession as declared by it (testamentary succession) instead of succession as per personal law (non-testamentary succession). The concept of transfer by a living person to another living person is wholly alien to a will.[1]

Power of disposition under wills

There is no direct authority in the texts of the Hindu law that a Hindu could not dispose of his property by law. In *Beer Pertab* v *Rajendra*[2] the Privy Council observed that "It is too late to contend that because the ancient Hindu treatises make no mention of wills, a Hindu cannot make a testamentary disposition of his property; decided cases, too numerous to be now questioned, have determined that the testamentary power exists and may be exercised at least within the limits which the law

---

1 *N. Ramaiah* v *Nagaraj S.* AIR 2001 Kant 395.
2 (1867) 12 MIA 37 (PC).

prescribes for alienation by gift *inter vivos*." In *Tagore* v *Tagore*,[3] the Privy Council held: "The law of wills among Hindus is analogous to the law of gifts; and even if wills are not universally to be regarded in all respects as gifts, to take effect upon death, they are generally so to be regarded as to the property which they can transfer and the persons to whom it can be transferred." Section 30 of the Hindu Succession Act 1956 provides that any Hindu may dispose of by Will or other testamentary disposition any property which is capable of being so disposed of by him in accordance with the provisions of the Indian Succession Act 1925 or any other law for the time being in force and applicable to Hindus.

Formalities

A Hindu who is of sound mind and major can dispose of his property by will. A will may be oral or in writing. There is no particular form for a will. A Hindu cannot dispose of property by a will which he cannot alienate by a gift. There is no bar for a Hindu to dispose of his self-acquired or separate property. Under the Dayabhaga law a coparcener can dispose of all his property by a will; but under the Mitakshara law a coparcener cannot dispose of his coparcenary interest by a will. A Hindu woman could dispose of all her property held as *stridhan* by will. But the Hindu Succession Act 1956 has radically changed the old law.

A will may be revoked orally or in writing.[4] Actual destruction of a will is not necessary. If there is definite intention of the testator of revocation of the will, that will constitute revocation.

Beneficiaries under a will

A person who is in existence either in fact or in the contemplation of law is capable of taking benefit under a will.[5] According to the Supreme Court there is no bar in Hindu law that a Hindu cannot make gift or bequest for the benefit of an unborn person.[6] A bequest to an idol whether in existence or not at the date of the *testator* is valid. This rule also applies to charities. A bequest to a class of persons some of whom are not in existence at the time of death of the testator is valid so far as those persons who are capable of taking under a will are concerned.[7]

---

3 (1872)9 Beng LR 377 (PC).
4 *Maharaja Pratab Narain* v *Subaho Koer* (1877)41 All 228 (PC).
5 *Tagore* v *Tagore* (1872)9 Beng LR 377 (PC).
6 *Raman Nader* v *Rasalamma* AIR 1970 SC 1759.
7 *Rai Bishen Chand* v *Mt. Asmadia Koer* (1884)11 IA 164 (PC).

Construction of a will

The general principles for construction of a will are as follows:

(1) In construing a document whether in English or in vernacular, the fundamental rule is to ascertain the intention from the words used; the surrounding circumstances are to be considered.

(2) In construing the language of the will the court is entitled to put itself into the testator's armchair and is bound to bear in mind also other matters than merely the words used.

(3) The true intention of the testator has to be gathered not by attaching importance to isolated expressions but by reading the will as a whole.

(4) The court must accept, if possible, such construction as would give to every expression some effect rather than that which would render any of the expressions inoperative.

(5) It is a cardinal principal of construction of wills that effect should be given to every disposition contained in the will unless the law prevents effect being given to it.[8]

(6) Section 88 of the Indian Succession Act 1925 provides that where two clauses of gift in a will are irreconcilable so that they cannot possibly stand together, the last shall prevail. This is the principle that the last clause represents the latest intention of the testator.[9]

Conditions and directions in a will

A direction to accumulate given in a will is valid unless it offends any rule of Hindu law. The direction to accumulate is invalid under the following circumstances: (*i*) The period during which accumulation is directed exceeds the period of absolute vesting of the entire estate. (*ii*) The corpus of the property becomes inalienable because of direction to accumulate. (*iii*) The course of devolution of property is directed and controlled by the testator. (*iv*) The object of direction is against the public policy.

A direction to accumulate is valid if it is for (*i*) the payment of debts, (*ii*) the benefit of minor, (*iii*) charitable purposes, or (*iv*) marriage expenses of the testator's children.[10]

---

8 *Nanveet Lal* v *Gokul* (1976)1 SCC 630.
9 *Balwant Kaur* v *Chanan Singh* AIR 2000 SC 1908.
10 *Amrita Lal* v *Suronoomani* (1898)25 Cal 662; *Nafar Chandra* v *Ratan* (1910)15 CWN 66.

Where property is given absolutely subject to a condition restraing the power of alienation by the legatee, the condition is void, but the bequest is valid.[11]

Illustration

A, a Hindu testator makes a will under which A's wife B shall be the full absolute owner of A's property on his death. A gives a direction in the will regarding the manner in which devolution shall take place after B's death. It has been held that such direction is inoperative and invalid, because that will be repugnant to the dominant intention of A to confer on B an absolute right to property.[12]

Factors to be considered for determination of intention of a testator

The primary duty of the court to ascertain the intention of the testator is to look into the language of the will.[13] It is also necessary for the court to consider the surrounding circumstances other than the words used in the will. These are—(*i*) the race and religious opinion of the testator, (*ii*) the law under which the disposition is made, (*iii*) the position of the testator, (*iv*) his family relations, and (*v*) the probability that he would use words in a particular sense. In short, "the court is entitled to put itself into the testator's armchair."[14]

No terms of will to be altered by executor

A probate when granted binds the whole world. The Executor has to administer the estate of the testator in terms of Will and not on the basis of any settlement arrived at by and between the parties which would be inconsistent with the terms of the Will.[15]

---

11 *Saraju Bala* v *Jyotirmoyee* AIR 1931 PC 179.
12 *Bai Kevli* v *Dalsukhram* AIR 1945 Bom 178.
13 *Nathu* v *Gangabai* AIR 1938 PC 228.
14 *Venkata* v *Partha Sarathy* (1913)41 IA 51; *Nathu Ram* v *Gangabhai* AIR 1938 PC 228.
15 *Chandrabhai K. Bhoir* v *Krishna Arjun Bhoir* AIR 2009 SC 1645.

CHAPTER
16

Religious and Charitable Endowments

Essentials of religious endowment

A religious endowment is a mass of property set apart either for the worship of certain deity, or for the establishment or maintenance of a religious or charitable institution, or for the benefit of the public or some section of the public in the advancement of religion, knowledge, commerce, health, safety or any other object beneficial to mankind.[1]

The essentials of a Hindu religious endowment are the following:

(*i*) The donor must dedicate the property absolutely.

(*ii*) The object of the endowment must be definite. It means that the donor must state clearly that the property will be used in perpetuity for the worship of definite idol or for a particular charitable object.

(*iii*) The property must also be definite, that is, the specific property must be set apart.

An endowment shall be created by a Hindu of sound mind and who is not a minor. He may set apart certain specific property for a definite object which must be either religious or charitable. No writing is necessary unless the endowment is created by a will. In such a case the will is required to be attested by at least two witnesses.

An endowment must be made for religious or charitable purpose. Where an estate is created by a grant which is secular in nature, the mere fact that motive for the grant is religious does not constitute it a religious

---

1 *Commissioner of Income-Tax* v *Pemsel* [1891] AC 531.

endowment.[2] The following grants or endowments have been held to be religious or charitable: (a) Feeding Brahmins and the poor;[3] (b) Dharmasalas;[4] (c) Goshala;[5] (d) Establishment of University;[6] or of hospital;[7] (e) Construction and maintenance of tanks, wells and reservoirs of water;[8] (f) Building and renovation of temples.[9]

Dedication

A dedication may be either complete or partial. A complete and absolute dedication is one where the property is absolutely given for the deity without any beneficial interest to any person. On the other hand, a partial dedication is one when the dedicated property is subjected to a charge in favour of the deity. The leading case on this distinction is *Sri Iswar Jew* v *Sushilabala Dasi*.[10]

A dedication to a temple which is to be construed for a deity as stated in a deed of trust is valid.[11] But if a dedication is made without mentioning the particular deity for whom it is made, the dedication is void.

Illustration

A made a dedication by stating to "the Thakurji in my Thakurdwara" without mentioning the particular deity to whom the bequest was made. It was held that the bequest was void for uncertainty.[12]

An endowment is not affected where the image is destroyed or mutilated. A new image in such case may be installed, and the endowment be kept up.[13] It is not essential to construct the temple and to actually instal the idol therein for the purpose of validating a settlement in favour of the idol.[14]

Proof of dedication

Whether there is any valid dedication of property or not is a question of fact. It depends on the construction of the deed or will dedicating the property. A house may be dedicated to a deity and the deity is installed

---

2 *Anantha* v *Nagamuthu* (1882)4 Mad 200.
3 *Dwarakanath* v *Burroda* (1879)4 Cal 443.
4 *Purmanundas* v *Venayak* (1883)9 IA 86 (PC).
5 *Lalita Prasad* v *Brahmanand* AIR 1953 All 449.
6 *Monorama* v *Kalicharan* (1901)31 Cal 166.
7 *Fanindra* v *Adm. Gen. of Bengal* (1901)6 Cal WN 321.
8 *Gauri Shankar* v *Hemant Kumari* AIR 1936 All 301.
9 *Khub Lal* v *Ajodhya* AIR 1916 Cal 792.
10 AIR 1954 SC 69.
11 *Panchamuthu Nader* v *TPT Charities* AIR 1971 Mad 253.
12 *Phundan Lal* v *Arya Prithi* (1911)33 All 793.
13 *Bijoychand* v *Kalipada* (1914)41 Cal 57.
14 *Sarab Sukh* v *Ram Prasad* (1924)46 All 130.

therein. The performance of ceremonies relating to *prathista* is presumed. Subsequently, if the idol is made to disappear, that does not wipe out the existence of the deity or invalidate the dedication.[15] The mere execution of a deed of endowment even if registered is not sufficient to create a valid endowment. There must be transfer of ownership from the donor to the donee. The deed will have no effect unless there is intention on the part of the maker to divest himself of the property.[16] Where dedication was oral and accounts show how the rents and profits were used, the presumption is that there was no complete dedication.[17] The divestment of property from a *guru* to *chella* does not lead to presumption that it is a religious property.[18]

Distinction between public and private endowments

Religious endowments may be of two kinds, namely public endowment and private endowment. A public endowment is one in which the dedication is for the use or benefit of the public, whereas in a private endowment the dedication is for the use or benefit of certain private individual persons to the exclusion of all other. In a public endowment the beneficial interest is vested in an uncertain and a fluctuating body of persons, but in a private endowment the beneficiaries are definite and ascertained individuals. The essence of a public endowment consists in its being dedicated to the public. But where property is set apart for the worship of a family God, the endowment is a private one.[19] Where the rents and profits of endowed property are exclusively utilised for public charity for a long time, the inference is that the dedication is to public charity.[20]

In *Radhakanta Deb* v *Commr. Hindu Religious Endowments, Orissa*[1] the following tests are laid down to provide sufficient guidelines for determination on facts of each case whether an endowment is of a private or of a public nature—(1) where the origin of the endowment cannot be ascertained, the question whether the user of the temple by members of the public is as of right; (2) the fact that the control and management vests either in a large body of persons or in the members of the public and the founder does not retain any control over the management; (3) where a

15 *Ganga Devi* v *Sita Ram* 1981 UPLT (NOC) 86.
16 *Jadu Nath* v *Thakore Sita Ramji* AIR 1917 PC 177.
17 *Mahasin* v *Pareshnath Thakur* AIR 1954 Ori 198.
18 *Parma Nand* v *Nihal Chand* AIR 1938 PC 195.
19 *Bihar State Board* v *Palat Lal* AIR 1972 SC 57.
20 *Ranchhoddas* v *Mahalaxmi* (1952)54 Bom LR 982.
1 AIR 1981 SC 798.

document is available to prove the nature and origin of the endowment; (4) where evidence shows that the founder did not make any stipulation for offerings from any member of the public to the temple, it is a private nature of endowment.

Illusory endowment

If the dedication of property is to appropriate the profits of the property by the executant for his own use and for the worship of an idol, it is an illusory endowment. In such case the dedication is inoperative. Similarly, where there is no real dedication of property to idol, but only an attempt to create a perpetuity in favour of the settlor's descendants, the dedication is illusory and void.[2] If the real object of executant of a deed of endowment is to defraud creditors or to defeat the provisions of ordinary law of succession or to restrain alienations and keep the property in perpetuity in the family, the endowment is illusory and as such inoperative. Whether a dedication is real or illusory is a question of facts depending on several factors, such as the construction of the deed or will, if any, the extent of property involved and other surrounding circumstances.[3]

Illustration

In a trust deed the settlor had stated that she had installed the deity Iswar Srigopal in her house and she had been worshipping the deity regularly since the installation of the deity. The settlor stated further for the construction of two temples, in one the deity Iswar Srigopal would be installed and in the other the marble image of her preceptor would be installed. The trust deed also provided for the establishment of a charitable hospital and dispensary for the gratuitous medical, surgical and maternity advice. The trustees consisted of five persons out of whom three were strangers to the family. It was held that the trusts were public endowment.[4]

Tests for public temple

The issue whether a religious endowment is a public or a private one is a mixed question of law and fact. The decision on the question depends on the following:

(1) Is the temple built in such manner that it may *prima facie* appear to be a public temple?

(2) Are the members of the public entitled to worship in that temple as of right?

---

2 *Promotho* v *Radhika* (1875)14 Beng LR 175.
3 *Ishwari Bhubaneshwari* v *Brojo Nath Dey* AIR 1937 PC 185.
4 *State of Bihar* v *Charusila Dasi* AIR 1959 SC 1002.

(3) Are the temple expenses met from the contributions made by the public?

(4) Whether the *sevas* and *utsavas* conducted in the temple are those usually conducted in public temples?

(5) Have the management and the devotees been treating that temple as a public temple?

If the answers to these tests are affirmative, the temple is a public temple.[5]

Deity and Image

A Hindu deity is a juristic person. On the consecration of the image in the temple, the Hindu worshippers believe that the Divine Spirit has descended into the image.[6]

Devasthan, Math, Shebait, Mohunt

Where the property is absolutely dedicated to *devasthan* or temple, the management of such property is carried out by a person who is technically known as *shebait*. A *shebait* is not a *pujari* or *archak* of the temple, but a manager of the estate dedicated completely and absolutely to the deity of the temple. *Math* is an abode or place of religious learning of students. The management and possession of the property belonging to *math* is carried out by a person who is called *mohunt*. In case of the property of the *math* it is vested in *mohunt*.[7] Property dedicated to the deity is called *debutter* property. In *Vidyapurna* v *Vidyanidhi*[8] it was held that the *mohunt* of an institution does not forfeit his office though he subsequently becomes insane. In *Krishna Singh* v *Mathura Ahir*[9] it has been held that a *math* is an institutional sanctum presided over by a superior who combines in himself the dual office of being the religious or spiritual head of the particular cult or religious fraternity, and of the manager of the secular properties of the institution of the *math*. The property belonging to a *math* is attached to the office of the *mahant* and passed by inheritance to no one who does not fill the office. It is well settled that succession to *mahantship* of a math or religious institution is regulated by custom or usage of a particular institution except where a rule of succession is laid down by the founder himself who created the endowment.

---

5 *Mahalaxmi Vahuji* v *Ranchhoddas* AIR 1970 SC 2025.
6 *Seshammal* v *State of T.N.* (1972)2 SCC 11.
7 *Jagadindra Nath Roy* v *Hemanta Kumari Debi* (1905)32 Cal 129.
8 (1904)27 Mad 435.
9 AIR 1980 SC 707.

Powers of shebait

It is incumbent on him to perform the proper or customary religious duties. So far as the sale of properties is concerned, he cannot do so without legal necessity. Mere benefit to the deity or the temple is not sufficient for alienation of property.

A contract made by a *shebait* is not binding on the endowment unless it is for legal necessity. A purchaser or lender is entitled to the benefit of the rule in *Hanooman Parsad* case.[10]

Similarly, a mortgage or a permanent lease of property by a *shebait* is invalid without legal necessity.

In *Vidyavaruti's* case[11] the position of the *shebait* and the *mohunt* has been described in the following terms: "Called by whatever name, he is only institution. In almost every case he is given the right to a part of the usufruct, depending again on usage or on custom. In no case was the property conveyed to or vested in him, nor is he a trustee in the English sense of the term although in view of the obligations and the duties resting in him, he is answerable as a trustee for maladministration." However, in one respect the *mohunt* has superior position to that of the *shebait*. The *mohunt* may exercise discretion in the application of the funds of the *math*. Offerings made to the *mohunt* belongs to him absolutely.

Generally, property given for the maintenance of religious worship is inalienable. The *shebait* or *mohunt* in charge of such property may borrow money on mortgage of the property for the purpose of keeping up the religious worship. This power of alienation is determined with reference to an existing necessity of religious worship. The power of a *shebait* to alienate *debutter* property is analogous to that of a manager for an infant heir as defined in the case of *Hanooman parsad* v *Mussamat Babooee*.[12] A *shebait*, it is held in the case, has no power to alienate *debutter* property except "in a case of need or for the benefit of the estate." He has no power to sell the property for the purpose of investing the price so as to enhance income. He cannot also grant permanent lease of *debutter* property except for legal necessity.

A *shebait* can alienate the *debutter* property for legal necessity.[13] The legal necessity means keeping up of *seva*, occasional festivies, repairs of

---

10 (1856)6 MIA 393 (PC).
11 48 IA 302.
12 (1856)6 MIA 393.
13 *Basudeo* v *Jugal Kishore* 22 CWN 841 (PC).

temple, restoration of the image, preserving the estate, paying Government revenue, necessary litigation, etc.

Illustrations

(1) A permanent lease was granted by a *shebait*. The lease was called in question after half a century from the date of the execution of the deed of the lease. The original parties to the transaction are dead. What is the effect of the lease? It was held that if all the parties to the transaction who could have given evidence as to the circumstances of the transaction passed away, the recital of the document assumes greater importance. The recitals gathered from the document go to show that the grant was made for legal necessity and the transaction is binding.[14]

(2) *Puja* Bye-law of a temple provides that whatever gift a piligrim is desirous of making and which is not connected with the offering to the deity shall be made outside the temple precincts and not inside it. The Bye laws were challenged. It was held that the Bye-laws are not repugnant to the general principles of Hindu law. This particular Bye-law does not take away the proprietary right of any person which is recognised under ordinary law.[15]

The *shebait* has the general power (*i*) to sue or defend legal proceedings, (*ii*) to contract debts, and (*iii*) to alienate properties for the benefit of the estate under the endowment. The *shebait* cannot delegate his duties to another person.[16] He cannot remove the idol except in the interest of the idol itself.[17] He cannot claim adverse possession against the idol as long as he continues to be *shebait*.[18]

Duties and liabilities of shebait

The duties of the *shebait* depend on the terms of the endowment creating the post of *shebait* and also on the usages prevailing in the similar religious institutions. He cannot delegate the duties of his office.[19]

The liability of the *shebait* is like that of a trustee to account for the property of the endowment.[20] He is personally liable for all acts done by him which are not for the purpose and benefit of the estate under the endowment.

---

14 *Sree Iswar Gopal Jieu Thakur* v *Pratapmal Bagaria* AIR 1951 SC 214.
15 *Nar Hari Shastri* v *Shri. Badrinath Temple Committee* AIR 1951 SC 245.
16 *Gopal Sridhar Mahadev* v *Shasheebhushan* AIR 1933 Cal 109.
17 *Pramatha Nath* v *Pradyumna* AIR 1925 PC 139.
18 *Ishwar Gridher Jew* v *Sushila Bala Dasi* AIR 1954 SC 69.
19 *Gopal Sridhar Mahadev* v *Shasheebhushan Sarkar* AIR 1933 Cal 109.
20 *Chotalal* v *Manohar* (1900)26 IA 199 (PC).

Pujari

A *'pujari'* has to perform the prescribed daily worship of the image as well as the special worship of a periodical nature on particular occasions.[1] The right of a hereditary priest or *'pujari'* in a temple amounts to property.[2] A female cannot perform the duties of a *pujari*.

Mathadhipati

A *mathadhipathi* is not a corporate body. He is the head of a spiritual fraternity. He performs the duties of a religious teacher. If any provision of law prevents him from propagating his doctrines, that would affect the provisions of Art. 25 of the Constitution.[3]

Legal status of idol and temple

An idol is a juridical person but a temple is not. It has been held in *Pramatha* v *Pradyumna*[4] that an idol is a juridical person and not a chattel. An idol is capable (*i*) of requiring and holding property, and (*ii*) has the capacity to sue and be sued. The property dedicated to *devasthana* is the property of the deity and not of the *shebait*.[5] Property of an idol includes offerings and rent of dedicated property.[6]

Since a temple is not a juristic person, no suit can be filed in the name of a temple.[7] An idol is regarded as an infant.[8] But an idol is not regarded as a minor for all purposes and the rule under s. 68 of the Indian Contract Act that a person who supplies necessaries to a minor is entitled to be reimbursed from the minor's estate does not apply to the case of idol of a temple.[9] Besides, an idol is not regarded as minor for the purpose of s. 6 of the Limitation Act 1963.[10] The court may, in the interest of *devasthana*, remove a *shebait*.

Ceremonies required to become "Sanyasi"

In order to prove that a person has adopted the life of a *sanyasi*, it must be shown that he has actually relinquished all worldly possessions or that

---

1. *Raj Kali* v *Ram Rattan* AIR 1955 SC 493.
2. *Raj Kali* v *Ram Rattan* AIR 1955 SC 493.
3. *Commr., H.R.E.* v *Lakshmindra* AIR 1954 SC 282.
4. AIR 1925 PC 139.
5. *Bimal* v *Jnanendra* AIR 1937 Cal 338.
6. *Chotalal* v *Manohar* (1900)26 IA 199.
7. *Mukundji* v *Parsotamlalji* AIR 1957 All 77.
8. *Bimal Krishna* v *Jnanendra* AIR 1937 Cal 338.
9. *Gopal* v *Shasheebhusan* AIR 1933 Cal 109.
10. *Chitar Mal* v *Panchu Lal* AIR 1926 All 392.

such ceremonies are performed which indicate the severance of his natural family and his secular life. In case of orthodox *sanyasis* it must be proved that all necessary ceremonies have been performed, such as *pindadans* or Birjahoma or Prajapathyesthi without which renunciation will not be complete. According to Manu giving up of all worldly property is essential.[11] The orthodox view is that a Sudra cannot become a *sanyasi* or ascetic. But the existing practice all over India is quite contrary to such orthodox view.[12] It is held in *Krishna Singh* v *Mathura Ahir*[13] that a Hindu of any caste may become a *sanyasi*. Right to ascetic life got extended to *sudras*.

Sale of one-half share in shebaiti right

A deed of sale by a co-*shebait* in favour of a stranger purporting to transfer her share in *shebaiti* right, along with the temple and the properties attached thereto was held to be void and illegal, because neither the temple nor the deities nor the *shebaiti* right can be transferred for pecuniary consideration.[14]

---

11 Sherring's *Hindu Tribes and Castes*, pp. 256-267.
12 *History of Dharmasastra* by Dr. P.V. Kane, vol. 2, pt. 1, p. 163.
13 AIR 1980 SC 707.
14 *K.K. Ganguly* v *P. Banerjee* AIR 1974 SC 1932.

CHAPTER
17

The Hindu Succession Act 1956

Changes made by the Act in the traditional Hindu law of succession

The Hindu Succession Act 1956 has brought about certain important changes in the traditional law relating to intestate succession among the Hindus. Some of them are noted below:

(1) The Act lays down a uniform and comprehensive system of inheritance. It applies equally to persons governed by the Mitakshara and Dayabhaga schools.

(2) Section 4 of the Act abrogates all the rules of the law of succession hitherto applicable to the Hindus either by any text of Hindu law or by custom having the force of law.

(3) Sections 8-13 of the Act lay down a set of general rules for succession to the property of a male Hindu dying intestate.

(4) Section 8 of the Act provides for abolition of separate or self-acquired property of a male intestate for the purpose of succession.

(5) The Hindu women's limited estate has been abolished and any property held by a female Hindu is now regarded as her absolute property (s. 14).

The Hindu Succession Act 1956 has altered the rule of survivorship in coparcenary property under the Mitakshara law. A male Hindu is entitled to dispose of his interest in Mitakshara coparcenary property by will. Under this Act sex or propinquity will not be made ground of preference for succession.

There is one exception which has been provided in s. 6 of the Hindu Succession Act 1956. By this section if a male Hindu dies after the commencement of this Act, his interest in a Mitakshara coparcenary property shall devolve by survivorship upon the surviving members of the coparcenary.

Abrogation of Hindu law on succession

Section 4 of the Hindu Succession Act 1956 provides that any text, rule or interpretation of Hindu law or any custom or usage relating to Hindu succession in force immediately before the commencement of the Hindu Succession Act shall cease to have any effect with the commencement of this Act. Thus, the Act abrogates the old Hindu law laid down by the *smritis*, the sruits or the commentators. The customary law of succession prevailing in the Punjab would stand abrogated.[1] But this Act would not take away any vested right of a Hindu widow by virtue of the provisions of the Hindu Women's Rights to Property Act 1937 before the commencement of this Act.[2] This Act abrogates matters only in respect of which provisions have been made in the Act and not other matters. Thus, the pious obligation of a son to pay his father's debt is not provided in the Act and as such this has not been abrogated by this Act.[3]

Any other law in force immediately before the commencement of the Hindu Succession Act 1956 shall also cease to apply to Hindus, so far as it is inconsistent with any of the provisions of this Act. Thus, the Hindu Inheritance (Removal of Disabilities) Act 1928, the Caste Disabilities Removal Act 1850 and the Hindu Women's Rights to Property Act 1937 have been abrogated by virtue of the provisions of s. 4 of the Hindu Succession Act 1956.

But this Act does not affect the provision of any law relating to (*i*) prevention of fragmentation of agricultural holdings, (*ii*) fixation of ceilings, or (*iii*) devolution of tenancy right in respect of such holdings.

Section 5 of the Act provides that any succession to property under the Indian Succession Act 1925 by reason of the provision of s. 21 of the Special Marriage Act 1954 shall not be in any way affected.

Illustrations

(1) A Hindu male marries a Hindu female under the Special Marriage Act 1954. The property of each of them on his or her death would be governed by the Indian Succession Act 1925. There will be no difference of succession law even if son or daughter born of such marriage has married under the Hindu Marriage Act.

---

1 *Ishwar Das* v *Raj Kumar* AIR 1961 Punj 275.
2 *Upendra* v *Chintamoni* AIR 1960 Cal 22.
3 *Nathubhai* v *Chhotubhai* AIR 1962 Guj 68.

(2) A Hindu male married a Hindu female under the Special Marriage Act 1954. They have a son S who marries according to Hindu law. S has a son M who survives on the death of S. M will inherit according to the Hindu Succession Act, provided he does not marry under the Special Marriage Act 1954 in respect of the property of S but he succeeds to the property of S's father according to the Indian Succession Act 1925.

Customs of tribals

Neither the Hindu Succession Act, nor succession Act nor even Shariat Law is applicable to custom for governing tribals as custom varies from people to people and region to region.[4] Where parties are Scheduled Tribe and factual evidence on record shows that they are following Hindu traditions and not following customary traditions, s. 2(2) of the Hindu Succession Act 1956 will not apply to exclude the parties from application of the Hindu Succession Act 1956.[5]

Sections 4(2), 14(2)[6]—Devolution of land on widow

Under s. 213 of Quanoon Mal a widow acquires limited right. She had executed a lease deed after remarriage and before coming into force of the Hindu Succession Act 1956. Such transfer did not confer any right on the tenant.

Devolution of interest in coparcenary property

The Original provisions of s. 6 of the Hindu Succession Act 1956 have been substituted by s. 3 of the Hindu Succession (Amendment) Act 2005 with effect from 09.09.2005. Under the new s. 6 of the Hindu Succession Act 1956 after substitution the following provisions have been made with regard to devolution of interest in coparcenary property: (1) In a joint Hindu family governed by the Mitakshara law, the daughter of a coparcener shall (*a*) by birth become a coparcener in her own right in the same manner as the son; (*b*) have the same rights in the coparcenary property as she would have had if she had been a son; (*c*) the subject to the same liabilities in respect of the said coparcenary property as that of a son. (2) Property to which a female becomes owner under sub-sec. (1) of s. 6 may be disposed of by her by testamentary disposition. (3) Where

---

4   *Madhu Kishwar* v *State of Bihar* AIR 1996 SC 1864.
5   *Labishwar Manjhi* v *Pran Manjhi* (2000)8 SCC 587.
6   Prior to the Hindu Succession (Amendment) Act 2005.

a Hindu governed by the Mitakshara law dies after the amending Act of 2005, his property shall not devolve on heirs by survivorship but is to be deemed to have been divided as if there was a partition and (*a*) the daughter is allotted the same share as the son; (*b*) the share of predeceased son or a predeceased daughter shall be allotted to the surviving child of such predeceased son or of such predeceased daughter; (*c*) the share of predeceased son or of a predeceased daughter shall be allotted to the child of such predeceased child of predeceased son or a predeceased daughter. (4) After the amendment of 2005 no court shall recognise any right to proceed against a son, grandson or great grandson for the recovery of any debt from his father or grandfather or great grandfather on the ground of pious obligation. But if the debt is contracted before the commencement of the amending Act of 2005, the right of the creditor shall not be affected, nor the alienation for the satisfaction of the debt would be unenforceable. (5) Nothing contained in this new s. 6 shall apply to a partition which has been effected before 20th December 2004.

General rules of succession in case of males

Section 8 of the Hindu Succession Act 1956 lays down general rules of succession in the case of a male Hindu dying intestate. The property of a male Hindu dying intestate shall devolve according to the provisions of chapter II of the Act. First, the property shall devolve upon the heirs being the relatives specified in class I of the Schedule.

The heirs in class I of the Schedule to the Hindu Succession Act 1956 are as follows: Son, daughter, widow, mother, son of a predeceased son, daughter of a predeceased son, son of a predeceased daughter, daughter of a predeceased daughter, widow of a predeceased son, son of a predeceased son of a predeceased son, daughter of a predeceased son of predeceased son, widow of a predeceased son of a predeceased son, son of a predeceased daughter of a predeceased daughter; daughter of predeceased daughter of a predeceased son.

Section 9 provides that the heirs specified in class I of the Schedule shall take simultaneously to the exclusion of all other heirs.

Section 10 provides that the property of an intestate shall be divided among the heirs in class I of the Schedule in accordance with the following rules:

Rule 1 lays down that if there are more widows than one of the deceased, all of them together shall take one share. Rule 2 lays down that the surviving sons and daughters and the mother of the intestate shall each take one share. Rule 3 lays down that the heirs in the branch of each predeceased son or each predeceased daughter of the intestate shall take between them one share. Rule 4 is a corollary to r. 3. It lays down that among the heirs in the branch of the predeceased son distribution shall be so made that the widow and the surviving sons and daughters get equal portions, and the branch of his predeceased sons gets the same portion. The distribution among the heirs in the branch of the predeceased daughter shall be so made that the surviving sons and daughters get equal portions.

Changes effected under section 8 of the Hindu Succession Act

The major changes brought about by s. 8 of the Hindu Succession Act 1956 are as follows:

(a) It introduces a uniform system of succession in all schools of the Mitakshara and the Dayabhaga.

(b) It excludes certain heirs recognised by the old system of law. A preceptor and disciple were heirs under certain circumstances.

(c) It removes the distinction between the theory of spiritual efficacy and *sapinda* relationship under the two schools of Hindu law. This section recognises both cognates and agnates as heirs without any specific reference to them.

Illustrations

(1) A Hindu died intestate leaving a widow and mother. Both of them would succeed together in equal shares.[7]

(2) A Hindu died after the commencement of the Hindu Succession Act 1956 leaving two widows, a mother, a son and two daughters. The property would be divided into five equal parts. The two widows together would take one fifth as one heir in equal shares under s. 10, r. 1, the mother one-fifth, the son one-fifth and two daughters one-fifth each.[8]

(3) A, a Hindu died intestate leaving M, the mother; W_1 and W_2 as two widows; B, a son; W_3, a widow, G and H as sons of a predeceased son, C of A; W_4, a widow, K, a son and L, a daughter of a predeceased grandson of a predeceased son D of A; E, a daughter of A; and I, a son and J, a daughter of a predeceased daughter F of A. The property of A will be divided into seven equal parts: M, (one seventh); W_1 and W_2 (together one-seventh); W_3, G and H (together one-seventh representing predeceased son C); W_4, K and L (together one seventh representing grandson of A); E (one-seventh); and I and J (together one-seventh representing F); and B (one seventh).

(4) Joint family constituted by father with his son. Son died leaving behind childless widow. Father expired later and mother died thereafter leaving behind

---

7 *Gurdit Singh* v *Darshan Singh* AIR 1973 Punj 262.
8 *Kishta Bai* v *Ratna Bai* (1979)1 Andh LT 250.

daughter-in-law and four daughters. It was held that share of daughter-in-law is one-third and of each daughter is one-sixth.[9]

(5) *No pre-existing legal right.* Chance of daughter to succeed to her father's estate in case father dying intestate is not a pre-existing right. Limited ownership confessed on daughter by her father's will would not mature into full ownership merely on the basis of such chance to succeed.[10]

Succession by Hindu females

Section 14 of the Hindu Succession Act 1956 is given retrospective effect. This section has enlarged a Hindu limited estate into an absolute estate in respect of property which had been acquired by her before the Act came into force. Under the Hindu Succession Act 1956 property succeeded by a female heiress would be her absolute property. Section 14 of the Hindu Succession Act 1956 confers the absolute ownership on all females in respect of all properties in their possession. No matter whether the property was acquired before or after the commencement of the Act.

By the term "property" the explanation to s. 14 of the Act includes both movable and immovable property.

Section 14 of the Hindu Succession Act 1956 provides for absolute ownership of property by a female Hindu. Section 15 lays down the rules for the devolution of such property of a female dying intestate. The rules are as follows:

(1) The property will devolve on the sons and daughters (including children of predeceased son or daughter) and the husband.

(2) In the absence of any one of them above-stated, the property will devolve upon the heirs of the husband.

(3) It will devolve upon the mother and father.

(4) In the absence of above classes of heirs, it will devolve upon the heirs of the father.

(5) Lastly, in absence of all the above it will go to the heirs of the mother.

There are certain exceptions to the above rules. First, if a female Hindu inherits property from her father or mother, on her death without issue the property will revert to the heirs of her father. Similarly, if she inherits property from her husband or father-in-law, it will devolve in absence of children or grand children of the deceased upon the heir of the husband.

---

9 *Lehja Bai* v *Sewanti Bai* (2009)6 SCC 800.
10 *Balwant Kaur* v *Chanan Singh* AIR 2000 SC 1908.

Besides, the heirs of a female Hindu include her illegitimate children and children born by remarriage.

Section 16 of the Act deals with the order of succession and the manner of distribution amongst the heirs of a female dying intestate.

A widow is disqualified to inherit under the Hindu Succession Act 1956 on the following grounds: (*i*) If she has remarried on the date of succession. (*ii*) If she commits murder or abets the commission of murder of her husband. (*iii*) If she ceases to be a Hindu.

Illustrations

(1) B, a Hindu Jat of Hissar District, alienated certain property in 1916. M, a reversioner obtained a declaratory decree in 1920 to the effect that the alienation was ineffective against his reversionary rights. B died in 1959 leaving behind him his widow, three sons and two daughters. It was held that the estate devolved on the widow, three sons and two daughters by virtue of the provisions of ss. 2 and 4(1) of the Hindu Succession Act 1956.[11]

(2) A preliminary decree was passed under which K was entitled to a share in the family estate. The said estate was a joint family property of which K was a member and in her joint possession. It was held that by virtue of s. 14(1) of the Hindu Succession Act 1956 the right declared in the decree includes possession of property by her.[12]

(3) A, the last owner of a property died in 1920 leaving a will under which B, the widow of A, was authorised to adopt a son. In compliance with the direction of the will B adopted C in 1942. D claiming to be the nearest reversioner challenged the validity of C's adoption in a declaratory suit. The suit was dismissed and on appeal the High Court affirmed the decision of the trial court. D appealed to the Supreme Court after the commencement of the Hindu Succession Act 1956. It was held that A's estate vested in B through constructive possession of C.[13]

(4) A Hindu female died leaving her daughter, a daughter of a predeceased son and his wife. It has been held that the former two and not the wife of a predeceased son would succeed to the property.[14]

(5) A Hindu female, died intestate leaving behind D, a daughter S, an adopted son, I, an illegitimate son, and M, a step son. The property of A will be inherited by D, S and I and not by M.[15]

(6) W, a Hindu female, had three children, namely, A, B and C from her first husband who died and W married another man and had one child D from him. On the death of her second husband W became the owner of his property as a successor. A, B and C claimed a share in the property inherited by W from her

---

11 *Giani Ram* v *Ramji Lal* AIR 1969 SC 1144.
12 *Munnalal* v *Rajkumar* AIR 1962 SC 1493.
13 *G.T.M. Kothurswami* v *S. Veeravva* AIR 1959 SC 577.
14 *Ramkatori* v *Prakashwati* ILR (1968)1 All 697.
15 *Gurbachan Singh* v *Kichar Singh* AIR 1971 Punj 240; *Mallappa* v *Shivappa* AIR 1962 Mys 140.

second husband on her death. It was held that A, B, C and D are entitled to equal shares.[16]

(7) A, a Hindu, died leaving two widows, W_1 and W_2, and N, a nephew. On W_1's death N claims her property. It was held that W_2 would be the heir of W_1 in preference to N.[17]

(8) A, a Hindu woman, dies intestate leaving behind H, the husband; B, a son; D a daughter; S and T, two sons of a predeceased son; P, a daughter of a predeceased daughter. The property of A will be divided in five equal parts. H, B and D will inherit one-fifth each. S and T will jointly inherit one-fifth. P will inherit one-fifth.

(9) *Remarriage of widow, effect.* A limited right of maintenance permeates into an absolute right under s. 14(1) of the Hindu Succession Act 1956, but in the event of there being a remarriage of the widow prior to 1956, the widow is divested of even, the limited ownership of her deceased husband's property. The Hindu Widow's Remarriage Act 1856 had its full play on the date of remarriage itself, as such the succession Act could not confer the widow who has already remarried any right in terms of s. 14(1) of the 1956 Act.[18]

(10) *Widow estate.* Under s. 14(1) of the Hindu Succession Act 1956 all that is necessary to be shown by a female Hindu is that she had a right in the property in question and she is possessed of that property. The possession may be physical, constructive or formal in a legal sense on the date of the coming into operation of the Act. But this is not the *sine qua non* for the acquisition of full ownership in the property. Where a Hindu Widow transferred all her right to third party through sale deed before the 1956 Act came into force and without any legal necessity, she could not be said to be possessed of this property. Thus, the sale deed does not restrict the enjoyment of the estate, it would full outside the purview of sub-sec. (2) and would full under sub-sec. (1) of s. 14 of the 1956 Act.[19]

(11) *Facts of the case.* In *Mangal Singh v Smt. Rattna*[20] the plaintiff instituted a suit for possession of land against the defendants Nos. 1-4. The suit was dismissed by the trial court but was decreed on appeal against defendants Nos. 1-3 only treating defendant No. 4 as proforma respondent on the pleadings of the parties. The defendants Nos. 1-3 preferred an appeal for reversal of decree against them impleading defendant No. 4 as respondent. The High Court of Punjab dismissed the appeal and thereupon the matter went up to the Supreme Court by special leave. During the pendency of the appeal one of the defendants-appellants died and his legal representatives were brought on the record as appellants. The defendant No. 4 who was respondent in the appeal also died. The application to bring his legal representatives on record was dismissed by the order of the court.

Point for decision. Is a Hindu widow who was illegally dispossessed of land belonging to her deceased husband entitled to bring a suit for possession?

Decision. Yes.

---

16 *Ram Kali v Sohanlal* AIR 1972 Punj 419.
17 *Kaibalo v Barojo* (1966)32 Cut LT 148.
18 *Velamuri Venkata Sivaprasad (dead) by L.Rs. v Kothuri Venkataeswarlu (dead) by L.Rs.* AIR 2000 SC 434.
19 *Smt. Naresh Kumari (dead) by L.Rs. v Shakshi Lal (dead) by L.Rs.* AIR 1999 SC 928.
20 AIR 1976 SC 1986.

Reasons for decision. Though during the pendency of the suit the Hindu Succession Act 1956 came into force and subsequently in 1958 the widow died and her legal representative was brought on record, s. 14(1) of the Act would govern her possession.

Points decided. (1) Even if a female Hindu is, in fact, out of possession, the property must be held to be possessed by her.

(2) The use of the expression "in possession of" in s. 14(1) of the Hindu Succession Act 1956 was intended to enlarge the meaning of this expression. This provision will become applicable to any property which is owned by a female Hindu, even though she is not in actual, physical or constructive possession of that property.

Validity of section 14 of the Hindu Succession Act 1956

Section 14 of the Hindu Succession Act was challenged as *ultra vires* Art. 31 of the Constitution in *Bhabani Prosad* v *Sarat Sundari*,[1] on the ground that this section in effect abolished the class of reversionary heirs depriving them of their right under the old Hindu Law to inherit property after the death of the limited heir. It was held in that case that s. 14 was covered by Art. 31(1) and (3) and as such was valid.

Section 14 was then attacked as *ultra vires* Art. 14 of the Constitution in *Joginder Singh* v *Kehar Singh*[2] on the ground that there were restrictions on the power of a male to alternate coparcenary property but no such restrictions were made on a Hindu female. It was held in that case that the women form a distinct category for the purpose of Art. 15(3) of the Constitution and as such s. 14 is valid.

In *Prema Devi* v *Jt. Direction*,[3] s. 14 of the Hindu Succession Act was assailed on the ground that it was *ultra vires* the Central Legislature regarding agricultural lands. But it was held that this section is valid and does not come in conflict with the provision of any other law.

Is section 14 prospective or retrospective?

Section 14 of the Hindu Succession Act 1956 is both prospective and retrospective. Section 14(1) provides that any property possessed by a female Hindu, whether acquired *before* or *after* the commencement of this Act, shall be held by her as full owner thereof and not as a limited owner. This section is retrospective in so far as it enlarges a Hindu woman's right to a limited estate into an absolute right of her ownership before the commencement of this Act.[4] Even when an appeal is pending at the

---

1 AIR 1957 Cal 527.
2 AIR 1965 Punj 407 (FB).
3 AIR 1970 All 238.
4 *Venkayamma* v *Veerayya* AIR 1957 AP 280.

commencement of this Act with regard to a limited right of a widow, it has been held that the widow must be deemed to have been held as a full owner of her limited right in an estate.[5] This section is not retrospective in case a Hindu female with limited right in an estate had died before the Act came into force.[6] Section 14 has no application to a Hindu woman who is in possession of a property without any right therein.[7]

Devolution of interest in coparcenary property

Under the law prevailing before the commencement of the Hindu Succession Act 1956 a coparcency could not make any alienation of his interest in undivided property by a will. If any such alienation was made, that was regarded as invalid. But now under s. 30 of the Hindu Succession Act a male Hindu in a Mitakshara coparcenary is competent to dispose of his interest in the coparcenary by a will. Section 8 prescribes that where a coparcener dies, the Mitakshara coparcenary property will not be disrupted but the surviving coparceners shall remain as members of the joint family without arriving at a partition. The undivided interest of a coparcener in the coparcenary property will devolve on his death by survivorship upon the surviving coparceners. According to the proviso to s. 6 of the Act the interest of a coparcener dying intestate will devolve upon the persons who are among the twelve preferential heirs set out in class I of the Schedule.

Illustrations

(1) A, a Hindu, dies leaving his widow W, one son, S and four daughters D, E, F and G. The widow W would get $\frac{1}{3}$ share in her own right, and $\frac{1}{8}$ share in $\frac{1}{3}$ share of her husband A. S will also get $\frac{1}{3}$ share plus $\frac{1}{8}$ share of his father. D, E, F and G will get $\frac{1}{8}$ share each.[8]

(2) A, B, C and D are four brothers and coparceners. A has three sons, B has two sons, C has one son and D has none. On partition of coparcenary property A, B, C and D will get $\frac{1}{4}$ share each. On further partition amongst A and his three sons, each of them will get $\frac{1}{4} \times \frac{1}{4}$, that is $\frac{1}{16}$ share each. Similarly, on further partition amongst B and his two sons, each will get $\frac{1}{12}$ share $\left(\frac{1}{4} \times \frac{1}{3}\right)$.[9]

---

5   *Dhirajkunwar* v *Lakhansingh* AIR 1957 MP 38.
6   *Andal* v *Sivaprakasa* AIR 1963 Mad 452.
7   *Eramma* v *Veerupana* AIR 1966 SC 1879.
8   *Vidyaben* v *Jagdish* AIR 1974 Guj 23.
9   *Dukhi* v *Mabdei* (1978)4 All LR 555.

(3) K dies leaving joint family property and his widow, two sons and three daughters. The widow files a suit for partition. She is entitled to $\frac{1}{4}$ share on partition in her own right and $\frac{1}{6}$ of the $\frac{1}{4}$ share of her husband. Thus, she is entitled to $\frac{7}{24}$ share in the property.[10]

(4) A dies leaving an undivided interest in the coparcenary property and some self-acquired property as well. A leaves behind two sons, B and C, a daughter D and a widow, W. B having separated from A during his life time is not entitled to any coparcenary property which will be divided into three equal parts among C, D and W. But A's separate property is divisible into four equal parts among B, C, D and W.

(5) *Female Hindu*. A female Hindu inherited property from her mother. On her death the property would devolve on his sister as per sub-sec. (2) of s. 15 of the Hindu Succession Act 1956 and not on heirs of her predeceased husband.[11]

Position of a female inheriting a share in a dwelling house

Section 23 of the Hindu Succession Act 1956 provided that where a Hindu intestate has left surviving him or her both male and female heirs specified in Class I of the Schedule and his or her property includes a dwelling house, the right of any such female heir to claim partition of the dwelling house shall not arise until the male heirs choose to divide their respective shares therein. But the female heir shall be entitled to a right of residence in that dwelling house if she is a daughter, and she is unmarried or a widow, or deserted by or separated from her husband.

The provisions of s. 23 are omitted by s. 4 of the Hindu Succession (Amendment) Act 2005 (w.e.f. 09.9.2005) as a result of which both the male and female heirs have equal right to partition of a dwelling house.

Section 23 proviso (prior to deletion w.e.f. 09.09.2005) and after— Effect

G. died intestate leaving behind one son and four daughters. Two of his daughters filed a partition suit on 11.3.1996. The son contested the suit on the ground that their father left a will. The son could not succeed in probate proceedings and as such the court allowed the daughter's partition suit and passed a preliminary decree of partition. The son preferred an appeal to the Supreme Court on the ground that the High Court erred in retrospectively applying s. 3 of the Hindu Succession (Amendment) Act 2005 without considering the bar of s. 23 of the Hindu Succession Act 1956. In dismissing the appeal the Supreme Court held that it is

---

10 *Gurupad* v *Hirabai* AIR 1978 SC 1239.
11 *Bhagat Ram (dead)* v *Teja Singh* AIR 1999 SC 1944.

evident from the 174th Report of the Law Commission and the Statement of Objects and Reasons of the Hindu Succession (Amendment) Act 2005 that Parliament intended to achieve the goal of gender equality. If after amendment the disability of female heir to inherit the equal share of property together with a male heir in a joint coparcenary property. Where a partition has not taken place, s. 6 of the 1956 Act would apply. In that case the statute is prospective in nature. Neither the 1956 Act nor the 2005 Act seeks to reopen vesting of a right where succession has already taken place.[12]

Right of a child in the womb

Section 20 of the Hindu Succession Act 1956 provides that a child who was in the womb at the time of the death of an intestate and is born subsequently alive shall have the same right to inherit the property of the intestate as if he or she had been born before the death of the intestate, and the inheritance shall be deemed to vest in such a case with effect from the date of the death of the intestate.

This section recognises children *ventre sa mere*. It adopts the old principle of Hindu law that a child in the womb is a person in actual existence. The right of such person relates back to the date of conception. Where no share is allotted to a child in the womb at the time of the death or partition of an estate either because the pregnancy was not manifest at the material point of time or otherwise, the child after the birth has a right to reopen a succession as well as a partition, as the case may be.

Presumption in cases of simultaneous deaths

Section 21 of the Hindu Succession Act 1956 provides that where two persons have died simultaneously, the presumption in such case is that until the contrary is proved, the younger survived the elder. This presumption will apply to all matters of succession to property. In case of simultaneous deaths son survived the father until the contrary is proved.

Illustrations

(1) A woman and her married daughter died in a fire in their house. There was no evidence as to who died first. It was held that the mother must be presumed to have died first. The daughter was, therefore, entitled to inherit the property of the mother. On the death of the daughter simultaneously with the mother in the facts and circumstances above, the husband of the daughter was entitled to the property.[13]

---

12 *G. Sekar* v *Geetha* (2009)6 SCC 99.
13 *Jayantilal* v *Mehta* AIR 1968 Guj 212.

(2) A Hindu woman and her daughter were murdered on the same day and at the same time and in the same case. It was held that the daughter, being the younger, survived the mother, being the elder.[14]

Right of pre-emption

Section 22 of the Hindu Succession Act provides for the right of pre-emption to acquire property in certain cases of devolution on more than one person specified in class I of the Schedule. If any one of such heirs has an interest in any immovable property of an intestate or in any business carried on by him or her, whether solely or in conjunction with others and any one of such heirs proposes to transfer his or her interest in the said property or business, the other heirs specified in class I of the Schedule shall have a preferential right to acquire the interest proposed to be transferred. This right of pre-emption is a personal right and cannot be transferred.

The consideration for the transfer of such interest, in the absence of any agreement between the parties, shall be determined by the court on an application being made to it in this behalf. If any person proposing to acquire the interest is not willing to acquire for the consideration so determined by the court, such person shall be liable to pay all costs of or incidental to the application.

If there are two or more heirs specified in class I of the Schedule proposing to acquire any interest as above, the heir who offers the highest consideration for the transfer is to be preferred.

The provisions of this section will not apply to a case where the property devolves by survivorship.

Illustrations

(1) B, a Hindu, died intestate leaving behind two sons, namely C and D, who took the property of B by survivorship. It was held that neither C nor D would have a right of pre-emption against the other.[15]

(2) A and B are two sons of A and have inherited the property of A on his death by way of succession. A sells the property of his share to D without any notice to B. It was held that such transfer was ineffective on proof that the transfer was made without notice of the proposal of the transfer.[16]

---

14 *Padmaraja* v *Gyanachandappa* AIR 1976 Mys 87.
15 *Bholanath* v *Santosh* AIR 1975 Pat 336.
16 *Ganesh* v *Rukmani* AIR 1971 Ori 65.

Persons disqualified to inherit

Section 24 of the Hindu Succession Act 1956 provides that a widow on remarriage shall not be entitled to succeed to the property of the intestate if on the date of succession she has remarried.

Section 24 of the Act has been omitted by s. 5 of the Hindu Succession (Amendment) Act 2005 which has come into effect on 9.9.2005. Consequent upon this amendment there will be no discrimination of unmarried widow and remarried widow for inheritance.

Section 25 provides that a person who commits murder or abets the commission of murder shall be disqualified from inheriting the property of the person murdered.

Section 26 lays down that where a Hindu has ceased or ceases to be Hindu by conversion to another religion, children born to him or her after such conversion and their descendants shall not be entitled to succeed the property of their Hindu relatives unless such children are Hindus at the time when the succession opens.

Illustrations

(1) A widow has succeeded to the property of her deceased husband and thereafter she remarries. The property already vested cannot be divested by subsequent disqualification.[17]

(2) A wife is charged with murder of her husband. She was subsequently acquitted by a competent court. It was held that she would not be disqualified from inheritance.[18]

Effects of disqualification and failure of any heir to succeed

Section 27 of the Hindu Succession Act 1956 provides that if any person is disqualified from inheriting any property under this Act, it shall devolve as if such person had died before the intestate.

Section 29 provides that if an intestate has left no heir qualified to succeed to his or her property in accordance with the provisions of this Act, such property shall devolve on the Government. The Government shall take the property subject to all the obligations and liabilities to which an heir would have been subject. This provision is technically known as escheat to the Government.

---

17 *Bhuri* v *Champi* AIR 1968 Raj 139.
18 *Chaman Lal* v *Mohan Lal* AIR 1977 Del 97.

Illustration

A Hindu bequeathed his property to his two sons as a class. One son had murdered the father. It was held that there was no intestacy with regard to the share of the murderer, the bequest being to a class, the property would go to the other son. Section 27 has no application to this case.[19]

Section 29A

The right conferred on unmarried daughter in HUF property by s. 29A which was introduced in 1985 would have no effect on computation of ceiling limits of her father on the notified date under the Land Ceiling Act.[20]

Testamentory succession

Section 30 of the Hindu Succession Act 1956 provides that any Hindu may dispose of his property by a Will, provided such person is competent to do so in accordance with the provisions of the Indian Succession Act 1925.

Illustration

A coparcener made a will prior to the commencement of the Hindu Succession Act 1956 but died afters the commencement of this Act. It was held that the will was valid, because it took effect from the death of the testator.[21]

---

19 *Mohinder* v *Wasson* AIR 1968 Punj 389.
20 *Makineni Venkata Sujatha* v *Land Reforms Tribunal* AIR 2000 SC 3191.
21 *Virabhatrappa* v *Irabayawwa* (1969)2 Mys LJ 105.

PART 3

Muslim Family Law

CHAPTER
18

Introduction

Schools of Mahomedan law

The Mahomedans are divided principally into two sects, namely, the Sunnis and Shias.

The Sunni sect is once again divided into four sub-sects, namely, the Hanafis, the Malikis, the Shafeis and the Hanbalis.

The Shia sect is sub-divided into three sub-sects, namely, Athna—Asharias, the Ismailyas and the Zaidyas.

A. Sunni law

(*i*) *The Hanafi school*. This school was founded by Abu Hanafi. This is the most important school. This school is also known as 'Kufe School'. Besides, Abu Hanafi, his two pupils, namely, Abu Yusuf and Imam Muhammad Ash Shaybani, contributed a lot for the development of this school. The *Fatawa-i-Alamgiri* contain the important doctrines of this school.

(*ii*) *The Maliki school*. The school was founded by Malik Ibn Anas. Malik's contributions to the Islamic law are the art of interpretation by reasoning and the development of Islamic jurisprudence based on the Koran and Hadis. The followers of Malik Ibn Anas are to be found in Upper Egypt, Central and West Africa, Spain and Eastern Arabian coast.

(*iii*) *The Shafei school*. This school was founded by Muhammed Ibn Idrisash-Shafii. Originally, he was a pupil of Malik Ibn Anas, but subsequently he founded a new school of Islamic law. His principal contributions are the doctrine of Qiyas, ijmaa as a source of law. His famous work is kitab-ul-umm. The followers of this school are to be found in Egypt, South Arabia, East Africa, Indonesia, Malaysia and South East Asia.

(iv) The Hanbali school. This is the school of the traditionists who followed the principle of law modified by Ahmed Ibn Hanbal, a pupil of Imam Shafii Ahmed Ibn. Hanbal's principal works are Musnad at Imam Hanbal, Taat-ur-Rasul and Kitab-ul-Alal. The followers of this school are to be found in Syria and Palestine.

Shia laws

The Shia school was founded by Imam Jafar Asadik. The advocates of this school do not agree with the advocates of the Sunni schools on many points. First, the Shias do not believe any tradition as propounded by the Sunnis unless such tradition originated in the house of the Prophet. The Shias do not endorse any view unless upheld by an Imam.

The followers of the Shia school are to be found in Persia (Iran).

Effect of change of sect

The Mahomedan law is applicable to each sect or sub-sect differently. A Mahomedan who has attained the age of puberty has right to change his sect or sub-sect and adopt the tenets of other sect or sub-sect. He will then be governed by the law of the new sect or sub-sect which he has adopted.[1]

A Sunni woman who contracts marriage with a Shia, does not become subject to the Shia law.[2] Similarly, if a Shia woman contracts marriage with a Sunni, she does not thereby become subject to the Sunni law.

Sources of Mahomedan law

The principal sources of Mahomedan law are, (1) the Koran, (2) the Hadis, (3) Jimaa, and (4) Kiyas.

(1) *The Koran.* It is the sacred book of the Mahomedans. The courts cannot put their own construction on the Koran repugnant to the express rulings of the Mahomedan commentators of ancient time and of high esteem.

(2) *The Hadis.* These are precepts, actions and sayings of the prophet Mahomed. These were not written down by the Prophet during his life time, but preserved by tradition and handed by authorised persons.

(3) *Ijmaa.* It means the concurrence of opinion of the companions of Mahomed and his disciples. No new exposition of law is permissible on the ancient texts or authorities of the law.[3]

---

1 *Hayat-un-Nissa* v *Muhammad* (1890)12 All 290.
2 *Nasrat* v *Hamidan* (1882)2 All 205.
3 *Baqar Ali* v *Anjuman* (1902)25 All 236.

(4) *Kiyas.* It means an analogical deduction derived from a comparison of the first three sources when they did not apply to a particular case.

(5) *Custom.* Custom is also recognised as one of the sources of the Mahommedan law.[4] In matters of inheritance and succession. The Khojas of Bombay, the Sunni Bohras of Gujarat, the Molesalam Giarasias of Broach and the Halovi Memon of Porbandar (Gujarat) were governed by the Hindu law of succession and inheritance.

In addition, the rules of equity are often referred to for the purpose of adjudication of cases under Mahomedan law.[5]

General rules of interpretation of the Hanafi law

The general rule of interpretation of the Hanafi law is that where there is a difference of opinion between Abu Hanifa, the great exponent of the Hanafi—Sunni law, and his two disciples, Abu Yusuf and Imam Muhammad or the opinion between Abu Hanifa and Imam Muhammad, that opinion is to prevail which coincides with the opinion of Abu Yusuf. When the two disciples differ between themseves and also with their master, the opinion of their master is generally preferred. Where there is no specific rule to guide the court, the court will follow the rule of justice, equity and good conscience.[6]

Application of Mahomedan law

The Mahomedan law is applicable to a Mahomedan. A Mahomedan is a person who professes the Mahomedan religion and believes in one God and Mahomed as the Prophet.[7] A person is a Mahomedan by birth or by conversion.[8]

Conversion to Mahomedanism and its effect on marital rights

The conversion of a person into the Islamic faith has effect on marital right. If a Hindu wife is converted to Mahomedanism, her marriage with the Hindu husband is not *ipso-facto* dissolved. Before legally dissolving the marriage if she marries for the second time a Mahomedan after her conversion into Mahomedanism, she commits an offence of bigamy under s. 494 of the Indian Penal Code.[9]

---

4 See Sir Abdur Rahim: *Mohamedan Jurisprudence*, (1911 Ed.), p. 136.
5 *Hamira Bibi* v *Zubaida Bibi* (1916)43 IA 294.
6 *Aziz Bano* v *Muhammed* (1925)47 All 823.
7 *Narantakath* v *Prakkal* AIR 1923 Mad 171.
8 *Abraham* v *Abraham* (1863)9 Moo IA 199.
9 In the matter of *Ram Kumari* (1891)18 Cal 264; *Mst. Nandi* v *The Crown* (1920)1 Lah 440.

Illustrations

(a) A Christian married a Christian woman. Subsequently the Christian man embraced Mahomedanism and went through a marriage ceremony with another woman. The Privy Council held that the latter marriage was of doubtful validity.[10]

(b) An Indian Christian domiciled in India married an Indian Christian woman. They were domiciled in India. The Christian man embraced the Mahomedan faith and went through a marriage ceremony with a Mahomedan woman during the subsistance of the former marriage. It was held that the latter marriage was valid.[11]

(c) A Zorostrain married woman embraced the Mulsim faith and asked her husband to embrace the Muslim faith which offer he declined. The woman sought for a declaration in a suit that her marriage with the Zorostrain husband was dissolved. It was held that the Muslim personal law did not apply where at the time of the marriage both the parties were non-Muslims.[12]

Effect of conversion to Mahomedanism on inheritance

Succession to the estate of a convert to Mahomedanism is governed by the Mahomedan law in absence of any custom or convention to the contrary.[13]

Illustration

A Hindu husband had a wife living and children. He then became a Muslim and married a Muslim wife and had also children by her. After his death his property passed to his Muslim wife and children and not to his Hindu wife and children.[14]

A person converted to Mahomedanism changes not only his religion but also his personal law. Such a rigid rule, however, applies to cases of individual conversions, for, in cases of wholesale conversion of a caste or a community, it is recognised that the converts might retain a part of their original personal law according to their hitherto held habits, traditions and surroundings.[15]

Excommunication

The Dawoodi Bohras form one of the several sub-sects of the Shia sect of Musalmans. The Dai-ul-Matlaq as the head of the Dawoodi Bohra Community has the right to excommunicate any member of the community.[16]

Religious practice

Cow slaughter on Bakri Idd day is not an essential religious practice.[17]

---

10 *Skinner* v *Orde* (1871)14 MIA 309.
11 *John Jiban Chandra* v *Abinash* (1939)2 Cal 12.
12 *Robasa Khanum* v *Khodadad Bomanji* AIR 1947 Bom 272.
13 *Mitar Sen Singh* v *Maqbul Hasan* (1930)57 IA 313.
14 *Poniah Nadar* v *Essaki Devania* AIR 1955 Trav Co. 180.
15 *Controller of Estate Duty* v *Haji Abdul Sattar* AIR 1972 SC 2229.
16 *Sardar Syedna* v *State of Bombay* AIR 1962 SC 853.
17 *State of West Bengal* v *Ashutosh Lahiri* AIR 1995 SC 464.

CHAPTER
19

The Muslim Personal Law (Shariat) Application Act 1937

Object

All the Muslim Women Organisation condemned prior to the passing of the Muslim Personal Law (Shariat) Application Act 1937 that the customary law adversely affected their rights. They demand that the Muslim Personal Law (Shariat) should be made applicable to them. Thus, this Act was passed to apply to all Muslims, men and women.[1]

Title, extent and applicability

This Act is called the Muslim Personal Law (Shariat) Act 1935. It extends to the whole of India, except the State of Jammu and Kashmir.[2] In all questions except question relating to agricultural land regarding intestate succession, special property of females including personal property inherited or obtained under a contract or gift or any other provisions of personal law, marriage, dissolution of marriage, maintenance, dower, guardianship, gifts, trusts and trust properties and wakf (other than charities and charitable institutions and charitable and religious endowments) the rule of decision where the parties are Muslims shall be the Muslim Personal Law (Shariat).[3]

Declaration in prescribed form, necessary

A person who satisfies the prescribed authority that (*a*) he is a Muslim and (*b*) he is competent to contract within the meaning of s. 11 of the

---

1 See Statement of Objects and Reasons, Gazette of India 1935, pt. v, p. 136.
2 Section 1, Muslim Personal Law (Shariat) Application Act 1937.
3 Section 2, *ibid*.

Indian Contract Act 1872 and (c) he is a resident of the territories to which this Act extends may by declaration in a prescribed form and filed before the prescribed authority declare that he desires to obtain the benefit of the provisions of the Act. The declarant may also declare that he as well as all his minor children and his descendants shall also be governed by the provisions of s. 2 of the Act. If the prescribed authority refuses to accept such a declaration, the aggrieved declarant may appeal to such officer as the State Government may appoint.[4]

Rule making powers of State Government

The State Government is empowered to make rules to carry into effect the purposes of the Act.

---

4   Section 3, *ibid*.

CHAPTER
20

Marriage and Sonship

Definition of marriage

A Muslim marriage (*nikah*) is defined as a contract for the object of the procreation and legalisation of children. A marriage under the Mahomedan law is not a sacrament but a civil contract. The rights and obligations under the contract of marriage arise immediately after the marriage and are not dependent on any condition precedent to the contract.[1]

Essentials of a valid Muslim marriage

Literally *nikah* means marriage. It is defined by the Mahomedan law as a contract which has for its objects the procreation and the legalising of children.

The following are essentials of a *nikah*:

(*i*) There should be a proposal made by or on behalf of one of the parties to the marriage.

(*ii*) There should be an acceptance of the proposal by or on behalf of the other party.

(*iii*) The offer and acceptance of the proposal must be made in the presence and hearing of two male or one male and two female witnesses who are competent persons in the Mahomedan law.

(*iv*) The proposal and acceptance must be made at one meeting. Writing or any religious ceremony is not necessary for valid marriage.[2]

There is a practice that a Nikah Register is maintained in every mosque in which the marriage is recorded and signed by the parties to the marriage

---

1   *Abdul Kadir* v *Salima* (1886)8 All 149.
2   *Jogu Bibi* v *Mesal Shaikh* (1936)63 Cal 415.

or their representatives and attested by the witnesses. A Mullah is invited for offering benediction on the newly weds.[3]

Marriage of fosterage

The marriage of fosterage is forbidden by Shia law. But the Sunnis recognise the marriage of fosterage in the following cases:

(1) The marriage of the father of the child with his child's foster-mother;

(2) With the daughter;

(3) The marriage of the foster-mother with the brother of the child whom she has fostered;

(4) The marriage of an uncle or aunt with the foster-mother.

Celebration of marriage

A Muslim marriage is generally celebrated in the house of the father or guardian of the bride in the presence of the agents (*wakils*)—of the parties. Some persons become witnesses to the deed of marriage. The document contains all the conditions to which the husband binds himself. The conditions are *inter alia* (1) the amount of anti-nuptial payment to the bride, (2) the amounts of *mahr* (dower), (3) the custody of children, etc. The document is signed by the *walis* (guardian), the *wakils* (agents), if any, of the bride and the bridegroom, and also by the witnesses.

Capacity for Muslim marriage

A person of sound mind may enter into a contract of Muslim marriage provided the party has attained puberty. Thus, three conditions determine the capacity for Muslim marriage. These are—(1) soundness of mind, (2) attainment of puberty, and (3) consent. The age of puberty in case of a Muslim girl is nine years.[4] In the case of a boy the age of puberty is twelve years. A marriage procured by force or fraud and without subsequent ratification by the aggrieved party is invalid.[5] A marriage without consent of the aggrieved party cannot be said to be valid even if there is consummation against the will of the aggrieved woman.[6]

Kinds of marriage

According to Mahomedan law there are three kinds of marriages, namely, valid (*sahih*), irregular (*fasid*), and void (*batil*). A marriage that fulfils the

---

3 See Ameer Ali: *Mahommedan Law*, 5th Ed., vol. 2, Appendix-1, p. 555.
4 *Sadiq Ali Khan* v *Jai Kishori* AIR 1929 PC 152.
5 *Abdul Latif* v *Nyaz Ahmed* (1909)31 All 343.
6 *Abdul Kasem* v *Jamila Khatun Bibi* AIR 1940 Cal 251.

essential conditions is a valid marriage. A marriage which is not valid is either irregular or void.

A void marriage is unlawful in itself. It is no marriage at all from the very beginning. Thus, when a marriage takes place with a woman prohibited by reason of consanguinity, affinity or fosterage, it is void. The prohibition against marriage with such woman is perpetual and absolute.

An irregular marriage is not unlawful in itself but unlawful "for something else". The prohibition in this case is not absolute but temporary. It arises from an accidental mistake, such as absence of witnesses. A marriage may be irregular due to the following circumstances: (*a*) A marriage is contracted without witness. (*b*) A marriage is contracted with a fifth wife by a person having four wives living. (*c*) A marriage is contracted with a woman who is undergoing *iddat*. (*d*) A marriage is contracted with one who is prohibited by reason of difference of religion. (*e*) A marriage is contracted with a woman who is related to the wife in such a way that if one of them had been a male, they could not have been lawfully married.

The above irregularities may be removed, and as soon as these are done, the irregular marriage is turned into a valid marriage.

Marriage by recognition

A Muslim marriage is presumed in absence of direct proof by acknowledgment of the children as legitimate by the father.

In order to make a valid acknowledgment the following conditions are to be satisfied.

(1) There must be a difference of at least twelve and a half years of age between the acknowledger and the acknowledged so as to admit the possibility of their standing as father and son.

(2) The person acknowledged must be of an unknown descent.

(3) The person acknowledged must believe himself to be the acknowledger's child.

Presumption of lawful marriage

There is a presumption of lawful marriage where there was prolonged and continued cohabitation as husband and wife and where there was no insurmountable obstacle to such a marriage. Some of those obstacles are: (*a*) prohibited relationship between the parties, (*b*) the woman being an undivorced wife of a husband who is alive. The presumption of lawful marriage does not apply if the conduct of the parties was incompatible with the existence of the relation of husband and wife nor did it apply if the woman was admittedly a prostitute before she was brought to the man's house. If, therefore, there was no insurmountable obstacle to such a marriage, and the man and woman had cohabited with each other continuously and for a prolonged period, the presumption of lawful marriage would arise and it would be sufficient to establish that there was a lawful marriage between them.[7]

In *Imambandi* v *Haji Mutsaddi*[8] one Ismail Khan died leaving three widows and several minor children. On his death one of his widows named Zohra sold her share including the shares of her minor children in respect of certain immovable property to the plaintiffs. The plaintiffs sued for possession and declaration of title. But the defendants alleged that Zohra was not the married wife of Ismail Khan and as such her children were not legitimate. In addition, Zohra had no power to transfer the shares of her minor children. The Subordinate Judge decreed the suit in favour of the plaintiffs. This was affirmed by the High Court of Calcutta on appeal. Then the matter went up to the Privy Council.

Points of decision. (1) Was Zohra a lawful wife of Ismail Khan? (2) Had Zohra any authority to sell the shares of her minor children?

Decision. (1) Yes. (2) No.

Reasons for decision. Though there was no direct evidence as to the marriage between Ismail Khan and Zohra, there was sufficient evidence to prove that Ismail Khan acknowledged her children as legitimate. Under the Mohammedan law a marriage between the parties in such circumstances must therefore be presumed.

Points decided. (1) Under the Mahomedan law the mother is entitled only to the custody of her minor children upto a certain age.

(2) A *de facto* guardian has no power to transfer or pledge the immovable property of the minor children except under imperative necessities.

(3) Where a Mohamedan has acknowledged children as his legitimate issues, there is a presumption that he had a valid marriage with their mother.

---

7   *Mohd. Amin* v *Vakil Ahmad* AIR 1952 SC 358.
8   (1918)45 IA 73.

Muta marriage

A *muta* or temporary marriage may be contracted by a Shia Muslim. It is essential to the validity of *muta* marriage that the period of cohabitation should be fixed and that some dowry should be specified.

The incidents of a *muta* marriage are the following:

(a) It does not create any right of inheritance on either spouse. But children conceived of *muta* marriage can inherit parent's property.[9]

(b) Where the term for *muta* marriage is fixed and cohabitation continues after that period, the presumption is that the term has been extended by mutual consent.

(c) A *muta* marriage is *ipso facto* dissolved after the expiry of the period for which it was fixed.

(d) Where a *muta* marriage is not consummated, the woman is entitled to half the dower.

(e) A woman of *muta* marriage is not entitled to maintenance under the Shia law. But she is entitled to maintenance under s. 125 of the Code of Criminal Procedure 1973.

The Sunni law does not recognise *muta* marriage.

Plurality of marriages

Right to plurality of marriage is not unconditionally conferred on husband. His capacity to do justice between co-wives is condition precedent.[10]

Second marriage by Hindu convert

Status of second wife and children born out of marriage by Hindu convert has not been gone into in the case of *Lily Thomas* v *Union of India*.[11]

Dower (mahr)

Mahr means dower. *Mahr* is a sum of money or other property which the wife receives from her husband in consideration of marriage. Under the Shia law, there is legal minimum fixed for dower. The amount of dower may be fixed either before or after or at the time of marriage.

Where a contract of dower is made by the father of the husband who is minor, it is binding on the husband. But under the Shia law the minor

---

9 *Shoarat Singh* v *Jafri Bibi* (1915)17 Bom LR 13.
10 *Lily Thomas* v *Union of India* AIR 2000 SC 1650.
11 AIR 2000 SC 1650.

son is not liable for the contract of dower made by his father if he has no means of his own.[12]

The wife is entitled to proper dowry even if the marriage was contracted on the express condition that she should not claim any dower. The proper dower under the Shia law shall not exceed 500 *dirhams*. The dower is an essential incident under the Mahomedan law to the status of marriage.[13]

The dower may be confirmed by any one of the following ways: (*a*) Consummation of marriage. (*b*) A valid retirement. (*c*) The death of either the husband or the wife.

Dower debt. A dower debt has no priority over other debts on any equitable consideration or on the ground that there is something inherent in its very nature which entitles it to priority.[14]

Disentitlement of dower. A Muslim woman is not entitled to any dower in any of the following cases if the separation takes place before consummation:

(1) When the marriage is contracted between two minors without the consent of their guardians.

(2) When a marriage between two minors is cancelled by them in exercise of their right of option.

(3) When the marriage is cancelled by order of the Judge.

(4) When a man enters into a contract of marriage while he is labouring under death, illness.

(5) When the wife enters into a contract of marriage while she is suffering from illness.

Restitution of conjugal rights. Mahomedan law lays down that a wife is bound (*i*) to live with her husband, and (*ii*) to follow him wherever he desires to go. If a Muslim wife refuses to do any one of them without any valid reason the Court of Justice on a suit for restitution by her husband shall order her to live with her husband. A Muslim wife cannot refuse to live with her husband on any of the following grounds:

(1) That she wishes to live with her parents.

(2) That the domicile of choice of the husband is different from the domicile of origin.

---

12 *Sabir Husain* v *Farzanel Khan* AIR 1938 PC 80.
13 *Hamira Bibi* v *Zubaida Bibi* (1916)43 IA 294.
14 *Kapore Chand* v *Kidar Nissa* AIR 1953 SC 413.

(3) That the climate of the domicile of choice of her husband is injurious to her health.

(4) That she detests her husband.

Divorce

A contract of marriage under the Mahomedan law may be dissolved (1) by the husband at his will, (2) by mutual consent of the husband and the wife, and (3) by a judicial decree.

Talak. Talak means dissolution of marriage.

A *talak* may be effected in any of the following ways:

(*i*) TALAK ASHAN. This consists of a single pronouncement of divorce made during a *tuhr* (period between menstruations) followed by abstinence from sexual intercourse for the period of *iddat*.

(*ii*) TALAK HASAN. This consists of three pronouncements made during successive *tuhrs* followed by abstinence from sexual intercourse.

(*iii*) TALAK-UL-BIDDAT OR TALAK-I-BADAI. This consists of: (1) three pronouncements made during a single *tuhr* either in one sentence or in separate sentences, or (2) a single pronouncement made during a *tuhr* clearly indicating an intention irrevocably to dissolve the marriage.[15]

A *khula* is a divorce with the consent and at the instance of the wife. The wife agrees to give a consideration to the husband for her release from the marriage tie. The terms of the bargain are settled between the husband and the wife.

A *mubarat* is a divorce by agreement. But it differs from *khula* on the point of consideration. In *mubarat* the aversion is mutual. Both the husband and wife mutually agree to separate from each other. The offer of mutual separation may flow either from the husband or from the wife. But once the offer is accepted by the other side, dissolution is complete.

Ila. Ila form of divorce is a constructive divorce which is effected by abstinence from sexual intercourse for more than four months in persuance of a vow.

Zihar. It is a form of inchoate divorce. In this kind of divorce husband looks at his wife as the replica of his mother or a female falling within the

---

15 *Sarabai* v *Rabiabai* (1905)30 Bom 537.

prohibited degree. The wife has right in such case to refuse to surrender to the husband until he performs penance.

Talak under compulsion. Repudiation of marriage under compulsion or threat is invalid according to Shia law under the following circumstances:

(1) That the compeller is able to do what he threatens.

(2) That there is strong probability of carrying out the threat.

(3) That the threat involves imminent and serious danger to the person concerned.

A "trifling injury" is not sufficient to establish compulsion.

Judicial decree. The Dissolution of Muslim Marriages Act 1939 provides the grounds for divorce by a wife which are the following (s. 2):

(a) The whereabouts of the husband are not known for a period of four years.

(b) Failure of the husband to provide for maintenance of the wife for a period of two years.

(c) Sentence of imprisonment of the husband for not less than seven years.

(d) Failure of the husband to perform marital obligation without reasonable cause for a period of three years.

(e) Impotency of the husband at the time of the marriage and even thereafter.

(f) Insanity of the husband for a period of two years or suffering of the husband from leprosy or a virulent venereal disease.

(g) Repudiation of the marriage by the wife before attaining the age of eighteen years and also before the consummation of the marriage where she was given in marriage by her father or other guardian before she attained the age of fifteen years.

(h) Cruelty of the husband such as (i) assaults, (ii) illicit connection with women of evil repute, (iii) leading of immoral life, (iv) disposal of her property, (v) obstruction to her performance of religious practices, (vi) discrimination between wives, and (vii) cruelty recognised by Muslim law.

Iddat. It is a period during which it is incumbent upon a woman whose marriage has been dissolved by divorce or death of her husband to remain in seclusion, and to abstain from marrying another person. When the marriage is dissolved by divorce, the duration of *iddat* is generally three lunar months. If it is dissolved by death, the duration is four months and ten days.

Lian. It means imprecation. The wife can sue her husband for falsely implicating her with a charge of adultery. She is required to file a suit for dissolution of marriage.

Effect of conversion of a Muslim wife to other faith

Section 4 of the Dissolution of Muslim Marriages Act 1939 provides that the renunciation of Islam by a married Muslim woman or her conversion to a faith other than Islam shall not by itself operate to dissolve her marriage. But after such renunciation or conversion, she is entitled to obtain a decree for the dissolution of her marriage on any ground mentioned in s. 2 of the Act.

The provisions of s. 4 shall not apply to a woman converted to Islam from some other faith who re-embraces her former faith.

Custody of child. The mother is of all persons the best entitled to the custody of her infant children during the connubial relationship as well as after its dissolution. (Fatawai 'Alamgiri', vol. 1, p. 728). According to the Hanafi school the mother retains the custody of her daughter until she attains the age of puberty. The Malikis and Hanbalis lay down that the custody of a daughter continues until she is married.

The right of *hizanat* or custody of a child is lost according to all schools of thought under the following circumstances:

(1) Subsequent marriage of the *hazina* with a person not related to the infant.

(2) Misconduct of the *hazina* to the child.

(3) Change of domicile of the *hazina* so as to present the father or tutor from exercising necessary supervision over the child.

(4) Abjuration of Islam.

(5) Neglect of or cruelty to the child.

CHAPTER
21
Gifts

Distinction between Hiba and Hiba-bil-iwej

A *hiba* in Mahomedan law means a gift. It may be defined as "a transfer of property made immediately, and without any exchange" by one person to another and accepted by or on behalf of the other.

There are three essentials of a *hiba*. First, there must be a declaration of gift by the donor. Secondly, there must be an acceptance of gift, express or implied, by or on behalf of the donee. Thirdly, there, must be delivery of possession of the subject of the gift by the donor to the donee. Unless these conditions are fulfilled, there cannot be a valid gift. On the other hand, if these conditions are satisfied, the gift is complete.[1]

A *hiba-bil-iwej* is a gift for consideration. In fact it is a sale or exchange. It has all the incidents of a contract of sale. Possession is not required to complete the transfer as it is required in the case of *hiba*. Two conditions must be satisfied for a valid *hiba-bil-iwej*.

First, there must be actual payment of consideration on the part of the donee.

Secondly, there must be *bona fide* intention on the part of the donor to divest himself of the property.

Where *hiba-bil-iwez* is in respect of immovable property of the value of Rs. 100 and upwards, it must be effected by a registered instrument as required by s. 54 of the Transfer of Property Act 1882. As a sale, it also gives rise to a right of pre-emption.[2]

---

1 *Sultan Begum* v *Ara Begum* (1933)57 Cal LJ 459.
2 *Satyendra Nath* v *Fulsom Bibi* 36 CWN 483.

Illustrations

(1) A plaintiff filed a suit for declaration that the owner of a house had given it to him by way of gift. But he failed to prove either the grant of the corpus or of the usufruct of the house to him by its owner. It was held that the very first condition of a valid gift, namely, the declaration of gift by the donor, was lacking in that transaction. Such a declaration must indicate, with reasonable clarity, what is really gifted.[3]

(2) The husband made a gift of his properties including immovable property to his minor wife who had attained puberty, by a registered deed. The husband was living at the time of the gift in the house of his mother-in-law. The wife was also living at her mother's house and in her care. The mother accepted the delivery of possession of the property on behalf of her daughter. On challenge against the validity of the said gift it was held that the intention to make the gift was clear and manifest, because it was made by a deed which was registered and handed over by the donor to his mother-in-law who accepted it on behalf of her minor daughter. There was an intention to divest ownership on the part of the donor and to transfer the property to the donee. If the donor had handed over the deed to his wife, the gift would have been complete under Mahomedan law. Both on texts and authorities such a gift must be held to be valid and complete.[4]

(3) A gift of property in the possession of a trespasser is made by a declaration of the donor and accepted by the donee. It was held that to validate the gift there must also be either delivery of possession or failing such delivery, some overt act by the donor to put the property in possession of a donee. If, apart from making a declaration, the donor does nothing else, the gift is invalid.[5]

(4) The Muslim Ruler of Bhopal State gave to one of his subjects a residential house in addition to pension by a firman in consideration of his services rendered to the State. The grantee was in the house until he died issueless and widowless. The house was thereafter occupied by one of his heirs. It was held that the intention of the Ruler was to grant only the right of residence for life to the grantee and the right of absolute estate in the house.[6]

Death-bed gifts

A Mahomedan may make a gift of his entire property even in favour of a stranger to the exclusion of his heirs. The only limitation imposed is in respect of death-bed gifts.[7]

A death-bed gift is one which a Mahomedan makes during *marz-ul-maut* or death illness. A *marz-ul-maut* is a malady or death illness. It is highly probable that the death will ultimately result from illness or malady. The limitation of such gift is that it cannot take effect beyond one-third of the estate of the donor after payment of funeral expenses and debts

---

3 *State of UP* v *Sayed Abdul Jalil* AIR 1972 SC 1290.
4 *Valia* v *Pathakkalan* AIR 1964 SC 275.
5 *Maqbool* v *Khodaija* AIR 1966 SC 1194.
6 *Mohsin Ali* v *State of MP* AIR 1975 SC 1518.
7 *Sahi Ullah* v *Ghulam Jabbar* (1955) Lah 57.

unless the heirs of the donor consent to the gift in excess of one-third of the estate after the death of the donor.

A gift made during *marz-ul-maut* by a Mahomedan cannot take effect unless the following conditions are fulfilled:

(1) A third of the estate of the donor after payment of funeral expenses are made is given. Beyond this prescribed limit property may be given only when the heirs give their consent after the death of the donor. Where such gift is made to an heir, it will not take effect unless other heirs consent there to after the donor's death.[8]

(2) There must be proximate danger of death and it must occur before long. In other words, the gift must be "under pressure of the sense of the imminence of death".[9]

(3) There must be delivery of possession by the donor to the donee.

Gift of mushaa

A gift of *mushaa* or an undivided share in property capable of division is valid under the following circumstances:

(a) The gift is made by one co-sharer to another.

Illustration

A Mahomedan female died leaving her mother, a son and a daughter as her heirs. The mother made a gift of her undivided share in the property inherited to the son of the deceased. It was held that the gift was valid.[10]

(b) The gift is in respect of a share in zamindari.

Illustration

M, N and R were co-sharers of a zamindari share and each co-sharer was separately assessed by the Government. M made a gift of his share to S without partition of the said zamindari. The gift was valid.[11]

(c) The gift is in respect of a share of freehold property in a city.

Illustration

M was the owner of a house in the city of Rangoon. M made a gift of one-third of that house to N. The gift was valid.[12]

(d) The gift is regarding shares in a company dealing with lands.

---

8 Mt. Sakina Begum v Khalifa Hafiz-ud-din (1914)194 IC 77.
9 Ibrahim Goolam Ariff v Saiboo (1908)35 Cal 1.
10 Mahomed Buksh v Hoossei Bibi (1881)15 IA 81.
11 Abdul Aziz v Fateh Mahomed (1911)38 Cal 518.
12 Ibrahim Goolam Ariff v Saido (1907)34 IA 167.

Conditions for making valid gift

The conditions to make a valid and complete gift under the Muhammedan law as restated in *Abdul Rahim* v *Sk. Abdul Zabar*,[13] are as under:

(a) The donor should be same and major and must be the owner of the property which he is gifting.

(b) The thing gifted should be in existence at the time of *hiba*.

(c) If the thing gifted is divisible, it should be separated and made distinct.

(d) The thing gifted should be such property to benefit from which is lawful under the Shariat.

(e) The thing gifted should not be accompanied by things not gifted, *i.e.*, should be free from things which have not been gifted.

(f) The thing gifted should come in the possession of the donee himself, or of his representative, guardian or executor.

Three pillars of a valid gift under the Muhammedan law are declaration, acceptance and delivery of possession.[14]

Revocation of gifts

A gift may be revoked at any time before delivery of the property by the donor.

A gift may be revoked after delivery of the property by the donor in the following cases:

(1) The gift is made by the husband to the wife and *vice versa*.

(2) The donee is related to the donor within the prohibited degree.

(3) The donee is dead.

(4) The subject-matter of the gift is lost or destroyed.

(5) The value of the subject-matter of the gift has increased.[15]

(6) The character or the subject-matter of the gift is changed and cannot be identified.[16]

(7) The donor has received consideration in exchange of the gift from the donee.

---

13 (2009)6 SCC 160. See *Abdul Rahim* v *Sk. Abdul Zabar* AIR 2010 SC 211.
14 *Maqbool Alam* v *Khodaija* AIR 1966 SC 1194.
15 *Mulani* v *Maula Baksh* AIR 1924 All 307.
16 *Maqbul* v *Ghafur-un-nissa* (1914)36 All 333.

A gift after delivery of possession can be revoked only by a decree of the court.

Hiba-ba-shart-ul-iwaz

When a gift is made with a stipulation for a return, it is called *hiba-ba-shart-ul-iwaz*. Delivery of possession is necessary to make this gift valid. It is revocable but becomes irrevocable on delivery.

Areeat

Where there is no declaration of gift, the transaction would amount to nothing more than the grant of licence, revocable at the grantor's option. Such grant is known as *'areeat'*. In one case, the plaintiff failed to prove that there was either grant of the *'corpus'* or of the *'usufruct'* of the house to him for his life by its ower. Thus, it was held to be *areeat*.[17]

---

17 *State of UP* v *Sayed Abdul Jalil* AIR 1972 SC 1290.

Chapter
22
Wakf

Conditions of valid wakf

Wakf is a religious or charitable endowment of a property dedicated permanently by a person professing the Islamic faith. In *Vidya Varuthi Thirtha Swamigal* v *Balusamy Iyer*,[1] the Judicial Committee of the Privy Council points out that wakf constitutes the "tying up of property in the ownership of God, the Almighty and the devotion of the profits for the benefit of human beings." Section 2 of the Mussalman Wakf Validating Act 1913 defines wakf as "the permanent" dedication by a person professing the Mussalman faith of any property for any purpose recognised by the Mussalman law as religious, pious or charitable." Section 3(*r*) of the Wakf Act 1995 defines wakf as "the permanent dedication by a person professing Islam, of any movable or immovable property for any purpose recognised by the Muslim law as pious, religious or charitable and includes—

(*i*) a wakf by user but such wakf shall not cease to be a wakf by reason only of the user having ceased irrespective of the period of such cesser;

(*ii*) "grants" including *mashrut-ul-khidmat* for any purpose recognised by the Muslim law as pious, religious or charitable; and

(*iii*) a *wakf-alal-aulad* to the extent to which the property is dedicated for any purpose recognised by Muslim law as pious, religious or charitable."

A wakf *inter vivos* may be completed by a mere declaration of endowment by the owner. According to Muhammad a wakf is not

---

1 AIR 1922 PC 123.

complete unless, besides a declaration of wakf, a *muttawalli* is appointed by the owner and possession of the endowed property is delivered to him. But the Allahabad High Court in a Full Bench decision has held that a mere declaration of endowment by the owner is sufficient to complete the wakf.[2]

The Mussalman Wakf Validating Act of 1913 has introduced an important change relating to private wakf. Section 3 of the Act provides that a wakf created by a Mahomedan will be valid if it conforms to all the Mussalman law and is made for the following purposes: (*a*) Maintenance and support wholly or partially of the wakif's children or descedants. (*b*) Where the creator of wakf is a Hanafi Mussalman, it can be created for his own maintenance and support or the payment of his debts out of rents and profits of the property dedicated.

Prior to this Act a wakf was valid if the effect of the deed of wakf was to give the property in substance to charitable uses only. Where the property in substance was given to the testator's family, it was not a valid wakf.

After passing of the Mussalman Wakf Validating Act 1913 which was made retrospective, the validity of a wakf made for the benefit of the settlor's family cannot be challenged.[3]

Illustrations

(1) Land is being used from time immemorial for religious purposes. There is no evidence for clear and express dedication. It has been held that no evidence for express dedication in such case is necessary. It is a wakf by user.[4]

(2) There had been long user of part of property for wakf. It was held that it did not convert the whole property into wakf property.[5]

Wakf, creation of

The directions for conduct "fateha" at the graveyard and to use the house for those purposes are certainly valid objects of a wakf. In *Wati Mohammed* v *Rahmat Bee*,[6] the offerings of prayers are not confined to prayers at the tombs of the grantor or his family members. The grant was by the head of the order and related to the prayers at a number of tombs in the graveyard. Thus, it is clear that a wakf of a public nature was created.

---

2   *Mohammad Yosin* v *Rahmat Ilahi* AIR 1947 All 201 (FB).
3   *Bibi Saddiqa Fatima* v *Saiyed Mohd. Mahmood Hasan* (1978)3 SCC 299.
4   *Mohd. Shah* v *Fasihuddin* AIR 1956 SC 713.
5   *Anjuman* v *Munshi* (1971)3 SCC 814.
6   AIR 1999 SC 1136.

Validity of wakfnama

A wakfnama was executed and duly registered by sub-registrar. Settlor was found to be in fit mental condition and was owner of properties mentioned in wakfnama. He executed wakf for religious benefit and thereafter property vested in God. He assumed the character as *mutawalli*. It is a valid wakf.[7]

Bequest creating wakf, when invalid

A bequest creating wakf is contingent upon life time of a lady. It is invalid. Disposition subject to contingency is invalid under Muslim law.[8]

Powers and functions of mutawalli

Mutawalli means a manager of wakf property. As soon as a wakf is created, all rights of property vest in the Almighty. The *mutawalli* has no right in the property belonging to the wakf. He merely acts as a superintendent or manager of the wakf property.

A *mutawalli* has no power to mortgage, sell or exchange the wakf property or any part thereof without the leave of the court. But he can do so if he is expressly authorised by the deed of wakf. A *mutawalli* has no power to grant a lease of wakf property for more than a specified period. If it is agricultural land, he cannot grant lease for more than three years. If it is non-agricultural, he cannot grant lease for more than one year (*i*) unless he is expressly empowered by the deed of wakf or (*ii*) unless he has obtained the leave of the court. A *mutawalli* in absence of authority in the deed of wakf has no power of alienation of property against a creditor's right.

He has also no power to increase the allowance of officers and servants fixed by the deed without the leave of the court.

The founder of a wakf may constitute himself the first *mutawalli* and when the founder and the *mutawalli* are the same person, no transfer of physical possession of property is necessary. Nor is it necessary that the property should be transferred from the name of the donor as owner into his name as *mutawalli*. An apparent transaction must be presumed to be real and the onus of proving the contrary is on the person alleging that the wakf was not intended to be acted upon.[9]

---

7 *Zubeda Begum* v *Syed Shah Khursheed Ahmad Hashmi* (1997)9 SCC 324.
8 *Punjab Wakf Board* v *Shakur Masih* AIR 1997 SC 104.
9 *Garib Das* v *M.A. Hamid* AIR 1970 SC 1035.

Alienation of wakf property

In case of wakf property, it is only the *mutawalli* or the trustee who can alienate the property. If he makes an alienation, it is binding on all concerned until and unless it is set aside. Thus, if a person sues to get such alienation declared to be void, he can do so by getting the deed invalidated. The relief claimed in such case may also include a consequential relief.[10]

Illustrations

(1) A Shia Muslim lady created a wakf of her entire property dividing them into 3 qurras. She appointed her husband as *mutawalli* of one of the qurras. The *mutawalli* obtained a permanent lease of land and constructed a building thereon with income from the wakf fund in the name of his wife. It was held that the building belonged to the wakf and the wife could not lay any claim on it.[11]

(2) A suit was filed for the removal of the *mutawalli* for non-compliance of direction made in the deed of wakf. It was held that the suit was not maintainable without the consent of the Advocate-General as required under s. 92, CPC.[12]

Revocation of wakf

A testamentary wakf may be revoked by the wakif (dedicator) at any time before his death.[13] In case of non-testamentary wakf, where the wakif reserves to himself the power of revoking the wakf, the wakf is invalid.[14]

According to Shia law the wakf is irrevocable after possession is given to the beneficiaries or the *mutawalli*. The settlor divests himself of the ownership of the property and of everything in the nature of usufruct from the moment the wakf is created. In purely metaphorical sense the expression "ownership of God" is used. The Shia authorities in such case consider the property as transferred to the beneficiaries or to the object of the wakf. Strictly speaking, the ownership of the wakf property has no jural conception with any exactitude. The corpus is tied down and is made inalienable. Only the usufruct and the income from the corpus of the wakf property is available for carrying out the objects of the wakf.[15]

---

10 *Shamsher v Rajinder* AIR 1973 SC 2457.
11 *Bibi Saddiqa Fatima v Saiyed Mohd. Hasan* AIR 1978 SC 1362.
12 *Sugra Bibi v Hazi Kummu* AIR 1969 SC 884.
13 *Muhammad Ahsan v Umardraz* (1906)28 All 633.
14 *Ashna Bibi v Awaljadi* (1917)44 Cal 698.
15 *Bibi Saddiqa Fatima v Saiyd Mohd. Mahmood Hasan* (1978)3 SCC 299.

Valid objects of wakf

The following are valid objects of a wakf:

(1) Mosques and provision for *imams* to conduct worship therein. (2) Colleges and provision for professors to teach in colleges. (3) Aquaducts, bridges and caravan serais. (4) Repairs of imambaras.

In *Nawab Zain* v *Director of Endowments*,[16] it has been held that the purpose for which a wakf can be created must be one which is recognised by Mahommedan law as pious, religious or charitable, and the objects of public utility which may constitute beneficiaries under the wakf must be objects for the benefit of the Muslim community.

The word 'charity' used in the Mussalman Wakf Validation Act 1913 is not intended to give a new meaning. In common parlance it is used to denote to give to some one in necessitious circumstances and in law it means to give for public good. A private gift to one's own self or kith and kin may be meritorious and pious but is not a charity in the legal sense and the courts in India have never regarded such gifts as for religious or charitable purposes even under the Mahommedan law.[17]

Imambara

An imambara is an apartment in a private house set apart like a private chapel for religious purpose. It is usually intended for use of the owner and members of his family. But the public are also admitted with the consent of the owner.

Office of imam. Mahommedan law does not recognise the hereditary right of being *imam*. Because an *imam* must possess certain special qualities and certain special knowledge of the scriptures before he can be allowed to lead the prayers. An *imam* is normally chosen under Mahommedan law by the Muslim community. The primary consideration should be the welfare of the wakf properties.[18]

Sajjadanashin

A Sajjadanashin is the head of a *khankah* which is a Mohamedan religious institution. He is a spiritual superior and the manager of the institution. He is the administrator of the charities of the institution.

---

16 AIR 1963 SC 985.
17 *Fazlul Rabbi* v *State of WB* AIR 1965 SC 1722.
18 *Syed Mohd. Salie* v *Mohd. Hanifa* AIR 1976 SC 1569.

Appointment of mutawalli

Generally the founder of a wakf may appoint himself or his children or his descendants or any other person including a female or a non-Mahomedan as *mutawalli* of wakf property. A person who is a minor or is of unsound mind cannot be appointed *mutawalli*.[19] But where the office of *mutawalli* is hereditary and the person entitled to the office is a minor, the court may appoint a *mutawalli* in place of the minor only during the period of his minority.[20]

The founder of the wakf may provide in the deed of trust creating the wakf the manner in which the succession to the office of *mutawalli* shall take place. If any appointed *mutawalli* dies, resigns or refuses to act or is removed by the court, the office of *mutawalli* falls vacant. In absence of specific provision in the deed of wakf for filling up the vacancy, a new *mutawalli* may be appointed (*a*) by the founder or (*b*) by his executor (if any), or (*c*) by the court. In appointing *mutawalli* by the court the following factors were taken into consideration: (*i*) direction of the founder, (*ii*) not to appoint a stranger where any member of the founder's family is alive, (*iii*) in case of contest between a lineal descendant and a non-lineal descendant of the founder, the former is preferred.

Position of mutawalli. As soon as a wakf is created, all rights or property pass out of the wakf and vest in the Almighty. The *mutawalli* has no right in the property belonging to the wakf. He is not a trustee in the technical sense. His position is merely that of a superintendent or a manager. A *mutawalli* has no power, without the permission of the court to mortgage, sell or exchange wakf property or any part thereof unless he is expressly empowered by the deed of wakf to do so.[1] Where power is given to *mutawalli* to fix stipends for his wife and children, he must exercise that power equally.[2] A *mutawalli* cannot set up adverse title to the trust and cannot confer any benefit out of the trust fund for his personal ends.[3]

Graveyard. Under the Mahommedan law the graveyards are of two kinds. One is family or private graveyard and the other is a public graveyard. A graveyard is a private one which is confined only to the burial of corpses of the founder, his relations or his descendants. In such burial

---

19 *Abdus Salam* v *Abdul Aziz* (1944)48 CWN 465.
20 *Ejaz Ahmad* v *Khatan Begam* (1917)39 All 288.
1 *Ahmed G. H. Ariff* v *CWT* AIR 1971 SC 1691.
2 *Bibi Saddiqa* v *Saiyed Mohd. Mahmood Hasan* AIR 1978 SC 1362.
3 *Mohd. Shah* v *Fasihuddin* AIR 1956 SC 713.

ground no person who does not belong to the family of the founder is permitted to bury the corpse. On the other hand, if any member of the public is permitted to be buried in a graveyard and this practice grows, then the presumption is that the dedication is complete and the graveyard has become a public graveyard where the Mahommedan public will have the right to bury their corpses.[4]

Mosque of public character. In order to create a valid dedication of a mosque of a public character the following conditions are to be fulfilled:

(1) That the founder must declare his intention to dedicate a property for the purpose of a mosque. No particular form of declaration is necessary.

(2) That the founder must divest himself completely from the ownership of the property. The divestment can be inferred from the fact that he had delivered possession of the mosque to the *mutawalli* or the *imam*. Even if there is no actual delivery of possession of the mosque by the founder, the mere fact that members of the Mahommedan public are permitted to offer prayers with *azans* and *ikamat*, would constitute a valid and complete wakf of irrevocable nature.

(3) That the founder must make a separate entrance to the mosque which may be used by the public.

If any additions or alterations, either structural or otherwise, are made which are incidental to the offering of prayers or for other religious purposes, those constructions would be deemed to be accretions to the mosque.[5]

Mosque. Mosque is not an essential part of the practice of Islam religion. Namaaz (prayer) can be offered anywhere even in open. Thus, acquisition of mosque is not prohibited by the Constitution of India.[6]

---

4 *Syed Mohd. Salie* v *Mohd. Hanifa* AIR 1976 SC 1569.
5 *Syed Mohd. Salie* v *Mohd. Hanifa* AIR 1976 SC 1569.
6 *M. Ismail Faruqui* v *Union of India* AIR 1995 SC 605.

Chapter 23

Wills

Conditions for a valid will

Every Mahomedan of sound mind and not a minor may dispose of his property by will. Majority is attained by a Mahomedan for the purpose of making a will when he completes the age of eighteen years. A will may be made either orally or in writing. The burden of proving an oral will is very heavy. It is required to be proved with the utmost precision. A Mahomedan cannot by will dispose of more than a third of the surplus of his estate after payment of funeral expenses and debts of the testator. If the bequests exceed the legal third, and the heirs refuse their consent, the bequests abate rateably.

A bequest to an unborn person at the testator's death is void. But a bequest may be made to a child in the womb, provided it is born within six months from the date of the will.

Limits of bequest by a will

A Mahomedan cannot by will dispose of more than one-third of the surplus of his estate after payment of funeral expenses and debts. Bequests in excess of the legal third cannot be operative unless the heirs consent thereto after the death of the testator.[1] The limit of one-third is not laid down in the Koran. This limit is imposed by subsequent sanction. But the Koran has provided that a Mahomedan should not dispose of his property by will as to leave his heirs destitute. The reason for the limits of testamentary power is to benefit solely the heirs. If the testator has no heirs, he may bequeath the whole of his property to a stranger. It is noted that once consent is given by the legal heirs, it cannot be rescinded.

---

1 *Khajooroonissa* v *Rowshan Jehan* (1876)2 Cal 184.

Illustrations

(1) A Muslim testator leaves a will and dies leaving behind a widow, two sons, a daughter and a son of a predeceased son. The will provides that the grandson, that is son of predeceased son, shall take a son's share in his inheritance. The division of the property will be as follows:

Widow $\frac{1}{8}$;   Daughter $\frac{1}{8}$;   Each son $\frac{1}{4}$;   Grandson $\frac{1}{4}$.

(2) A Muslim testator dies after making a will leaving behind a widow, a son, a daughter and a son of a predeceased son. The will provides that the grandson, that is son of predeceased son, shall take share of a son in his inheritance. The division of property will be as follows:

Widow $\frac{1}{8}$;   Daughter $\frac{7}{40}$;   Son $\frac{21}{60}$;   Grandson $\frac{21}{60}$.

Kinds of executors

There are three kinds of executors. The first is a trustee. Such executor performs all the duties assigned to him by the testator. His appointment is fixed and he cannot be removed by the Judge without proof of breach of trust. The second executor is a trustworthy person. But he is unable to do the work of an executor. He is weak and inefficient. The Judge should associate another person with him for assisting him. The third testator is a *fasik* (corrupt or unworthy person). He may be a non-Muslim or a bondman of another. It is necessary for the Judge to remove him and appoint some other person in his place.

Powers of executor

The power of an executor under Mahommedan law is similar to that of an executor under English law. When the heirs of a testator are minors, the powers of the executor are to be exercised cautiously. In case of necessity he has the power to sell the property and invest the proceeds after payment of debts of the testator and incurring all the expenses of maintenance of minor heirs, into profitable property. The sale must be for adequate consideration. The executor cannot sell the property to himself or to any of his relatives. He can enter into partition with the co-sharers of the testator. An executor cannot buy anything for the minor excepting food and clothes which are necessaries to life. Where the heirs of the testators are *sui juris*, the executor cannot effect any partition of immovable property in their absence. Unless any remuneration is fixed by the testator an executor cannot take anything for himself from the estate.

Revocation of bequest

A bequest may be revoked either expressly or by implication. A bequest is revoked by a bequest in a subsequent will of the same property to a person other than the former. A bequest may be revoked by any act which occasions an addition to the subject of the bequest or an extinction of the right of the testator.

CHAPTER
24

Pre-emption

Origin of pre-emption under Mahommedan law

The law of pre-emption was introduced in India by the Mahommedans. There is no indication of the conception of pre-emption under the Hindu law. During the rule of Mughal emperors the law of pre-emption was administered as a rule of common law of the land in those parts of the country which were under the domination of the Mahommedan rulers. Gradually this right received the blessing of statutes in some provinces like Punjab, Agra and Oudh during the British rule.

Under the Mohammedan law the right of pre-emption is confined to persons of a particular religious persuation.[1]

Definition of pre-emption and persons entitled to pre-emption

The right of *shufaa* or pre-emption is a right which the owner of an immovable property acquires by purchase of another immovable property which has been sold to a stranger. The following three classes of persons can claim pre-emption:

 (*a*) A co-sharer in the property.

 (*b*) A participator in immunities and appendages.

 (*c*) Owners of adjoining immovable property.

The right of pre-emption arises out of a valid, complete and *bona fide* sale. The conditions for claiming pre-emption are the following:

 (*a*) The person claiming pre-emption has declared his intention to assert the right immediately.

---

1 *Audh Behari* v *Gajadhar* AIR 1954 SC 417.

(b) He has without delay affirmed the intention and has made a formal demand (i) either in the presence of the buyer or the seller, and (ii) in the presence of at least two witnesses. This formality is called *talab-i-ishhed*.[2]

Formality for pre-emption

A person is not entitled to the right of pre-emption unless the following conditions are fulfilled:

(a) He has demanded pre-emption immediately after the receipt of information of the sale of the property. This is known as *talab-i-mowasibat*.

(b) Alternatively, he may within a reasonable time make a formal demand (i) either in presence of the buyer, (ii) or the seller, (iii) or at the place of the sale; and in presence of two witnesses. This formality is called *talab-i-ishhad* (demand in presence of witnesses).[2]

In *Ram Saran* v *Domini*,[3] it has been held that one of the requisites before the right of pre-emption can be exercised is the preliminary demand by the pre-emptor and that such demand must be made after the completion of the sale. In *Munni Lal* v *Biswanath*,[4] it has been held that under the Mahommedan law of pre-emption there must be full ownership in the land pre-empted. The right of pre-emption does not arise on the sale of lease-hold interest in land.

The Mahommedan law relating to demand before filing a suit for pre-emption is of highly technical nature. The *talab-i-mowasibat* is the first demand and the *talab-i-ishad* is the second demand. The third demand consists of the institution of the suit for pre-emption. Both the *talabs* are conditions precedent to the exercise of the right of pre-emption. The first demand (*talab*) should be made as soon as the fact of sale is known to the claimant. Any unreasonable or unnecessary delay will be construed as an election not to pre-emption.[5]

Illustration

A house of a deceased Mahommedan was divided into east and west portions by his heirs as a result of partition. K purchased the west portion of the house from its co-sharers. Thereafter K entered into agreement with the rest of the co-sharers of the east portion but that could not be materialised. The co-sharers of the east portion then executed an agreement of sale in favour of M. One of the co-sharers

---

2 *Narayana* v *Karthiayani* AIR 1962 Ker 122.
3 AIR 1961 SC 1747.
4 AIR 1968 SC 450.
5 *Sheikh Mohd. Rafi* v *Khalilul Rahman* AIR 1972 SC 2162.

B changed her mind and executed a sale deed in favour of K. Two suits were filed. The first suit was by M against B for specific performance of the agreement, and the second suit was by K for possession by pre-emption. It was held by the Supreme Court that the suit for pre-emption would succeed and the suit for specific performance would fail.[6]

Loss of right of pre-emption

The right of pre-emption is lost by the death of the pre-emptor. But if he dies during the pendency of the suit, it can be continued by substitution. The right is also lost by acquiescence.[7] The right of pre-emption is lost by joinder of plaintiffs who are not entitled to pre-emption. But it will not be lost if the co-plaintiff is also a pre-emptor who has failed to make the demand for pre-emption in time.[8]

Pre-emption by a shafi

Where a sale is made by a shafi to another shafi or to a shafi and a stranger, the other shafis are entitled to claim pre-emption.

Illustrations

(a) A, B and C are co-shares of certain property. A sells his share to B. C is entitled to claim pre-emption of one-half of the property sold.[9]

(b) A, B and C are co-sharers of certain property. A sells his share to B and S. C is entitled to claim pre-emption of one-half of the property sold.[10]

---

6 *Sheikh Mohd. Rafi v Khalilul Rahman* AIR 1972 SC 2162.
7 *Narayandas v Jagan Nath* AIR 1950 MB 85.
8 *Narayana v Karthiayani* AIR 1962 Ker 122.
9 *Enatullah v Kowsher Ali* (1927)54 Cal 265.
10 *Saligram v Raghubar dyal* (1887)15 Cal 244.

CHAPTER
25

Succession, Administration and Partition

Administration of estate of a deceased Mahomedan

On the death of a Mahomedan, his estate will be first applied successively for the following purposes;

(1) The funeral expenses and death-bed charges.

(2) Expenses for obtaining probate, letters of administration or succession certificate.

(3) Wages payable to labourers or domestic servants for a period of three months immediately prior to death.

(4) Other debts of the deceased.

(5) Legacies not exceeding one-third of the remaining estate after payment of the above claims.

(6) The residue is to be distributed amongst the heirs of the deceased according to the Mahomedan law.

Under s. 211 of the Indian Succession Act 1925 the estate of a deceased Mahomedan vests in the executor if he leaves a will even though no probate has been obtained.[1]

An heir of a deceased Mahomedan may transfer his own share to a third party who will acquire a good title to it even before distribution of the estate, provided the purchaser buys for a valuable consideration and *bona fide*.[2]

---

1 *Venkata Subbamma* v *Ramayya* (1932)59 IA 112.
2 *Bazayet Hossein* v *Dooli Chand* (1878)5 IA 211.

Illustrations

(1) A Mahomedan dies leaving behind two sisters as his only successors. A creditor of the sisters obtained a decree against them for the debt of deceased Mahomedan. The property then came into the hands of P who acquired the property in execution of the decree. C, another creditor of the deceased cannot attach the property in the hands of P.[3]

(2) A Mahomedan died leaving a widow, a daughter and two sisters. A creditor of the deceased instituted a suit against the widow and the daughter who were in possession of the property for the debt of the deceased. The decree passed in such suit was binding on all the heirs including the two sisters.[4]

(3) A creditor of a deceased Mahomedan instituted a suit against his widow for a claim without making his two daughters parties to the proceedings. The creditor obtained a decree and attached the immovable property of the deceased lying in joint possession of the widow and two daughters. The daughters then filed a suit for declaration. It was held that the decree was not binding on their shares.[5]

(4) A mortgagee instituted a suit against the minor son of a deceased Mahomedan represented by his guardian and mother for possession without making two daughters as parties to the proceedings. The suit was decreed *ex parte* and possession of the mortgaged property was obtained. The decree was binding on the daughters because they were not entitled to redeem the mortgage.[6]

Guardian for minor and his property

Mother of minor cannot act or be appointed as guardian. Equally in Mohammadan law, mother cannot act nor be appointed as property guardian of the minor. She cannot act as legal guardian.[7]

Devolution of property on death

It is well settled principle of Mahommedan law that the estate of a deceased Mahommedan devolves on his heirs in specific shares at the moment of his death, and the devolution is not suspended by reason of debts due from the deceased, nor is the distribution of the shares inherited postponed till the payment of the debts. It is also well recognised proposition of law that property vests in the heirs under the Mahommedan law, unlike the Indian Succession Act, without the intervention of an administrator.[8]

The estate of a Muslim dying intestate devolves under the Islamic law upon his heirs at the moment of his death. In other words, the estate vests

---

3 *Wahidunnissa* v *Shubrattun* (1870)6 Beng LR 54.
4 *Muttyjan* v *Ahmed Ally* (1882)8 Cal 370.
5 *Bishambhar Nath Gopi Nath* v *Hashim Begam* AIR 1949 Oudh 56.
6 *Devalava* v *Bhimaji* (1895)20 Bom 208.
7 *Mahboob Sahab* v *Syed Ismail* AIR 1995 SC 1205.
8 *Ebrahim Aboobaker* v *Tek Chand* AIR 1953 SC 298.

immediately in each heir in proportion to the shares obtained by the personal law and the interest of each heir is separate and distinct. Each heir under the personal law is liable to satisfy the debts of the deceased only to the extent of the debt proportionate to his share in the estate. A creditor of a Muslim dying intestate may sue all the heirs of the deceased. Where the estate of the deceased has not been distributed between the heirs, he may execute the decree against the property as a whole without regard to the extent of the liability of the heirs *inter se*. The creditor is not bound to sue all the heirs. He may sue only some of the heirs and obtain a decree against those heirs, and the liability for satisfaction of the decree may be enforced against individual heir in the property held by him proportionate to his share in the estate.[9]

Illustration

K, a Mahommedan, died leaving behind one widow and 5 sons. K was heavily indebted before his death. Three sons of K who were quite well off paid the debts of their father and obtained two deeds of relinquishment from the other two sons of K to the effect that the executants had received cash and movables and they would have no right in future to the properties mentioned in the said deeds. After the death of K, one of the executants of the deeds filed a suit for partition. It was held that a renunciation by an expectant heir in the life-time of his ancestor is not valid or enforceable against him after the vesting of the inheritance. But if the expectant heir had received consideration and acted himself as to mislead an owner, he would be debarred from setting up his right.[10]

Partition

In Mahommedan law the doctrine of partial partition is not applicable. Because the heirs under Mahommedan law are tenants-in-common and the heirs of a deceased Muslim succeed to the definite fraction of every part of his estate. The shares of heirs under Mahommedan law are definite and known before actual partition. Thus, on partition of properties there is division by metes and bounds in accordance with the specific share of each heir being already determined by law.[11]

---

9 *Mohd. Sulaiman Sahib* v *Mohd. Ismail Saheb* AIR 1966 SC 792.
10 *Gulam Abbas* v *Haji Kayyum* AIR 1973 SC 554.
11 *Syed Shah Ghulam Ghouse* v *Syed Shah Ahmed Mohiuddin* AIR 1971 SC 2184.

CHAPTER
26
Inheritance

General rules

There are certain rules of inheritance under the Mahomedan law. They are as follows:

(1) *No distinction between ancestral and self acquired property.* In the Mahommedan law there is no distinction between ancestral and self-acquired property for the purpose of inheritance.

(2) *Doctrine of representation.* The Sunni law does not recognise the doctrine of representation for the purpose of succession. Unlike the Sunni law, the Shia law recognise this doctrine.

Illustration

A, a Sunni Mahommedan had two sons, namely M and N. M died during the life time of A leaving behind his only son P. Subsequently, A died leaving behind him his son N and the grandson P, the surviving son of M. The property of A passed to N to the exclusion of P.[1]

(3) *No transfer of the right of spes successionis.* A *spes successionis* cannot transfer his right of succession to the property.

Illustration

A had a daughter D and a son S. A paid Rs. 500 to D in lieu of her relinquishment to inherit A's property. A died. D could sue S for her share in A's property. D was a *spes successionis* and as such her right could not be transferred. But D was bound to return Rs. 500 to the estate of A for distribution.[2]

---

1 *Moolla Cassim* v *Moolla Abdul* (1905)33 Cal 173.
2 *Sumsuddin* v *Abdul Hussein* (1906)31 Bom 165.

(4) *Life estate not recognised.* The creation of life estate is not recognised by the Mahommedan law. There ought to be very clear proof of such unusual transaction.[3]

(5) *Joint family.* Unlike the Hindu law members of a Mahomedan family living together do not form a joint family under the Mahomedan law.[4] Similarly, members of a Mahomedan family carrying on business jointly do not form a joint family firm as is found under the Hindu law.[5]

(6) *Homicide.* Homicide under the Shia law is not a bar to succession unless the murder is caused with *mens rea*.

Classes of heirs

There are three classes of heirs under the Hanafi law of inheritance. They are (1) Sharers. (2) Residuaries, and (3) Distant kindred. Sharers are persons who are entitled to prescribed shares under inheritance. Residuaries are persons who do not take any prescribed shares but are entitled to succeed to the property of the deceased out of the estate after satisfying the claims of sharers. Distant kindred are persons who fall neither in the category of sharers nor in the category of residuaries. They are the blood relations of the deceased.[6] Father having child or children of son gets prescribed share.[7]

Sharers

The following are the sharers under the Sunni law and the nominal share inherited by each of them is shown against each sharer:

(1) Father is entitled to one-sixth share when there is a child or a child of a son. But if there is no child or a child of a son, the father takes the rest of the property as a residuary.

(2) True grandfather is entitled to one-sixth share when there is a child or a child of a son of the deceased but there is no father. But if there is no child or child of a son or father of the deceased, the true grandfather inherits as a residuary.

(3) Husband inherits one-fourth share where there is a child or a child of a son. But he inherits one-half share when there is no child or child of a son.

---

3 *Humeeda* v *Budhim* (1872)17 WR 525.
4 *Hakim Khan* v *Gool Khan* (1882)8 Cal 826.
5 *Solema* v *Hafez* (1927)54 Cal 687.
6 *Abdul Serang* v *Pulee Bibi* (1902)29 Cal 738.
7 *Newnness alias Mewajannessa* v *Shaikh Mohamad* AIR 1996 SC 702.

(4) Wife or wives collectively inherit one-eighth share where there is a child or a child of a son of the deceased. But wife or wives collectively take one-half share when there is no child or child of a son.

(5) Mother inherits one-sixth share where there is child or child of a son or where there are two or more brothers or sisters or one brother and sister. But mother takes one-third where there is no child or child of a son or brother or sister more than one. If there are wife or husband and the father, mother takes one-third of the remaining estate after satisfaction of the claim of wife or husband.

(6) True grandmother or grandmothers jointly inherit one-sixth share when there is no paternal or maternal mother or paternal father or nearer true grandmother, paternal or maternal.

(7) Daughter, if one, inherits one-half share; but in case of two or more daughters, they jointly inherit two-thirds share when there is no son. When there is a son, the daughter becomes a residuary.

(8) Son's daughter, if one, inherits one half, in case of two or more, they jointly inherit two-thirds if there is no son, daughter or higher relation than son's daughter. When there is a daughter or a higher relation than son's daughter, the son's daughter will take one-sixth share.

(9) Uterine brother or sister, if one, inherits one-sixth and in case of two or more, they jointly inherit one-third when there is no child or child of a son or father or true grandfather.

(10) Full sister, if one, inherits one-half share; in case of two or more full sisters, they jointly inherit two-thirds when there is no child, child of a son, father, true grandfather, or full brother. If there is a full brother, she becomes a residuary.

(11) Consanguine sister, if one, inherits one-half; and in case of two or more, they jointly inherit two-thirds if there is no child, child of a son, father, true grandfather, full brother, full sister or consanguine brother. If there is a consanguine brother, she becomes a residuary.

EXAMPLES

(a) There are husband, mother and father of a deceased. They inherit in the following manner:

Husband $\frac{1}{2}$, Mother $\frac{1}{6}$ and Father $\frac{1}{3}$ as residuary.

(b) There are widow, mother and father of the deceased. They inherit in the following manner:

Widow $\frac{1}{4}$, Mother $\frac{1}{4}$, Father $\frac{1}{2}$.

Increase (Aul). According to Hanafi law of succession where it is found on assigning the respective shares to the shares that the total of the shares exceeds unity, the share of each sharer is proportionately diminished by reducing the fractional share to a common denominator, and the denominator is increased in such a manner that it equalises the sum or the numerators.

Illustration. A woman dies leaving behind her husband, two daughter's and a mother. Their respective shares will be one-fourth, two-thirds and one-sixth. The common division in this case is twelve. Thus, the shares will be divided as follows:

Husband 3; Daughter 8; Mother 2. But 3, 8 and 2 make thirteen. The Sunnis in order to give the exact number of shares to each heir shall divide the property into thirteen shares.

In another example—

$$\text{Husband } \frac{1}{2} = \frac{3}{6} \text{ reduced to } \frac{3}{7}$$

$$\text{2 sisters } \frac{2}{3} = \frac{4}{6} \text{ reduced to } \frac{4}{7}$$

$$\text{Total } = \frac{7}{6} \ldots\ldots 1$$

Return (Radd). According to Hanafi law of inheritance where there is any residue left after satisfying the claims of sharers and there is no residuary, the residue reverts to the sharers in proportion to their shares. This right of reverter is technically known as return or *radd*.

EXAMPLE

A person dies leaving a mother, an uterine sister and a consanguine sister. The division will be as follows:

Mother $\frac{1}{6}$; Uterine sister $\frac{1}{6}$; Consanguine sister $\frac{1}{2}$.

The remainder is returned to them in the same proportion.

Thus, finally the share will be—

Mother $\dfrac{1}{5}$; Uterine sister $\dfrac{1}{5}$; Consanguine sister $\dfrac{3}{5}$.

There may be a return among the following persons: (a) mother; (b) grandmother; (c) daughter; (d) son's daughter; (e) full sister; (f) half sister by his father; (g) half brother; or (h) sister by the mother. A return may take place in respect of one, two or three classes at the same time and no more.

Illustrations

(1) When there are two widows, a mother and three daughters, the widows take between them $\dfrac{1}{8}$. Mother takes $\dfrac{7}{48}$ (that is $\dfrac{1}{6}$ or $\dfrac{7}{8}$). Three daughters take $\dfrac{28}{48}$ (that is $\dfrac{4}{6}$ of $\dfrac{7}{8}$).

Therefore, two widows will get $\quad 9 \times 2 = 18$
Mother will get $\quad\quad\quad\quad\quad\quad\quad\quad\;\; 21$
Three daughters will get $\quad\;\; 35 \times 3 = \underline{105}$
$\quad\quad\quad\quad\quad\quad\quad\quad\quad\quad\quad\quad\quad\quad\;\; 144$

(2) There is a grandmother with sister by the same mother of the deceased. The shares are $\dfrac{1}{6}$ each. The residue is divided among them equally.

(3) There are a daughter and mother. The shares are $\dfrac{1}{2}$ and $\dfrac{1}{6}$. The residue is divided between them in proportion to their shares which will be $\dfrac{3}{12}$ and $\dfrac{1}{12}$.

(4) If a Muslim dies leaving behind his widow as the sole successor, she takes $\dfrac{1}{4}$ as sharer and the residue $\dfrac{3}{4}$ by "return". If he leaves behind his widow and mother as heirs/successors, the wife takes $\dfrac{1}{4}$ as sharer and the mother takes $\dfrac{1}{6}$ as the sharer and the residue $\dfrac{7}{12}$ by "return", that is the wife gets $\dfrac{1}{4}$ and the mother gets $\dfrac{3}{4}$.

Residuaries

When there is no sharer, the entire estate is distributed amongst the residuaries. Even when there are sharers, any residue left after satisfying their claims is distributed amongst the residuaries.

Examples

(a) There are two sons and three daughters of a deceased.

Sons inherit 4/7 and daughters 3/7 as residuaries.

(b) There are a widow, a son and a daughter of the deceased. They inherit in the following manner:

Widow: 1/8 as sharer. Son $\frac{2}{3}$ of $\frac{7}{8} = \frac{7}{12}$ as a residuary;

Daughter: $\frac{1}{3}$ of $\frac{7}{8} = \frac{7}{24}$ as a residuary.

(c) There are one son and one daughter of the deceased. They inherit as residuaries in the following manner : Son $\frac{2}{3}$; Daughter $\frac{1}{3}$.

(d) A dies leaving two daughters, a son's son and a daughter of a son. The division will be thus:

Daughters $\frac{2}{3}$; Son's son and son's daughter (as residuaries) $\frac{1}{3}$;

Son's son $\frac{2}{3} \times \frac{1}{3} = \frac{2}{9}$; Son's daughter $\frac{1}{3} \times \frac{1}{3} = \frac{1}{9}$.

(e) The deceased leaves a mother, three sisters, a brother and a widow. The division will be as follows:

Widow $\frac{1}{4}$; Mother $\frac{1}{6}$; Brother and sisters (as residuaries) $\frac{14}{24}$;

Brother $\frac{2}{5} \times \frac{14}{24} = \frac{14}{60}$; Each sister $\frac{1}{5} \times \frac{14}{24} = \frac{7}{60}$.

(f) A dies leaving a widow, an uterine sister and four nephews (brother's sons). The division will be as follows:

Widow $\frac{1}{4}$; Sister $\frac{1}{2}$; Nephews (as residuaries) $\frac{1}{4}$.

(g) A dies leaving behind father, mother and daughter. The division will be as follows:

$$\left.\begin{array}{ll} \text{Father} & \frac{1}{6} \\ \text{Mother} & \frac{1}{6} \\ \text{Daughter} & \frac{1}{2} \end{array}\right\} = \frac{5}{6}$$

The residue goes to the father.

(h) A person dies leaving behind him his father, mother and two daughters. The division will be as follows:

Father $\frac{1}{6}$; Mother $\frac{1}{6}$; Two daughters $\frac{4}{6}$.

There will be no residue.

(i) A person dies leaving father, mother, a son and a daughter. The inheritance will be in the following manner:

Father $\frac{1}{6}$; Mother $\frac{1}{6}$; Son $\frac{4}{9} = \left(\frac{2}{3} \times \frac{2}{3}\right)$;

Daughter $\frac{2}{9} = \left(\frac{1}{3} \times \frac{2}{3}\right)$.

(j) A dies leaving behind her husband, father and mother. The division will be as follows:

Husband $\frac{1}{2}$; Mother $\frac{1}{6} = \left(\frac{1}{3} \times \frac{1}{2}\right)$; Father (as residuary) $\frac{1}{3}$.

(k) A dies leaving behind mother, father and a sister. The division will be as follows:

Mother $\frac{1}{3}$; Father (as residuary) $\frac{2}{3}$.

Sister is excluded by father.

(l) A person dies leaving father, mother, daughter and two granddaughters (son's daughters). The division will be as follows:

Father $\frac{1}{6}$; Mother $\frac{1}{6}$; Daughter $\frac{1}{2}$;

Two granddaughters $\frac{1}{6}$.

(m) A dies leaving behind father, mother, two daughters and two granddaughters (son's daughters). The division will be as follows:

Father $\frac{1}{6}$; Mother $\frac{1}{6}$; Two daughters $\frac{2}{3}$.

Two granddaughters are excluded by two daughters.

(n) A woman dies leaving behind husband, two daughters, a sister and a son of father's paternal uncle. The division will be as follows:

Husband $\frac{1}{4}$; Daughters $\frac{2}{3}$; Sister $\frac{1}{12}$.

The son of father's paternal uncle is excluded by the sister.

Distant kindred

If there is no sharer or residuary, the estate of a deceased Mahomedan is distributed amongst distant kindred. Distant kindred are divided into four classes. They are: (1) Descendants of the deceased other than sharers and residuaries; (2) Ascendants of the deceased other than sharers and residuaries; (3) Descendants of parents other than sharers and residuaries; and (4) Descendants of ascendants other than residuaries.

Descendants of the deceased as in class (1) are daughter's children and their descendants; children of son's daughters.

Ascendants of the deceased as in class (2) above are false grandfathers; false grandmothers.

Full brothers' daughters and their descendants, consanguine brothers' daughters and their descendants etc. are the examples of class (3) of distant kindred.

Full paternal uncles' daughters and their descendants, consanguine paternal uncles' daughters and their descendants, uterine paternal uncles and their children and their descendants are some of the examples of class (4) of distant kindred.

Rules of preference amongst distant kindred. The first rule is that the nearer of the kindred of the deceased excludes the more remote kindred. The second rule is that the children of sharers or residuaries are preferred to other kindred amongst the kindred in the same degree of relationship.

Example of order of succession

The order of succession amongst the distant kindred of class (1) will be in the following way:

(1) Daughter's children. (2) Son's daughter's children. (3) Daughter's grandchildren. (4) Son's daughter's children. (5) Daughter's great grandchildren and son's daughter's grandchildren.

Definition

 (a) *True grandfather* is a male ancestor between whom and the deceased no female intervenes.

 (b) *True grandmother* is a female ancestor between whom and the deceased, no false grandfather intervenes.

 (c) *False grandfather* is a male ancestor between whom and the deceased a female intervenes.

 (d) *False grandmother* is a female ancestor between whom and the deceased a false grandfather intervenes.

Posthumous child. If a child is born after the death of its father within the ordinary period of gestation, it will succeed to its father. But if the child is born dead, it does not inherit. There is no other legal effect in such case. If half of the child is protruded, and it then dies, it is entitled to succeed.

Simultaneous death. If two persons die in a sudden calamity, it is presumed that both of them have died together. The property of each goes to his or her respective heirs unless it is known in what order they died. The person who died last will inherit to the property of the person who died first.

CHAPTER
27

Maintenance under Muslim Law

A Muslim husband is under obligation to provide for maintenance of his divorced wife who is unable to maintain herself. Section 125, Cr PC provides that a person who is possessed of sufficient means neglects or refuses to maintain amongst others his wife who is unable to maintain herself may be ordered by a Magistrate of the first class upon proof of such refusal or neglect to pay monthly allowance to such person. The Muslim personal law limits the husband's liability to provide for maintenance of the divorced wife upto the period of *iddat*. It does not contemplate or countenance the situation envisaged by s. 125, Cr PC. The true position as laid down by the Supreme Court in this regard. In *Mohd. Ahmed Khan* v *Shah Bano Begum*[1] it has been held that if the Muslim divorced wife is able to maintain herself, the husband's liability to provide maintenance for her ceases with the expiration of the period of *iddat*. But if she is unable to maintain herself, she is entitled to take recourse to s. 125, Cr PC. There is no conflict between the provisions of s. 125, Cr PC and those of the personal law of Muslim on this issue. *Mahr* is not the amount payable by the husband to the wife on divorce. Though deferred *mahr* is payable at the time of dissolution of marriage, yet it cannot be said to be the maintenance of the wife after dissolution of marriage. *Mahr* is an obligation imposed upon the husband payable to the wife as a mark of respect for her. The view of the Supreme Court received the support even from the decision of the Division Bench of the Bangladesh High Court made on 9th January 1995. The Supreme Court reiterated its view in *Danial Latifi* v *Union of India*[2] that the maintenance of divorced Muslim

---

1   AIR 1985 SC 945.
2   AIR 2001 SC 3958.

wife would confine not only to the period of *iddat* but also extend to her entire life if she does not remarry. In *Subarn* v *A.M. Abdul Gafoor*[3] a question arose as to whether a Muslim wife has any right of maintenance after her husband had contracted a second marriage or taken a mistress under s. 125, Cr PC. It has been held in that case that Explanation to the second proviso to s. 125(3), Cr PC contemplated two kinds of matrimonial injury to a wife, *viz.*, by the husband either marrying again or taking a mistress. The explanation places a second wife and a mistress on the same footing, because the husband breaks his vows of fidelity. Thus, a right is conferred on the wife under the said Explanation to live separately and claim maintenance from the wife for causing any of the aforesaid matrimonial injury.

3   AIR 1987 SC 1103.

CHAPTER
28

The Muslim Women (Protection of Rights on Divorce) Act 1986

Objectives of the Act

After the decision of the Supreme Court in *Mohd. Ahmed Khan* v *Shah Bano Begum*[1] some controversy arose as to the obligation of Muslim husband to pay maintenance to his divorce wife. For solution of this controversy the Muslim Women (Protection of Rights on Divorce) Bill was introduced in Parliament which was passed and received the assent of the President on 19th May 1986. The Muslim Women (Protection of Rights on Divorce) Act 1986 has laid down the provisions for protection of rights of Muslim women on divorce.

Applicability and definitions of some terms

The Muslim Women (Protection of Rights on Divorce) Act 1986 extends to the whole of India except the State of Jammu and Kashmir.[2]

"Iddat period" means in the case of a divorced woman—(*i*) three menstrual courses after the date of divorce, if she is subject to menstruation; (*ii*) three lunar months after the divorce, if she is not subject to menstruation; and (*iii*) if she is enceiente at the time of divorce, the period between the divorce and the delivery of her child or the termination of her pregnancy, whichever is earlier.[3]

---

1 AIR 1985 SC 945.
2 Section 1(2), Muslim Women (Protection of Rights on Divorce) Act 1986.
3 Section 2(*b*), *ibid*.

The expression "divorced women" means a Muslim woman who was married according to Muslim law and has been divorced by or has obtained divorce from her husband in accordance with Muslim law.[4]

Return of mohr and other properties of Muslim woman on divorce

A Muslim woman on her divorce is entitled to (*a*) a reasonable and fair provision and maintenance payable to her within the iddat period by her former husband; (*b*) maintenance of her children born to her before or after divorce for a period of two years from the respective dates of birth of such children; (*c*) an amount equal to the sum of *mahr* or dower agreed to be paid to her; and (*d*) all the properties given to her before or at the time of marriage or after her marriage. In the event of failure or refusal by the husband to comply with the above obligation, the divorced Muslim woman may institute a criminal proceedings before a Magistrate of first class for making appropriate order within one month from the date of filing of the application. The said period of one month may be extended on reasonable ground. If that order is not carried out, the Magistrate may issue a warrant against the person concerned and sentence him to imprisonment for a term not exceeding one year.[5]

An application under section 3 of the said 1986 Act can be made only before a Magistrate of the First Class. The Family Court has no jurisdiction to entertain an application from a divorced Muslim woman for the sum of *mahr* or dower.[6]

The provisions of s. 125, Cr PC are not affected by cl. (*b*) of s. 3(1) of the 1986 Act and it would be unreasonable, unfair, inequitable and even preposterous to deny the benefit of s. 125, Cr PC to the children on the ground that they were born of Muslim parents. Right to maintenance to Muslim children are available till they attain majority or are able to maintain themselves. This right is not restricted, affected or controlled by s. 3(1)(*b*) of the Muslim Women (Protection of Rights on Divorce) Act 1986.[7]

Order of maintenance to divorced Muslim woman by others

Where a divorced Muslim woman is unable to maintain herself even after the expiry of the *iddat*, the Magistrate, on being satisfied that the divorced woman has not remarried, may make an order directing such of her

---

4 Section 2(*a*), *ibid*.
5 Section 3, *ibid*.
6 *Anjum Hasan Siddiqui* v *Salma* AIR 1992 All 332.
7 *Noor Saba Khatoon* v *Mohd. Quasim* AIR 1997 SC 3280.

relatives who would be entitled to inherit her property according to Muslim on her death, shall pay a reasonable and fair maintenance amount to her having regard to the needs of the divorced woman. Where such divorced woman has children the Magistrate shall order only such children to pay maintenance to her. If such children are unable to pay such maintenance, the Magistrate shall order the parents of such divorced woman to pay maintenance to her. Where any of the parents is unable to maintain her, the Magistrate shall order some other relatives to share the maintenance. If a divorced woman is unable to maintain her in accordance with the foregoing provisions the Magistrate may, by order, direct the State Wakf Board functioning in the area in which the divorced woman resides to pay maintenance as determined by him.[8] In one and same proceeding, one or more orders can be passed in favour of the divorced Muslim woman subject of course to her not remarrying and remaining unable to maintain herself. A Muslim woman is entitled to plead and prove relevant facts in one proceeding as to inability of her relations mentioned in s. 4(1) of the Act of 1986 to maintain her by directing her claim against State Wakf Board.[9]

Option for sections 125 to 128, Cr PC

If on the date of the first hearing of the application under s. 3(2) of the Muslim Women (Protection of Rights on Divorce) Act 1986 a divorced woman and her former husband declare, by affidavit or any other declaration in writing in prescribed form either jointly or separately that they opt to be governed by the provisions of ss. 125-128 of the Code of Criminal Procedure 1973 and file such affidavit or declaration in the court, the Magistrate shall dispose of such application.[10] The expression "date of the first hearing of the application" means the date fixed in the summons for the attendance of the respondent to the application.[11]

Some illustrative cases

(a) The Muslim Women (Protection of Rights on Divorce) Act 1986 applies only to divorced Muslim women and not to a woman who is not divorced. Proceedings under s. 125, Cr PC are of civil nature. If the court notices that there is a divorced Muslim woman who has made an application under s. 125, Cr PC, it is open to the court to treat the same as a petition

---

8   Section 4, Muslim Women (Protection of Rights on Divorce) Act 1986.
9   *Secy., T.N. Wakf Board* v *Syed Fatima Nachi* AIR 1996 SC 2423.
10 Section 5, Muslim Women (Protection of Rights on Divorce) Act 1986.
11 Explanation to s. 5, *ibid*.

under the 1986 Act considering the beneficial nature of the legislation, especially since proceedings under s. 125, Cr PC and claims made under the 1986 Act are tried by the same court.[12]

(b) The right to claim maintenance by a divorced Muslim wife for her children from her former husband under s. 125, Cr PC is recognised even after enactment of the 1986 Act.[13]

(c) When an application is filed by Muslim wife for maintenance under s. 125, Cr PC on the ground of desertion and cruelty by husband, the plea of previous divorce in written statement is not sustainable.[14]

Section 6 of the Muslim Women (Protection of Rights on Divorce) Act 1986 empowers the Central Government by notification in the Official Gazette to make rules for carrying out the purposes of the Act. By virtue of this power the Central Government has made the rules called the Muslim Women (Protection of Rights on Divorce) Rules 1986.

Meaning of expression

Expression "maintenance to be made and paid to the wife within iddat period by her former husband" appearing in s. 3(1)(a) of the Muslim Women (Protection of Rights on Divorce) Act 1986 does not include past maintenance payable to her prior to her divorce.[15]

---

12 *Iqbal Bano* v *State of U.P.* (2007)6 SCC 785.
13 *Mst. Bilkis Begum* v *Majid Ali Gazi* 2002 (2) Cal HN 151 (SC).
14 *Shamim Ara* v *State of U.P.* (2002)7 SCC 518.
15 *Thoombath Haris* v *Khadeeja Sherbin* AIR 2010 NOC 230 (Ker).

PART 4

Christian Family Law

CHAPTER
29

The Indian Christian Marriage Act 1872

Preliminary

The Indian Christian Marriage Act 1872[1] is an Act to consolidate and amend the law relating to solemnisation in India of the marriages of persons professing the Christian religion.[2] It extends to the whole of India, except the territories which, immediately before 1st November 1956, were comprised in the States of Travancore-Cochin, Manipur and Jammu and Kashmir.[3] Every marriage between persons, one or both of whom is or are a Christian or Christians, shall be solemnised in accordance with the provisions of the Indian Christian Marriage Act 1872.[4] Where a marriage between a Hindu and a Christian was performed before a Marriage Registrar under the Indian Christian Marriage Act, it would not be invalid merely on the ground that rites and ceremonies prescribed by the Hindu law were not performed.[5] Any marriage solemnised not in accordance with the provisions of the Indian Christian Marriage Act 1872, but otherwise, the District Court may pass a decree under s. 4 of the said Act subject to confirmation by the High Court.[6]

Persons by whom marriages may be solemnised

Marriages may be solemnised in India (*i*) by any person who has received episcopal ordination; (*ii*) by any Clergyman of the Church of Scotland; (*iii*) by any Minister of Religion licensed under this Act; (*iv*) by or in the

---

1   Act 15 of 1872.
2   See Preamble to Act 15 of 1872.
3   Section 1 of Act 15 of 1872.
4   Section 4, *ibid*.
5   (*Mrs.*) *Dubey* v (*Mr.*) *Dubey* AIR 1951 All 529.
6   *Mariasoosai* v *Clara Mary* AIR 1995 Mad 35.

presence of a Marriage Registrar appointed under this Act; (v) by any person licensed under this Act to grant certificates of marriage between Indian Christians.[7] Where a person alleges that a marriage has not been solemnised by any person authorised under s. 5 of the Indian Christian Marriage Act, the onus of proof lies on that person.[8] No Christian during the continuance of valid marriage can enter into a second marriage with another woman and any child born of such second marriage is termed as illegitimate.[9] The decision of the ecclesiastical tribunal cannot affect the civil rights of the parties arising out of marriage solemnised under s. 5 of the Indian Christian Marriage Act.[10] The State Government may grant and revoke any licence to Ministers of Religion to solemnise marriages within its territories by notification in the Official Gazette.[11] When there are more than one Marriage Registrar in any District, the State Government shall appoint one of them as the Senior Marriage Registrar.[12] The State Government may also grant a licence to any Christian, either by name or as holding any office for the time being authorising him to grant certificate of marriage between Indian Christians.[13]

Time and place of solemnisation of marriage

(A) *Time.* Every marriage solemnised under this Act shall be made between 6 a.m. and 7 p.m. except under the following circumstances.[14]

    (a) a Clergyman of the Church of England solemnising a marriage under a special licence permitting him to do so at any hour other than between 6 a.m. and 7 p.m. under the hand and seal of the Anglican Bishop of the Diocese or his Commissary, or

    (b) a Clergyman of the Church of Rome solemnising a marriage between the 7 p.m. and 6 a.m. when he has received a general or special licence in that behalf from the Roman Catholic Bishop of the Diocese or Vicariate, or

    (c) a Clergyman of the Church of Scotland solemnising a marriage according to the rules, rites, ceremonies and customs of the Church of Scotland.

---

7 Section 5 of the Indian Christian Marriage Act 1872.
8 K.J.P. *David* v *Nilmoni Devi* AIR 1960 Ori 164.
9 *Chakko* v *Daniel* AIR 1953 Trav-Co. 61.
10 *Jose* v *Alice* 1989 Cr LJ 1527.
11 Section 6 of the Indian Christian Marriage Act 1872.
12 Section 7, *ibid*.
13 Section 9, *ibid*.
14 Section 10, *ibid*.

(B) *Place*. No Clergyman of the Church of England shall solemnize a marriage in any place other than a Church where worship is generally held according to the forms of the Church of England unless there is no such Church within a radius of five miles by the shortest road from such place or unless he has received a special licence authorising him to do so under the hand and seal of the Anglican Bishop of the Diocese or of his Commissary.[15]

Marriages solemnised by licensed Ministers of Religion

Whenever a marriage is intended to be solemnised by a licensed Minister of Religion under this Act, one of the parties to the intending marriage shall give notice in writing according to the prescribed form or to the like effect, to the Minister of Religion whom he or she desires to solemnise the marriage and shall state therein (*a*) the name and surname, and the profession or condition of each party to the intending marriage, (*b*) the dwelling place of each of them, (*c*) the time during which each has dwelt there, (*d*) the Church or private dwelling in which the marriage is to be solemnised.[16] If it is intended that the marriage is to be solemnised in a private dwelling house, the Minister of Religion shall forward the notice of intended marriage to the Marriage Registrar of the District who shall affix the same to some conspicuous place in his own office.[17] When one of the parties to the intending marriage is a minor, the Minister of Religion shall send by post or otherwise a copy of such notice to the Marriage Registrar of the district or if there be more than one Registrar of such district, to the Senior Marriage Registrar.[18] The Marriage Registrar or Senior Marriage Registrar, as the case may be, on receipt of such notice, shall affix it to some conspicuous place in his office and if there are more than one Marriage Registrar, the Senior Marriage Registrar shall send copy of such notice to each of the other Marriage Registrar who shall likewise publish the same on the above manner.[19] A Minister of Religion consenting to solemnise such intending marriage shall issue under his hand a certificate of notice and of a declaration provided—(*a*) that no such certificate shall be issued until the expiration of four days after the date of the receipt of the notice by such Minister, (*b*) that there is no lawful impediment to the issue of certificate; (*c*) that the issue of such

---

15 Section 11 of the Indian Christian Marriage Act 1872.
16 Section 12, *ibid*.
17 Section 14, *ibid*.
18 Section 15, *ibid*.
19 Section 16, *ibid*.

certificate has not been forbidden by any person authorised to do so.[20] But no certificate shall be issued until one of the parties to the intended marriage appears before the Minister of Religion personally and makes a solemn declaration (a) that there is no impediment to the said marriage, (b) that the consent or consents required by law has or have been obtained or that there is no person resident in India having authority to give such consent as the case may be.[1] The consent on behalf of minor to an intending marriage may be given by the father, if living, or if the father is dead, by the guardian of the person of such minor, and in case there is no such guardian, then the mother of such minor.[2] Every person whose consent is required to a marriage with a minor has power to prohibit by notice from issuing the certificate by the Minister of Religion.[3] After the issue of the certificate by the Minister, marriage may be solemnised between the parties as the Minister thinks fit to adopt provided that the marriage is solemnised in presence of atleast two witnesses besides the Minister.[4] When the marriage is not solemnised within two months after the date of issue of the Certificate by the Minister, it shall be void.[5]

Registration of marriages solemnised by Minister of Religion

Every Clergyman of the Church of England shall keep a register of marriages in which the marriage solemnised under this Act shall be registered.[6] Every Clergyman of the Church of England shall send quarterly returns in duplicate authenticated by his signature, of the entries in the register of marriages to the Registrar of the Archdeaconry to which he is subject.[7] Every marriage solemnised by a Clergyman of the Church of Rome shall be registered according to the form directed in that behalf by the Roman Catholic Bishop of the Diocese or Vicariate in which such marriage is solemnised and the person authorised to make the entry in the register shall send quarterly returns of the entries of all marriages registered by him to the Registrar General of Births, Deaths and Marriages.[8]

---

20 Section 17 of the Indian Christian Marriage Act 1872.
1 Section 18, *ibid*.
2 Section 19 of the Indian Christian Marriage Act 1872. (For the definition of minor, see s. 3 of the Indian Christian Marriage Act 1872 which provides that a person is a minor who has not completed the age of 21 years and who is not a widower or a widow.)
3 Section 20 of the Indian Christian Marriage Act 1872.
4 Section 25, *ibid*.
5 Section 26, *ibid*.
6 Section 28, *ibid*.
7 Section 29, *ibid*.
8 Section 30, *ibid*.

Every Clergyman of the Church of Scotland shall keep a register of marriages and shall register therein every marriage which he solemnises under this Act and shall forward quarterly returns to the Registrar General of Births, Deaths and Marriages through the Senior Chaplain of the Church of Scotland.[9] The entry of each marriage in both the certificate and marriage register-book shall be signed by the person solemnising the marriage and also the persons married and shall be attested by two credible witnesses present at the time of its solemnisation.[10]

Marriages solemnised by or in the presence of a Marriage Registrar

When a marriage is intended to be solemnised by, or in the presence of a Marriage Registrar, one of the parties to such marriage shall give a notice in writing in the prescribed form to any Marriage Registrar of the District within which the parties have dwelt or if the parties dwell in different districts, the like notice shall be given to a Marriage Registrar of each district and the notice shall contain (*a*) the name and surname, (*b*) the profession or condition of each of the parties, (*c*) the dwelling place of each of them and the duration of dwelling therein, and (*d*) the place at which the marriage is to be solemnised.[11] Every Marriage Registrar shall on receiving any notice of intended marriage, cause a copy of the said notice to be affixed in some conspicuous place in his office, but in case a party to the intending marriage is a minor, the Marriage Registrar shall within twenty-four hours after the receipt by him of the notice of such marriage a copy of such notice is to be sent to any other Marriage Registrar (if any) in the same district who shall likewise affix the copy in some conspicuous place in his own office.[12] The Marriage Registrar shall file all notices and keep them with the records of his office and shall also forthwith enter a true copy of all such notices in a book to be furnished to him for that purpose by the State Government which is called the "Marriage Notice Book."[13] If a party by whom notice is given requests the Marriage Registrar to issue the certificate, he shall issue it under his hand on oath having been made.[14] The oath shall be made by a party to the intending marriage before the Marriage Registrar to the effect (*a*) that he or she believes that there is not any impediment of kindred or affinity or other lawful hindrance to the said marriage; (*b*) that both the parties have or

---

9 Section 31, Indian Christian Marriage Act 1872.
10 Section 33, *ibid*.
11 Section 38, *ibid*.
12 Section 39, *ibid*.
13 Section 40, *ibid*.
14 Section 41, *ibid*.

had or the party making the oath has, had their, his or her usual place of abode within the district of such Marriage Registrar; (c) that the consent or consents to such marriage required by law has or have been obtained thereto or that there is no person resident in India authorised to give such consent, as the case may be.[15] Where a marriage is otherwise valid, the mere fact that the bridegroom induced the Marriage Registrar to solemnise the marriage by false declaration as to the age and residence of the bride would not render the marriage illegal or void.[16] If a party to the intending marriage is a minor and both the parties reside either in Calcutta, Madras and Bombay, they may apply by a petition to the concerned High Court to order upon the Marriage Registrar to issue his certificate before the expiration of the prescribed period of fourteen days.[17] Any person who is entitled to consent under the Act to a marriage may enter a protest against the issue of certificate by the Marriage Registrar and on receipt of such protest no certificate is issued until the Marriage Registrar has examined into the matter of protest and is satisfied that it ought not to obstruct the issue of the certificate of the said marriage.[18]

Where consent of a party is required under the Act is of unsound mind or if any person other than the father withholds the consent to the marriage for just cause the parties to the intending marriage may apply to a Judge of High Court of Calcutta, Madras and Bombay if the contending party resides within the jurisdiction of such High Court, otherwise to the District Judge having jurisdiction over the consenting person and the competent court on being satisfied would pass order declaring the marriage to be a proper marriage.[19] When a Marriage Registrar refuses to issue a certificate, either of the parties to the intending marriage may apply to a Judge in the High Court of Calcutta, Madras and Bombay if the district of such Marriage Registrar is within the town of the said respective city, otherwise to a District Judge within which such Registrar resides, and the said Judge of the High Court or the District Judge as the case may be, shall examine the allegations of the petition in a summary way and decide thereon which shall be final and binding on the Marriage Registrar.[20] When the Marriage Registrar has doubt about the authority of the person applying for forbidding the issue of certificate, Marriage

15 Section 42, Indian Christian Marriage Act 1872.
16 *Lala Gokuldas* v *John Kantaraj* AIR 1937 Mad 895 (DB).
17 Section 43, Indian Christian Marriage Act 1872.
18 Section 44, *ibid*.
19 Section 45, *ibid*.
20 Section 46, *ibid*.

Registrar may apply by a petition where his district is within any of the towns of Calcutta, Madras and Bombay to a Judge of that High Court or if such district is within the town elsewhere then, he will apply to the concerned District Judge who shall examine into the allegations of the petition and declare whether the person forbidding the issue of certificate is legally authorised or not and if the decision is in the negative, such certificate shall be issued.[1] Every person making frivolous protest against issue of certificate shall be liable for all costs of proceedings in relation thereto and for damages as well.[2] The certificate is issued by the Marriage Registrar in the form prescribed in the Second Schedule to the Act.[3] After the issue of such certificate the Marriage Registrar shall solemnise. The marriage in presence of two credible witnesses according to such form or ceremony as the parties think fit and proper.[4] Where a marriage is not solemnised within two months after the notice being entered by the Marriage Registrar, any certificate issued thereafter shall be void.[5] A Marriage Registrar before whom the marriage is solemnised may ask the parties to the intending marriage several particulars required to be registered touching the marriage.[6] The Marriage Registrar shall forthwith separate the certificate from the Marriage Register Book and send it, at the end of every month to the Registrar General of Births, Deaths and Marriages.[7] The Marriage Registrar shall ascertain that notice and certificate are understood by an Indian Christian.[8] When any Indian Christian is married under the provision of part V of the Act the person solemnising the marriage shall make every effort to make Indian Christians to understand the declarations in English language.[9] The registration of marriages between Indian Christians under Part V shall be made in conformity with the rules laid down in s. 37 so far they are applicable and not otherwise.[10]

Marriage of Indian Christians

A certificate for a marriage between Indian Christians may be granted without the preliminary notice required under Part III of the Indian

---

1 Section 48, Indian Christian Marriage Act 1872.
2 Section 49, *ibid*.
3 Section 50, *ibid*.
4 Section 51, *ibid*.
5 Section 52, *ibid*.
6 Section 53, *ibid*.
7 Section 55, *ibid*.
8 Section 57, *ibid*.
9 Section 58, *ibid*.
10 Section 59, *ibid*.

Christian Marriage Act 1872 under Part VI of the said Act if the following conditions are fulfilled:[11] (*i*) the age of the man intending to be married shall not be under twenty one years and the age of the woman intending to be married shall not be under eighteen years of age; (*ii*) neither of the person intending to be married shall have a wife or husband living; (*iii*) in the presence of a person licensed under s. 9 of the said Act and atleast two credible witnesses other than such person, each of the parties shall say to the other "I call upon these persons here present to witness that I, A.B. in the presence of Almighty God, and in the name of our Lord Jesus Christ, do take thee, C.D., to be my lawful wedded wife or husband" or words to the like effect. If the aforesaid conditions are fulfilled, the person licensed under s. 9 of the said Act in whose presence the above declaration is made, shall on application of either of the parties to the marriage, and on payment of prescribed fees, grant a certificate of the marriage.[12] Every such licensed person shall keep in English or in the vernacular language in ordinary use in the district or State in which marriage is solemnised, a register book of all marriages solemnised under Part VI of the Act in his presence and shall deposit in the office of the Registrar General of Births, Deaths and Marriages duly authenticated extracts from his register-book of all entries made therein.[13] Such licensed person shall allow searches in the said register book at all reasonable times and shall, on payment of proper fees, give a copy certified under his hand.[14] Part VI of the said Act shall not apply to marriages between Roman Catholics except certain marriages.[15]

Penalties

If anybody for the purpose of procuring a marriage or licence of marriage intentionally (*i*) takes a false oath, or (*ii*) makes false declaration, or (*iii*) signs a false notice or certificate, he or she shall be deemed to have committed the offence punishable under s. 193 of the Indian Penal Code, with imprisonment for a term not exceeding three years and with fine.[16] Whoever forbids the Marriage Registrar the issue of a Certificate by falsely representing himself to be a person whose consent to the marriage is required by law, knowing or believing such representation to be false is

---

11   Section 60, Indian Christian Marriage Act 1872.
12   Section 61, *ibid*.
13   Section 62, *ibid*.
14   Section 63, *ibid*.
15   Section 65, *ibid*.
16   Section 66, *ibid*.

guilty of an offence under s. 205 of the Indian Penal Code.[17] Whoever solemnises any Christian Marriage without due authority shall be punished with imprisonment which may extend to ten years or with transportation for a term of not less than seven years and not exceeding ten years and shall also be liable to fine.[18] Whoever knowingly and wilfully solemnises a marriage out of proper time or without witnesses shall be punishable with imprisonment for a term which may extend to three years and shall also be liable to fine.[19] Any Minister of Religion licensed to solemnise marriage under this Act solemnises marriage without notice or within fourteen days after notice or with a minor, he shall be punished with imprisonment for a term which may extend to three years and shall also be liable to fine.[20] A Marriage Registrar commits an offence (*i*) if he issues a Certificate for marriage without publication of notice, (*ii*) solemnises marriage after expiry notice; (*iii*) solemnises marriage with minor within fourteen days without authority of a competent court; (*iv*) issues Certificate against authorised prohibition.[1] Any Marriage Registrar who knowingly and wilfully issues Certificate for marrige after expiry of notice, or in case of a minor within fourteen days after notice or against authorised prohibition, shall be deemed to have committed an offence under s. 166 of the Indian Penal Code.[2] Whoever being authorised to solemnise (other than clergy of churches of England, Scotland or Rome) issues a Certificate for marriage without publishing any notice or after expiry of two months, or issues a Certificate for marriage with minor within fourteen days after notice or issues any certificate authorisedly forbidden or solemnises any marriage authorisedly forbidden, he shall be punished with imprisonment for a term which may extend to four years and shall also be liable to fine.[3] If an unlicensed person grants a Certificate of marriage under Part-VI of the Act pretending to be a licensed person, then he shall be punished with imprisonment for a term which may extend to five years and shall also be liable to fine.[4] Whoever, by himself or another wilfully destroys or injuries any register book or inserts any false entry in such register book shall be punished with imprisonment for a term which may extend to seven years and shall also be liable to fine.[5]

---

17 Section 67, Indian Christian Marriage Act 1872.
18 Section 68, *ibid*.
19 Section 69, *ibid*.
20 Section 70, *ibid*.
1 Section 71, *ibid*.
2 Section 72, *ibid*.
3 Section 73, *ibid*.
4 Section 74, *ibid*.
5 Section 75, *ibid*.

The prosecution of every offence punishable under this Act shall be commenced within two years after the offence is committed.[6]

Miscellaneous

If a marriage is solemnised in accordance with the provisions of ss. 4 and 5 of the Act, it shall not be void on account of any of the following irregularities: (*a*) any statement made in regard to the dwelling of the persons married or to the consent of any person whose consent is required by law, (*b*) the notice of the marriage; (*c*) the certificate or translation thereof; (*d*) the time and place at which the marriage is solemnised; (*e*) the registration of the marriage.[7] Every person charged with the duty of registering any marriage may, on discovery of any error as to form or substance, correct the error within the prescribed time.[8] Every person solemnising a marriage, every Marriage Registrar or Registrar General of Births, Deaths and Marriages shall, on payment of proper fees, at all reasonable times, allow searches to be made in the register or for certificate or duplicate or copies of any entry.[9] Every certified copy of entry in marriage register signed by the person entrusted under this Act shall be received as evidence of the marriage.[10] A true copy of the extract from the Register Book of Marriages kept by Cathedral Church duly certified by the Senior Chaplain showing the registration of marriage is the conclusive proof of the marriage.[11] Certificates of certain marriages are to be sent at the end of every quarter in each year to the Central Government.[12] The State Government is empowered to prescribe fees,[13] to make rules,[14] to declare who shall be the District Judge.[15] Nothing in this Act shall apply to any marriage performed by any Minister. Consul or Consular Agent between subjects of the State which he represents and according to the laws of such State.[16] Nothing in this Act shall be deemed to validate any marriage which is forbidden by personal law of either of the parties.[17]

---

6 Section 76, Indian Christian Marriage Act 1872.
7 Section 77, *ibid*.
8 Section 78, *ibid*.
9 Section 79, *ibid*.
10 Section 80, *ibid*.
11 *Ranjit Kumar Bhattacharyya* v *Sabita Bhattacharya* AIR 1996 Cal 301.
12 Section 81, Indian Christian Marriage Act 1872.
13 Section 82, *ibid*.
14 Section 83, *ibid*.
15 Section 85, *ibid*.
16 Section 87, *ibid*.
17 Section 88, *ibid*.

CHAPTER
30
The Divorce Act 1869

Objects and reasons of the Act

The principal object of the Divorce Act 1869 is to amend the law of divorce of persons professing Christian religion and to confer upon certain courts jurisdiction in matrimonial matters. The provisions of the said Act are based on the prevailing provisions of the (English) Matrimonial Causes Act 1859 and the Matrimonial Causes Act 1860.[1]

Amendments

The (Indian) Divorce Act 1869 was subsequently amended by Acts 6 of 1909, 10 of 1912, 18 of 1919, 11 of 1923, 32 of 1925, 25 of 1926, 34 of 1926, 15 of 1927, 30 of 1931, 8 of 1935, 40 of 1949, 3 of 1951, 72 of 1952, the Marriage Laws (Amendment) Act 2001 (Act 49 of 2001) and the Indian Divorce (Amendment) Act 2001 (Act 51 of 2001). By the latest two amendments attempts have been made to introduce uniformity of matrimonial laws in India in certain matters, such as right of wife to apply for "expenses of proceedings and alimony pending suit," disposal of application for maintenance and education of minor children within sixty days from date of service, dissolution of marriage by mutual consent, etc.

Test of Christianity

A petitioner is not entitled to any relief under the Divorce Act 1869 unless he or she professes the Christian religion, the marriage of the parties was solemnised in India or the parties domiciled or last resided together in India at the time of presentation of the petition. Professing the Christian religion by the parties is the primary consideration for the purpose of invoking the provisions of the said Act. Although a person is

---

1   Calcutta Gazette, 1863, p. 173.

excommunicated by the Sect. or the Church to which he belongs, he does not thereby cease to profess Christianity. The question of professing Christianity is a question of his own action and not the action of his Church.[2]

Test of domicile

The question of domicile is a mixed question of fact and law. When a European claims to be domiciled in India, it will be pertinent to enquire where his father lived and died or resides, where he and his father were born, the circumstances under which he comes and resides in India. These enquiries will assist the court to ascertain whether there exists an *animus revertendi* or an *animus manendi*. His object of residing in India and generally as to the conditions under which he lives and habits of life are the determining factors for domicile of a person.[3] A woman upon her marriage acquires the domicile of her husband. If the husband deserts her the original domicile of the wife is not automatically revived and as such the domicile acquired by her on her marriage does not come to an end.[4]

Test of residence

Residence ordinarily means abode. From various decisions the following propositions relating to residence emerge.[5]

(1) To constitute residence it is not necessary that the party or parties must have his or their own home.

(2) To constitute residence the stay need not be permanent.

(3) That residence will not take a casual stay in or flying visit to a particular place with no intention of remaining is not covered by the word "reside".

(4) Residence implies some intention to remain at a place.

(5) To constitute residence the intention must be to make it his or their abode or residence either permanent or temporary.

(6) The expression "last resided" also means the place where the person had his last abode or residence.

(7) Where there has been residence together of a more permanent character and a casual or brief residence together, courts have

---

2 *Pakkiam Solomon* v *Chelliah Pillai* AIR 1924 Mad 18 (FB).
3 *Wright* v *Wright* AIR 1931 Cal 313 (SB). See also *Satya* v *Teja Singh* AIR 1975 SC 105 where the question of domicile has been elaborately dealt with.
4 *Prem Pratap Singh* v *Jagat Pratap Kunwar* AIR 1944 All 97 (DB).
5 *T.J. Poonen* v *Rathi Varghese* AIR 1967 Ker 1 (FB).

taken the view that it is only the former that can be considered as "residence".

(8) Choice of place as residence depends on facts and circumstances of each case.

Jurisdiction of court

Jurisdiction of court under the Divorce Act 1869 is conferred on the High Court and district court.[6] A suit based on the ground of non-observance of essential ceremonies is to be instituted in the ordinary court of original civil jurisdiction and not in the High Court.[7]

Dissolution of marriage

A marriage solemnised whether before or after the commencement of the Indian Divorce (Amendment) Act 2001 may be dissolved on a petition presented either by husband or wife to the District Court, on any of the following grounds:[8]

(i) has committed adultery; or

(ii) has ceased to be a Christian; or

(iii) has been incurably of unsound mind for a continuous period of not less two years; or

(iv) has been suffering from a virulent and incurable form of leprosy for a period of not less than two years; or

(v) has been suffering from venereal disease in a communicable form for a period of not less than two years; or

(vi) has not been heard of as being alive for a period of seven years or more; or

(vii) has wilfully refused to consummate the marriage; or

(viii) has failed to comply with a decree for restitution of conjugal rights for a period of two years or upwards; or

(ix) has deserted the petitioner for at least two years; or

(x) has treated the petitioner with cruelty.

The wife has a right to present a petition for divorce on the ground that her husband has been guilty of rape, sodomy or bestility.

The definition of "adultery" as given in Latey on *Divorce* and Murray's *Oxford Dictionary* is the true meaning in which the word "adultery" has

---

6 Section 4, Divorce Act 1869.
7 *Jorden Dienadah* v *Swarnjit Singh Chopra* (1982)1 DMC 224.
8 Section 10, Divorce Act 1869.

been used in s. 10 of the Divorce Act 1869.[9] Latey has defined "adultery" as willing sexual intercourse between a husband or wife and one of the opposite sex while marriage subsists."[10] In Murray's *Oxford Dictionary* adultery is defined as "violation of the marriage bed". Free movement is not necessarily adulterous course of conduct nor intimate connection is adulterous connection.[11] If there is unrebuttable evidence that the wife is living with another person in one room accommodation for more than seven months, she is guilty of adultery.[12] In *B.D. Charles v Nara Benjamin*[13] it has been laid down that (*i*) direct proof adultery is very rare; (*ii*) adultery can be established by circumstantial evidence; and (*iii*) circumstances must be such as would lead the guarded discretion of a reasonable and just man to a conclusion of adultery.

Cruelty has not been defined in the Act. Halsbury's *Laws of England*[14] defines cruelty as the coduct of such a character as to cause danger to life, limb or health (bodily or mental) or as to give rise to a reasonable apprehension of such danger. This definition is borrowed from the definition of "legal cruelty" given in *Russell v Russell*.[15]

Section 11 of the Divorce Act provides that on a petition for dissolution of marriage on the ground of adultery, the adulterer or adulterors must be made co-respondent or co-respondents to the petition.

Divorce by mutual consent

Section 10A of the Divorce Act provides for dissolution of marriage by mutual consent. A petition for dissolution of marriage by mutual consent is to be presented to the District Court by both the parties to a marriage together on the ground that (*i*) they have been living separately for a period of two years or more, (*ii*) they have not been able to live together, and (*iii*) they have mutually agreed that the marriage should be dissolved. On presentation of the joint petition to the District Court not earlier than six months after the date of presentation of the petition and not later than eighteen months after the said date, if the petition is not withdrawn in the meantime, the court shall, on being satisfied, after hearing the parties and making inquiry, if necessary, pass a decree of divorce with effect from the date of the decree. But in a case[16] it has been held that a decree for divorce

---

9 *Olga Thelma Gomes v Mark Gomes* AIR 1959 Cal 541 (SB).
10 Latey on *Divorce*, 14th Ed., p. 74.
11 *Ramish Francis Toppo v Violet Francis Toppo* AIR 1989 Cal 128.
12 *Peter Masih v Anguina Masih* AIR 1992 Del 20.
13 AIR 1979 Raj 156 (SB).
14 4th Ed., vol. 13, para 1269.
15 [1895] p. 315.
16 *Sherly Thomas v Johny* AIR 2002 Ker 280.

on mutual consent can be granted by waiving the statutory period of waiting for six months.

Power of court to dismiss petition for dissolution

If the court, on the evidence in relation to any petition for dissolution of marriage, is not satisfied, the petition shall be dismissed.[17] The court is also to be satisfied that there is no collusion between the parties or the petitioner has been accessory to or connive at or condoned the matrimonial offence. The word "satisfied" used in ss. 12 and 13 of the Act means preponderance of probabilities and not beyond reasonable doubt.[18]

Power of court in dissolving marriage

When the court is satisfied on the evidence that (1) the petitioner has proved his/her case for dissolution of marriage and that (2) (*a*) the petitioner is not accessory to or (*b*) conniving at or (*c*) adultery of the other party to the marriage or (*d*) has not condoned the adultery of the respondent or that (3) there is no collusion between the parties to the petition, the court shall pronounce a decree declaring the dissolution of the marriage. The court is not bound to pronounce decree if it finds that the petitioner (*i*) has been guilty of adultery, or (*ii*) has been guilty of unreasonable delay in presenting or prosecuting the petition, or (*iii*) is guilty of cruelty towards the respondent, or (*iv*) has deserted or left the respondent without reasonable excuse, or (*v*) is guilty of wilful neglect or misconduct towards the other party. The word "condonation" for adultery will mean that conjugal cohabitation has been resumed or continued.[19] The words "satisfied on evidence" imply that the duty of the court is to pronounce a decree if satisfied that the case of the petitioner has been proved, otherwise to dismiss the petition if not so satisfied.[20]

Under section 15 of the Divorce Act the court can grant relief in case of opposition to the respondent on his or her application had he or she presented a petition seeking such relief.[1]

Section 16 of the Act provides that every decree for dissolution of marriage made by High Court shall be at the first instance a decree *nisi* and not to be made absolute till after the expiration of such time, not less than six months from the pronouncing thereof. Whenever a decree *nisi* has been made and the petitioner fails, within a reasonable time, to move

---

17 Section 13, Divorce Act 1869.
18 See *Pasumpon Gandhi* v *Shirley Gandhi* AIR 2003 NOC 239 (Mad).
19 Section 14, Divorce Act 1869.
20 *Earnest John White* v *Kathleen Olive White* AIR 1958 SC 441.
1 Section 15, Divorce Act 1869.

to have such decree made absolute, the High Court may dismiss the suit.[2] Decree of dissolution of Christian marriage passed by Family Court under the Family Courts Act 1984 would not need any confirmation from the High Court. Such decree would operate as a final decree subject to the right of appeal under s. 19 of the Family Courts Act.[3]

Nullity of marriage

Any husband or wife may present a petition to the District Court praying for a declaration that his or her marriage is null and void.[4] A decree for nullity of marriage can be made on any of the following grounds[5]: (1) that the respondent was and still is impotent; (2) that the parties are within the prohibited degree of consanguinity or affinity; (3) that either party was a lunatic or idiot at the time of the marriage; (4) that the former husband or wife was living at the time of the marriage. A petitioner cannot urge any ground in a nullity proceeding which is not specified in s. 19 of the Act.[6]

Nothing in s. 19 shall affect the jurisdiction of the District Court to make decrees of nullity of marriage on the ground that the consent of either party was obtained by force or fraud. The reasons for putting restrictions on a void marriage are four folds. These are based on (*i*) religious considerations, (*ii*) natural law, (*iii*) genetic consideration, and (*iv*) social policy.

Where a marriage is annulled on the ground that the former husband or wife was living and it is adjudged that the subsequent marriage was contracted in good faith and with full belief of the parties that the former husband or wife was dead or when a marriage is annulled on the ground of insanity, children begotten before the degree shall be treated as legitimate children and shall be entitled to succeed to the estate of their parents.[7]

Judicial separation

No decree shall be made for divorce a *mensa et toro*, but the husband or wife may obtain a decree of judicial separation on the ground of adultery, cruelty or desertion for two years or upwards, and such decree shall have the effect of a divorce a *mensa et toro* under the existing law.[8] Where the

---

2 Section 16, Divorce Act.
3 *Jyotsna* v *Suresh John Jagtop* 2000 (1) Civ LJ 471 (Bom).
4 Section 18, Divorce Act.
5 Section 19, *ibid*.
6 *Lakshmi Dhar* v *Sachit Kumar Dhar* 73 Cal WN 1001 (DB).
7 Section 21, Divorce Act.
8 Section 22, *ibid*.

petitioner fails to prove the grounds for decree for divorce, but the ground for judicial separation, the court can grant the same even if it is not asked for in the petition. An oral request in this regard would be enough.[9]

After the judicial separation under the Divorce Act, the wife shall be considered as spinster with respect to every property which she may acquire or which may come to or devolve upon her.[10] The separated wife in case of judicial separation under this Act shall be deemed to be spinster for purposes of contract and suing.[11] If any decree of judicial separation is obtained during absence of husband or wife, it may be reversed on the application of the aggrieved respondent concerned.[12]

Restitution of conjugal rights

When either the husband or the wife has, without reasonable excuse, withdrawn from the society of the other, either wife or husband may apply, by a petition to the District Court for restitution of conjugal rights and the court, on being satisfied of the truth of the statements made in such petition, may grant a decree for restitution of conjugal rights.[13] In answer to such a petition, nothing should be pleaded which would not be ground for a suit for judicial separation or for a decree of nullity of marriage.[14]

Alimony

In any suit under this Act whether it is instituted by husband or a wife and whether or not she has obtained an order of protection, the wife may present a petition for expenses of the proceedings and alimony pending the suit. Such petition shall be served on the husband and the court, on being satisfied, may make an order on the husband for payment to the wife of the expenses of the proceedings and alimony pending the suit. Such petition for expenses of the proceedings and alimony *pendente lite* should be disposed of within a period of sixty days.[15] In fixing quantum of temporary alimony, the court should take into consideration the earnings of the wife also. If she is able to support herself by her own earnings, she will not be entitled to any alimony *pendente lite*.[16]

---

9 *Prem Prakash* v *Sarla* AIR 1989 MP 326 (SB).
10 Section 24, Divorce Act.
11 Section 25, *ibid*.
12 Section 26, *ibid*.
13 Section 32, *ibid*.
14 Section 33, *ibid*.
15 Section 36, Divorce Act.
16 *Leelavathy* v *Sunder Athmaseelam* AIR 1977 Mad 409.

Where a decree of dissolution of the marriage or a decree of judicial separation is obtained by the wife, the District Court may order that the husband shall pay to the wife such gross sum of money or such annual sum of money for any term not exceeding her own life, having regard to her fortune, to the ability of the husband and to the conduct of the parties and for that purpose the court may cause a proper instrument to be executed by all necessary parties.

In every such case the court may make an order on the husband for payment to the wife either monthly or weekly sums for her maintenance and support. If the husband afterwards shows any cause for his inability to make such payments, it shall be lawful for the court to discharge or modify the order.[17] Order for permanent alimony at the time of passing the decree *nisi* for dissolution of marriage is premature.[18] The court may direct the payment of alimony either to the wife herself or to any trustee on her behalf to be approved by the court.[19]

Custody of children

In a suit for obtaining a judicial separation the court may, from time to time, before making its decree, make interim order with respect to the custody, maintenance and education of the minor children of the parties to the suit. The application for making such interim order shall be disposed of preferably within sixty days from the date of service of notice on the respondent.[20] The court will always consider the long interest of a child[1] and the wishes of a child confine to immediate interest. The court after the decree of judicial separation may, upon application, make such orders and provisions with respect to the custody, maintenance and education of minor children of the parties to the decree.[2] Orders relating to custody of children are not final but interlocutory and subject to modification at any future time upon proof of change of circumstances requiring change of custody, but such change in custody must be proved to be in paramount interest of the child.[3]

Where a decree of dissolution or nullity of marriage has been passed, the District Court may, upon application by petition, make from time to time all such orders and provision with respect to the custody, maintenance and education of the minor children of the parents to the decree, or for

---

17 Section 37, Divorce Act.
18 *Santhammal* v *Thangaraj* AIR 1975 Kant 23 (SB).
19 Section 38, Divorce Act.
20 Section 41, *ibid*.
1 See Re S. (*Infants*) [1967]1 WLR 396.
2 Section 43, Divorce Act.
3 *Jai Prakash Khadria* v *Shyam Sunder Agarwala* AIR 2000 SC 2172.

placing such children under the protection of the said court.[4] Where the petitioner to whom the custody of children was granted died, her parents could intervene and pray for the custody of the children. The court, if it appeared just, could grant such custody.[5]

Procedure

Subject to the provisions of the Divorce Act, all proceedings under this Act shall be governed by the Code of the Civil Procedure 1908.[6] Forms of petitions and statements are set forth in the Schedule to the Act.[7] Every petition for a decree of dissolution of marriage, or of nullity of marriage or of judicial separation shall state that there is no collusion or connivance between the parties thereto.[8] The word "shall" used in s. 47 of the Act ought not to be understood in a rigid manner. Collusion between the parties can be easily discovered even if the pleadings are silent about the prescribed norms in s. 47.[9]

When the husband or wife is a lunatic or idiot, a suit under this Act (other than a suit for restitution of conjugal rights) may be brought on his or her behalf by the committee or person entitled to his or her custody.[10] If the petitioner is minor, he or she shall sue by his or her next friend to be approved by the court.[11] An appeal shall lie to the Supreme Court from a decree (other than a *decree nisi*) or under this Act of a High Court made on appeal, and from any decree (other than a *decree nisi* or order made in the exercise of original jurisdiction by judges of a High Court or of any Division Court.[12]

Remarriage

Where a decree for dissolution or nullity of marriage has been passed and the time for appeal has expired without an appeal having been presented to any court including the Supreme Court or an appeal, if preferred, has been dismissed and the decree has become final, it shall be lawful for either party to the marriage to marry again.[13] The provisions of s. 57 of the Act are mandatory. When a new marriage is contracted without compliance of the provisions of s. 57 of the Act, it can be declared null and void.[14]

---

4 Section 44, Divorce Act.
5 *Pryor* v *Pryor* [1947]1 All ER 381.
6 Section 45, Divorce Act.
7 Section 46, *ibid*.
8 Section 47, *ibid*.
9 *Christinamary* v *Vijay Siddharaj* AIR 1979 Mad 100 (SB).
10 Section 48, Divorce Act.
11 Section 49, *ibid*.
12 Section 56, *ibid*.
13 Section 57, *ibid*.
14 *Jackson* v *Jackson* (1912)34 All 203.

CHAPTER
31

The Intestate Succession to Christian under the Indian Succession Act 1925

As to what property deceased considered to have died intestate (section 30)

A person is deemed to die intestate in respect of all property of which he has not made a testamentary disposition which is capable of taking effect.

Illustrations

(*i*) A has left no will. He has died intestate in respect of the whole of his property.

(*ii*) A has left a will, whereby he appointed B his executor, but the will contains no other provisions. A has died intestate in respect of the distribution of his property.

(*iii*) A has bequeathed his whole property for an illegal purpose. A has died intestate in respect of the distribution of his property.

(*iv*) A has bequeathed 1,000 rupees to B and 1,000 rupees to the eldest son of C, and has made no other bequest and has died leaving the sum of 2,000 rupees and no other property. C died before A without having ever had a son. A has died intestate in respect of the distribution of 1,000 rupees.

Devolution of property of an intestate (section 32)

The property of an intestate devolves upon the wife or husband or upon those kindred of the deceased in the order and according to rules contained in Chapter II of Part V of the Indian Succession Act 1925. "Kindred" or "consanguinity" is defined in s. 24 of the Indian Succession Act 1925 as the connection or relation of persons descended from the same stock or common ancestor.

(A) *Where intestate has left widow and lineal descendants or widow and kindred only or widow and no kindred the following rule shall apply (section 33).* Where the intestate has left a widow—(*a*) if he has also left any lineal descendents, one-third of his property shall belong to his widow and the remaining two-thirds shall go to his lineal descendants; (*b*) save as provided by s. 33A if he has left persons who are kindred to him, one-half of his property shall belong to his widow and the other half shall go to those who are kindred to him, (*c*) if he has left none who are kindred to him, the whole of his property shall belong to his widow.

(B) *Special provision where intestate has left widow and no lineal descendants (section 33A).* Where the intestate has left a widow but no lineal descendants and the net value of the property does not exceed five thousand rupees, the whole of the property shall belong to the widow. Where the net value of the property exceeds rupees five thousand, the widow shall be entitled to five thousand rupees thereof and shall have a charge upon the whole of such property for such sum of five thousand rupees with interest thereon from the date of the intestate at 4% per annum until payment. This right of widow shall be in addition and without prejudice to her interest and share in the residue of the estate of such intestate remaining after payment of the sum of five thousand rupees with interest thereon as aforesaid and such residue shall be distributed in accordance with the provisions of s. 33. The net value of the property shall be ascertained by deducting from the gross value thereof all debts and all funeral and administrative expenses of the intestate and all other lawful liabilities and charges to which the property shall be subject. The provisions of s. 33A shall not apply (*a*) to the property of (*i*) any Indian Christian, (*ii*) any child or grandchild of any male person who is or was at the time of his death an Indian Christian, or (*iii*) any person professing the Hindu, Buddhist, Sikh, Jain a religion, the succession to whose property is, under s. 24 of the Special Marriage Act 1872 regulated by provisions of that Act; (*b*) unless the deceased dies intestate in respect of all his property.

(C) *Where intestate has left no widow, and where he has left no kindred (section 34).* Where the intestate has left no widow, his property shall go to his lineal descendants or to those who are of kindred to him, not being lineal descendants; and if he has left none who are kindred to him, it shall go to the Government.

(D) *Right of widower (section 35).* A husband surviving his wife has the same rights in respect of her property, if she dies intestate, as a widow has in respect of her husband's property, if he dies intestate.

Distribution of intestate property where there are lineal descendants

Section 36 of the Indian Succession Act 1925 provides that the rules for the distribution of intestate's property after deducting the widow's share if he has left any widow, amongst his lineal descendants shall be those contained in ss. 37 to 40 of the Act.

(A) *Where intestate has left child or children only (section 37).* Where the intestate has left surviving him a child or children, but no more remote lineal descendant through a deceased child, the property shall belong to his surviving child, if there is only one, or shall be equally divided among all his surviving children.

(B) *Where intestate has left no child, but grandchild or grandchildren (section 38).* The property of the intestate in such case shall belong to his surviving grandchild, if there is one, or shall be equally divided among all his surviving grandchildren.

Illustrations

(*i*) A has three children and no more, John, Mary and Henry. They all die before the father, John leaving two children, Mary three and Henry four. Afterwards, A dies intestate leaving those nine grandchildren and no descendant of any deceased grandchild. Each of his grandchildren will have one-ninth.

(*ii*) But if Henry has died, leaving no child, then the whole is equally divided between the intestate's five grandchildren, the children of John and Mary.

(C) *Where intestate has left only great-grandchildren or remoter lineal descendants (section 39).* In like manner the property shall go to the surviving lineal descendants who are nearest in degree to the intestate, where they are all in the degree of great-grandchildren to him or are all in a more remote degree.

(D) *Where intestate leaves lineal descendants not all in the same degree of kindred to him, and those through whom the more remote are descended are dead (section 40).* In such a case the property of the intestate shall be divided into such a number of equal shares as may correspond with the number of the lineal descendants of the intestate who either stood in the nearest degree of kindred to him at his decease, or having been of the like degree of kindred to him, died before him, leaving lineal descendants who survived him. One of such shares shall be allotted to each of the lineal descendants who stood in the nearest degree of kindred to the intestate at his decease; and one of such shares shall be allotted in respect of each of such deceased lineal descendants; and the share allotted in respect of each of such deceased lineal descendants shall belong to his surviving child or children or more remote lineal descendants always taking the share which his or their parent or parents would have been entitled to respectively if such parent or parents had survived the intestate.

Illustrations

(*i*) A had three children, John, Mary and Henry; John died leaving four children, and Mary died, leaving one and Henry alone survived the father. On the death of A, intestate, one-third is allotted to Henry, one-third to John's four children, and the remaining third to Mary's one child.

(*ii*) A left no child but left eight grandchildren, and two children of a deceased grandchild. The property is divided into nine parts, one of which is allotted to each grandchild, and the remaining one-ninth is equally divided between the two great-grandchildren.

(*iii*) A has three children, John, Mary and Henry; John dies leaving four children, and one of John's children dies leaving two children. Mary dies leaving one child. A afterwards dies intestate. One-third of his property is allotted to Henry, one third to Mary's child and one-third is divided into four parts, one of which is allotted to each of John's three surviving children, and the remaining part is equally divided between John's two grandchildren.

(*iv*) A has two children and no more, John and Mary. John dies before his father, leaving his wife pregnant. Then A dies leaving Mary surviving him and in due time a child of John is born. A's property is to be equally divided between Mary and the posthumous child.

Distribution of property of intestate where there are no lineal descendants

Rules of distribution where intestate has left no lineal descendants are contained in ss. 42 to 48. This distribution shall be made after deducting the widow's share, if he has left a widow (section 41).

(A) *When intestate's father living (section 42).* In such a case the father shall succeed to the property of the intestate.

(B) *Where intestate's father dead, but his mother, brothers and sisters living (section 43).* In such a case if there is no child living of any deceased brother or sister, the mother and each living brother or sister shall succeed to the property in equal shares.

Illustration

A dies intestate, survived by his mother and two brothers of the full blood, John and Henry and a sister Mary, who is the daughter of his mother, but not of his father. The mother takes one-fourth, each brother takes one-fourth and Mary, the sister of half-blood takes one-fourth.

(C) *Where intestate's father dead and his mother, a brother or sister and children of any deceased brother or sister, living (section 44).* In such case the mother and each living brother or sister, and the living child or children of each deceased brother or sister shall be entitled to the property in equal shares, such children (if more than one) taking in equal shares only the shares which their respective parents would have taken if living at the intestate's death.

Illustration

A, the intestate, leaves his mother, his brothers, John and Henry, and also one child of a deceased sister, Mary, and two children of George, a deceased brother of half blood who was the son of his father but not of his mother. The mother takes one-fifth, John and Henry, each takes one-fifth, the child of Mary takes one-fifth and the two children of George divide the remaining one-fifth equally between them.

(D) *Where intestate's father dead and his mother and children of any deceased brother or sister living (section 45).* In such case the mother and the child or children of each deceased brother or sister shall be entitled to the property in equal shares, such children (if more than one) taking in equal shares only the shares which their respective parents would have taken if living at the intestate's death.

Illustration

A, the intestate, leaves no brother or sister but leaves his mother and one child of a deceased sister, Mary and two children of a deceased brother, George. The mother takes one-third, the child of Mary takes one-third and the children of George divide the remaining one-third equally between them.

(E) *Where intestate's father dead, but his mother living and no brother, sister, nephew or niece (section 47).* In such case the property of the intestate shall belong to the mother.

(F) *Where intestate has left neither lineal descendant nor parents, nor brother nor sister (section 48).* In such case the property of the intestate shall be divided equally among those of his relatives who are in the nearest degree of kindred to him.

Illustrations

(i) A, the intestate, has left a grandfather, and a grandmother and no other relative standing in the same or a nearer degree of kindred to him. They, being in the second degree, will be entitled to the property in equal shares, exclusive of any uncle or aunt of the intestate, uncles and aunts being only in the third degree.

(*ii*) A, the intestate, has left a great-grandfather or a great-grandmother, and uncles and aunts, and no other relative standing in the same or a nearer degree of kindred to him. All of these being in the third degree will take equal shares.

(*iii*) A, the intestate, left a great-grandfather and uncle and a nephew, but no relative standing in a nearer degree of kindred to him. All of these being in the third degree will take equal shares.

(*iv*) Ten children of one brother or sister of the intestate, and one child of another brother or sister of the intestate, constitute the class of relatives of the nearest degree of kindred to him. They will each take one-eleventh of the property.

Children's advancements not brought into hotchpot (section 49)

Where a distributive share in the property of a person who has died intestate is claimed by a child, or any descendant of a child, of such person, no money or other property which the intestate may, during his life, have paid, given or settled to, or for the advancement of, the child by whom or by whose descendant the claim is made shall be taken into account in estimating such distributive share.

CHAPTER
32

The Converts' Marriage Dissolution Act 1866

Preliminary

The Converts' Marriage Dissolution Act 1866 was passed to legalise, under certain circumstances the dissolution of marriages of converts to Christianity.[1]

Convert deserted by the spouse

If a husband changes his religion for Christianity, and if in consequence of such change, his wife for a continuous period of six months deserts or repudiates her, she may sue him for conjugal society.[2] If a wife changes her religion for Christianity, and if in consequence of such change her husband for a continuous period of six months deserts or repudiates her, she may sue him for conjugal society.[3]

Jurisdiction of court

If the respondent, at the time of commencement of a suit resides within the local limits of the ordinary original civil jurisdiction of any of the High Courts of Judicature, the suit shall be commenced in such court; otherwise it shall be commenced in the principal Civil Court of original jurisdiction of the district in which the defendant resides at the commencement of the suit.[4]

---

1 See Preamble to the Converts' Marriage Dissolution Act 1866.
2 Section 4, the Converts' Marriage Dissolution Act 1866.
3 Section 5, *ibid*.
4 Section 6, *ibid*.

Procedure

The suit shall be commenced by a petition in the form in the first schedule to the Act, or as near thereto as the circumstances of the case will allow.[5] A copy of the petition shall be served upon the respondent and the court shall thereupon issue a citation under the seal of the court and signed by the Judge.[6] In the ordinary cases, the citation shall be in the form given in the second schedule to the Act or as near thereto as the circumstances of the case will allow.[7] A copy of the citation sealed with the seal of the court shall be served on the respondent and the provisions of the Code of Civil Procedure as to the service and endorsement of summons shall apply *mutatis mutandis*, to citation under the Act.[8] If the respondent does not obey such citation and comply with every other requirement made upon her or him under the provisions of this Act, she or he shall be liable to punishment under s. 174 of the Indian Penal Code.[9] On the day fixed in the citation, the petitioner shall appear in the court and prove the following points:[10] (a) the identity of the parties, (b) the marriage between the petitioner and the respondent, (c) the male party to the suit has completed the age of sixteen years and that the female party to the suit has completed the age of thirteen years, (d) the desertion or repudiation of the petitioner by the respondent, (e) that such desertion or repudiation was in consequence of the petitioner's change of religion, (f) and that such desertion or repudiation had continued for six months immediately before the commencement of the suit. If these points are proved to the satisfaction of the Judge, the respondent is asked whether she or he refuses to cohabit with the petitioner, and if so, what is the ground of such refusal.[11] Every interrogation made by the Judge may, at his discretion, take place in open Court or in his private room.[12] If the respondent is a female and in answer to the interrogatories of the Judge or Commissioner appointed by the Judge refuses to cohabit with the petitioner, the Judge

---

5 Section 7 read with the Form of Petition in the First Schedule of the Converts' Marriage Dissolution Act 1866.
6 Section 8, *ibid*.
7 Section 9, read with the Form of Citation in ordinary cases in the Second Schedule and read with the Form of Citation in cases of Respondent exempt from appearance in court as given in the Third Schedule of the Converts' Marriage Dissolution Act 1866.
8 Section 10, *ibid*.
9 Section 11, *ibid*.
10 Section 12, *ibid*.
11 Section 13, *ibid*.
12 Section 14, *ibid*.

considering the respondent's answers and the facts and circumstances of the case which have been proved by the petitioner and shall form an opinion whether the ground for refusal is the petitioner's change of religion and, thereafter, shall make an order adjourning the case for a year with direction to the parties in the interim period to meet in presence of some person or persons as selected by the Judge to ascertain whether or not the respondent freely and voluntarily persists in such refusal.[13] At the expiration of the said adjournment period of one year. The petitioner shall again appear in court and shall prove that the said desertion or repudiation had continued and shall satisfy the Judge as to the points mentioned in s. 12 of the said Act and if the respondent on being interrogated by the Judge once again refuses to cohabit with the petitioner, the respondent shall be taken to have deserted or repudiated finally the petitioner and the Judge shall pass a decree under his hand and seal declaring that the marriage between the parties is dissolved.[14] If the respondent is a male and in answer to the interrogatories of the Judge or Commissioner appointed by the Judge, he refuses to cohabit with the petitioner, the Judge upon consideration of the respondent's answers and the facts which have been proved by the petitioner shall form an opinion that the ground for his refusal is the petitioner's change of religion and in that case the Judge shall adjourn the matter for a year and at the end of the adjournment period the petitioner shall again appear in the court and if the respondent on being interrogated by the Judge refuses again to cohabit with the petitioner, the Judge shall thereupon pass a decree under his hand and seal declaring that the marriage between the parties is dissolved.[15] Where it appears to the Judge at any stage of the suit that both or either of the parties has not attained puberty at the date of the marriage and that such marriage has not been consummated and if in answer to the interrogatories, the respondent refuses to cohabit with the petitioner on the ground of change of religion, the Judge shall thereupon pass a decree declaring that the marriage between the parties is dissolved.[16] After the passing of the decree for dissolution of marriage it shall be lawful for the respective parties thereto to marry again.[17] The provisions of the Code of Civil Procedure as to summoning and examining a witness shall apply in suits instituted under the Act.[18] If at any stage of the suit

---

13   Section 15, Converts' Marriage Dissolution Act 1866.
14   Section 16, *ibid*.
15   Section 17, *ibid*.
16   Section 18, *ibid*.
17   Section 19, *ibid*.
18   Section 22, *ibid*.

either party under the age required by the Act or parties are cohabiting as man and wife or the respondent as willing to cohabit, the court shall pass a decree dismissing the suit on stating the ground for such dismissal.[19] At any time within twelve months after a decree of dismissal of the suit the respondent again deserts or repudiate the petitioner on the ground of his or her change of religion, the suit may be revived by summoning the respondent and upon proof of the former decree and of such renewed repudiation or desertion, the suit shall recommence at the stage at which it had arisen immediately before the passing of such decree and after the proof, interrogatories, interview and adjournment as required under the Act, the Judge shall thereupon pass a decree dissolving the marriage between the parties.[20] If at any stage of the suit it is proved that the respondent has deserted or repudiated the petitioner solely or partly in consequence of the petitioner's cruelty or adultery, the court shall pass a decree dismissing the suit on stating the ground of such dismissal.[1] If the petitioner, being male has at the time of institution of the suit two or more wives, he shall make them all respondents and if it is proved that he is cohabiting with one of such wives as man and wife, the court shall pass a decree dismissing the suit and stating the ground of such dismissal.[2]

Status of children

A dissolution of marriage under the provisions of this Act shall not operate to deprive the respondent's children, if any by the petitioner of their status as legitimate children or of any right or interest which they would have had, according to the personal law applicable to them, by way of maintenance, inheritance or otherwise, in case the marriage had not been so dissolved.[3]

Alimony

Where a suit is commenced under the provisions of the Converts' Marriage Dissolution Act 1866[4] and it appears to the court that the wife has no sufficient separate property to enable her to maintain herself suitably to her life and to prosecute or defend the suit, the court may, pending the suit, order the husband to furnish the wife sufficient funds to enable her to prosecute or defend the suit and also order for her maintenance

---

19 Section 23, Converts' Marriage Dissolution Act 1866.
20 Section 24, *ibid*.
1   Section 25, *ibid*.
2   Section 26, *ibid*.
3   Section 27, *ibid*.
4   Act 21 of 1866.

pendente lite and permanent alimony which shall cease from any time of any subsequent marriage of the wife.[5]

Reference of question of conversion to High Court

No appeal has lie against any order or decree made or passed by a court in a suit under this Act; but the Judge may state a case raising the question whether conversion has dissolved the marriage and submit it with his own opinion thereon for the decision of the High Court.[6] Every such case shall concisely state the facts and set forth documents as may be necessary to enable the High Court to decide the question raised and the suit shall be stayed until the judgement of the such court is received.[7] Every such case shall be decided by atleast three Judges of the High Court and if such High Court situates at any of the Presidency Towns, the petitioner and the respondent may appear and be heard either in person or by an advocate.[8] The High Court may refer the case to the Judge for such additions or alterations in the statements as the High Court may direct in that behalf.[9] The High Court may decide the question raised and Judge shall, on receiving the judgement from the High Court, dispose of the case conformably to such judgment.[10]

---

5   Section 28, Converts' Marriage Dissolution Act 1866.
6   Section 29, *ibid*.
7   Section 30, *ibid*.
8   Section 31, *ibid*.
9   Section 32, *ibid*.
10 Section 33, *ibid*.

PART 5

Parsi Family Law

CHAPTER
33

The Parsi Marriage and Divorce Act 1936

Object of Parsi Marriage and Divorce Act 1936

The primary object of this Act was to amend the law relating to marriage and divorce among the Parsis. This Act has been amended by the Parsi Marriage and Divorce (Amendment) Act 1988 and the Marriage Laws (Amendment) Act 2001.

Requisites of valid Parsi marriages

No Parsi marriage shall be valid if—(a) the contracting parties are related to each other in any of the degrees of consanguinity or affinity set forth in Schedule I; or (b) such marriage is not solemnised according to the Parsi form of ceremony called "Ashirvad" by a priest in the presence of two Parsi witnesses; or (c) in the case of any Parsi (whether such Parsi has changed his or her religion or domicile or not) who, if a male, has not completed twenty-one years of age, and if a female has not completed eighteen years of age. Notwithstanding that a marriage is invalid for not compliance with the requisites stated above, any child born of such marriage shall be legitimate.[1]

Any formal irregularity of marriage contracted under this Act shall not make the marriage invalid. Such irregularities are (i) that the marriage was not certified under s. 6, or (ii) that the certificate was not sent to the Registrar, or (iii) that the certificate was defective.[2]

---

1 Section 3, Parsi Marriage and Divorce Act 1936.
2 Section 17, *ibid*.

Unlawful remarriage and punishment of bigamy

No Parsi shall contract any marriage under this Act during the life time of his or her wife or husband except after his or her lawful divorce from such wife or husband or after his or her marriage has been lawfully declared null and void or dissolved.[3] When a Parsi during the subsistence of his or her marriage marries again, he or she shall be subjected to punishment provided in ss. 494 and 495 of the Indian Penal Code for the offence of bigamy.[4]

Registration of marriage

Every marriage contracted under this Act shall be certified by the officiating priest in the prescribed form. The certificate shall be signed by the said priest, the contracting parties and two witnesses present at the marriage. The said certificate is thereafter sent with requisite fees to the Registrar of the place at which such marriage is solemnised. The Registrar on receipt of such certificate enter it in the Register maintained for that purpose.[5] The Register of marriages is kept open for inspection at all reasonable times.[6] There are also provisions for registration of divorces.[7]

Penalty for breach of certain provisions of the Act

There are some penal provisions for non-compliance with certain provisions of the Act. Solemnisation of marriage in violation of s. 4 of the Act is subjected to penalty.[8] Any priest neglecting to comply with the requirements of s. 6 is liable to penalty.[9] Every person required by s. 6 to subscribe or attest the said certificate is liable to pay fine.[10] Every person making or signing or attesting any certificate containing a statement which is false is also liable to penalty.[11] Any Registrar failing to enter the said certificate pursuant to s. 6 is liable to punishment.[12] A person secreting, destroying or dishonestly altering the said Register in any part thereof shall be liable to punishment.[13]

---

3   Section 4, Parsi Marriage and Divorce Act.
4   Section 5, *ibid*.
5   Section 6, *ibid*.
6   Section 8, *ibid*.
7   Section 10, *ibid*.
8   Section 11, *ibid*.
9   Section 12, *ibid*.
10 Section 13, *ibid*.
11 Section 14, *ibid*.
12 Section 15, *ibid*.
13 Section 16, *ibid*.

Parsi Matrimonial Courts

For purposes of hearing of suits under the Parsi Marriage and Divorce Act 1936 a special court shall be constituted in each of the Presidency-towns of Calcutta, Madras and Bombay and in such other places where the State Governments shall think fit.[14] There are two types of Parsi Matrimonial Courts. The Courts established in Presidency-towns will be called Parsi Chief Matrimonial Courts and every court constituted at a place other than a Presidency-town shall be called Parsi District Matrimonial Court of such place. The local limits of the jurisdiction of a Parsi Chief Matrimonial Court shall be conterminous with the local limits of the ordinary original civil jurisdiction of the High Court.[15] The local limits of jurisdiction of Parsi District Matrimonial Courts shall be conterminous with the limits of the district.[16] The Judge of Parsi Matrimonial Court shall be aided by five delegates in trial of cases under this Act except in regard to: (*a*) interlocutory applications and proceedings; (*b*) alimony and maintenance, both permanent as well as *pendente lite*; (*c*) custody, maintenance and education of children, and (*d*) all matters and proceedings other than the regular hearing of cases.[17] All delegates appointed under this Act shall be treated as public servants within the meaning of the Indian Penal Code.[18] All legal practitioners shall be entitled to practise in Parsi Matrimonial Courts.[19] All suits instituted under this Act shall be brought in the court within the limits of whose jurisdiction (*i*) the defendant resides at the time of institution of the suit, or (*ii*) where the marriage under the Act was solemnised, or (*iii*) where the plaintiff and the defendant last resided together in case of leaving the territory by the defendant, or (*iv*) where the plaintiff resides in case the defendant has left the territory after recording the reasons in writing by the court.[20]

Notwithstanding contained in s. 19 or s. 20 of the Act where in case of trial in Parsi Matrimonial Court not less than three delegates have attended throughout the proceedings, the trial shall not be invalid by reason of absence of the other delegates.[1] Provisions of the Code of Civil Procedure 1908 shall apply to the proceedings in suits instituted under this Act.[2]

---

14 Section 18, Parsi Marriage and Divorce Act.
15 Section 19, *ibid*.
16 Section 20, *ibid*.
17 See ss. 19, 20, *ibid*.
18 Section 26, *ibid*.
19 Section 28, *ibid*.
20 Section 29, *ibid*.
 1 Section 44, *ibid*.
 2 Section 45, *ibid*.

Nullity of marriage

In case of non-consummation of marriage due to impossibility of natural causes, such marriage may, at the instance of either party thereto, be declared to be null and void.[3]

Dissolution of marriage

A suit for dissolution of marriage may be instituted at the instance of either party thereto if a husband or a wife shall have been continually absent from his or her wife or husband for a period of seven years.[4] Other grounds for divorce are as follows: (*a*) wilful refusal to consummate marriage within one year after solemnisation of marriage; (*b*) unsound mind of defendant at the time of marriage; (*c*) incurable unsound mind of defendant for a period of two years or more immediately preceding the filing of the suit; (*d*) mental disorder of defendant causing apprehension in the mind of the plaintiff; (*e*) pregnancy of defendant at the time of marriage by some one other than the plaintiff; (*f*) adultery or fornication or bigamy or rape or an unnatural offence committed by the defendant; (*g*) treating the plaintiff with cruelty; (*h*) voluntarily causing grievous hurt to the plaintiff; (*i*) the defendant infected with venereal disease; (*j*) the defendant undergoing a sentence of imprisonment for seven years or more; (*k*) desertion of the plaintiff for at least two years; (*l*) no marital intercourse for one year or more since passing of an order against the defendant for maintenance of the plaintiff; (*m*) conversion to other religion of the defendant.[5]

Either party to a marriage may also sue for divorce on the ground (*i*) that there has been no resumption of cohabitation as between the parties to the marriage for a period of one year or upwards after the passing of a decree for judicial separation; or (*ii*) that there has been no restitution of conjugal rights as between the parties to the marriage for a period of one year or upwards. No decree for divorce shall be granted if the plaintiff has failed or neglected to comply with an order for maintenance passed against him.[6]

In every suit for divorce on the ground of adultery, the plaintiff shall make the person with whom adultery is alleged to have been committed a co-defendant unless the court orders otherwise.[7]

---

3 Section 30, Parsi Marriage and Divorce Act.
4 Section 31, *ibid*.
5 Section 32, *ibid*.
6 Section 32A, *ibid*.
7 Section 33, *ibid*.

Divorce by mutual consent[8]

A suit for mutual divorce may be filed by both the parties to the marriage together on the grounds (*i*) that they have been living separately for a period of one year or more, (*ii*) that they have not been able to live together, and (*iii*) that they have been mutually agreed that the marriage should be dissolved. No such suit shall be filed unless at the date of filing of the suit one year has lapsed since the date of the marriage. The court shall, on being satisfied, after hearing the parties and after making such inquiry as it thinks fit, (*a*) that the marriage has been solemnised under this Act and the averments in the plaint are true and (*b*) that the consent of either party to the suit was not obtained by force or fraud, pass a decree of divorce with effect from the date of the decree.

Suit for judicial separation

Any person married under this Act may sue for judicial separation on any of the grounds for which such person could have filed a suit for divorce.[9] Grounds for divorce have been set out in s. 32 of the Act. The safest criterion is to consider by the court as to the course of conduct of the parties towards each other during their married lives and to consider whether the party has shown just and lawful grounds for living separately from the other.[10]

No bar to grant decrees in certain cases

In any suit under s. 30 (suit of nullity), s. 31 (suit for dissolution), s. 32 (grounds for dissolution), s. 32A (non-resumption of cohabitation) or s. 34 (suit for judicial separation), whether defended or not, the court will not withhold relief if any of the following grounds does not exist:

(*a*) The act or omission set forth in the plaint has not been condoned; (*b*) the husband and wife are not colliding together; (*c*) the plaintiff has not connived at or been accessory to the said act or omission; (*d*) (save where a definite period of limitation is provided by this Act) there has been no unnecessary or improper delay in instituting the suit; and (*e*) there is no other legal ground why relief should not be granted.[11]

---

8 Section 32B, Parsi Marriage and Divorce Act.
9 Section 34, *ibid*.
10 *Pistonji Kekobund Bharucha* v *Aloo* AIR 1984 Bom 75.
11 Section 35, *ibid*.

Suit for restitution of conjugal rights[12]

Where a husband has deserted or without lawful cause has ceased to cohabit with his wife or where a wife has deserted or has without lawful cause ceased to cohabit with her husband, the party so deserted may sue for restitution of conjugal rights. The court, on being satisfied of the truth of the allegations contained in the plaint, may proceed to decree such restitution of conjugal rights.

Counter-claim and documentary evidence

In any suit under the Act the defendant may make a counter-claim for any relief he or she is entitled to under the Act.[13] No document shall be inadmissible in evidence in any proceeding at the trial of a suit under the Act on the ground that it is not duly stamped or registered.[14]

Alimony pendente lite

When in any suit under this Act, it appears to the court that either the wife or the husband, as the case may be, has no independent income sufficient for her or his support and the necessary expenses of the suit, the court may, on an application of the wife or the husband, order the defendant to pay to the plaintiff the expenses of the suit and such weekly or monthly sum, during the pendency of the suit, as, having regard to the plaintiff's own income and the income of the defendant.[15] Such application should be disposed of preferably within sixty days from the date of service of notice.

Permanent alimony and maintenance

A court exercising jurisdiction under this Act may, at any time of passing any decree or at any time subsequent thereto, on an application made to it for the purpose by either the wife or the husband, order that the defendant shall pay to the plaintiff such gross sum or such monthly or periodical sum for a term not exceeding the life of the plaintiff as having regard to the defendant's own income and other property, the income and other property of the plaintiff, the conduct of the parties and other circumstances of the case. The court may secure such payment by charge on the movable or immovable property of the defendant. The court may also vary, modify or rescind any such order when there is a change in the circumstances of the party after the original order was made. The court,

---

12 Section 36, Parsi Marriage and Divorce Act.
13 Section 37, *ibid*.
14 Section 38, *ibid*.
15 Section 39, *ibid*.

if it is satisfied that the party in whose favour the order was made has remarried, that she has not remarried chaste or if such party is the husband that he had sexual intercourse with any woman outside the wedlock, may vary, modify or rescind any such order.[16] The court has power to make an order for payment of a lump sum in full satisfaction of permanent alimony.[17] The court may make any decree or order for payment of alimony to wife or to her trustee approved by the court.[18]

Disposal of joint property

The court may make provision in the final decree with respect to property presented at or about the time of marriage which may belong jointly to both the husband and wife.[19]

Liberty to parties to remarry

When the time limited for appealing against any decree granting divorce or nullity or dissolving any marriage has expired and no appeal has been preferred against such decree or when such appeal has been dismissed or when in the result of an appeal a divorce has been granted or marriage has been declared to be annulled or dissolved, but not sooner, it shall be lawful for the respective parties thereto to marry again.[20]

Custody of children

The court may from time to time pass such interim orders and make such provisions in the final decree with respect to custody, maintenance and education of the children under the age of eighteen years. The court may, after the final decree upon application by the petitioner, make, revoke, suspend or vary from time to time all such orders and provisions with respect to custody, maintenance and education of such children. The application with respect to maintenance and education of children shall be disposed of by the court preferably within a period of sixty days from the date of service of notice on the respondent.[21] Where there is bitter relationship between the husband and the wife, the best way to serve the welfare and interest of the minor girl is to remove her from the unhealthy atmosphere at home and to put her up in Boarding School under the custody of the mother.[22]

---

16 Section 40, Parsi Marriage and Divorce Act.
17 *Tehmi* v *Dinyar* AIR 1976 Bom 246.
18 Section 41, Parsi Marriage and Divorce Act.
19 Section 42, *ibid*.
20 Section 48, *ibid*.
21 Section 49, *ibid*.
22 *Thirty Hoshie Dolikuka* v *Hoshiam Shavaksha Dolikuka* AIR 1982 SC 1276.

Chapter 34

The Intestate Succession to Parsi under the Indian Succession Act 1925

General principles relating to intestate succession among Parsis (section 50)

(a) There is no distinction between those who were actually born in the lifetime of a person deceased and those who at the date of his death were only conceived in the womb, but who have been subsequently born alive;

(b) A lineal descendant of an intestate who has died in the lifetime of the intestate without leaving a widow or widower of any lineal descendant or a widow or widower of any lineal descendant shall not be taken into account in determining the manner in which the property of which the intestate has died intestate shall be divided; and

(c) Where a widow or widower of any relative of an intestate has married again in the lifetime of the intestate, such widow or widower shall not be entitled to receive any share of the property of which the intestate has died intestate and such widow or widower shall be deemed not to be existing at the intestate's death.

Division of intestate's property among widow, widower, children and parents (section 51)

Where a Parsi dies leaving one or both parents in addition to children or widow or widower and children, the property of which such Parsi dies intestate shall be so divided that the parents or each of the parents shall receive a share equal to half the share of each child. Subject to this provision of law, the property of which a Parsi dies intestate shall be divided— (a) where such Parsi dies leaving a widow or widower and children, among the widow or widower and children so that the widow or widower and each child receive equal shares; (b) where such Parsi dies leaving children, but no widow or widower, among the children in equal shares.

Division of share of predeceased child of intestate leaving lineal descendants (section 53)

In all cases where a Parsi dies leaving any lineal descendant, if any child of such intestate has died in the lifetime of the intestate, the division of the share of the property of which the intestate has died intestate which such child would have taken if living at the intestate's death shall be in accordance with the following rules, namely:

(a) If such deceased child was a son, his widow and children shall take shares in accordance with the provisions of this chapter III as if he had died immediately after the intestate's death. But where such deceased son has left a widow or widower of a lineal descendant, the residue of his share after such distribution shall be divided in accordance with the provisions of this Chapter as property of which the intestate has died intestate and in making the division of such residue the said deceased son of the intestate shall not be taken into account.

(b) If such deceased child was a daughter, her share shall be divided equally among her children.

(c) If any child of such deceased child has also died during the lifetime of the intestate, the share which he or she would have taken if living at the intestate's death shall be divided in like manner in accordance with clause (a) or clause (b) as the may be.

(d) Where a remoter lineal descendant of the intestate has died during the lifetime of intestate, the provisions of clause (c) shall apply *mutatis mutandis* to the division of any share to which he or she would have been entitled if living at the intestate's death by reason of predeceased of all the intestate's lineal descendants directly between him or her and the intestate.

Division of property where, intestate leaves no lineal descendant but leaves a widow or widower or a widow or widower of any lineal descendant (section 54)

Where a Parsi dies without leaving any lineal descendant but leaving a widow or widower or a widow or widower of lineal descendant, the property of which the intestate dies intestate shall be divided in accordance with the following rules, namely:

(a) If the intestate leaves a widow or widower, but no widow or widower of a lineal descendant, the widow or widower shall take half the said property.

(b) If the intestate leaves a widow or widower and also a widow or widower of any lineal descendant, his widow or her widower shall receive one-third of the said property and the widow or widower of any lineal descendant shall receive another one-third or if there is more than one such widow or widower of lineal descendants, the last mentioned one-third shall be divided equally among them.

(c) If the intestate leaves no widow or widower, but one widow or widower of a lineal descendant, such widow or widower of the lineal descendant shall receive one-third of the said property or if the intestate leaves no widow or widower, but more than one widow or widower of lineal descendants, two-thirds of the said property shall be divided among such widows or widowers of the lineal descendants in equal shares.

(d) The residue after the division specified in (a) or (b) or (c) above has been made, shall be distributed among the relatives of the intestate in the order specified in Part I of Schedule II; and the next-of-kin standing first in Part I of that Schedule shall be preferred to those standing second, the second to the third and so on in succession, provided that the property shall be so distributed that each male and female standing in the same degree of propinquity shall receive equal shares.

(e) If there are no relatives entitled to the residue under (d) above the whole of the residue shall be distributed in proportion to the shares specified among the persons entitled to receive shares under s. 54 of the Act.

Division of property where intestate leaves neither lineal descendants nor a widow or widower nor a widow or widower of any lineal descendant (section 55)

When a Parsi dies leaving neither lineal descendants nor a widow or widower nor a widow or widower of any lineal descendants, his or her next-of-kin, in the order set forth in Part II of Schedule II, shall be entitled to succeed to the whole of the property of which he or she dies intestate. The next-of-kin standing first in Part II of that Schedule shall be preferred to those standing second, the second to the third, and so on in succession, provides that the property shall be distributed that each male and female standing in the same degree of propinquity shall receive equal shares.

Division of property where there is no relative entitled to succeed under other provisions (section 56)

Where there is no relative entitled to succeed under the other provisions of Chapter III of Part V of the Indian Succession Act 1925 to the property of which a Parsi has died intestate, the said property shall be divided equally among those of the intestate's relatives who are all in the nearest degree of kindred to him.

Part 6

Secular Law of Family

CHAPTER
35

The Special Marriage Act 1954

Objects of the Act

The main object of the Special Marriage Act 1954 is to provide (a) special form of marriage in certain cases irrespective of caste and religion and its registration under this Act. It is an attempt to introduce uniformity of family laws in matrimonial matters. The Act also contains among others the provisions for dissolution of marriage, maintenance custody and education of minor children.[1]

Amendments

This Act has been amended by the Marriage Laws (Amendment) Act 1976, 1999, 2001 and 2003.

Application and commencement of the Act

This Act applies to the whole of India except the State of Jammu and Kashmir and applies to all citizens of India domiciled in territories to which this Act extends who are in the State of Jammu and Kashmir.[2] The provisions of the Act shall apply to all citizens of India whether residing at home or abroad. This Act has come into force on and from 1st January 1955.

Conditions for solemnisation of special marriages

A marriage between any two persons may be solemnised under this Act if the following conditions are fulfilled:

(1) Neither party has a spouse living.

---

1 See Statement of Objects and Reasons, Published in Gazette of India Extra, pt. II, s. 2, p. 41.
2 Section 1(2), Special Marriage Act.

(2) Neither party is incapable of giving valid consent.

(3) Neither party is incapable for marriage as a result of suffering from mental disorder and procreation of children.

(4) Neither party has been subject to recurrent attacks of insanity.

(5) The male has completed the age of twenty one years and the female the age of eighteen years.

(6) The parties are not within the degrees of prohibited relationship unless the custom of one party permits of such marriage between them.

(7) Where the marriage is solemnised in the State of Jammu and Kashmir, both parties are citizens of India domiciled in the territories.[3]

Marriage under this Act may be solemnised between two citizens of India or two foreigners or between a citizen of India and a foreigner.[4]

Notice of intended marriage

When a marriage is intended to be solemnised under the Special Marriage Act 1954, the parties to the marriage shall give notice thereof in writing in the form specified in the Second Schedule to the Marriage Officer of the district in which at least one of parties to the marriage has resided for a period of not less than thirty days immediately preceding the date on which such notice is given.[5] Question of notice under s. 5 of the Act cannot be raised after the issuance of the certificate of marriage, because certificate of marriage is conclusive proof of valid marriage.[6]

Marriage Officer, Marriage Notice Book and publication

For the purpose of this Act the State Government may, by notification in the Official Gazette, appoint one or more Marriage Officers for the whole or any part of the State. For application of this Act to the citizens of India domiciled in territories to which this Act extends who are in the State of Jammu and Kashmir, the Central Government may, by notification in the Official Gazette, specify such officers of the Central Government as the Marriage Officers for the State or part thereof.[7] The Marriage Officer shall keep all notices given under s. 5 of the Act with the records of his office

---

3 Section 4, Special Marriage Act.
4 *Marian Eva* v *State* AIR 1993 HP 7.
5 Section 5, Special Marriage Act.
6 *Purabi Banerjee* v *Basudeb Mukherjee* AIR 1969 Cal 293 (DB).
7 Section 3, Special Marriage Act.

and shall also enter a true copy of every such notice in Marriage Notice Book which is open for inspection at all reasonable time without any fee. The Marriage Officer shall cause every such notice to be published by affixing a copy thereof to some conspicuous place in his office. Where a party to an intended marriage is not permanently residing within the local limits of the District Officer to whom notice has been given under s. 5, the Marriage Officer shall transmit a copy of such notice to the Marriage Officer of that district within whose jurisdiction such party is permanently residing and that Marriage Officer shall, thereupon cause a copy thereof to be affixed to some conspicuous place in his office.[8]

Objection to marriage and procedure on receipt of objection

Any person may, before the expiration of thirty days from the date of publication of the notice, object to the marriage on the ground that it would contravene one or more of conditions relating to solemnisation of special marriage under s. 4 of the Act. If no any objection is received, after expiration of thirty days from the date of publication of the notice of the intended marriage the marriage may be solemnised. If any objection is received, the nature of objection shall be recorded in writing by the Marriage Officer in the Marriage Notice Book and shall be signed by him.[9] When an objection to the intended marriage is received by the Marriage Officer, he shall not solemnise the marriage until he has inquired into the matter of objection and is satisfied that it ought not to prevent the solemnisation of marriage, or the objection is withdrawn by the person making it. But the Marriage Officer shall not take more than thirty days in completing the process of inquiry to arrive at a decision from the date of objection. If the Marriage Officer upholds the objection and refuses to solemnise the marriage, either party to the intended marriage may, within a period of thirty days from the date of refusal prefer an appeal to the district court within the local limits of whose jurisdiction the Marriage Officer has his office and the decision of the district court shall be final and the Marriage Officer shall act accordingly.[10] Where objection is made to a Marriage Officer in the State of Jammu and Kashmir in respect of intended marriage he shall make inquiry into the matter and if he entertains a doubt, he shall not solemnise the marriage and he shall transmit the record in the matter to the Central Government. The Central

---

8 Section 6, Special Marriage Act.
9 Section 7, *ibid*.
10 Section 8, *ibid*.

Government shall, thereafter after making inquiry, give decision thereon in writing to the Marriage Officer who shall act accordingly.[11]

Powers of Marriage Officer in respect of inquiry

The Marriage Officer shall have all the powers vested in a civil court under the Code of Civil Procedure 1908 while inquiring an objection to an intended marriage. The Marriage Officer shall have the following powers of a civil court: (a) summoning and enforcing the attendance of witness and examining them on oath; (b) discovery and inspection; (c) compelling the production of documents; (d) reception of evidence on affidavits; and (e) issuing commission for examination of witness. The proceeding before the Marriage Officer shall be deemed to be a judicial proceeding within the meaning of s. 193 of the Indian Penal Code. The jurisdiction of the Marriage Officer extends to local limits of his district for the purpose of enforcing attendance of any person. If it appears to the Marriage Officer that the objection to the intended marriage is false, he may impose penalty on the person objecting for a sum not exceeding one thousand rupees as compensation payable in whole or part thereof to parties to the intended marriage and may also order for costs. The arrears of such compensation and costs may be executed in the manner as a decree passed by the district court.[12]

Solemnisation of marriage

Before the marriage is solemnised the parties and three witnesses shall in presence of the Marriage Officer, sign a declaration in the form signed in the Third Schedule of the Act and the declaration shall be counter-signed by the Marriage Officer.[13] The marriage may be solemnised at the office of the Marriage Officer or at any other convenient place as the parties may desire upon payment of additional fees as prescribed. The marriage may be solemnised in any form which the parties may choose to adopt. But the marriage shall not be complete unless each party says to the other in presence of the Marriage Officer and three witnesses and in any language understood by the parties—"I, (A), take the (B) to be my lawful wife (or husband)".[14] When the marriage is solemnised, the Marriage Officer shall enter a certificate thereof in the form specified in the Fourth Schedule in a book to be called the Marriage Certificate Book and such certificate shall be signed by the parties to the marriage and three

---

11 Section 10, Special Marriage Act.
12 Section 9, *ibid*.
13 Section 11, *ibid*.
14 Section 12, *ibid*.

witnesses. The certificate of marriage is the conclusive evidence of the fact that the marriage under the Act has been solemnised after compliance with all the formalities.[15] There is no difference in the effect of the expression "conclusive evidence" from that of "conclusive proof", the aim of the both being to give finality to the establishment of the existence of a fact from the proof of another.[16]

New notice is required to be given in the manner laid down in the Act when a marriage is not solemnised within three months from the date on which notice thereof has been given to the Marriage Officer.[17]

Under s. 49 of the Act the Marriage Officer has power to rectify any error in the form or substance of any entry in the Marriage Certificate Book.

Registration of marriages celebrated in other forms

Any marriage celebrated in other forms may be registered under Chapter III of the Act by a Marriage Officer, provided the following conditions are fulfilled: (a) a ceremony of marriage has been performed between the parties and they have been living together as husband and wife ever since; (b) neither party has at the time of registration more than one spouse living; (c) neither party is an idiot or a lunatic at the time of registration; (d) the parties have completed the age of twenty-one years at the time of registration; (e) the parties are not within the degrees of prohibited relationship; (f) the parties have been residing within the district of the Marriage Officer for a period of not less than thirty days.[18] Where the essential ceremonies of a Hindu marriage, mere issuance of a certificate of registration under s. 15 of the Special Marriage Act would not validate the marriage in view of the provisions of s. 24(2) of the Act.[19] Upon receipt of an application signed by both the parties to the marriage for registration of their marriage under this Chapter, the Marriage Officer shall give public notice thereof in the prescribed manner and after allowing thirty days for objections and after hearing any objection received within that period, shall, after being satisfied, enter a certificate of the marriage in the Marriage Certificate Book in the form specified in the Fifth Schedule and such certificate shall be signed by the parties to the marriage and by three witnesses.[20] Regarding registration of second marriage of a Muslim,

---

15 Section 13, Special Marriage Act.
16 *Sonawanti* v *State of Punjab* AIR 1963 SC 151.
17 Section 14, Special Marriage Act.
18 Section 15, *ibid*.
19 *Sanjay Mishra* v *Eveline* (1987)1 DMC 318 (MP).
20 Section 16, Special Marriage Act.

certificate of divorce of first marriage from concerned Juma-Ath in accordance with Muslim personal law is sufficient.[1]

A person aggrieved by any order of a Marriage Officer refusing to register a marriage under Chapter III may, within thirty days from the date of the order, prefer an appeal to district court within the local limits of whose jurisdiction the Marriage Officer has his office and the decision of the district court shall be final and the Marriage Officer shall act in conformity with such order.[2] Subject to the provisions contained in s. 24(2) of the Act, where a certificate of marriage has been finally entered in the Marriage Certificate Book under this Chapter shall, from the date of such entry, be deemed to be marriage solemnised under this Act and all children born after that date of the ceremony of marriage shall in all respects be deemed to be the legitimate children of their parents. But it will not confer upon any such children any right to property of any person other than their parents, in any case where, but for the passing of this Act, such children would have been incapable of possessing or acquiring any such rights by reason of their not being legitimate children of their parents.[3]

Consequences of marriage under the Act

The marriage solemnised under this Act of any member of an undivided family who professes the Hindu religion shall be deemed to effect his severance from such family.[4] Subject to provisions of s. 19, any person whose marriage is solemnised under this Act shall have the same right of succession to any property to whom the Caste Disabilities Removal Act 1850 applies.[5] Notwithstanding any restriction contained in the Indian Succession Act 1925 with respect to its application to members of certain communities, succession to property of any person whose marriage is solemnised under this Act shall be regulated by the provisions of the said Act and for the purposes of this Act shall have effect as if Chapter III of Part V (Special Rules for Parsi Intestates) had been omitted therefrom.[6] The provision contained in s. 21 of the Special Marriage Act does not in any way affect or negative the exception made under s. 213(2) of the Indian Succession Act 1925.[7]

---

1 *Alungaparambil Abdul Khader Shud* v *State of Kerala* AIR 2007 DOC 126 (Ker).
2 Section 17, Special Marriage Act.
3 Section 18, *ibid*.
4 Section 19, *ibid*.
5 Section 20, *ibid*.
6 Section 21, *ibid*.
7 In re, *Hasima Latifi* AIR 1962 Bom 227.

Where the marriage is solemnised under this Act of any person who is a Hindu with a person who is also Hindu, s. 19 and s. 21 shall not apply and so much of s. 20 as creates a disability shall not also apply.[8] Where the marriage of a person whose property was claimed by succession was solemnised before the amendment of s. 21A and the person died after the amendment, the succession opened on the date of death and it was to be governed by the law that was in force on that date and not on the date of solemnisation of marriage.[9]

Restitution of conjugal rights

When either the husband or the wife has, without any reasonable excuse, withdrawn from the society of the other the aggrieved party may apply by a petition to the district court for restitution of conjugal rights. The court, on being satisfied of the truth of the statements made in the petition and also considering of the absence of legal bar, may decree restitution of conjugal rights: where the question of reasonable excuse for withdrawal from the society arises, the burden of proving reasonable excuse shall be on the person who has withdrawn from the society.[10]

Judicial separation

A petition for judicial separation may be presented to the district court either by the husband or the wife (*a*) on any of grounds specified in sub-sec. (1) and sub-sec. (1A) of s. 27 on which a petition for divorce might have been presented; or (*b*) on the ground of failure to comply with a decree for restitution of conjugal rights. The court, on being satisfied of the truth of the statements made in such petition, and that there is no legal bar to grant the relief, may decree judicial separation. Where the court grants a decree for judicial separation, it shall not be obligatory for the petitioner to cohabit with the respondent. The court may, on the application by petition of either party and on being satisfied of the truth of the statements made in such petition, rescind the decree.[11] Impotency of husband amounts to cruelty. Thus, the wife is entitled to maintenance under s. 125, Cr PC and is justified for refusing to live with her husband.[12]

---

8   Section 21A, Special Marriage Act.
9   *Maneka Gandhi* v *Indira Gandhi* AIR 1984 Del 428.
10 Section 22, Special Marriage Act.
11 Section 23, Special Marriage Act.
12 *Sirajmohmed Khan* v *Hafizunnisa Yasinkhan* AIR 1981 SC 1972.

Void marriage

A marriage solemnized under this Act becomes null and void and may, on a petition presented by either party thereto against the other party, be so declared by a decree of nullity if—

(i) any of conditions specified in cls. (*a*), (*b*), (*c*) and (*d*) of s. 4 has not been fulfilled; or

(ii) the respondent was impotent at the time the marriage and at the time of the institution of the suit.[13]

Nothing in s. 24 shall apply to any marriage deemed to be solemnised under this Act within the meaning of s. 18, but the registration of any such marriage under Chapter III may be declared to be of no effect if the registration was in contravention of any condition specified in cls. (*a*) to (*e*) of s. 15.[14] No declaration shall be made in any case where an appeal has been preferred under s. 17 of the Act and in such case the decision of the district court shall be final.[15] No legal consequences flow from a void marriage. The court merely declares such marriage as null and void. Void marriages cannot be either approbated or ratified.[16] Section 24(1)(*ii*) of this Act providing the ground of impotency cannot be availed of by a third person.[17]

Voidable marriage

A marriage solemnised under this Act shall be voidable and may be annulled by a decree of nullity if—(*i*) the marriage has not been consummated owing to wilful refusal of the respondent; or (*ii*) the respondent was at the time of marriage pregnant by some person other than the petitioner; or (*iii*) the consent of either party to the marriage was obtained by coercion or fraud as defined in the Indian Contract Act 1872. But in case of ground (*ii*) the court shall not grant a decree unless it is satisfied—

(*a*) That the petitioner was at the time of marriage ignorant of the alleged facts; (*b*) that the proceedings were instituted within a year from the date of the marriage; and (*c*) that the marital intercourse with the consent of the petitioner has not taken place since the discovery of that ground for a decree. In case of ground (*iii*) the court shall not grant decree

---

13 Section 24(1), Special Marrige Act.
14 Section 24(2), *ibid*.
15 Proviso to s. 24(2), *ibid*.
16 *Nirmal Dass Bose* v *Mamta Gulati* AIR 1997 All 401.
17 *Prafulla Bala Biswas* v *Ila Das* Cal LT 1996(2) HC 315.

if (*a*) proceedings have not been instituted within one year after the coercion has ceased or fraud has been discovered; or (*b*) the petitioner has with his or her free consent lived with the other party to the marriage as husband and wife after the coercion has ceased or the fraud had been discovered.[18]

Some illustrative cases

(1) Where parties are living together for about five months and letter written by husband to wife expressing his satisfaction of sexual relations with her, it cannot be a ground of wilful refusal to consummate marriage for a decree of annulment of marriage under s. 25(1) of the Act.[19]

(2) Wife conceals the fact before the marriage that she is older by 3 years than her husband. It amounts to fraud as contemplated in s. 25(*iii*) of the Act.[20]

(3) Suppression of fact by wife that she was married before and a widow at the time of her second marriage is a material fact and as such it amounts to fraud exercised on her second husband and he is entitled to decree of nullity.[1]

Legitimacy of children of void and voidable marriages

Where a marriage is null and void under s. 24 of the Act, any child of such marriage shall be legitimate. Similarly, where a decree of nullity is granted in respect of voidable marriage under s. 25 of the Act, any child begotten or conceived before the decree is made, shall be deemed to be their legitimate child. A child of marriage which is null and void under s. 24 or which is annulled by a decree of nullity under s. 25, shall not acquire any right in or to the property of any person other than its parents.[2]

Divorce and alternative relief in proceedings

A petition for divorce may be presented to the District Court either by the husband or by the wife on any of the grounds that the respondent—(*a*) has after the marriage had voluntary sexual intercourse with a person other than the petitioner; or (*b*) has deserted the petitioner for a continuous period of not less than years immediately preceding the presentation of the petition; or (*c*) is undergoing a sentence of imprisonment for seven

---

18 Section 25, Special Marriage Act.
19 *Sunil K. Mirchandani* v *Reena S. Mirchandani* AIR 2000 Bom 66.
20 *Gitika Bagchi* v *Subhabrata Bagchi* AIR 1996 Cal 246.
1 *Asha Qureshi* v *Afaq Qureshi* AIR 2002 MP 263.
2 Section 26, Special Marriage Act.

years or more for an offence under the Indian Penal Code; (*d*) has after the marriage treated the petitioner with cruelty; or (*e*) has been incurably of unsound mind or has been continuously or intermittently suffering from mental disorder of such a kind that the petitioner cannot reasonably be expected to live with the respondent; or (*f*) has been suffering from venereal disease in a communicable form; or (*g*) has been suffering from leprosy, the disease not having been contracted from the petitioner; or (*h*) has not been heard of alive for a period of seven years or more. In this context "mental disorder" means mental illness, arrested or incomplete development of mind, psychopathic disorder. The expression "psychopathic disorder" means persistent disorder or disability of mind which results in abnormally aggressive or seriously irresponsible conduct. The expression "desertion" means desertion of the petitioner by the respondent to the marriage without reasonable cause.[3]

A wife in addition to the above grounds may also file a petition for divorce to the district court on the ground (*i*) that her husband has, after the marriage, been guilty of rape, sodomy or bestiality; (*ii*) that in a suit under s. 18 of the Hindu Adoptions and Maintenance Act 1956 or in a proceeding under s. 125, Cr PC 1973, a decree or order has been passed against the husband awarding maintenance to the wife and since then she has been living apart and there is no cohabitation between the parties for one year or more.[4] Besides, either party to a marriage may present a petition to the district court on the ground—(*i*) that there has been no resumption of cohabitation between the parties to the marriage for a period of one year or more after passing the decree for judicial separation, or (*ii*) that there has been no restitution of conjugal rights between the parties to the marriage for a period of one year or upwards after passing a decree for restitution of conjugal rights.[5]

Some illustrative cases

(*a*) The essential elements of desertion are *factum* and *animus*. The *factum* or physical separation and the *animus deserendi* or intention to desert must continue throughout the period.[6]

(*b*) In suitable case the court can dissolve marriage under s. 27(1)(*d*) of the Act by awarding suitable permanent alimony to the wife.[7]

---

3 Section 27(1), Special Marriage Act.
4 Section 27(1A), *ibid*.
5 Section 27(2), *ibid*.
6 *Ramchandra Anand Suryavanshi* v *Kalindi Ramchandra Suryavanshi* AIR 1991 Bom 315.
7 *Pranay Majumdar* v *Bina Majumdar* 2007(2) CHN 13 (SC).

(c) Wife's attitude towards the relations of the husband showing her bitterness amounts to cruelty.[8]

(d) In case of consent by the wife to the act of sodomy on her, the onus is on the husband to prove it.[9]

Irretrievable breakdown of marriage

The time has come for complete reform of the law of marriage and make a uniform law applicable to all people irrespective of religion or caste. It is necessary to introduce irretrievable breakdown of marriage and mutual consent as grounds of divorce in all cases.[10]

Alternative relief

In any proceedings under this Act on a petition for dissolution of marriage by a decree of divorce the court may, except a petition founded on ground mentioned in s. 27(1)(h), pass instead a decree for judicial separation.[11] Section 27(1)(h) deals with presumption of death of a person for being heard of alive for a period of seven years or more.

Divorce by mutual consent

A petition for divorce may be presented to the District Court by both the parties to the marriage together on the ground (1) that they have been living separately for a period of one year on more, (2) that they have not been able to live together and (3) they have mutually agreed that the marriage should be dissolved. On the motion of both the parties not earlier than six months after the presentation of the petition and not later than eighteen months after the said date, if the petition is not withdrawn in the meantime, the court shall on being satisfied, after, hearing the parties and after making inquiries that the averments in the petition are true, pass a decree declaring the marriage to be dissolved from the date of the decree.[12]

Even in a petition for divorce by mutual consent it is incumbent on the court to comply with the mandatory provisions of s. 34(2) of the Act to make attempt for reconciliation between the parties.[13]

---

8   *Iris Paintal* v *Avtar Singh Paintal* AIR 1988 Del 121.
9   *Keogh* v *Keogh* [1962]1 WLR 191.
10 *Jorden Diengdeh* v *S.S. Chopra* AIR 1985 SC 935.
11 Section 27A, Special Marriage Act.
12 Section 28, *ibid*.
13 *Pramila Bhagat* v *Ajit Raj Sinha* AIR 1989 Pat 163.

Restriction for divorce during first year of marriage and remarriage

No petition for divorce shall be presented to the district court before expiry of one year from the date of entering the certificate of marriage in the Marriage Certificate Book. But the court may allow a petition to be presented before one year on the ground that the case is one of exceptional hardship suffered by the petitioner or of exceptional depravity on the part of the respondent. If it appears to the district court at the hearing of the petition that the petitioner obtained the leave to present the petition by any misrepresentation or concealment of the nature of the case, the district court may pronounce a decree which will be effective after expiry of one year from the date of the marriage or may dismiss the petition without prejudice to any petition which may be brought after expiration of one year on the same or substantially the same grounds. In disposing such petition the district court shall have regard to the interest of any children of the marriage and also the question whether there is a reasonable probability of reconciliation between the parties.[14]

When a marriage has been dissolved by a decree of divorce and there is no right of appeal against the decree or if there is such a right of appeal, the time for appeal has expired or an appeal has been presented, but the same has been dismissed, either party to the marriage may marry again.[15] A party who has won in High Court and got a decree of dissolution of marriage cannot marry again after the High Court's decree till the time for presenting an application for special leave to the Supreme Court by the losing party has expired.[16]

Jurisdiction and procedure

Every petition under Chapter V (Restitution of conjugal rights and judicial separation) or Chapter VI (Nullity of marriage and divorce) shall be presented to the district court within local limits of whose original civil jurisdiction—(*i*) the marriage was solemnised; or (*ii*) the respondent at the time of the presentation of the petition resides; or (*iii*) the parties to the marriage last resided together; or (*iv*) in case the petitioner is wife, where she is residing on the date of presentation; or (*v*) the petitioner is residing at the time of presentation of the petition, in a case where the respondent is, at that time residing outside the territories to which this Act extends or has not been heard of as being alive for a period of seven years. The district court may entertain a petition by a wife domiciled in

---

14 Section 29, Special Marriage Act.
15 Section 30, *ibid*.
16 *Chandra Mohini Srivastava* v *Avinash Prasad Srivastava* AIR 1967 SC 581.

the territories to which the Act extends for nullity of marriage or for divorce if she is resident in that territory and has been ordinarily resident therein for a period of three years and the husband is not resident in the said territories.[17]

Some illustrative cases

(1) Both husband and wife are Indian citizens but are married in U.S.A. according to Hindu rites, District court or Family court in India can exercise jurisdiction to entertain matrimonial suit either under s. 31 of the Special Marriage Act or under s. 19 of the Hindu Marriage Act.[18]

(2) If a court rendering a judgment suffers from want of jurisdiction, its judgment is a nullity and may be ignored.[19]

Proceedings to be in camera

Every proceeding under this Act shall be conducted *in camera* and it shall not be lawful for any person to print or publish any matter in relation to any such proceeding except a judgment of the High Court or of the Supreme Court without previous permission of the court. If any person contravenes these provisions, he shall be punishable with fine which may extend to one thousand rupees.[20]

Duty of court in passing decrees

In any proceeding under Chapter V or Chapter VI of this Act whether defended or not if the court is satisfied as to the following matters, it shall decree the relief as asked for that (*a*) any of the grounds for granting relief exists, and (*b*) where the petition is founded on the grounds specified in cl. (*a*) of sub-sec. (1) of s. 27, the petitioner is not to or connived at or condoned the act of sexual intercourse referred to therein or where the ground of the petition is cruelty, the petitioner has not condoned the cruelty; and (*c*) when divorce is sought on ground of mutual consent, such consent has not been obtained by force, fraud or undue influence; and (*d*) the petition is not presented or prosecuted in collusion with the respondent; and (*e*) there has not been any unnecessary or improper delay in instituting the proceedings; and (*f*) there is no other legal bar to grant the relief.[1] Before proceeding to grant any relief under this Act, the court shall make every endeavour to bring about a reconciliation between

---

17 Section 31, Special Marriage Act.
18 *Navin Chander Advani* v *Leena* AIR 2005 Bom 277.
19 *Kiron Singh* v *Chaman Paswan* AIR 1954 SC 340.
20 Section 33, Special Marriage Act.
1 Section 34(1), *ibid*.

the parties.[2] But such duty of court shall not apply to cases where relief is sought on any of the grounds specified in cl. (*c*) (undergoing sentence of imprisonment), cl. (*e*) (unsoundness of mind), cl. (*f*) (suffering from venereal disease), cl. (*g*) (suffering from leprosy) and cl. (*h*) (not heard of to be alive) of sub-sec. (1) of s. 27 of the Act. For the purpose of bringing about reconciliation the court may adjourn in proceedings for a period not exceeding fifteen days if the parties so desire and refer the matter to any person named by the parties or to any person nominated by the court with direction to report to the court as to the consequences thereof.[3] In every case where the marriage is dissolved by a decree of divorce, the court shall supply a copy of the decree free of cost to each party.[4]

Some illustrative cases

(1) Generally, the burden of proving connivance is on the person alleging it. But if there is a *prima facie* case of presumption of connivance, the burden of disproving connivance is on the petitioner.[5]

(2) Where the dissolution of marriage is sought by a joint petition of the parties under s. 28 of the Act, it is incumbent on the court to comply with the mandatory provisions of s. 34(2) of the Act to make an attempt for reconciliation between the parties.[6]

(3) The fact that under s. 34(4) of the Act the court is bound to give a certified copy of the decree to each party free of cost is immaterial for the purpose of appeal.[7]

Counter-claim by respondent

In any proceeding for divorce or judicial separation or restitution of conjugal rights the respondent may not only oppose the relief, but also make a counter-claim for any relief under this Act on the ground of petitioner's adultery, cruelty or desertion. The court, if satisfied, may grant relief to the respondent.[8]

Alimony pendente lite

In any proceeding under Chapter V or Chapter VI it appears to the District Court that the wife has no independent income for her support

---

2 Section 34(2), Special Marriage Act.
3 Section 34(3), *ibid*.
4 Section 34(4), *ibid*.
5 *Blyth* v *Blyth* [1966]2 WLR 634 (HL).
6 *Pramila Bhagat* v *Ajit Raj Singh* AIR 1989 Pat 163.
7 *Jyoti Malhotra* v *Kewal Kishore Malhotra* AIR 1983 Del 14.
8 Section 35, Special Marriage Act.

and the necessary expenses of the proceeding, it may, on the application of wife, order the husband to pay to her the expenses of the proceedings, weekly or monthly during the pendency of the proceedings having regard to the income of the husband. Such application shall be disposed of within sixty days from the date of service of notice.[9] In estimating the independent income of the wife derived from her property, service, occupation and other sources, the income of the wife's parents or other relations cannot be taken into consideration.[10]

Permanent alimony and maintenance

The court in passing a decree in any proceedings under Chapter V or Chapter VI of the Act or at any time thereafter, on an application made to it may pass an order that the husband shall secure to the wife for her maintenance and support by a charge on the husband's property, such gross sum or such monthly or periodical payment of money for a term not exceeding her life, as having, regard to her own property, if any, husband's property and ability, the conduct of the parties and other circumstances of the case. The district court may, on the application of either party, vary, modify or rescind the order under changed circumstances. The district court may also vary, modify or rescind the order if the wife has remarried or is leading an unchaste life.[11]

The two terms "maintenance" and "support" are comprehensive in nature and of wide amplitudes. They include a claim for medical expenses.[12]

The decree for permanent alimony passed under s. 37 of the Act does not extinguish on the death of the husband. The assets left behind by him are liable to be proceeded against in the hands of his legal heirs for satisfaction of the decree for maintenance.[13]

Custody of children

In any proceeding under Chapter V or Chapter VI, the district court may, from time to time, pass interim order and make such provisions in the decree with respect to the custody, maintenance and education of minor children consistently with their wishes wherever possible. The district court may, after the decree upon application by petition, revoke, suspend or vary, from time to time, any order and provision with respect to the

---

9 Section 36, Special Marriage Act.
10 *Mahalingam Pillai* v *Amsavalli* (1952)2 MLJ 289.
11 Section 37, Special Marriage Act.
12 *Rajesh Burman* v *Mitual Chatterjee* (2009)1 SCC 398.
13 *Aruna Basu* v *Dorothea Mitra* AIR 1983 SC 916.

custody, maintenance and education of such children. Any such application shall be disposed of within sixty days from the date of service of notice.[14]

Appeals from decrees and orders

Any decree made by the court in any proceeding under Chapter V or Chapter VI shall be appealable except on the subject of costs. Such appeals shall lie to the court to which appeals ordinarily lie from the decision of the court exercising original civil jurisdiction. Any interim order passed under s. 37 or s. 38 of the Act is not appealable. Every appeal shall be preferable within a period of ninety days.[15]

Enforcement of decree and order

All decrees or orders made in any proceeding under Chapter V or Chapter VI shall be enforced in the like manner as the decrees and orders of the court made in the exercise of its original civil jurisdiction.[16] A suit for execution can be converted into an execution application as a measure of *ex debito justitiae*.[17]

Power to transfer petition

Where a petition under this Act has been presented to the district court having jurisdiction praying for a decree for judicial separation or for a decree of divorce and another petition under this Act has been presented thereafter by the other party for the same relief in the same district court or in a different district court in the same State or in a different State, the petitions shall be dealt with in the following manner. If the petitions are presented to the same district court, both the petitions shall be tried together by that district court. If the petitions are presented to different district courts, the petition presented later shall be transferred to the district court in which the earlier petition was presented and both the petitions shall be heard and disposed of together. The court or the Government competent under the Code of Civil Procedure 1908 to transfer any suit or proceeding from the district court in which the later petition has been presented to the district court in which the earlier petition is pending shall exercise its powers to transfer such later petition under the said Code.[18]

---

14 Section 38, Special Marriage Act.
15 Section 39, *ibid*.
16 Section 39A, *ibid*.
17 *Nandarani Majumdar* v *Indian Airlines* AIR 1983 SC 1201.
18 Section 40A, Special Marriage Act.

Disposal of petition and appeal

The trial of the petition under this Act shall be concluded consistently with the interests of justice preferably within six months from the date of service of notice without granting unnecessary adjournment. Every appeal shall be heard and disposed of within three months from the date of service of notice of appeal on the respondent.[19]

Documentary evidence

No document is inadmissible in evidence in any proceeding at the trial of a petition under this Act on the ground that it is not duly stamped or registered.[20]

Penal provisions

Save as otherwise provided in Chapter III every person who marries again during the subsistence of the earlier marriage is guilty of an offence under s. 494 or s. 495 of the Indian Penal Code 1860.[21] Every person whose marriage is solemnised under this Act during the subsistence of earlier marriage is guilty of bigamy.[1] Every person making, signing or attesting any false declaration or certificate shall be guilty of an offence under s. 199 of the Indian Penal Code 1860.[2] Marriage Officer who knowingly and wilfully solemnises marriage wrongfully is liable for punishment.[3]

---

18 Section 40B, Special Marriage Act.
19 Section 40C, *ibid*.
20 Section 43, *ibid*.
1 Section 44, *ibid*.
2 Section 45, *ibid*.
3 Section 46, *ibid*.

CHAPTER
36

The Foreign Marriage Act 1969

Objects and reasons

This Act sought to implement the twenty-third Report of the Law Commission on the law relating to foreign marriages. There was uncertainty as to law on the subject. Any problem in the field of foreign marriages was previously governed by the principles of private international law which were by no means well-settled. The Special Marriage Act 1954 sought to remove some uncertainty in respect marriages solemnised abroad between citizens of India. This Act is also intended to apply to marriages abroad where one of the parties alone is an Indian citizen. The Act was based on the model of the Special Marriage Act 1954. Besides, the English and Australian legislations on the subject were resorted to for modification. The special features of the Foreign Marriage Act 1969 are that the form of marriage, rules relating to capacity of parties and conditions of validity of marriage and matrimonial reliefs are more or less similar to those of the Special Marriage Act 1954.

Preliminary

Section 2(*a*) of the Foreign Marriage Act 1969 defines "degree of prohibited relationship" as that in the Special Marriage Act 1954. "Foreign Country" is defined in s. 2(*c*) of the 1969 Act as a country or place outside India, and also a ship which is for the time being in the territorial waters of such a country or place. Section 3 of the said Act provides that for the purpose of this Act the Central Government may, by notification in the Official Gazette, appoint a diplomatic or consular as Marriage Officer for any foreign country.

Conditions for solemnisation of foreign marriage

Section 4 of the Foreign Marriage Act 1969 provides that a marriage between parties one of whom is at least a citizen of India may be solemnized under this Act by or before a Marriage Officer in a foreign country if the following conditions are fulfilled:

(a) Neither party has a spouse living.

(b) Neither party is an idiot or a lunatic.

(c) The bridegroom has completed the age of twenty-one years and the bride the age of eighteen years at the time of the marriage.

(d) The parties are not within the degrees of prohibited relationship.

Other formalities of foreign marriage

Section 5 of the Foreign Marriage Act 1969 provides that the parties to the intended marriage shall give notice thereof in prescribed form as specified in the First Schedule to the Marriage Officer of the District in which at least one of parties to the marriage has resided for a period of not less than thirty days immediately preceding the date on which such notice is given and the notice shall state that the party has so resided. Under s. 6 of the said Act it is obligatory on the part of the Marriage Officer to keep all such notices with the records of his office and shall enter a true copy of every notice in a book called "Marriage Notice Book" which shall be kept open for inspection at all reasonable times without any fee. According to s. 7 of the said Act a notice under s. 5 of the Act received by a Marriage Officer is to be published (a) in his own office by affixing a copy thereof to a conspicuous place, (b) in India and in the country in which a party is an ordinarily respondent in prescribed manner. If any objection to the marriage is received by the Marriage Officer, the Marriage Officer shall record the nature of objection in his Marriage Notice Book (section 8). But where no objection is made within thirty days from the date of publication of the notice, then on expiry of that period the marriage may be solemnised (section 9). Section 10 of the said Act provides that if any objection is received, the Marriage Officer shall not solemnise the marriage until he inquires into the matter and transmit the record along with his statement to the Central Government. The Central Government shall thereafter making further inquiry into the matter and after obtaining such advice as it thinks fit shall give its decision thereon in writing to the Marriage Officer, who shall act in conformity with the decision of the Central Government. Section 11 of the said Act provides that no such marriage shall be solemnised in contravention of local laws. Section 12 of the said Act provides that before the marriage is solemnised, the parties and three witnesses shall, in the presence of the Marriage Officer, sign a declaration in the form specified in the Second Schedule and such declaration shall be counter-signed by the Marriage Officer. Section 13 of the Act provides that the place of such marriage is at the official house of the Marriage Officer with open doors between the prescribed hours in presence of at least three witnesses. The marriage may be solemnised in any form which the parties may choose to adopt. Section 14 of the said Act provides that whenever a marriage is solemnised under this Act, the Marriage Officer shall enter a certificate in the form specified in the Third Schedule which is called Marriage Certificate Book. Such certificate shall be signed by the parties to the marriage and three witnesses. Section 15 of the Act provides that a marriage solemnised under this Act shall be good and valid in law in India. Section 16 provides that if a marriage is not solemnised within six months from the date of notice of the intended marriage, new notice has to be given for intended marriage between the same parties.

Registration of foreign marriages

Section 17 of the Foreign Marriages Act 1969 provides for registration of marriage solemnised under the law of a foreign country. But there cannot be any registration of marriage unless the marriage is solemnised in compliance with the conditions laid down in s. 4 of the Foreign Marriage Act 1969. Section 17 provides also the mode of registration and consequences thereof. Once a marriage is registered under this Act, it will be deemed to have been solemnised under this Act. In view of deeming provisions of s. 17(6) of the Act, the registration absolves the parties of proving that the marriage was in fact solemnised in accordance with the provisions of the Foreign Marriage Act 1969.[1] Section 17(6) further provides that the marriage registered under this section shall, as from the date of registration, be deemed to have been solemnised under this Act. Thus, it applies to marriages solemnised even prior to the commencement of the Act.[2]

Matrimonial reliefs in respect of foreign marriages (section 18)

Section 18 of the Foreign Marriage Act 1969 deals with matrimonial reliefs in respect of foreign marriages with reference to provisions contained in the Special Marriage Act 1954. The provisions of Chapters IV, V, VI and VII of the Special Marriage Act 1954 shall apply in relation to marriages solemnised under the Foreign Marriage Act 1969. As a result of all the

---

1 *Joyce Sumathi* v *Robert Dickson Brodie* AIR 1982 AP 389.
2 *Abdur Rahim* v *Padma* AIR 1982 Bom 341.

provisions of Chapter VI of the Special Marriage Act 1954 relating to divorce etc. and of Chapter VII relating to jurisdiction and procedure shall ordinarily apply to and govern all marriages taking place in a foreign country, however, solemnised, provided one of the spouses is a citizen of India.[3]

Under s. 18(3)(a)(i) of the Foreign Marriage Act 1969 a court can exercise jurisdiction if the petitioner wife has been residing in India for a period of not less than three years immediately preceding the presentation of the petition for a decree of dissolution of marriage. If the petitioner remains away from India for a short period, that will not make the petitioner disentitled to file petition.[4]

Penalty

Section 19 of the Foreign Marriage Act 1969 provides for punishment for bigamy. Section 20 lays down punishment for contravention of condition specified in cl. (c) or cl. (d) of s. 4 of the Act. Section 21 provides for punishment for false declaration for the purpose of procuring a marriage.

Miscellaneous

Section 23 of the Foreign Marriage Act 1969 deals with recognition of marriages solemnised under the law of other countries. Section 24 relates to certification of documents of marriages solemnised in accordance with local law in a foreign country. Section 26 is concerned with correction of errors. Section 28 confers power on the Central Government to make rules for carrying out the purposes of this Act.

---

[3] *Sachindra Paul* v *Kalpana Paul* 93 CWN 404.
[4] *M* v *A* AIR 1993 Bom 110.

CHAPTER
37

The Family Courts Act 1984

Aims and objects

The Family Courts Act 1984 aims at establishing Family Courts for the purpose of promoting conciliation in, and, securing speedy settlement of disputes relating to marriage and family affairs and for matters connected therewith.[1] Order 32A of the Code of Civil Procedure 1908 as amended in 1976 provides for suits relating to matters concerning the family. The word "family" has not been defined in the Family Courts Act 1984, but the meaning of "family" as given in r. 6 of Or. 32A of the Code of Civil Procedure may be assigned to "family" in view of the provision in s. 2(*e*) of the Family Courts Act 1984. Rule 6 of Or. 32A, CPC defines that each of the following shall be treated as constituting a family, namely—(*a*) (*i*) a man and his wife living together, (*ii*) any child or children being issue of theirs or of such man or such wife, (*iii*) any child or children being maintained by such man and wife; (*b*) a man not having a wife or not living together with his wife, any child or children, being issue of his and any child or children being maintained by him; (*c*) a woman not having a husband or not living together with her husband any child or children being maintained by her; (*d*) a man or woman and his or her brother, sister, ancestor or lineal descendant living with him or her; and (*e*) any combination of one or more of groups specified in cl. (*a*), cl. (*b*), cl. (*c*) or cl. (*d*) of this rule. Besides, the concept of "family" used in any personal law or any other law for the time being in force shall also apply. In *K.A. Abdul Jaleel* v *T.A. Shahida*[2] it has been held that the approach for settlement

---

1 See Preamble to the Family Courts Act 1984.
2 (2003)4 SCC 166.

of disputes through the Family Court is different from that adopted in ordinary civil proceedings.

Extent and applicability of the Act

The Family Courts Act 1984 extends to the whole of India except the State of Jammu and Kashmir. It applies to Hindus, Sikhs and Jains under the Hindu Marriage Act 1955, all other persons under the Special Marriage Act 1954. People professing Christian, Muslim and Parsi religion do not invoke the jurisdiction of the Family Court for their matrimonial disputes.

Family Courts

For the purpose of exercising the jurisdiction and powers by the Family Court, the State Government after consultation with the High Court and by notification shall establish for every area in the State comprising a city or town whose population exceeds one million, a Family Court. The State Government may also establish Family Courts for such other areas in the State as it may deem necessary. The Government shall, after consultation with the High Court, specify by notification the local limits of the area to which the jurisdiction of a Family Court shall extend.[3] There are eighty seven Family Courts Functioning in India.

Appointment of Judges

The Judges of the Family Courts are appointed by the State Government with concurrence of the High Court. A Family Court may consist of more than one Judge. In such case the State Government may, with the concurrence of the High Court, appoint any of the Judges to be the Principal Judge and any other Judge to be the Additional Principal Judge. A person shall not be qualified for appointment as a Judge of a Family Court unless he—(*a*) has for at least seven years held judicial office in India or any post under the Union or a State requiring special knowledge of law; or (*b*) has for at least seven years been an advocate of a High Court; or (*c*) possesses such other qualification as the Central Government may, with the concurrence of the Chief Justice of India, prescribe. In selecting persons as Judge every endeavour shall be made to protect and preserve the institution of marriage and promote welfare of children. Preference shall be given to appoint women as Judges. No person shall be appointed as, or hold office of, a Judge of a Family Court after he has attained the age of sixty two years. The salary and other allowances

---

[3] Section 3, Family Courts Act.

payable to and the other conditions of service of a Judge shall be decided by the State Government in consultation with the High Court.[4]

Shifting of Family Court

The State has discretion to establish or not to establish a Family Court. But when a Family Court is established in a city or town whose population exceeds one million, then the State has no power to shift the Family Court from one place to another within the area.[5]

Counsellors, officers and employees of Family Court

The State Government in consultation with the High Court shall determine. The number and categories of counsellors, officers and other employees for the purpose of assisting the Family Court in discharge of its functions.[6] This is an indirect ban on advocates to practise in the Family Court.

Jurisdiction of Family Court

Jurisdiction of a Family Court is laid down in s. 7 of the Family Courts Act 1984. A Family Court shall (*a*) have and exercise all the jurisdiction exercisable by any district court or any subordinate civil court under any law for the time being in force in respect of suits or proceedings; (*b*) be deemed for the purposes of exercising such jurisdiction under such law, to be a district court or, as the case may be, such subordinate civil court for the area to which the jurisdiction of Family Court extends. Explanation to sub-sec. (1) of s. 7 defines the expression "suits and proceedings". It means the following:

(*i*) a suit or proceeding between the parties to a marriage for a decree of nullity of marriage or restitution of conjugal rights or judicial separation or dissolution of marriage;

(*ii*) a suit or proceeding for a declaration as to the validity of marriage or as to the matrimonial status of a person;

(*iii*) a suit or proceeding as to property of parties to marriage;

(*iv*) a suit or proceeding for an order of injunction arising out of marital relationship;

(*v*) a suit or proceeding for a declaration as to legitimacy of a person;

(*vi*) a suit or proceeding for maintenance;

(*vii*) a suit or proceeding in relation to guardianship of the person or the custody of or access to a minor.

---

4 Section 4, Family Courts Act.
5 *M.P. Gangadharan* v *State of Kerala* AIR 2006 SC 2360.
6 Section 6, Family Courts Act.

A Family Court shall also have jurisdiction (*a*) exercisable by a First Class Magistrate under Chapter IX (relating to maintenance of wife, children and parents) of the Code of Criminal Procedure 1973; and (*b*) such other jurisdiction as may be conferred by any other enactment.

Some illustrative cases

(*a*) After constitution of the Family Court for the Madras area the original jurisdiction of the High Court in respect of matters that may fall under the Explanation to s. 7 of the Act is not ousted.[7] Both the Family Court as well as the High Court (on its original jurisdiction) will have concurrent jurisdiction.[8]

(*b*) The Family Court on evidence found that the plaintiff wife was ill treated by the defendant husband and was forced to live separately. There was no evidence to show that the plaintiff had any independent income of her own. The husband was earning Rs. 6,500 per month as driver. Grant of maintenance of Rs. 1,300 to the plaintiff was held to be proper.[9]

(*c*) The Family Court has no jurisdiction to appoint a guardian or manager in respect of property of a minor.[10]

(*d*) The Family Court can, in its inherent powers, direct medical examination of a party to matrimonial proceedings in appropriate cases.[11]

Exclusion of jurisdiction

Where a Family Court is established in any area—(*a*) no district court or any subordinate civil court shall, in relation to such area, have to exercise any jurisdiction in respect of any suit or proceeding as referred to in Explanation to sub-sec. (1) of s. 7; (*b*) no magistrate shall, in relation to such area, have or exercise any jurisdiction of powers under Chapter IX of the Code of Criminal Procedure 1973; (*c*) every suit or proceeding of the nature described in Explanation to s. 7(1) and every proceeding under Chapter IX of Cr PC, 1973 (*i*) which is pending immediately before the establishment of such Family Court before any district court or subordinate court or before any magistrate under the said Code; and (*ii*) any suit or proceeding which was instituted or taken before the commencement of

---

7 *Mary Thomas* v *K.E. Thomas* AIR 1990 Mad 100 (FB).
8 *Mary Sheila* v *Vincent Thamburaj* AIR 1991 Mad 180 (SB); see *Kanak Vinod Mehta* v *Vinod Dulerai Mehta* AIR 1991 Bom 337 (DB).
9 *Mohd. Ibrahim* v *Mehrunisa Begum* AIR 2004 Kant 261.
10 *Sushila Nath* v *Judge Family Court* AIR 1998 Ori 61.
11 *Lalit Kishore* v *Meeru Sharma* AIR 2010 SC 1240.

this Act shall stand transferred to such Family Court on the date on which it is established.[12] Thus, an order of maintenance passed by Magistrate before establishment of Family Court shall be executed by the Family Court after it has been established. The Magistrate has no jurisdiction to execute the said order after such establishment of the Family Court.[13]

Duty of Family Court to endeavour for settlement

In every suit or proceeding it will be the duty of Family Court to endeavour for settlement of the dispute between parties. If it appears to the Family Court that there is a possibility of a settlement between the parties, the Family Court may adjourn the proceeding for a reasonable period.[14] Presence of husband in person can be insisted for settlement talk. Husband cannot be represented by power of attorney-holder.[15]

Procedure for Family Court

Generally, the provisions of the Code of Civil Procedure, 1908 and of any other law for the time being in force shall apply to the suits and proceedings other than the proceedings under Chapter IX of the Code of Criminal Procedure 1973 before a Family Court and for that purpose a Family Court shall be deemed to be a Civil Court. The provisions of the Code of Criminal Procedure 1973 or rules made thereunder shall apply to the proceedings under Chapter IX of that Code before a Family Court. The Family Court in any such case is empowered to make its own procedure with a view to arrive at a settlement in respect of the subject-matter of the suit or proceeding.[16]

Family Court has all the attributes and satisfies all the ingredients of a court. It has been declared by s. 7 of the Act to be district court or subordinate civil court to which provisions of the CPC and Cr PC have been applied by s. 10 of the Act. It will not cease to be a court merely because some restrictions are imposed by ss. 11-16 of the Act.[17]

Every suit or proceeding under this Act may be held *in camera* if the Family Court so desires and shall be so held if either party so desires.[18]

---

12 Section 8, Family Courts Act.
13 *Mahapratap Rudra Das* v *Pravabati Das* (1993)2 DMC 54 (Ori).
14 Section 9, Family Courts Act 1984.
15 *Puthiyapurayil Abdul Salam* v *P.P. Mariyumma* AIR 2007 Ker 68.
16 Section 10, Family Courts Act 1984.
17 *Munna Lal* v *State of UP* AIR 1991 All 189.
18 Section 11, Family Courts Act 1984.

It is open to Family Court to secure the services of a medical expert or such persons as welfare experts as the court may think fit for the purpose of assisting the Family Court in discharging its functions.[19] In the interest of justice the Family Court may seek the assistance of legal expert as *amicus curiae*. But no party to a suit or proceeding before Family Court shall be entitled, as of right, to be represented by a legal practitioner.[20] The scheme of the Act does not show that there is any complete prohibition on representation by a legal practitioner before the Family Court.[21] A Family Court may receive as evidence any report or document or matter that may, in the opinion of the court, assist it to deal effectually with a dispute whether the same is otherwise relevant or admissible under the Evidence Act 1872.[1]

In a suit or proceeding before the Family Court it is not necessary to record the evidence of witness at length, the Judge may record or cause to be recorded the substance of what the witness has deposed and the same shall be signed by the Judge and the witness.[2] The evidence of formal character may be given on affidavit.[3] The judgment of the Family Court shall contain concise statement of the case, the point for determination, the decision thereon and the reasons for such decision,[4] Family Court should not prolong proceeding in writing lengthy judgment.[5]

Execution of decree and order

A decree or order other than one made under Chapter IX of the Code of Criminal Procedure 1973 passed by Family Court shall have the same force and effect as a decree or order of a civil court and shall be executed in the same manner as prescribed by the Code of Civil Procedure 1908 for the execution of decree or order. An order passed by a Family Court under Chapter IX of the Code of Criminal Procedure 1973 shall be executed in the manner prescribed for the execution of such order by that Code. A decree or order passed by the Family Court may be executed by that court or by the Family Court or ordinary civil court to which it is sent for execution.[6]

---

19 Section 12, Family Courts Act.
20 Section 13, *ibid*.
21 *Bansidhar* v *Seema* 1992 Cr LJ 1562 (All).
1 Section 14, Family Courts Act.
2 Section 15, *ibid*.
3 Section 16, *ibid*.
4 Section 17, *ibid*.
5 *Shashi Shah* v *Kiran Kumar Shah* 1999(2) Civ LJ 65 (All).
6 Section 18, Family Courts Act.

No inconsistency between s. 8 and s. 18

The district court can also execute a decree or order passed by a Family Court provided no Family Court is established for that area. When such meaning is assigned to sub-sec. (3) of s. 18 of the Act, there will be no inconsistency between s. 8 and s. 18 of the Act.[7]

Appeal

An appeal shall lie from every judgment or order, not being an interlocutory order, a Family Court to the High Court both on facts and on law. No appeal shall lie from a decree or order passed by the Family Court with the consent of the parties or from an order passed under Chapter IX of the Code of Criminal Procedure 1973. Every appeal shall be preferred within a period of thirty days from the date of the judgment or order of the Family Court. The High Court may, of its own motion or otherwise, call and examine the record of any proceeding in which the Family Court situate within its jurisdiction passed an order under Chapter IX of the Code of Criminal Procedure 1973 for the purpose of satisfying itself as to the correctness, legality or propriety of the order, not being an interlocutory order. Except the above provisions, no appeal or revision shall lie to any court from any judgment, order or decree of a Family Court. An appeal preferred to the High Court shall be heard by a Bench consisting of two or more judges.[8]

Some illustrative cases

(*a*) An order passed on application challenging the jurisdiction of the Family Court is not an interim order and as such appeal will lie against that order.[9]

(*b*) Writ petition by way of remedy against interlocutory order passed by Family Court is maintainable.[10]

(*c*) A Family Court dealing with procedure under Chapter IX of the Cr PC passes an order in exercise of jurisdiction of a Judicial Magistrate First Class, it is a final order and as such it is revisable under s. 19(4) of the Family Courts Act as criminal revision.[11]

---

7 *Marya Tersa Martin* v *E. Martin* AIR 1994 Ker 264.
8 Section 19, Family Courts Act.
9 *Vinod Goyal* v *Sarita Goyal* AIR 2006 Uttaranchal 37.
10 *Anusha* v *K. Shankar Raman* 1998(4) Civ LJ 389 (Kant).
11 *Rajesh Shukla* v *Smt. Meena R. Shukla* AIR 2006 NOC 268 (All).

Some illustrative cases

The Family Courts Act 1984 has a overriding effect notwithstanding anything inconsistent therewith contained in any other law for the time being in force.[12] A petition by a divorced Muslim woman under s. 125, Cr PC (2 of 1974) for maintenance against husband before the Family Court is maintainable even after iddat period as long as she does not remarry.[13]

The High Court is empowered to make rules as it deems necessary by notification in the Official Gazette.[14] The Central Government may, with the concurrence of the Chief Justice of India, by notification in the Official Gazette, make rules prescribing the other qualifications for appointment of a Judge referred to in s. 4(3)(c) of the Act.[15] The State Government may, after consultation with the High Court, by notification in the Official Gazette, make rules for carrying out the purposes of this Act.[16]

---

12 Section 20, Family Courts Act.
13 *Shabana Bano* v *Imran Khan* AIR 2010 SC 305.
14 Section 21, *ibid*.
15 Section 22, *ibid*.
16 Section 23, *ibid*.

CHAPTER
38

The Dowry Prohibition Act 1961

Origin and object

"The dowry system, as originally devised, provided post marital security to an otherwise hapless (*abala*) bride."[1] The primary object of the Dowry Prohibition Act 1961 is to include customary presents at marriage, to ensure that any dowry given would be for the benefit of the wife and at the same time to discourage the dowry system by declaring it as a punishable offence.[2]

Evil effects of dowry

The evil effects of dowry are (*a*) decline in birth rate of female child and (*b*) murder, suicide, burning, harassment and torture of newly married young girls. In well-off States like Maharashtra, Gujarat, Punjab and Haryana in India it is recorded that more than 50 points have declined in the child sex ratio.[3] The Supreme Court in *Vikas* v *State of Rajasthan*[4] has observed: "Daily, demon of dowry is devouring lives of young girls, who marry with high hopes of having heavenly abode in their husbands' house. In few cases, guilty are punished but it has no deterrent effect on mothers-in-law or sisters-in-law who might have suffered similar cruelty/tyranny. This deep rooted social evil requires to be controlled not only by effective implementation of the Dowry Prohibition Act 1961, but also by the society."

---

1 Report of the Joint Committee of the Houses to examine the question of the working of the Dowry Prohibition Act 1961 presented on August 11, 1982, p. 5.
2 See Statement of Objects and Reasons, Gazette of India, 1959, Ext. Pt. II, s. 2, p. 397.
3 See *State of Haryana* v *Santra* AIR 2000 SC 1888.
4 AIR 2002 SC 2830 (para 1).

Applicability of the Dowry Prohibition Act 1961

The Dowry Prohibition Act 1961 extends to the whole of India except the State of Jammu and Kashmir. It applies to all communities of people irrespective caste, creed and religion.

Definition of dowry

Section 2 of the Dowry Prohibition Act 1961 defines "dowry". It means any property or valuable security given or agreed to be given either directly or indirectly—(a) by one party to a marriage to the other party to the marriage; or (b) by the parents of either party to a marriage or by any other person, to either party to the marriage or to any other person at or before or at any time after the marriage in connection with the marriage of the parties. But it does not include dower or mohr in case of persons to whom the Muslim Person Law (Shariat) applies. In *Satvir Singh* v *State of Punjab*[5] the Supreme Court has dealt with the meaning of dowry. There are three occasions related to dowry. One is before the marriage, second is at the time of marriage and the third is "at any time" after the marriage. It cannot be said that there would be conviction for dowry death if there is agreement for dowry. Even demand of dowry on other ingredients being satisfied is punishable.[6]

Illustrative cases

(1) Persistent demands for T.V. and scooter made from the bride after the marriage or from her parents would mean dowry within the meaning of s. 304B, IPC.[7]

(2) Furnishing a list of ornaments and other house-hold goods at the time of settlement of marriage amounts to demand of dowry within the meaning of s. 2 of the Act.[8]

Penalty for dowry

If any person gives or takes or abets the giving or taking of dowry, he shall be punishable with imprisonment for a term of not less than five years and with a fine for a sum which shall not be less than fifteen thousand rupees or the amount of the value of such dowry, whichever is more. The court may, for special reason, impose a sentence of

---

5 AIR 2001 SC 2828 (para 21). See *Koppisatti Subbharao* v *State of A.P.* AIR 2009 SC 2684 (para 15).
6 *Baldev Singh* v *State of Punjab* AIR 2009 SC 913.
7 *Pawan Kumar* v *State of Haryana* AIR 1998 SC 958.
8 *Madhusudan Malhotra* v *Kishore Chand Bhandari* (1988)1 SCWR 167.

imprisonment for a term less than five years. But no penalty shall be imposed in relation to (a) presents which are given at the time of marriage without any demand provided that such presents are entered in a list maintained in accordance with the rules made under this Act; (b) presents which are given at the time of marriage to the bridegroom without any demand provided that such presents are entered in the list in accordance with the rules under this Act. Where presents are given by any person related to the wife and such presents are of customary nature and not of excessive value should not be treated as dowry.[9]

If any person demands directly or indirectly from the parents or other relatives or guardian of a bride or bridegroom any dowry, he shall be punishable with imprisonment for a term which shall not be less than six months and not more than two years and with fine which may extend to ten thousand rupees. The court may, however for special reasons, impose a sentence of imprisonment for a term less than six months.[10]

Demand for dowry by itself is punishable. Agreement for dowry is not *sine quo non* for conviction. It can be inferred from circumstantial evidence.[11] Agreement for giving or taking dowry is void.[12]

Advertisement in any newspaper, periodical journal or other media offering share in property or in business or any money as consideration of marriage of son or daughter is totally banned. If any person does so, he is liable to be punished with imprisonment for a term which shall not be less than six months and not more than five years or with fine which may extent to fifteen thousand rupees. The court may impose a sentence for a term of less than six months in exceptional cases.[13]

Where any dowry is received by any person other than the woman in connection with whose marriage it is given, the person shall transfer it to the woman, because he holds it in trust for the benefit of the woman or her heirs in case of her death.[14]

Cognizance of offence

No court inferior to that of a Metropolitan Magistrate or a Judicial Magistrate of the first class shall try any offence under this Act. No court shall take cognizance of an offence under this Act except upon (i) its own

9 Section 3, Dowry Prohibition Act 1961.
10 Section 4, *ibid*.
11 *State of Andhra Pradesh* v *Raj Gopal Asawa* AIR 2004 SC 1933.
12 Section 5, Dowry Prohibition Act.
13 Section 4A, *ibid*.
14 Section 6, *ibid*.

knowledge or a police report of the facts which constitute such offence, or (ii) a complaint by the person aggrieved by the offence or a parent or other relative of such person, or by any recognised welfare institution or organisation. It shall be lawful for the competent Magistrate to pass sentence prescribed by this Act on any person convicted of any offence under this Act. Nothing in Chapter XXXVI of the Code of Criminal Procedure 1973 shall apply to any offence under this Act. A statement made by the person aggrieved by the offence shall not subject such person to a prosecution under this Act.[15] Offences under this Act are cognizable for certain purposes and are to be non-bailable and non-compoundable.[16] Burden of proof for the offence under s. 3 or under s. 4 of the Act is on that person that he had not committed an offence under those sections.[17] The State Government shall appoint Dowry Prohibition Officers for different jurisdictions with statutory powers assigned to them under this Act.[18]

The Central Government as well as the State Government are empowered to make rules for carrying out the purposes of this Act.[19]

Illustrative cases

(a) In *Sakhi Mandalani* v *State of Bihar*[20] there was a demand for dowry coupled with harassment. The main part of the charge under s. 304B, IPC was not established. In such case conviction under ss. 3 and 4 of the Dowry Prohibition Act was not proper. Thus, the conviction under the said sections of the Act was set aside.

(b) Testimony of brother and father of deceased as to payment of part of dowry cannot be discarded on the ground that they failed to establish that there was an agreement to pay the dowry.[21]

(c) A joint account was opened in the name of bride and bridegroom and a sum of Rs. 10,000 was deposited after settlement of marriage. Reasonable inference of demand for dowry can be made. Thus, it is an offence under s. 4 of the Dowry Prohibition Act 1961.[22]

---

15 Section 7, Dowry Prohibition Act 1961.
16 Section 8, *ibid*.
17 Section 8A, *ibid*.
18 Section 8B, *ibid*.
19 Sections 9 and 10, *ibid*.
20 (1999)5 SCC 705.
21 *State of Karnataka* v *M.V. Manjunathegowda* AIR 2003 SC 809.
22 *Vijayabai* v *State of Maharashtra* 1995 Supp (2) SCC 734.

(d) The cruel conduct of husband causing the deceased to commit suicide was not based on demand of dowry and as such the accused was not liable under the provisions of the Dowry Prohibition Act, but was liable for abetment of committing suicide.[23]

(e) *Satbir Singh* v *State of Haryana*[24] it was held by the Supreme Court that the ingredients of s. 304B of the Indian Penal Code dealing with dowry death were established and as such the conviction of the accused persons under that section was proper.

(f) In *Narayanamurthy* v *State of Karnataka*[25] the Supreme Court held that there was nothing to show that the demand for dowry was soon before the death of the wife-neighbours were not supporting the prosecution case. The accused husband was liable to be acquitted.

---

23   K. *Prema S. Rao* v *Yadla Srinivasa Rao* [2002]4 LRI 918.
24   AIR 2005 SC 3546.
25   AIR 2008 SC 2377.

CHAPTER
39

The Guardians and Wards Act 1890

Introduction

From the early Roman law to the modern law, the King and the State are under a duty to care for the class of persons who are incompetent to take care of themselves because of their immature intellect and imperfect discretion arising from their age. Under the Hindu Law as in English Law, the King is regarded as *"parens patriae"*. The protection of infants by the King is taken by the courts as representatives of the sovereign. Before the passing of the Guardians and Wards Act 1890, the law on the subject was scattered in several Acts and Regulations. The Guardians and Wards Act 1890 was passed with a view to consolidating and amending the law relating to Guardians and Wards. This Act has been amended by the Code of Civil Procedure 1908, the Guardians and Wards (Amendment) Act 1926, the Guardians and Wards (Amendment) Act 1929, etc.

Right of natural guardian to custody of child

The right of natural guardian to custody of child is not always absolute. Welfare of the child is paramount importance while considering the grant of custody of child. In *Anjali Kapoor* v *Rajiv Baijal*,[1] father married a second time having a child with a meagre income. The mother of the child died during child birth. The child is living in the custody of grandmother who is financially sound. It was held that the custody of the child would be allowed to be retained by the appellant grandmother.

---

1   (2009)7 SCC 322.

CHAPTER
40

The Religious Endowments Act 1863

Introduction

The Religious Endowments Act 1863 was passed for appropriation of rents and produce of lands granted for the support of mosques, temples, colleges and other purposes. In order to relieve the Boards of Revenue and local agents from such duties, so far as those duties related to the superintendence of lands granted for the support of mosques or temples and for other religious uses; the appropriation of endowments made for the maintenance of such religious establishments and the appointment of trustees or managers thereof and to enable the Government to divest itself of the management of such institutions.

No power to grant perpetual lease of math properties

In the absence of legal necessity the previous *mathadhipathi* had no power to grant a perpetual lease of math properties at a fixed rent. But the *mathadhipathi* had power to grant a lease which could endure for his life time.[1]

No dedication of property before gift

The owner who has constructed a temple and installed a deity therein makes a gift of the property expressing a desire that the donee should enter possession and occupation of the gifted property and perform *seva puja* and *rajbhog* of the deity. When there is no dedication before making the gift and it is only after the transfer that the donee by his own actings makes the property *devottar* constituting himself the *shebait* of the deity.

---

1 *Sarangadeva* v *Ramaswami* AIR 1966 SC 1603.

The deed of gift passes an interest in the donee so that his heirs would succeed to the shebaitship.[2]

Filling in vacancy in Committee of Wakf

The District Judge has no jurisdiction or power to fill in vacancies in the Committee constituted under the Religious Endowments Act 1863 for Wakf of a Dargah which is governed by the U.P. Muslim Wakfs Act 1960. Only the Board has full powers with regard to inspection of accounts, their auditing, administration of wakf funds and all such matters.[3]

---

2 *Shahzad Kunwar* v *Ram Karan* AIR 1965 SC 254.
3 *UPSC Wakf Board* v *Mohd. Alim* AIR 1971 SC 1396.

CHAPTER
41

The Indian Succession Act 1925

TESTAMENTARY SUCCESSION

Introduction

Section 57 provides that the provisions of Past VI of the Indian Succession Act 1925 which are set out in Schedule III, shall apply, subject to the restrictions and modifications specified therein apply (*a*) all Wills and codicils made by any Hindu, Buddhist, Sikh or Jaina on or after 1st September 1870 within the territories under the Lieutenant-Governor of Bengal or within the local limits of the ordinary original civil jurisdiction of the High Courts of Judicature at Madras and Bombay; and (*b*) to all such wills and codicils made outside those territories and limits relating to immovable property situate within those territories; and (*c*) to all Will and codicils made by Hindu, Buddhist, Sikh or Jaina on or after 1st January 1927. Marriage shall not revoke any such Will or codicil.

Schedule III as referred to in s. 57 of the Indian Succession Act 1925 specifies the following sections, namely, 59, 61-64, 68, 70, 71, 73-90, 95, 96, 98, 101-117, 119-190.

Restrictions and modifications in application of forgoing sections are as follows:

1. Nothing therein contained shall authorise a testator to bequeath property which he could not have alienated *inter vivos* or to deprive any persons of any right of maintenance of which, but for the application of these sections, he could not deprive them by will.

2. Nothing therein contained shall affect any law of adoption or intestate succession.

3. In applying s. 70 the words "than by marriage or" shall be omitted.

4. In applying any of the sections, namely sections 75, 76, 105, 109, 111, 112, 113, 114, 115, 116 to such Wills and codicils the words "son", "sons", "child" and "children" shall be deemed to include an adopted child, and the word "grand-children" shall be deemed to include the children whether adopted or natural born, of a child whether adopted or natural born, of a child, whether adopted or natural born; and the expression "daughter-in-law" shall be deemed to include the wife of an adopted son.

General application of Part VI dealing with succession (section 58)

The provisions of this Part shall not apply to testamentary succession to the property of any Muhammadan nor, save as provided in s. 57 to testamentary succession to the property of any Hindu, Buddhist, Sikh or Jaina, nor shall they apply to any Will made before 1st January 1866. Save and except the above restrictions, the provisions of this Part shall constitute the law of India applicable to all cases of testamentary succession.

Person capable of making Wills (section 59)

Every person of sound mind not being a minor may dispose of his property by Will. A married woman, a deaf or dumb or blind, an insane during the period of sound mind may make a Will. A person in intoxication or suffering from such illness that he does not know what he is doing cannot make a Will.

Illustrations

(*i*) A can perceive what is going in his immediate neighbourhood and can answer familiar questions, but has not a competent understanding as to the nature of his property, or the persons who are kindred to him or in whose favour it would be proper that he should make his Will. A cannot make a valid Will.

(*ii*) A executes an instrument purporting to be his Will, but he does not understand the nature of the instrument, nor the effect of its provisions. This instrument is not a valid Will.

(*iii*) A, being very feeble and debilitated, but capable of exercising a judgment as to the proper mode of disposing of his property, makes a Will. This is a valid Will.

Effect of Will. Normally, a Will becomes effective after demise of testator. But in case of nomination of *Shebait*, nomination takes effect from the date of execution of the Will.[1]

Testamentary guardian (section 60)

A father may be Will appoint a guardian or guardians for his child during minority.

---

1 *Rambir Das* v *Kalyan Das* 1997(2) Scale 499.

Effect of Will obtained by fraud, coercion or importunity (section 61)

A Will or any part of a Will, the making of which has been caused by fraud or coercion or by such importunity as takes away the free agency of the testator, is void.

Illustrations

(i) A, falsely and knowingly, represents to the testator, that the testator's only child is dead, or that he has done some undutiful act and thereby induces the testator to make a Will in his, A's favour, such Will has been obtained by fraud, and is invalid.

(ii) A, by fraud and deception, prevails upon the testator to bequeath a legacy to him. The bequest is void.

(iii) A, being a prisoner by lawful authority, makes his Will. The Will is not invalid by reason of the imprisonment.

(iv) A threatens to shoot B, or to burn his house or to cause him to be arrested on a criminal charge, unless he makes a bequest in favour of C. B, in consequence, makes a bequest in favour of C. The bequest is void, the making of it having been caused by coercion.

(v) A, being of sufficient intellect, if undisturbed by the influence of others, to make a Will yet being so much under the control of B that he is not a free agent, makes a Will, dictated by B. It appears that he would not have executed the Will but for fear of B. The Will is invalid.

(vi) A, being in, so feeble a state of health as to be unable to resist importunity, is pressed by B to make a Will of a certain purport and does so merely to purchase peace and in submission to B. The Will is invalid.

(vii) A, being in such a state of health as to be capable of exercising his own judgment and volition. B uses urgent intercession and persuasion with him to induce him to make a Will of a certain purport. A, in consequence of the intercession and persuasion, but in the free exercise of his judgment and volition, makes his Will in the manner recommended by B. The Will is not rendered invalid by the intercession and persuasion of B.

(viii) A, with a view to obtaining a legacy from B, pays him attention and flatters him and thereby produces in him a capricious partiality to A. B, in consequence of such attention and flattery, makes his Will, by which he leaves a legacy to A. The bequest is not rendered invalid by the attention and flattery of A.

A Will is not illegal on ground that the executor could not have willed away right of management of temple properties to person other than his lineal descendant.[2]

Revocation of Will (section 62)

A Will is liable to be revoked or altered by the maker of it at any time when he is competent to dispose of his property by Will.

---

2 *Palanivelayutham Pillai* v *Ramchandran* (2000)6 SCC 151.

Execution of unprivileged Wills (section 63)

Every testator, other than a soldier, airman, mariner at sea shall execute his Will according to the following rules: (*a*) The testator shall sign or shall affix his marks to the Will or it shall be signed by some other person in his presence and by his direction. (*b*) The signature of mark of the testator or the signature of the person signing for him, shall be so placed that it shall appear that it was intended thereby to give effect to the writing as a Will. (*c*) The Will shall be attested by two or more witnesses, each of whom has seen the testator sign or affix his mark to the Will or has seen some other person sign the Will, in the presence and by direction of the testator, or has received from the testator a personal acknowledgment of his signature or mark, or of the signature of such other person, and each of the witnesses shall sign the Will in the presence of the testator, but it shall not be necessary that more than one witness be present at the same time and no particular form of attestation shall be necessary.

A disputed Will attested by three witnesses out of which scribe was examined in court. It was held that the execution of the Will was proved.[3]

Suspicious circumstances

In *Niranjan Umeshchandra Joshi* v *Mrudula Jyoti Rao*,[4] it has been held that there are several circumstances which have been described by the Supreme Court as suspicious circumstances. There are—(*i*) when a doubt is created in regard to the condition of mind of the testator despite his signature in the Will. (*ii*) When the disposition appears to be unnatural or wholly unfair in the light of the relevant circumstances. (*iii*) Where the propounder himself takes prominent part in execution of Will which confers on him substantial benefit.

Incorporation of papers by reference (section 64)

If a testator, in a Will or codicil duly attested, refers to any other document then actually written as expressing any part of his intentions, such document shall be deemed to form a part of the Will or codicil in which it is referred to.

Privileged Wills (section 65)

Any soldier employed in an expedition or engaged in actual warfare, an airman, so employed or engaged or any mariner being at sea, may if he

---

3 *Palanivelayutham Pillai* v *Ramchandran* (2000)6 SCC 151; see also *Mathew Ommen* v *Suseela Mathew* AIR 2006 SC 786.
4 AIR 2007 SC 618.

has completed the age of eighteen years, dispose of his property by a Will. Such Wills are called privileged Wills.

Illustrations

(*i*) A, a medical officer attached to a regiment is a soldier and can make a privileged Will.

(*ii*) A, is at sea in a merchant ship of which he is purser. He can make a privileged Will as a mariner.

(*iii*) A, a soldier engaged in actual warfare and as such he can make a privileged Will.

(*iv*) A, a mariner of a ship in the course of a voyage can make a privileged Will.

(*v*) A, an admiral who commands a naval force lives on shore and occasionally goes on board his ship, cannot make a privileged Will.

(*vi*) A, a mariner, serving on a military operation, but not being at sea, is considered as a soldier and can make a privileged Will.

Mode of making and rules for executing, privileged Wills (section 66)

A privileged Will may be made in writing or by word of mouth. The execution of privileged Wills shall be governed by the following rules: (*a*) If the Will is wholly written by the testator with his own hand, it does not require his signature or attestation. (*b*) If the Will is wholly or in part written by another person and signed by the testator, it does not require attestation. (*c*) If an instrument purporting to be Will is written wholly or in part by another person and not signed by the testator it shall be deemed to be a Will if it was written by the testator's directions or that he recognised it as his Will. (*d*) If the execution of an instrument was not completed by the testator, it shall be deemed to be his Will if it can be reasonably ascribed to some cause other than abandonment of the testamentary intentions expressed in the instrument. (*e*) If a soldier, airman or mariner has written instructions for the preparation of his Will, but has died before it could be prepared and executed, such instrument shall be considered to constitute his Will. (*f*) If a soldier, airman or mariner has, in presence of two witnesses, given verbal instructions for the preparation of his Will, and they have been reduced into writing in his lifetime, but he has died before the instrument could be prepared and executed, such instruments shall be considered to constitute his Will although they may not have been reduced into writing in his presence, nor read over to him. (*g*) The soldier, airman or mariner may make a Will by word of mouth by declaring his intentions before two witnesses present at the same time. (*h*) A Will made by word of mouth shall be null at the expiration of one month after the testator, being still alive has ceased to be entitled to make a privileged Will.

Gift to attesting witness (section 67)

A Will shall not be deemed to be insufficiently attested by reason of any benefit thereby given either by way of bequest or by way of appointment to any person attesting it, or to his or her wife or husband; but the bequest or appointment shall be void so far as concerns the person so attesting or the wife or husband of such person or any person claiming under either of them. It is to be noted however that a legatee under a Will does not lose his legacy by attesting a codicil which confirms the Will.

Witness not disqualified by interest or by being executor (section 68)

No person having interest in, or by being executor of, a Will shall be disqualified as a witness to prove the execution of the Will or to prove the validity or invalidity thereof.

Revocation of Will or Codicil (sections 69, 70)

A Will is revoked by the marriage of the maker except a Will is made in exercise of a power of appointment. An unprivileged Will may be revoked by some writing declaring intention to revoke the same by executing another unprivileged Will, or by burning, tearing or otherwise destroying the same by the testator or by some person in presence and by his direction with the intention of revoking the same.

Illustrations

(*i*) A has made an unprivileged Will. Afterwards, A makes unprivileged Will which purports to revoke the first. This is a revocation.

(*ii*) A has made an unprivileged Will. Afterwards, A being entitled to make a privileged Will, which purports to revoke the privileged Will. This is revocation.

Revocation of privileged Will or codicil (section 72)

A privileged Will or codicil may be revoked by the testator by an unprivileged Will or codicil or by any act expressing an intention to revoke it or by the burning, tearing or otherwise destroying the same by the testator.

Revival of unprivileged Will (section 73)

No unprivileged Will or codicil, nor any part thereof which has been duly revoked, shall be revived otherwise than by re-execution thereof or by a codicil executed in a manner showing an intention to revive the same.

Construction of Wills

The provisions relating to the construction of Wills are laid down in Chapter VI of Part V of the Indian Succession Act 1925. The main rules of construction of Wills are as follows:

(*i*) The wordings of the Wills should be such the intentions of the testator can be known therefrom. The propounder of the Will is to clear all doubts and disputes of it.[5]

(*ii*) An error in the name or misdescription of object shall not prevent legacy from taking effect.

(*iii*) Intrinsic evidence is not admissible in cases of patent ambiguity or deficiency.

(*iv*) Meaning of a clause in a Will is to be collected from the entire instrument.

(*v*) Where a clause is susceptible of two meanings according to one of which it has some effect and according to one other of which it can have more, the former shall be preferred.

Principles of construction of a will, *inter alia*, are laid down in ss. 74 and 82 of the Indian Succession Act 1925. It is well-settled that the will should be read as a whole and the surrounding circumstances may be given effect to for the purpose of ascertaining the intention of the testator from the words used and the surrounding circumstances wherefore the court will put itself in the armchair of the testator.[6]

(*vi*) No part of the Will shall be rejected if it is possible to put a reasonable construction upon it.

(*vii*) The last of two inconsistent clauses shall prevail.

(*viii*) A Will or bequest not expressive of any definite intention is void for uncertainty.

Representative title to property of testator

Under section 211 of the Indian Succession Act 1925 the executor or administrator, as the case may be, of a deceased person is his legal representative for all purposes and all the property of the deceased person vests in him as such. But if the deceased was a Hindu, Muhammadan, Buddhist, Sikh, Jaina or Parsi or an exempted person, no property of deceased person shall vest in an executor or administrator which would

---

5 *Surendra Bhatia* v *Smt. Punam Bhatia* AIR 2001 Raj 338.
6 *Bhagwan Krishan Gupta* v *Prabha Gupta* 2009(3) CHN 198 (SC).

have otherwise passed by survivorship to some other person. Section 212 provides that no right to any part of property of a person who died intestate can be established in any court of justice unless letters of administration have been granted by a court of competent jurisdiction. But this will not apply in case of intestacy of a Hindu, Muhammadan, Buddhist, Sikh, Jaina, Indian Christian or Parsi. Section 213 provides that no right of executor or legatee can be established unless a court of competent jurisdiction in India has granted probate of the Will or has granted letters of administration with the Will or with an authenticated copy of the Will annexed. These provisions shall not apply in case of Wills made by Muhammadans or Indian Christians. They shall only apply to the Wills made by any Hindu, Buddhist, Sikh or Jaina; and in the case of Wills made by any Parsi dying after the commencement the Indian Succession (Amendment) Act 1962. In *Chiranjilal Shirilal Goenka (Deceased) through LRs v Jasjit Singh*,[7] it was held that the applicant could not consent to refer the dispute for arbitration in the pending proceedings. Sections 214 of the 1925 Act provides that the proof of the representative title is a condition precedent for recovery of debts through courts from the debtors of the deceased person. Section 215 provides that a grant of probate or letters of administration in respect of an estate shall supersede the grant of succession certificate. Section 216 provides that the grantee of probate or administration alone can sue or prosecute any suit until the same is revoked.

Grant of probate and letters of administration

Section 218 provides for the grant of administration of the estate of the deceased to any person according to the rules for distribution where the deceased was a Hindu, Muhammadan, Buddhist, Sikh or Jaina or an exempted person. Where he was not so, under s. 219 the administration shall be granted to such person who is connected with the deceased either by marriage or by consanguinity. Under s. 220 letters of administration entitle the administrator to all rights belonging to the estate. According to s. 221 probate is to be granted only to the executor appointed by the Will. Section 223 provides that no probate can be granted to a minor, insane or an association of individuals. Section 227 provides that the probate of a Will when granted establishes the Will from the death of the testator and renders valid all intermediate acts of the executor as such. Once the probate is granted, it is the conclusive proof on the validation of the Will unless it is revoked in accordance with the law.[8]

---

7 1993 AIR SCW 1439.
8 *Ramesh Nivrutti Bhagat v Dr. Surendra Manohar Parekhe* AIR 2001 Bom 461.

Alteration and revocation of grants

Under section 261 of the Indian Succession Act 1925 the court can rectify errors in names and descriptions or in setting forth the time and place of the deceased's death or the purpose in a limited grant. Section 263 provides the ground for revocation or annulment of the grant of probate or letters of administration—for just cause. "Just cause" shall be deemed to exist in the following cases: (*a*) The proceedings to obtain the grant were defective in substance; (*b*) the grant was obtained fraudulently by making a false suggestion or by concealing material from the court; (*c*) the grant was obtained by means of an untrue allegation of a fact; (*d*) the grant has become useless and inoperative; (*e*) the person to whom the grant was made has wilfully and without reasonable cause omitted to exhibit an inventory or account in accordance with the provisions of law.

Illustrations

(*i*) The court by which the grant was made had no jurisdiction.

(*ii*) The grant was made without citing parties who ought to have been cited.

(*iii*) The Will of which the probate was obtained was forged or revoked.

(*iv*) A obtained letters of administration to the estate of B, as his widow, but it has since transpired that she was never married to him.

(*v*) A has taken administration to the estate of B as if he had died intestate, but a Will has since been discovered.

(*vi*) Since probate had been granted, a latter Will has been discovered.

(*vii*) Since probate was granted, a codicil has been discovered which revokes or adds to the appointment of executors under the Will.

(*viii*) The person to whom probate was or letters of administration were, granted has subsequently become of unsound mind.

Petition for probate (section 276)

Application for probate or for letters of administration, with the Will annexed shall be made by a petition containing the following particulars:

(*a*) The time of the testator's death. (*b*) The writing annexed is his last Will and testament. (*c*) It was duly executed. (*d*) The amount of assets which are likely to come to the petitioner's hands. (*e*) When the application is for probate the petitioner is the executor named in the Will. In addition to these particulars, the petition shall further state—(*a*) When the application is to the District Judge, that the deceased at time of his death had a fixed place of abode or had some property situate within the jurisdiction of the Judge; and (*b*) when the application to a District Delegate that the deceased at the time of his death a fixed place of abode within the jurisdiction of such Delegate. Where the application is to the District

Judge and any portion of assets likely to come to the petitioner's hands is situate in another State, the petition shall state further the amount of such assets in each State and the District Judges within whose jurisdiction such assets are situate.

An unregistered Will is not unnatural, nor surrounded by suspicious circumstances, grant of probate is proper.[9]

Petition for letters of administration (section 278)

Application for letters of administration shall be made by petition stating—

(a) The time and place of the deceased's death;

(b) the family or other relatives of the deceased, and their respective residences;

(c) the right in which the petitioner claims;

(d) the amount of assets which are likely to come to the petitioner's hands;

(e) when the application is to the District Judge, that the deceased at the time of his death had a fixed place of abode, or had some property, and situate within the jurisdiction of the Judge; and

(f) when the application is to a District Delegate, that the deceased at the time of his death had a fixed place of abode, within the jurisdiction of such delegate.

Where the application is to the District Judge and any portion of the assets likely to come to the petitioner's hands is situate in another state, the petition shall further state the amount of such assets in each State and the District Judges within whose jurisdiction such assets are situate.

Petition for probate or letters of administration to be signed and verified (sections 280, 281)

The petition for probate or letters of administration shall, in all cases be subscribed by the petitioner and his Advocate and shall be verified by the petitioner in the prescribed form. The petition shall also be by at least one of the witnesses in the prescribed manner.

No change in terms of Will

In *Chandrabhai K. Bhoir* v *Krishna Arjun Bhoir*,[10] it has been held by the Supreme Court that a probate when granted binds the whole world. It is

---

9   E.M. *Pallikkaramma* v *K.V.P. Nair* AIR 2001 SC 435.
10 (2009)2 SCC 315.

a judgment *in rem*. The executor has to administer the estate of the testator in terms of the Will and not on the basis of the settlement arrived at by and between the parties which would be inconsistent with the terms of the Will. In case of any conflict between the terms of the Will and the settlement, the former will prevail.

Succession certificates

Under section 371 of the Indian Succession Act 1925, the District Judge within whose jurisdiction the deceased ordinarily resided at the time of his death, or if at that time he had no fixed place of residence, the District Judge within whose jurisdiction any part of the property of the deceased may be found, may grant a certificate. Section 372 provides that an application for such certificate shall be made to the District Judge by a petition signed and verified by or on behalf of the applicant in the manner prescribed by the Code of Civil Procedure 1908. The petition shall contain the following particulars:

(a) The time of the death of the deceased.

(b) The ordinary residence of the deceased at the time of his death, and if such residence was not within the local limits of the jurisdiction of the Judge to whom the application was made, then the property of the deceased within those limits.

(c) The family or other near relatives of the deceased and their respective residences.

(d) The right in which the petitioner claims.

(e) The absence of any impediment under s. 370 or any other law for the time being in force.

(f) The debts and securities in respect of which the certificate is applied for.

If the person verifying the averment in the petition knows or believes it to be false, he is guilty of an offence under s. 198 of the Indian Penal Code 1860. Application for such certificate may be made in respect of any debt or debts due to the deceased creditor or in respect of any portion thereof.

Findings given on an application for grant of succession certificate do not operate as *res judicata*.[11]

---

11 *Joginder Pal* v *Indian Red Cross Society* AIR 2000 SC 3279.

Revocation of succession certificate (section 383)

A certificate granted under Part X of the Indian Succession Act 1925 may be revoked on any of the following grounds:

(a) The proceedings to obtain the certificate were defective in substance.

(b) The certificate was obtained fraudulently by making of a false suggestion or by the concealment from the court of something material to the case.

(c) The certificate was obtained by means of an untrue allegation of a fact essential in point of law to justify the grant thereof, though such allegation was made in ignorance or inadvertently.

(d) The certificate has become useless and inoperative through circumstances.

(e) A decree or order made by a competent court in a suit or other proceeding with respect to effects comprising debts or securities specified in the certificate renders it proper that the certificate should be revoked.

CHAPTER
42
Maintenance under Code of Criminal Procedure 1973

Scope of section 125, Cr PC

Duty of parents to maintain their child does not disable them to claim damages from negligent doctor who performed an unsuccessful sterilisation operation giving birth to a child.[1] To claim maintenance under s. 125, Cr PC by a wife it is necessary to prove a valid or factum of marriage.[2] Section 125, Cr PC is a measure of social justice and specially enacted to protect women and children and falls within the sweep of Art. 15(3) reinforced by Art. 39 of the Constitution of India.[3] Even an illegitimate minor child is entitled to maintenance under s. 125, Cr PC.[4]

Statutory liability to maintain

Once the right under s. 125, Cr PC is established by proof of necessary conditions mentioned therein, it cannot be defeated by reference to personal law governing the parties.[5] Section 3(1)(*b*) of the Muslim Women (Protection of Rights on Divorce) Act 1986 (Act 25 of 1986) does not in any way affect the rights of the minor children of divorced Muslim parents to claim maintenance from their father under s. 125, Cr PC till they attain majority or are able to maintain themselves, or in the case of females till

---

1 *State of Haryana* v *Santra* AIR 2000 SC 1888; 2000 AIR SCW 1491.
2 *Sumitra Devi* v *Bhikan Choudhary* AIR 1985 SC 765; (1985)1 SCC 637; *Bakulabai* v *Gangaram* (1988)1 SCC 537.
3 *Captain Ramesh Chander Kaushal* v *Mrs. Veena Kaushal* AIR 1978 SC 1807; (1978)4 SCC 70.
4 *Sumitra Devi* v *Bhikan Choudhary* AIR 1985 SC 765.
5 *Yamunabai* v *Anantrao* AIR 1988 SC 644; see *Saira Banu* v *AM Abdul Gafoor* AIR 1987 SC 1103.

they are married.[6] A second wife is not entitled to maintenance but her children can claim maintenance under s. 125, Cr PC.[7]

The provision for maintenance *pendente lite* in s. 24 of the Hindu Marriage Act 1955 does not stand as a bar to grant relief under s. 125, Cr PC, 1973.[8]

Interim maintenance

The Magistrate may insist upon an affidavit being filed by or on behalf of the applicant stating the grounds in support of the claim for interim maintenance to satisfy himself that there is a *prima facie* case for making an order of interim maintenance.[9] The Supreme Court to do complete justice and considering the claim of the wife and daughter was maintainable under s. 125, Cr PC declared the amount awarded by the High Court under s. 24 of the Hindu Marriage Act 1955 should be treated as one under s. 125, Cr PC.[10]

Quantum of maintenance

Amount awarded under s. 125, Cr PC is adjustable against the amount awarded in matrimonial proceedings under s. 24 of the Hindu Marriage Act 1955 as alimony to wife.[11] The words "in the whole" occurring in s. 125, Cr PC cannot be interpreted to mean the total award for wife, child, mother and father together cannot exceed Rs. 500. What the section plainly means is that the court cannot grant more than Rs. 500 for each of the claimants.[12]

Cancellation or alteration of order of maintenance

An order granting maintenance can be revoked only prospectively having regard to the subsequent development in the form of order passed by the civil court.[13] On proof of sufficient charge the order of maintenance can be altered or modified.[14] Where it appears to the Magistrate that in consequence of any decision of a competent civil court any order made

---

6. *Noor Saba Khatoon* v *Mohd Quasin* AIR 1997 SC 3280; (1997)6 SCC 233.
7. *Khem Chand Om Prakash Sharma* v *State of Gujarat* (2000)3 SCC 753.
8. *Anand Ruia* v *Vidhas Ruia* 2004(1) Cal HN 685.
9. *Smt. Savitri* v *Govind Singh Rawat* (1985)4 SCC 337.
10. *Chigurupati Bambasiva Rao* v *Chigurupati Vijayalaxmi* (1997)11 SCC 84.
11. *Sudeep Chaudhary* v *Radha Chaudhary* AIR 1999 SC 536; 1999 Cr LJ 466.
12. *Captain Ramesh Chander Kaushal* v *Mrs. Veena Kaushal* AIR 1978 SC 1807; (1978)4 SCC 70.
13. *T.M. Narayanan* v *Nishad* 1990 (Supp) SCC 163(1).
14. Section 127(1), Cr PC 1973.

under s. 125, Cr PC should be cancelled or altered, the Magistrate shall cancel the order or, as the case may be, alter the same accordingly.[15]

Limitation

It is the duty of the High Court to dispose of a revision application against the order of maintenance under s. 125, Cr PC on merit by condoning the delay.[16] Provision under s. 125, Cr PC is a speedy remedy and tentative subject to find determination of rights in Civil Court.[17]

Forum for maintenance proceedings

Proceedings under s. 125, Cr PC may be taken against any person in any district (*a*) where he is, or (*b*) where he or his wife resides, or (*c*) where he last resided with his wife, or as the case may be, with the mother of the illegitimate child.[18] Where the wife filed an application under s. 125, Cr PC at the place of her residence, it cannot be dismissed by the Magistrate on the ground that the husband is not residing within his jurisdiction.[19]

Recovery of maintenance

An order of maintenance may be enforced by any Magistrate in any place where the person against whom it is made provided such Magistrate is satisfied as to the identity of the parties and non-payment of the allowance.[20] Sending husband to jail is a mode of enforcement and not a mode of satisfaction of the payment of allowance and as such the liability to pay arrears of maintenance allowance is not discharged merely because the defaulting husband prefers to go to jail.[21]

Award of maintenance from date of application or order

When wife does not stay with her husband and claims maintenance, the only question which the court is called upon to consider is whether she was justified to live separately from her husband and still claim maintenance from him? If the reply is in the affirmative, she is entitled to claim maintenance. It is therefore open to the Magistrate to award maintenance from the date of application and there is nothing which requires recording of "special reasons". It can also be awarded from the date of the order.[22]

---

15 Section 127(2), Cr PC 1973.
16 *Shilpa* v *Madhukar* JT 2000(10) SC 282.
17 *Inderjit Kaur* v *Union of India* (1991)2 Pat LJR 104 (SC).
18 Section 126, Cr PC 1973; *Darshan Kumari* v *Surinder Kumar* 1995 Supp (4) SCC 137.
19 *Kumutham* v *Kannappan* AIR 1999 SC 839; (1998)5 SCC 693.
20 Section 128, Cr PC 1973.
21 *Kuldip Kaur* v *Surinder Singh* AIR 1989 SC 232.
22 *Shail Kumari Devi* v *Krishan Bhagwan Pathak* AIR 2008 SC 3006.

CHAPTER
43

The Maintenance and Welfare of Parents and Senior Citizens Act 2007

Objects of the Maintenance and Welfare of Parents and Senior Citizens Act 2007

Traditional norms and culture of the Indian society laid stress on providing care for elderly persons particularly widowers and widowed women. Owing to the decline in joint family system a large number of elderly people in a family are not being looked after by other members of the family including sons and daughters, whether married or unmarried. They are, therefore, forced to spend their twilight years all alone and are exposed to emotional neglect and to lack of physical and financial support. This clearly reveals that ageing has become a major social challenge and there is necessity to give more attention to the care and protection for the older persons. Though, the parents can claim maintenance under the Code of Criminal Procedure 1973, yet the procedure is both time-consuming as well as expensive. Thus, the Maintenance and Welfare of Parents and Senior Citizens Act 2007 was passed with the view of simplifying the procedure making the relief available with less expense and providing for speedy disposal of the matter. This Act casts obligations on the persons who inherit the property of their aged relatives to maintain them. The provisions have also been made for setting up old age homes for providing maintenance to the indigent older persons and also for providing medical facilities to senior citizens.

Extent, applicability and some definitions of the Act

This Act applies to the whole of India except the State of Jammu and Kashmir. It also applies to the citizens of India outside India.

Section 2(*a*) of the Act defines children which includes son, daughter, grandson and granddaughter but does not include a minor.

Section 2(*b*) of the Act defines "maintenance" which includes provision for food, clothing, residence and medical attendance and treatment.

The word "parent" is defined in s. 2(*d*) of the Act which means father or mother, whether biological, adoptive or step-father or step-mother, as the case may be, whether or not the father or the mother is a senior citizen.

Section 2(*f*) of the Act defines "property" which means property of any kind, whether movable or immovable, ancestral or self-acquired, tangible or intangible and includes rights or interests in such property.

"Relative" according to s. 2(*g*) for the purpose of the Act means any legal heir of the children senior citizen who is not a minor and is in possession of or would inherit his property after his death. Section 2(*h*) of the Act defines "senior citizen" which means a person being a citizen of India who has attained the age of sixty years or above. "Welfare" is defined in s. 2(*k*) of the Act as the provision for food, health, care, recreation centres and other amenities necessary for senior citizens.

Overriding effect of the Act

The provisions of this Act shall have effect notwithstanding anything inconsistent therewith contained in any enactment other than this Act or in any instrument having effect by virtue of any enactment other than this Act (s. 3). Section 27 of the Act bars the jurisdiction of the civil court in respect of any matter to which the provisions of this Act apply.

Maintenance of parents and senior citizens

Section 4 of the Act provides that a parent or a senior citizen who is unable to maintain himself or herself from his or her own earning or out of property owned by him or her shall be entitled to make application under s. 5 of the Act in case of—(*i*) parent or grand-parent against one or more of his children not being minor; (*ii*) a childless senior citizen against relative as defined in s. 2(*g*) of the Act.

The obligation of the children or relative, as the case may be, to maintain a senior citizen extends to the needs of such citizen to lead a normal life. The obligation of the children to maintain the parent extends to the needs of such parent, father or mother or both, as the case may be, so that such parent may lead a normal life. Any person being a relative of a senior citizen and having sufficient means shall maintain such senior citizen provided he is in possession of the property of such senior citizen or he would inherit the property of such senior citizen. But where more than one relatives are entitled to inherit the property of a senior citizen, the maintenance shall be payable by such relative in the proportion in which they would inherit his property.

Section 5 provides for application for maintenance. An application for maintenance can be made (*a*) by a senior citizen or a parent, as the case may be; or (*b*) if he is incapable, by any other person or organisation authorised by him; or (*c*) the tribunal may take cognizance *suo motu*. An organisation here means any voluntary association registered under the Societies Registration Act 1860 or any other law for the time-being in force. The tribunal may, during the pendency of the proceeding regarding monthly allowance for maintenance order such children or relative to make a monthly allowance for the interim maintenance of such senior citizen including parent to pay the same to such senior citizen including parent as the tribunal may direct from time to time. On receipt of an application for maintenance, a notice thereof is to be given to the children or relative and after giving the parties an opportunity of being heard, hold an inquiry for determining the amount of maintenance. Such application shall be disposed of within ninety days from the date of service of notice of the application. The tribunal may extend the said period once for a maximum period of thirty days in exceptional circumstances for reasons to be recorded in writing. Such application may be filed against one or more persons, provided such children or relative are liable to maintain parent or senior citizen. Where an order of maintenance is made against more than one person, the death of one of them does not affect the liability of others to continue paying maintenance. Any such allowance for maintenance and expenses for proceeding shall be payable from the date of the order or if so ordered, from the date of filing of the application. If children or relative so ordered fail, without sufficient cause to comply with the order, the tribunal may, for every breach of the order, issue a warrant for levying the amount due in the manner provided for levying fines and may sentence such person for the whole or any part of each month's allowance for the maintenance and expenses of proceeding, as the case may be, remaining unpaid after the execution of the warrant, to imprisonment for a term which may extend to one month or until payment if sooner made whichever is earlier. But no warrant shall be issued for the recovery of any amount due unless application be made to the tribunal to levy such amount within a period of three months from the date on which it became due.

Jurisdiction and procedure

Section 6 of the Act deals with jurisdiction and procedure. The proceedings under s. 5 of the Act may be initiated against any children or relative in a District. (*a*) where a senior citizen or parent resides or last resided; or (*b*) where children or relative resides. On receipt of the application the tribunal shall issue a process for procuring the presence of children or relative against whom the application is filed. The tribunal shall have the power of a Judicial Magistrate of first class as provided in the Code of Criminal Procedure 1973 for securing attendance of such children or relative. All evidence to such proceedings shall be taken in presence of the children or relative against whom order for payment of maintenance is proposed to be made and shall be recorded in the manner prescribed for summons cases. But if the tribunal is satisfied that the children or relative against whom order is sought to be made is wilfully avoiding service or wilfully neglecting to attend the tribunal, the tribunal may proceed to hear and determine the case *ex parte*. Where the children or relative is residing outside India, the summons shall be served by the Tribunal through such authority as the Central Government may, by notification, specify in this behalf. The Tribunal may, before hearing the application, refer the same to a Conciliation Officer who shall submit his findings within one month and if amicable settlement is arrived at, the tribunal shall pass an order to that effect. In this context the term "Conciliation Officer" means (*a*) any person or representative of an organisation which is a voluntary association registered under the Societies Registration Act 1860 or any other law for the time-being in force; or (*b*) the Maintenance Officer designated by the State Government under s. 18(1) of the Act; or (*c*) any other person nominated by the Tribunal for this purpose.

Section 8 provides that in holding any inquiry under this Act the Tribunal may follow such summary procedure as it deems fit and for the purpose of taking evidence on oath and enforcing the attendance of witnesses and compelling the discovery and production of document the tribunal shall have the powers of a Civil Court. The tribunal shall be deemed to be a Civil Court for the purposes of s. 195 and Chapter XXVI of the Code of Criminal Procedure 1973.

(*a*) *Constitution of Maintenance Tribunal and Appellate Tribunal (sections 7, 15).* Section 7 provides that the State Government shall, by notification in the Official Gazette, constitute one or more Tribunals for each Sub-Division and the Tribunal shall be presided over by an officer not below the rank of Sub-Divisional Officer of a State. Where two or more Tribunals are constituted for any area the State Government may, by general or special order, regulate the distribution of business among them. Section 15 provides for constitution of Appellate Tribunal. The State Government may, by notification in the Official Gazette, constitute one Appellate Tribunal for each district to hear the appeal against the order of the Tribunal. The Appellate Tribunal shall be presided over by an officer not below the rank of District Magistrate.

(b) Order of maintenance (section 9). If children or relatives, as the case may be, neglect or refuse to maintain a senior citizen being unable to maintain himself, the Tribunal, on being satisfied of such neglect or refusal, order such children or relatives to make a monthly allowance at such monthly rate for the maintenance of such senior. The Tribunal may order the maintenance allowance as may be prescribed by the State Government by rules which shall not exceed ten thousand rupees per month.

(c) Alteration in allowance (section 10). On proof of misrepresentation or mistake of fact or a change in the circumstances of any person receiving monthly allowance, the tribunal may make order for alteration in the allowance for maintenance as it thinks fit. The tribunal may also cancel or vary the order of maintenance in consequence of an order of a Civil Court.

(d) Enhancement of order of maintenance (section 11). A copy of the order of maintenance and expenses of proceedings shall be given to the senior citizen or parent free of cost and such order may be enforced by any Tribunal in any place where the person against whom it is made. A maintenance order made under this Act shall have the same force and effect as an order passed under Chapter IX of the Code of Criminal Procedure 1973 and shall be executed in the manner prescribed for execution of such order by that Code.

(e) Option regarding maintenance in certain cases (section 12). Where a senior citizen or a parent is entitled to maintenance under this Act and also under Chapter IX of the Code of Criminal Procedure relating to maintenance of wives, children and parents, a senior citizen or a parent may, without prejudice to the provisions of Chapter IX of the said Code, claim such maintenance under either of those Acts but not under both.

(f) Deposit of maintenance amount (section 13). The children or relatives who are required to pay any amount of maintenance ordered by the Tribunal shall deposit the entire amount within thirty days in such manner as the Tribunal may direct.

(g) Award of interest where any claim is allowed (section 14). The Tribunal may also direct the payment of interest of not less than five per cent and not more than 18 per cent per annum in addition to the amount of maintenance. Where an application for maintenance under Chapter IX of the Code of Criminal Procedure 1973 is pending before a court at the

commencement of this Act; then such court shall allow the withdrawal of such application on the request of the parent or senior citizen.

(h) Right of legal representation (section 17). The legal practitioners shall not participate in any of the proceedings before the Tribunal and Appellate Tribunal.

(i) Maintenance Officer (section 18). The State Government shall designate the District Social Welfare Officer of an Officer not below the rank of District Social Welfare Officer as Maintenance Officer who shall represent a parent if he so desires before a Tribunal or Appellate Tribunal.

Appeals (section 16)

Any senior citizen or a parent, as the case may be, aggrieved by an order of a Tribunal may, within sixty days from the date of the order, prefer an appeal to the Appellate Tribunal. But on appeal the children or relative who is required to pay any amount in terms of such maintenance order shall continue to pay to such parent the amount so ordered in the manner directed by the Appellate Tribunal. The Appellate Tribunal may entertain the appeal after the expiry of the period of sixty days, if it is satisfied that the appellant was prevented by sufficient cause from preferring the appeal in time. On receipt of the appeal the Appellate Tribunal shall cause a notice to be served on the respondent. The Appellate Tribunal shall call for the records of the proceedings from the Tribunal against whose order the appeal is preferred. The Appellate Tribunal may, after examining the appeal and the records, either allow or reject the appeal. The order of the Appellate Tribunal shall be final. But no appeal shall be rejected unless an opportunity has been given to both the parties. The Appellate Tribunal shall make an endeavour to pronounce its order in writing within one month of the receipt of the appeal. A copy of every order passed by the Appellate Tribunal shall be sent to both the parties free of cost.

Establishment of old age homes (section 19)

The State Government may establish and maintain the old age homes in a phased manner for senior citizens having no sufficient means. The State Government may prescribe a scheme for management of old age homes including the standard and various types of services provided by them which are necessary for medical care and entertainment.

Medical support for senior citizens (section 20)

The State Government shall ensure that beds be provided for all senior citizens in Government hospitals or hospitals funded fully or partially by the Government as far as possible. Separate queues be arranged for senior citizens, facility for treatment of chronic, terminal and degenerative diseases; research activities for chronic diseases shall be expanded and facilities for geriatric patients in every district hospital shall be earmarked.

Measures for publicity, awareness, etc. for welfare of senior citizen (section 21)

The State Government shall take measures to give wide publicity through public media including the television, radio and the print at regular intervals the provisions of the Act. The State Government shall ensure that the officers of the Central Government and State Government including the police officers and the members of the judicial service are given periodic sensitisation and awareness training on the issues relating to the Act and effective co-ordination between the services provided by the concerned Ministers or Departments dealing with law, home affairs, health and welfare.

Authorities to be specified for implementing the provisions of the Act (section 22)

The State Government may confer such powers and impose such duties on District Magistrates to ensure that the provisions of the Act are properly carried out and the District Magistrates may specify the officers subordinate to them who shall exercise any of the powers and perform all or any of the duties conferred and local limits within which such powers and duties shall be carried out. The State Government shall also make a comprehensive action plan for providing protection of life and property of senior citizens.

Transfer of property to be void in certain circumstances (section 23)

If a senior citizen after the commencement of this Act transfers his property by way of gift or otherwise with the condition that the transferee shall provide basic amenities and basic physical needs and such transferee fails or refuses to provide such amenities and physical needs, the said transfer of property shall be deemed to have been made by fraud or coercion or under undue influence and the transfer be declared void by the Tribunal at the option of the senior citizen. Where a senior citizen has a right to receive maintenance out of an estate or part thereof and such estate or part thereof is transferred, the right may be enforced against the transferee. If a senior citizen is incapable of enforcing the rights, action may be taken on his behalf by any of the voluntary association registered under the Societies Registration Act 1860 or any other law for the time being in force.

Offences and procedure for trial and Miscellaneous matters

(a) Exposure and abandonment of senior citizen (section 24). Any person who is having care or protection of any senior citizen, intentionally abandons a senior citizen shall be liable for punishment of imprisonment which may extend to three months or with fine which may extend to five thousand rupees.

(b) Cognizance of offences (section 25). The offences under this Act are cognizable and bailable and shall be tried summarily by a Magistrate.

(c) Officers to be public servant (section 26). Every officer or staff appointed to exercise the functions under this Act shall be deemed to be a public servant within the meaning of s. 21 of Indian Penal Code 1860.

(d) Protection of action taken in good faith (section 28). No suit, prosecution or other legal proceedings shall lie against the Central Government, the State Government or the local authority or any officer of the Government in respect of anything which is done in good faith or intended to be done in pursuance of this Act and rules or orders made thereunder.

(e) Powers of Central Government (sections 30, 31). The Central Government is empowered to give directions to the State Government for carrying into execution of the provisions of this Act. The Central may make periodic review and monitor the progress of the implementation of the provisions of this Act by the State Government.

(f) Powers of State Governments (sections 29, 32). The State Government by notification in the Official Gazette may remove any difficulty which may arise in implementing the provisions of this Act. The said power may be exercised by the State Government within a period of two years from the date of commencement of this Act. Besides, the State Government may, by notification in the Official Gazette, make rules for carrying out the purposes of this Act.

Chapter 44

The Protection of Women from Domestic Violence Act 2005

Objects of the Protection of Women from Domestic Violence Act 2005

Domestic violence is undoubtedly a serious interference with the human rights. The Vienna Accord of 1994 and the Beijing Declaration and Platform for Action (1995) have acknowledged that domestic violence is an important human rights issue. The United Nations Committee on Convention on Elimination of All Forms of Discrimination Against Women (CEDAW) in its General Recommendation No. XII (1989) has recommended that State parties should act to protect women against violence of any kind especially that occurring within the family. The phenomenon of domestic violence is widely prevalent but has remained largely invisible in the public domain. Presently, where a woman is subjected to cruelty by her husband or his relatives, it is an offence under s. 498A of the Indian Penal Code. The civil law does not provide any remedy for such act of cruelty. Keeping in view the rights guaranteed under Arts. 14, 15 and 21 of the Constitution of India the Protection of Women from Domestic Violence Act 2005 was passed to implement the following objectives amongst others.

(*i*) It covers those women who are or have been in relationship with the abuser where both parties live together in a shared household and are related by consanguinity, marriage or adoption. Besides, family members living together as a joint family are included. Women who are sisters, widows, mothers, single women living with the abuser are entitled to legal protection under this Act.

(*ii*) The expression "domestic violence" would include not only actual abuse or threat but also harassment by way of unlawful demand for dowry.

(*iii*) The Act would provide for rights of women to secure housing. It also provides for the right of women to reside in her matrimonial home or shared household.

(*iv*) It empowers the Magistrate to pass protection orders in favour of the aggrieved person.

(*v*) It provides for appointment of Protection Officers.

This Act in short, provides for more more effective protection of the rights of women guaranteed under the Constitution who are victims of violence of any kind occurring within the family.

Extent of and some definitions in the Act

The Protection of Women from Domestic Violence Act 2005 came into force on 26th October 2006. It extends to the whole of India except the State of Jammu and Kashmir.

Domestic incident report [s. 2(e)]. Section 2(*e*) defines the expression "domestic incident report" as a report made in the prescribed form on receipt of a complaint of domestic violence from an aggrieved person.

Domestic relationship [s. 2(f)]. It means a relationship between two persons who live or have, at any point of time, lived together in a shared household, when they are related by consanguinity, marriage or through a relationship in the nature of marriage, adoption or are family members living together as a joint family.

Respondent [s. 2(q)]. The definition of "respondent" as defined in s. 2(*q*) of the Act clearly goes to show that any adult male person can only be shown as respondent when the aggrieved person has sought any relief under the Act. But the proviso to s. 2(*q*) has given an expanded meaning. It says that an aggrieved wife or female living in a relationship in the nature of marriage may also file a complaint against a relative of the husband or male partner. Thus, the proviso deals with complaint against two categories of persons, *i.e.*, (1) a relative of the husband or (2) the male partner.[1]

Shared household [s. 2(s)]. It means a household where the person aggrieved lives or at any stage has lived in a domestic relationship either singly or along with the respondent and includes such a household whether owned or tenanted either jointly by the aggrieved person and the respondent or owned or tenanted by either of them in respect of which either the

---

1 *Afzalunnisa Begum* v *State of A.P.* 2009 Cr LJ 4191 (AP).

aggrieved person or the respondent or both jointly or singly have any right, title, interest or equity and includes such a household which may belong to the joint family of which the respondent is a member, irrespective of whether the respondent or the aggrieved person has any right, title or interest in the shared household.

In *S.R. Batra* v *Taruna Batra*,[2] it has been held that mother-in-law's house does not become "shared household" only because the applicant wife had shared that house with her husband earlier.

Domestic violence (s. 3). Any act, omission or commission or conduct of the respondent shall constitute domestic violence in case it—

(*a*) harms or injures or endangers the health, safety, life, limb or well being, whether mental or physical of the aggrieved person or tends to do so and includes causing physical abuse, sexual abuse, verbal or emotional abuse and economic abuse; or

(*b*) harasses, harms, injures or endangers the aggrieved person with a view to coerce her or any other person related to her to meet any unlawful demand for dowry or other property or valuable security; or

(*c*) has the effect of threatening the aggrieved person or any person related to her by any conduct mentioned in cl. (*a*) or cl. (*b*);

(*d*) otherwise injures or causes harm, whether physical or mental, to the aggrieved person.

Explanation I to s. 3 explains the meanings of "physical abuse", "sexual abuse", "verbal and emotional abuse" and "economic abuse".

Explanation II states that in determining whether there is "domestic violence" it is necessary to take into consideration the overall facts and circumstances of the case.

Powers and duties of Protection Officer

Section 8 of the Protection of Women from Domestic Violence Act 2005 provides for appointment of Protection Officers. The State Government shall, by notification appoint a number of Protection Officers in each district. The Protection Officer shall as far as possible be women and shall possess prescribed qualifications. The terms and conditions of service of the Protection Officer and officers subordinate to him shall be prescribed by the State Government. Section 9 deals with the duties and functions of

---

2 AIR 2007 SC 1118.

the Protection Officers. It shall be the duty of the Protection Officer—(a) to assist the Magistrate; (b) to make a domestic incident report to the Magistrate; (c) to make an application in the prescribed form to the Magistrate if the aggrieved person so desires; (d) to ensure that the aggrieved person is provided legal aid or counselling, shelter home and medical facilities; (e) to make available a safe shelter home and to get medically examined if the aggrieved person has sustained bodily injuries and to forward a copy of the medical report to the police station and the Magistrate having jurisdiction in the area; (f) to ensure that the order for monetary relief under s. 20 of the Act is complied with and executed in accordance with the procedure prescribed under the Code of Criminal Procedure 1973; (g) to perform such other duties as may be prescribed. The Protection Officer shall act under the control and supervision of the Magistrate.

Duties and powers of service provider

The expression "service providers" is defined in s. 10 of the Act as any voluntary association registered under the Societies Registration Act 1860, or a company registered under the Companies Act 1956 or any other law for the time being in force with the object of protecting the rights and interests of women by any lawful means. Section 5 provides duties of police officers, service providers and Magistrate. When a complaint of domestic violence is received by him, he shall inform the aggrieved person—(a) of her right to make an application for obtaining a relief by way of a protection order; (b) of the availability of service of service-provider; (c) of the availability of services of the Protection Officer; (d) of her right to free legal services under the Legal Services Authorities Act 1987; (e) of his right to file complaint under s. 498A of the Indian Penal Code. But in spite of all those duties, a police officer is not relieved from his duty to proceed in accordance with law upon receipt of information as to the commission of a cognizable offence. Section 6 provides that a protection officer or service provider may request the person in charge of a shelter home to provide shelter to the aggrieved person. Under s. 7 it is the duty of Protection Officer or service provider to request a person in charge of medical facility to provide any medical aid to the aggrieved person. Section 10(2) of the Act deals with the power of the survice provider. A service-provider shall have the power to—(a) record the domestic incident report in prescribed form; (b) get the aggrieved person medically examined and forward a copy thereof to the Protection Officer and the police station situate within jurisdiction; (c) ensure that the aggrieved person is provided shelter in a shelter home and forward a report of the lodging of the aggrieved person in the shelter home to the police station within the local limits of which the domestic violence took place. No suit, prosecution or other legal proceeding shall lie against any service provider for anything done under this Act in good faith.

Duties of Government (section 11)

The Central Government and every State Government shall take all measures to ensure that—

(a) the provisions of this Act are given wide publicity through public media;

(b) the concerned officers including the police officers and members of the judicial services are given periodic sensitisation and awareness training;

(c) effective co-ordination between the services provided by concerned Ministers and Departments dealing with law, home affairs including law and order, health and human resources;

(d) protocols for the various Ministries concerned with the delivery of services to women under this Act.

Procedure for obtaining orders of reliefs application to Magistrate (section 12)

An aggrieved person or a Protection Officer or any other person on behalf of the aggrieved person may present an application to the Magistrate seeking one or more reliefs under this Act. Before passing an order the Magistrate shall take into consideration domestic incident report, if any. The relief may include a relief for issuance of an order for payment of compensation or damages. Every application shall be in prescribed form and contain all particulars. The Magistrate shall fix the first date of hearing which shall not ordinarily be beyond three days from the date of receipt of the application. The Magistrate shall endeavour to dispose of every such application within a period of sixty days from the date of first hearing.

Service of notice (section 13). A notice of date of hearing shall be given by the Magistrate through the Protection Officer.

Counselling (section 14). The Magistrate may order for counselling the respondent or the aggrieved person.

Assistance of welfare expert (section 15). The Magistrate may secure the services a person, preferably a woman, to assist him in discharging his functions.

Proceedings to be held in camera. Section 16 provides that the Magistrate may conduct the proceedings under this Act *in camera*.

Right to reside in a shared household (section 17). Every woman in a domestic relationship shall have the right to reside in the shared household, whether or not she has any right, title or beneficial interest in the same. The aggrieved person shall not be evicted or excluded from the shared household or any part thereof by the respondent except in accordance with the procedure established by law.

Protection orders (section 18). The Magistrate after hearing both the aggrieved person and the respondent is *prima facie* satisfied that domestic violence has taken place or is likely to take place, he may pass a protection order in favour of the aggrieved person and prohibit the respondent from—(*a*) committing any act of domestic violence; (*b*) aiding or abetting in the commission of acts of domestic violence; (*c*) entering the place of employment of the aggrieved person; (*d*) attempting to communicate in any form with the aggrieved person telephonic contract; (*e*) alienating any assets, operating bank lockers or back accounts; (*f*) causing violence to the dependants or other relatives of the aggrieved person; (*g*) committing any other act as specified in the protection order.

Residence orders (section 19). The Magistrate on being satisfied that domestic violence has taken place, may pass a residence order— (*a*) restraining the respondent from dispossessing the aggrieved person from the shared household; (*b*) directing the respondent to remove himself from the shared household; (*c*) restraining the respondent or any of his relatives from entering any portion of the shared household in which the aggrieved person resides; (*d*) restraining the respondent from alienating or disposing of the shared household; (*e*) restraining the respondent from renouncing his rights in the shared household; (*f*) directing the respondent to secure same level of alternative accommodation for the aggrieved person. The Magistrate may impose any additional conditions or pass any other direction to protect or to provide for the safety of the aggrieved person or any child of such aggrieved person. The Magistrate may require from the respondent to execute a bond. An order may also be passed by the Magistrate imposing on the respondent the obligations relating to the discharge of rent and other payments. The Magistrate may also direct the officer-in-charge of the police station in whose jurisdiction the Magistrate has been approached to assist in the implementation of the protection order.

Monetary reliefs (section 20). The Magistrate may direct the respondent to pay monetary relief to meet the expenses incurred or suffered by the aggrieved person.

Custody orders (section 21). The Magistrate at any stage of hearing of the application for protection order or for any other relief may grant temporary custody of any child or children to the aggrieved person.

Compensation orders (section 22). The Magistrate may, on application made by the aggrieved person, pass an order directing the respondent to pay compensation and damages for the injuries caused to the aggrieved person.

Grant of interim and ex parte orders (section 23). The Magistrate may pass such interim order as he may deem just and proper. The Magistrate may also grant *ex parte* order on the basis of the affidavit in the prescribed form made by the aggrieved person under s. 18, s. 19, s. 20, s. 21 or, as the case may be, s. 22 against the respondent.

Court to give copies of order free of cost (section 24). The Magistrate shall, in all cases, order that a copy of such order shall be given free of cost, to the parties to the application, the police-officer-in-charge of the police station in the jurisdiction of which the Magistrate has been approached.

Duration and alteration of orders (section 25). A protection order made under s. 18 shall remain in force till the aggrieved person applies for discharge. If the Magistrate on receipt of an application from the aggrieved person or the respondent, is satisfied that there is a change in the circumstances requiring alteration, modification or revocation of any order made under this Act, he may, for reasons to be recorded in writing pass such as he may deem appropriate.

Relief in other suits and legal proceedings (section 26). Section 26 provides that any relief available under the Act may also be sought in any legal proceeding before a civil court, family court or a criminal court. In case any relief has been obtained by the aggrieved person in any proceeding under this Act she shall be bound to inform the Magistrate of the grant of such relief.

Jurisdiction (section 27). Section 27 lays down that the court of judicial Magistrate of the first class or the Metropolitan Magistrate, as the case may be, within the local limits of which (*a*) the person aggrieved permanently or temporarily resides, carries on business or is employed; or (*b*) the respondent resides or carries on business or is employed; or (*c*) the cause of action has arisen, shall be the competent court to grant protection order and other orders under this Act and to try offences under this Act. Any order made under this Act shall be enforceable throughout India.

Procedure (section 28). All proceedings under ss. 12, 18, 19, 20, 21, 22 and 23 and offences under s. 31 shall be governed by the provisions of the Code of Criminal Procedure 1973. The Court can lay down its own procedure for disposal of an application under s. 12 or under sub-sec. (2) of s. 23 of the Act.

Appeal (section 29). An appeal shall lie to the Court of Session within thirty days from the date on which the order made by the Magistrate is served on the aggrieved person or the respondent, as the case may be, whichever is later. Where the right of residence is granted to wife at the house occupied by the husband, the mother-in-law who is the absolute owner of that house has right of appeal against that order although she was not a party in the trial court. It was because that she was adversely affected by the said order.[3]

Miscellaneous

(*a*) Protection Officers and members of service providers while acting in pursuance of any the provisions of this Act or any rules or orders made thereunder shall be deemed to be public servants within the meaning of s. 21 of the Indian Penal Code 1860. (section 30).

(*b*) Section 31 provides that a breach of protection order or an interim protection order by the respondent shall be an offence under this Act punishable with imprisonment which may extend to one year or with fine which may extend to twenty thousand rupees or with both. The offence of breach of protection order or interim order shall be tried as far as practicable by the Magistrate who had passed the order. The Magistrate while framing charges regarding breach of order may also frame charge under s. 498A or any other provision of the Indian Penal Code or the Dowry Prohibition Act 1961.

(*c*) Section 32 provides that the offence of breach of protection order by the respondent shall be cognizable and not bailable offence and the court may conclude on the sole testimony of the aggrieved person that the offence has been committed.

(*d*) If a Protection Officer fails or refuses to discharge his duties as directed by the Magistrate, he shall be punished with imprisonment which

---

3 *Asifa Khatoon* v *Rubina* 2009(4) Cal HN 490.

may extend to one year or with fine which may extend to twenty thousand rupees or with both (s. 33). No prosecution or other legal proceeding shall lie against the Protection Officer except on a complaint filed with the previous sanction of the State Government or an officer authorised by the State Government (s. 34). Section 35 provides that no suit or other legal proceeding shall lie against the Protection Officer for any damage caused or likely to be caused by anything done or intended to be done in good faith under the Act or any rule or order thereunder.

(*e*) Section 36 provides that the provisions of this Act shall be in addition to and not in derogation of the provisions of any other law, for the time being in force.

(*f*) *Power of Central Government to make rules (s. 37).* The Central Government may, by notification, make rules for carrying out the provisions of this Act. It is obligatory on the part of the Central Government to lay all those rules made under this before each House of Parliament.

By virtue of the powers conferred by s. 37 of the Protection of Women from Domestic Violence Act 2005, the Central Government has rules called the Protection of Women from Domestic Violence Rules 2006. The said Rules contain among others—(*i*) qualification and experience of Protection Officer; (*ii*) information to Protection Officer; (*iii*) duties and functions of Protection Officer; (*iv*) application to the Magistrate; (*v*) affidavit for obtaining *ex parte* orders of Magistrate; (*vi*) means of service of notices; (*vii*) form of domestic incident report under ss. 9(*b*) and 39(2)(*c*) of the Act; (*viii*) form of application to the Magistrate under s. 12 of the Act; (*ix*) form of affidavit under s. 23(2) of the Act; (*x*) form for registration as service provider under s. 10(1) of the Act; (*xi*) notice for appearance under s. 13(1) of the Act.

CHAPTER
45

The Prohibition of Child Marriage Act 2006

Objects and reasons of the Act

The Child Marriage Restraint Act 1929 was passed with a view to restraining solemnisation of child marriages. The said Act was subsequently amended in 1949 and 1978 in order, *inter alia*, to raise the age limit of the male and female persons for the purpose of the marriage. The Act, though restrained solemnisation of child marriages, yet it did not declare them to be void or invalid. There had been a growing demand for making the provisions of the Act more effective and the punishment thereunder more stringent so as to eradicate or effectively prevent the evil practice of solemnisation of child marriages in the country. This will enhance the health of children and the status of women. The National Commission for Women in its Annual Report for the year 1995-96 recommended that the Government should appoint Child Marriage Prevention Officers immediately. It further recommended that—
(*i*) punishment should be made more stringent; (*ii*) marriages performed in contravention of the Act should be made void; and (*iii*) the offences under the Act should be made cognizable. The National Human Rights Commission Act and made recommendations for comprehensive amendments therein in its Annual Report of 2001-2002. The Central Government after consulting the State Governments and Union territory Administrations on the recommendations of the National Commission for Women and the National Human Rights Commission decided to present a Bill on Prohibition of Child Marriage in Parliament. The salient features of the Bill were as follows: (*i*) provision to declare child marriage as voidable at the option of the contracting party to the marriage who was a child; (*ii*) provision to pay maintenance to the minor girl until her remarriage; (*iii*) provision for custody and maintenance of children born

of child marriage; (*iv*) child born of such marriage shall be legitimate; (*v*) power of district court to add, to modify or revoke any order relating to maintenance; (*vi*) declaring child marriage as void in certain circumstances; (*vii*) to empower the court to issue injunction; (*viii*) to make offences cognizable; (*ix*) to appoint Child Marriage Prevention Officer; (*x*) to empower State Governments to make rules.

The Prohibition of Child Marriage Bill 2006 was passed by the Rajya Sabha on December 2006 and by the Lok Sabha on 19th December 2006. The Act is called the Prohibition of Child Marriage Act 2006. The Act of 2006 extends to the whole of India except the State of Jammu and Kashmir. It applies to all citizens of India without and beyond India. It does not apply to the Renoncants of the Union Territory of Pondicherry.

Child marriages to be voidable at the option of contracting party being a child

Section 3 of the Prohibition of Child Marriage Act 2006 provides that every child marriage, whether solemnized before or after commencement of this Act, shall be voidable at the option of the contracting party who was a child at the time of the marriage. A "child" according to s. 2(*a*) of the Act means a person who, if a male, has not completed twenty one years of age, and if a female, has not completed eighteen years of age. A petition for annulling a child marriage by a decree of nullity may be filed in the district court only by a contracting party who was a child at the time of marriage. If at the time of filing a petition the petitioner is a minor, the petition may be filed through his or her guardian or next friend along with the Child Marriage Prohibition Officer the petition may be filed at any time but before the child filing the petition completes two years of attaining majority. While granting a decree of nullity the district court make an order directing parties to the marriage, their parents or their guardians to return to the other party the money, valuables ornaments and other gifts received on the occasion of marriage by them from the other side. No order shall be passed under s. 3 of the Act unless the concerned parties are given notices to appear before the district courts and show cause why such order should not be passed.

Provision for maintenance and residence to female contracting party to child marriage (section 4)

While granting a decree of nullity under s. 3 of the Act, the court may also order to make contracting party or his guardian to pay maintenance and make provision for residence for female contracting party till her remarriage.

Custody and maintenance of children of child marriage (section 5)

The district court shall also make appropriate order for the custody and maintenance of children born of the child marriage keeping in view the paramount welfare and best interests of the child.

Legitimacy of children born of child marriage (section 6)

A child begotten or conceived of child marriage shall be deemed to be a legitimate child in spite of such marriage being annulled by a decree of nullity under s. 3 of the Act.

Power of district court to modify orders

Section 7 of the Act provides that the district court has power to modify, add or revoke any order made under s. 4 or s. 5 of the Act if there is any change in the circumstances at any time during the pendency of the petition and even after the final disposal of the petition.

Jurisdiction

Section 8 provides that for the purpose of reliefs under ss. 3, 4 and 5, the district court having jurisdiction shall include the district court having jurisdiction over the place where the defendant or the child resides or where the marriage was solemnised or where parties last resided together or the petitioner is residing on the date of presentation of the petition.

Punishment for male adult marrying a child (section 9)

Marrying a child by a male adult above eighteen years of age is punishable with rigorous imprisonment which may extend to two years or with fine which may extend to one lakh rupees or with both.

Punishment for solemnising a child marriage (section 10)

Whoever performs, conducts or directs or abets any child marriage shall be punishable with rigorous imprisonment which may extend to two years and shall be liable to fine which may extend to one lakh rupees unless he proves that he had reasons to believe that the marriage was not a child marriage.

Punishment for promoting or permitting solemnisation of child marriages (section 11)

Where a child contracts a child marriage, any person having charge of the child whether as parent or guardian or any other person or in any other capacity, lawful or unlawful, including any member of an organisation or association of persons who does any act to promote the marriage or permits it to be solemnised, or negligently fails to prevent it from being solemnised, including attending or participation in a child marriage, shall be punishable with rigorous imprisonment which may extend to two years and shall also be liable to fine which may extend upto one lakh rupees. But in such offence no woman shall be punishable with imprisonment.

Marriage of minor child to be void in certain cases (section 12)

Where a child being a minor—(a) is taken or enticed out of the keeping of the lawful guardian; or (b) by force compelled or by any deceitful means induced to go from any place; or (c) is sold for the purpose of marriage, such marriage shall be null and void.

Power of court to issue injunction prohibiting child marriage (section 13)

If on an application of the Child Marriage Prohibition Officer or on receipt of information through a complaint or otherwise from any person a Judicial Magistrate of the First Class or a Metropolitan Magistrate is satisfied that a child marriage in contravention of this Act has been arranged or is about to be solemnised, such Magistrate shall issue an injunction against any person including a Member of an organisation or association of persons prohibiting such marriage. The court of Judicial Magistrate of the first class or the Metropolitan Magistrate may also take *suo motu* cognizance on the basis of reliable report or information. For the purpose of preventing solemnisation of mass child marriage on certain days, such as Akshaya Trutiya, the District Magistrate shall be deemed to be Child Marriage Prohibition Officer with all his powers under this Act. Generally, under s. 16 of the Act the State Government shall, by notification in the Official Gazette, appoint for the whole state or such part thereof, an officer or officers to be known as the Child Marriage Prohibition Officer having jurisdiction over his arrear. The State Government may also request a respectable member of the locality or an officer of the Gram Panchayat or Municipality or the Government or the Public Sector undertaking or an office bearer of any non-governmental organisation to assist the Child Marriage Prohibition Officer.

No injunction shall be issued unless the court has previously given notice to the person or organisation an opportunity to show cause against the issue of injunction. The court may issue interim injunction without giving any notice under this section. An injunction may be confirmed or vacated and giving notice and hearing the party against whom injunction was issued. On an application of the person aggrieved or on its own motion, the court shall rescind or alter an injunction. If any one disobeys an injunction knowing that injunction has been issued, shall be punishable with imprisonment for a term which may extend to two years or with fine which may extend to one lakh rupees or with both. But no woman shall be punishable with imprisonment.

Section 14 provides that any marriage solemnised in contravention of an injunction order under s. 13 of the Act shall be void *ab inito*. Section 15 says that an offence punishable under this Act is cognizable and non-bailable.

Duties of Child Marriage Prohibition Officer

Sub-section (3) of s. 16 lays down the duties of the Child Marriage Prohibition Officer. These are—(*a*) to prevent solemnisation of child marriages; (*b*) to collect evidence for the effective prosecution of persons contravening the provisions of this Act; (*c*) to advise either individual cases or counsel the residents of locality not to indulge in promoting, aiding or allowing the solemnisation of child marriages; (*d*) to create awareness of the evil of child marriages; (*e*) to sensitize the community on the issue of child marriages; (*f*) to furnish periodical returns and statistics as the State Government may direct; and (*g*) to discharge such other functions and duties as may be assigned to him by the State Government.

The State Government may, by notification in the Official Gazette, invest the Child Marriage Prohibition Officer with powers of a Police Officer. The Child Marriage Prohibition Officer shall have power to move the court for an order under ss. 4, 5 and 13 and along with the child under s. 3 of the Act.

Section 17 provides that the Child Marriage Prohibition Officer shall be deemed to be public servant within the meaning of s. 21 of the Indian Penal Code 1860. Under s. 18 of the Act no suit, prosecution or other legal proceeding shall lie against the Child Marriage Prohibition Officer in respect of anything done or to be done under the Act in good faith.

Power of State Government to make rules (section 19)

The State Government may, by notification in the Official Gazette, make rules for carrying out provisions of this Act. Every rule made under this Act shall be laid before the State Legislature.

Amendment and repeal

Section 20 of the Act provides for substitution of cl. (*a*) of s. 18 of the Hindu Marriage Act 1955, by the clause given in s. 20 of the Act. Section 21 provides that the Child Marriage Restraint Act 1929 is hereby repealed. In spite of such repeal no pending proceeding under that Act of 1929 shall be affected.

Index

Anand Marriage Act 1909
exemption of marriages from, 28

Arya Marriage Validation Act 1937
passed to recognise and remove doubts, 29

Caste Disabilities Removal Act 1850
effect of, 30
preamble to, 30

Converts' Marriage Dissolution Act 1866
alimony, 247
children, status of, 247
convert deserted by spouse, 244
High Court, reference of question of conversion, 248
jurisdiction of court, 244
passed to legalise dissolution of marriages of converts to Christianity, 244
procedure under, 245
punishment under s. 174, IPC, when, 245

Divorce Act 1869
alimony, 235
amendments to, 229
custody of children, 236
dissolution of marriage under, 231
divorce by mutual consent, 232
judicial separation, 234
jurisdiction of court under, 231
no decree for divorce *mensa at toro*, 234
nullity of marriage, 234
objects of, 229
power of court
    in dissolving marriage, 233
    to dismiss petition, 233

Divorce Act 1869—*continued*
procedure under, 237
reasons of, 229
remarriage, 237
restitution of conjugal rights, 235
test of Christianity, 229
    domicile, 230
    residence, 230

Dowry Prohibition Act 1961
applicability of, 293
cognizance of offence, 294
dowry
    definition of, 293
    evil effects of, 292
    penalty for, 293
object of, 292
origin of, 292

Family
a generic term, 3
consisting of, 4
construed, 3
defined, 3
elements to constitute, 5
includes, 4
marriage rooted in, 4
means technically, 4

Family Courts Act 1984
aims of, 284
appeal under, 290
applicability of, 285
counsellors in, 286
duty of settlement of family court, 288
employees of family court, 286
exclusion of jurisdiction under, 287
execution of decree and order under, 289

Family Courts Act 1984—*continued*
extent of, 285
family court, shifting of, 286
family, not defined in, 284
judges, appointment of, 285
jurisdiction of family court, 286
no inconsistency between s. 8 and s. 18 ... 290
objects of, 284
officers in, 286
procedure for family court, 288

Family law
concerned with, 4
denotes, 3
English, 5
German Civil Code, under, 4
meaning of, 3
USA, in, 5

Foreign Marriage Act 1969
conditions for solemnisation of, 281
matrimonial relief under, 282
objects, 280
other formalities of, 281
penalty, 283
preliminary, 280
reasons, 280
recognition of, 283
registration of, 282

Gift
accumulation, of, 134
definition of, 135
essentials of valid, 134
formalities, 133
immovable property and registration, of, 135
limitation, 133
nature, 133
properties of bhumidar, of, 136
registration of, 135
revocation of, 135
unborn person, to, 134

Guardians and Wards Act 1890
consolidating and amending law, 297
natural guardian, right of, to custody of child, 297

Hindu Adoptions and Maintenance Act 1956
aged parents, maintenance of, 89
applicability of, 78
capacity of giving in adoption, 80
capacity to adopt, 79
changes in, 77
children, maintenance of, 89
classes of dependants for maintenance, 90
commencement of, 78
conditions of, valid adoption, 81
effect of adoption, 83
extends to, 78
introduction, 77
maintenance, charge of, 93
maintenance concerned, 77
maintenance of dependants, 91
maintenance of widowed daughter in law, 88
no application of, 78
no presumption of adoption, when, 84
old law on, 77
performance of *datta homam*, 82
person to be adopted, 81
priority of debts, 94
prohibition of payments in adoption, 86
quantum of maintenance, 92
requisite of valid adoption, 79
saving of, 95
transfer of property on right of maintenance, 94
void, adoption, when, 78
wife, maintenance of, 86
wife's right to live separately, 87

Hindu Disposition of Property Act 1916
bequest to unborn person, 31
preliminary, 31

Hindu Inheritance (Removal of Disabilities) Act 1928
no retrospective effect, 31
preliminary, 31

Hindu law
important legislations on, 25
judicial interpretation on sources of, 22
means, 19
school of, 23
sources of, 20
was, 19

INDEX

Hindu Law of Marriage
ancient, 32
ceremonies of, 33
dissolution of, 33
forms of, 32
person competent under, 32

Hindu Marriage Act 1955
appeals, 72
bigamy and punishment, 60
ceremonies of, 38
children, custody of, 70
conditions of valid, 37
decree, enforcement of, 73
decree in proceedings, 64
disposal of joint property, 71
divorce, 49
    additional grounds for, 54
    conversion, 52
    cruelty, 50
    desertion, 51
    disappearance, 53
    leprosy, 52
    mutual consent, by, 57
    renunciation, 53
    unsoundness of mind, 52
    venereal disease, 52
irretrievable break down of, 56
judicial separation under, 43
jurisdiction and procedure, 61
legitimacy of children, 59
maintenance interim, 67
    permanent, 69
necessary changes made under, 36
nullity of marriage, 44
object of, 35
operation of, 35
punishment for contravention of s. 9 ... 61
rape, 55
remarriage, 59
restitution of conjugal rights under, 40
restriction on presentation of petition for divorce, 58
resumption of cohabitation, 43
right to make counter-claim, 66
sodomy, 55
territorial jurisdiction of, 36
void marriage, 44
voidable marriage, 46

Hindu marriage and divorce
legislations on, 34

Hindu Marriage Disabilities Removal Act 1946
preliminary, 29

Hindu Marriages (Validation of Proceedings) Act 1960
introduction, 75
validation of proceedings of courts, 76

Hindu Minority and Guardianship Act 1956
applicability of, 97
considerations for appointment of guardian, 102
custody of minor child to father, when, 103
limitations on guardians, 102
mother entitled to custody of child, 99
natural guardian of Hindu minor, 98
objects of, 96
paramount consideration of child in custody, 103
powers of natural guardian, 100
powers of testamentary guardians, 101
principal changes in, 96
testamentary guardians, 101

Hindu Succession Act 1956
abrogation of Hindu law, 151
changes effected under s. 8 of, 152
changes made by, 150
customs of tribals and, 152
devolution of interest in coparcenary property, 159
effect of disqualification, 163
failure of heir to succeed, 163
female inheriting share in dwelling house, 160
persons disqualified to inherit, 163
prospective and retrospective effect of s. 4 of, 158
right of child in womb, 161
right of pre-emption, 162
rules of succession for males, 153
simultaneous deaths, presumption in, 161
succession of Hindu females under, 155
testamentary succession, 164
validity of s. 14 of, 158

Hindu Widows' Remarriage Act 1856
preamble, 25
rights of widow on remarriage, 26

Indian Christian Marriage Act 1872
consent of marriage under, 224
marriage, not void for irregularities under, 228
marriage of Indian Christian under, 225
marriages solemnised by licensed Ministers of Religion, 221
marriages solemnised in presence of Marriage Registrar, 223
offence of Marriage Registrar, 227
penalties, 226
persons by whom marriages may be solemnized, 219
registration of marriages, 222
time and place of solemnization of, 220
to consolidate and amend law relating to Christian marriage, 219

Indian Succession Act 1925
alteration and revocation of grant, 308
gift to attesting witness, 305
grant of probate and letters of administration, 307
incorporation of papers by reference, 303
no change in terms of will, 309
no disqualification of person to be witness or executor of will, 305
person capable of making will, 301
petition for letters of administration, 309
petition for probate, 308
privileged will, 303
revival of unprivileged will, 305
revocation of privileged will, 305
revocation of succession certificate, 311
revocation of unprivileged will, 305
revocation of will, 302, 305
rules for executing privileged will, 304
succession certificates, 310
suspicious circumstances, when, 303
testamentary guardian, 301
testamentary succession, 300
introduction, 300
title to property of testator, 306
unprivileged will, execution of, 303
will, construction of, 306
will obtained by fraud, effect of, 302

Inheritance (Muslim)
ancestral and self-acquired, 202
aul, 205
classes of heirs, 203
distant kindred, 209
doctrine of representation, 202
general rules of, 202
homicide no bar to, 203
joint family, not recognised, 203
life estate, not recognised, 203
posthumous child, 210
property, no distinction, 202
radd, 205
residuaries, 206
sharers, 203
simultaneous death, 210
spes successionis, no transfer of right, 202

Intestate Succession to Christian under Indian Succession Act 1925
children's advancements not brought into hotchpot, 243
devolution of property of an intestate, 238
distribution of intestate property, 240
no lineal descendants for distribution, 241
property of deceased dying intestate, 238
right of widower, 239

Intestate Succession to Parsi under Indian Succession Act 1925
division of intestates property, 258
division of property where no relative, 260
division of share of predeceased child, 259
intestate succession, 258
no lineal descendant of intestate, 259

Joint family property and partition
alienation of impartible estate, 132
ancestral property, meaning of, 118
scope of, 118
impartible estate and, 131
impartible estate and self acquired property, 132
incidents of impartible estate, 131
joint family property,
burden of proof, 121
presumption of, 122

Joint family property and partition
—*continued*
joint family property and joint property, distinction, 117
joint, meaning of, 113, 114
Partition Act 1893 ... 132
partition, meaning of, 113, 116
    agreement, by, 128
    effect of, 126
    mode of effecting, 129
    partial, 128
    person entitled to, 125
    presumption in, suit, 128
    sham, 131
    under Dayabhaga system, 124
    under Mitakshara law, 124
property, meaning of, 113, 114
    division of, 130
reunion, 127
separate property, 123

Joint Hindu family
composition of, 104
coparcener, liability of, 111
    remedies of, 112
father to alienate coparcenary property, 106
leading case on, 108
management of, 110
manager, powers of, 106, 110, 111
    right of, 110
presumptions of, 105
property and separate property, 105
rights of coparceners, 109
tie of, 104

Mahomedan Law
application of, 169
change of sect, effect of, 168
conversion to Mahomedanism, 169
excommunication, 170
Hanafi law, rules of interpretation, 169
marital rights on conversion to Mahomedanism, 169
religious practice, 170
schools of, 167
    shia, 168
    sunnia, 167
sources of, 168

Maintenance and Welfare of Parents and Senior Citizens Act 2007
appeal, 320
applicability of, 315
authorities for implementation, 321
definitions of terms, 315
extent of, 315
jurisdiction of, 317
maintenance of parents, 316
    of senior citizens, 316
measures for publicity, 321
objects of, 315
offences, 322
old age homes, establishment of, 320
overriding effect of, 316
procedure for trial, 332
procedure of, 317
senior citizens, medical support for, 320
transfer of property, when void, 321

Maintenance under Code of Criminal Procedure 1973
alteration of order of maintain award of maintenance from date of, 314
cancellation of order of maintenance, 313
forum for maintenance proceedings, 314
interim maintenance, 313
limitation, 314
quantum of maintenance, 313
recovery of maintenance, 314
scope of s. 125, Cr PC, 312
statutory liability to maintain, 312

Maintenance under Muslim law
Muslim husband under obligation for, 211
section 125, Cr PC for, 211

Marriage
asura from of, 11
Christian, 7
civil, 8
classified in Roman law, 12
communal, 6
concept of, 6, 7
definition of, 7
Hindu, 7
institution of, 6
Muslim, 8
prohibited degrees for, 13

Muslim gifts
areeat, 186
conditions for making valid, 185
death-bed, 183
hiba and *hiba-bil-iwej*, distinction, 182
hiba-ba-shart-ul-iwez, 186
hiba means, 182
hiba-bil-iwej is, 182
mushaa, of, 184
revocation of, 185

Muslim marriage
capacity for, 174
celebration of, 174
custody of child, 181
definition of, 173
divorce, 179
dower, 177, 178
effect of conversion Muslim wife to other faith, 181
essentials of valid, 173
fosterage, of, 174
hizamat, 181
iddat, 180
ila, 179
irregular, 174, 175
judicial decree, 180
khula, 179
kinds of, 174
lian, 181
mubarat, 179
muta, 177
plurality of, 177
presumption of lawful, 175
recognition, by, 175
restitution of conjugal rights in, 178
second, by Hindu convert, 177
talak, 179
valid, 174
void, 174, 175
zihar, 179

Muslim Personal Law (Shariat) Application Act 1937
applicability of, 171
declaration in prescribed form, 171
extent of, 171
object of, 171
rule making powers of State Government, 172

Muslim Women (Protection of Rights on Divorce) Act 1986
applicability of, 213
definitions of terms under, 213
meaning of expression under, 216
objectives of, 213
option of a divorced woman, 215
order of maintenance to divorced Muslim woman by others, 214
return of mohr on divorce, 214
properties of Muslim women on divorce, 214

Parsi Marriage and Divorce Act 1936
alimony
  pendente lite, 256
  permanent, 256
counter-claim, 256
custody of children, 257
decree, no bar to grant, when, 255
dissolution of marriage, 254
divorce by mutual consent, 255
documentary evidence, 256
joint property, disposal of, 257
nullity of marriage, 254
object of, 251
parsi matrimonial courts, 253
penalty for breach of provisions of, 252
punishment for unlawful remarriage, 252
registration of marriages, 252
remarry liberty to parties, 257
requisites of valid, 251
suit for judicial separation, 255
suit for restitution of conjugal rights, 256
suits to be instituted under, 253
unlawful remarriage, 252

Personal law
Hindu, 14
Indian Christian, 14
is, 14
Muslim, 14
Parsis, 14

Pre-emption (Muslim)
definition of, 196
formality for, 197
loss of right of, 198
origin of, 196
persons entitled to, 196
shafi, by, 198

Prohibition of Child Marriage Act 2006
amendment and repeal, 336
child marriage prohibition officer, duties of, 336
child marriage, voidable, when, 333
custody and maintenance of children, 334
injunction by court, 335
jurisdiction under, 334
legitimacy of children, 334
maintenance to female, 333
marriage of minor child, 335
objects of, 332
power of district court, 334
    State Government, 336
punishment for child marriage, 334
    promoting child marriage, 334
reasons of, 332
residence to female, 333

Protection of Women from Domestic Violence Act 2005
Central Govt., to make rules, 331
definitions in, 324
extent of, 324
Govt., duties of, 327
magistrate to grant order of relief, 327
objects of, 323
protection officer,
    duties, 325
    powers, 325
    public servant, 330
service provider,
    duties, 326
    powers, 326
    public servant, 326

Religious and charitable endowment
dedication, 142
    proof of, 142
deity, 145
devasthan, 145
essentials of, 141
idol, legal status of, 148
illusory endowment, 144
image, 145
Math, 145
    Mathadhipati, 148
    Mohunt, 145

Religious and charitable endowment
—*continued*
private and public endowment distinction, 143
public temple, test for, 144
Pujari, 148
sanyasi, ceremonies to become, 148
shebait, 145
    duties and liabilities of, 147
    powers of, 146
    sale of, right, 149
temple, legal status of, 148

Religious Endowments Act 1863
committee of Wakf, filling in vacancy, 299
introduction, 298
math properties, perpetual lease of, 298
no dedication of property before gift, 298

Secular law
refers to, 15

Special Marriage Act 1954
alimony *pendente lite*, 276
    permanent, 277
alternative relief in divorce proceedings, 271
amendments to, 263
appeal, 278
application of, 263
break down of marriage, irretrievably, 273
children, custody of, 277
children, legitimacy of, 271
commencement of, 263
conditions for solemnisation of special marriages, 263
consequences of marriage under, 268
counter-claim, 276
disposal of appeal, 279
divorce by mutual consent, 273
enforcement of decree, 278
judicial separation, 269
jurisdiction, 274
marriage notice book and publication, 264
marriage officer, 264
notice of intended marriage, 264
object of, 263

Special Marriage Act 1954—*continued*
objection to marriage, 265
passing of decree, duty of court, 275
penal provisions, 279
powers of marriage officer, 266
procedure, 274
procedure on receipt of objection, 265
proceedings in camera, 275
registration of marriages, 267
restitution of conjugal rights, 269
restriction for divorce, 274
solemnisation of marriage, 266
transfer petition, power to, 278
void marriage, 270
voidable marriage, 270

Succession, administration and partition (Muslim)
administration of estate, 199
devolution of property on death, 200
doctrine of partial partition, 201
guardian for minor, 200
    minor's property, of, 200

Wakf (Muslim)
alienation of, property, 190
bequest creating, when valid, 189
conditions of valid, 187
creation of, 188
graveyard, 192
imambara, 191

Wakf (Muslim)—*continued*
mosque, not essential part of practice, 193
    public character, of, 193
mutawalli
    appointment of, 192
    functions of, 189
    position of, 192
    power of, 189
revocation of, 190
sajjadanashim, 191
valid objects of, 191
wakfnama, validity of, 189

Wills
beneficiaries under, 138
conditions in, 139
construction of, 139
definition, 137
directions in, 139
formalities of, 138
intention of testator in, 140
no terms of, to be altered, 140
power of disposition under, 137
scope, 137

Wills (Muslim)
conditions for valid, 194
executors
    kinds of, 195
    powers of, 195
limits of bequest by, 194
revocation of bequest by, 195

PADMAPRIYA SRIVATSA
ADVOCATE
Flat No 201, Suramya Apartments
Opp: Shirdi Sdyasai Mandira,
Kunjibettu UDUPI - 576 102.